1991
Science Year

The World Book Annual Science Supplement

A review of Science and Technology
During the 1990 School Year

World Book, Inc.

a Scott Fetzer company

Chicago London Sydney Toronto

The Year's Major Science Stories

From the discovery of a previously unknown dinosaur to the devastation of Hurricane Hugo to the launch of the *Hubble Space Telescope,* it was an eventful year for science and technology. On these two pages are the stories that *Science Year* editors picked as the most memorable, the most exciting, or the most important of the year, along with details about where you will find information about them in the book.   The Editors

Earthquake Rocks San Francisco Area

An earthquake shook a large area of northern California in October 1989, killing at least 62 people and causing up to $6 billion in damage. In the Special Reports section, see EARTH'S DEADLY MOVEMENTS. In the Science News Update section, see GEOLOGY.
▼

◄ Gigantic New Dinosaur

The discovery of the fossils of a dinosaur large enough to have swallowed a big cow in one gulp was announced in January 1990. In the Science News Update section, see PALEONTOLOGY.

◄ Cystic Fibrosis Gene Found

Researchers reported in September 1989 finding the gene that causes most cases of cystic fibrosis, one of the most common inherited diseases among Caucasians. In the Special Reports section, see TRACKING DOWN A DEADLY GENE. In the Science News Update section, see GENETICS.

Deadly Hurricane

Hurricane Hugo—the worst tropical storm to hit the United States since 1969—struck the U.S. mainland in September 1989. In the Science News Update section, see METEOROLOGY.
▼

ISBN 0-7166-0591-0

ISSN 0080-7621
Library of Congress Catalog Number: 65-21776
Printed in the United States of America

Hubble Space Telescope Launched
Space shuttle astronauts in April 1990 launched the *Hubble Space Telescope*, which has been termed the biggest single step in astronomy since Galileo used his first telescope. In the Special Reports section, see AN ORBITING EYE ON THE UNIVERSE. In the Science News Update section, see SPACE TECHNOLOGY.

Computing with Light
An "optical processor" that uses beams of laser light to carry out its operations was unveiled in 1990. Though still experimental, such devices may lead to desktop supercomputers. In the Science News Update section, see COMPUTER HARDWARE.

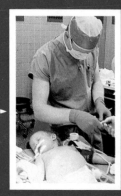

Liver-Donor Liver Transplant
The first United States liver transplant using tissue from a live donor took place in November 1989. In the Science News Update section, see MEDICAL RESEARCH.

Wonders of Neptune and Triton
The interplanetary probe *Voyager 2* sailed past Neptune in August 1989, finding six new moons, then made surprising discoveries about the moon Triton. In the Special Reports section, see NEPTUNE: LAST STOP ON A GRAND TOUR. In the Science News Update section, see SPACE TECHNOLOGY.

Contents

See page 246

See page 276

See page 344

Staff

Editorial Advisory Board

Special Reports

Fifteen articles give in-depth treatment to significant and timely subjects in science and technology.

See page 82   See page 130

See page 112

See page 187

Geologists have learned a great deal about
earthquakes and how to protect buildings and
other structures from their destructive force.

Earth's Deadly Movements

BY ELDRIDGE M. MOORES

It was 5:04 p.m. on Oct. 17, 1989, and the third game of baseball's
World Series between the San Francisco Giants and the Oakland
Athletics was about to begin at San Francisco's Candlestick Park.
Geologist Marty Giaramita was sitting in the bleachers. Suddenly, he
felt a vibration and heard a loud rocking and clicking sound moving
toward him from the left. As he stood up to see what was causing the
commotion, the bleacher seats around him began to rock violently.
He felt as if he were shooting the rapids of a river—while standing
up in the raft.

Giaramita had experienced one of the most devastating of all
nature's forces—an earthquake. The quake that rocked San Francisco, as well as nearby cities such as Santa Cruz, was the latest in a
series of large earthquakes that have occurred along California's San
Andreas Fault. This huge break in Earth's crust extends more than
1,200 kilometers (750 miles) from off the coast of northwestern
California to the southeastern part of the state near the Mexican
border. The October quake—named the Loma Prieta quake after a
nearby mountain—began about 97 kilometers (60 miles) southeast of
San Francisco in a section of the fault that passes through the Santa
Cruz Mountains. This earthquake killed at least 62 people and
caused an estimated $6 billion in damage.

Earthquakes are among the most powerful events on Earth. One
large earthquake may release more energy than six hydrogen bombs.
Earthquakes occur everywhere in the world except in areas where the
bedrock is very old and stable, such as Antarctica and central Canada.

Opposite page: Rescu-
ers search for survivors
in a collapsed section of
the double-decked Nim-
itz Freeway in Oakland
after an earthquake
jolted northern Califor-
nia on Oct. 17, 1989.

Scientists have learned much about where and why earthquakes occur and what happens during a quake. This information has helped them design structures that can stand up to even violent earthquakes, saving lives and minimizing property damage. And although the ultimate goal of earthquake research—predicting precisely when a quake will strike—remains elusive, even there scientists have made some surprising gains.

Earthquakes are sudden vibrations in Earth's outer layers. They always occur along *faults* (breaks in the rock). Sometimes, faults are visible at the surface. More often, however, they remain hidden beneath overlying rock.

Most faults occur along or near the boundaries between huge, irregularly shaped *tectonic plates* that make up Earth's outer layers. These plates are in slow, continual motion in relation to each other. Geologists believe the motion of the plates is driven by rising and falling currents of hot puttylike rock far below. Nearer the surface, the rock becomes cooler and more rigid. As this rigid rock near the edge of a plate is squeezed and stretched by the motion of the plates, it breaks, forming a fault.

It is the motions of the plates that give rise to earthquakes along a fault. Sometimes, the two sides of a fault slide past each other easily. But sometimes the sides of a fault are squeezed together so tightly by the weight of the rock that they cannot move. And sometimes, the jagged edges of a fault become locked together. As the plates try to move, this causes a build-up of pressure, which eventually becomes so great that the two sides of the fault suddenly spring past each other, releasing energy that makes Earth "quake."

Geologists classify faults according to the motion at plate boundaries, or the way in which two plates are moving relative to each other. There are three types of plate boundaries, and examples of all of these are found on the North American Plate, on which most North Americans live.

Horizontal, or *slip-strike*, *faults* are vertical cracks in the rock along which one side slides past the other. They are usually found where two plates are moving past each other, such as along the San Andreas Fault. There, the Pacific Plate is creeping north past the North American Plate. Some California cities, such as Los Angeles, San Diego, and Santa Barbara, actually sit on the Pacific Plate.

Normal faults and *thrust faults* are diagonal cracks in the rock. A normal fault occurs if one side of a fault drops below the other side. Normal faults generally occur where two plates are moving apart. For example, they are common along the eastern edge of the North American Plate, which lies beneath the middle of the Atlantic Ocean. There, the North American Plate is moving away from the plates that make up the eastern Atlantic Ocean, Africa, and Europe.

A thrust fault occurs if one side of the fault is thrust up and over the other side. Thrust faults generally occur at *subduction zones*, where

The author:
Eldridge M. Moores is professor of geology at the University of California, Davis.

The Making of a Quake

Earthquakes always occur along *faults,* breaks in Earth's outer layers. Often, the two sides of a fault move past each other smoothly. But sometimes the rock gets "stuck," and the sudden movement when it breaks free sets off an earthquake.

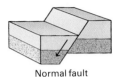
Normal fault

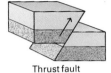
Thrust fault

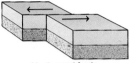
Horizontal fault

There are three kinds of faults, all of which move in different ways to create an earthquake. At a *normal fault,* one side of the fault drops below the other side. At a *thrust fault,* one side moves up and over the other. At a *horizontal*, or *slip-strike, fault,* one side moves sideways past the other.

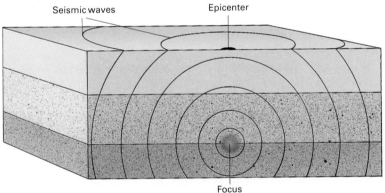
Seismic waves · Epicenter · Focus

Earthquakes usually occur deep in the ground. The point at which the fault begins to move is called the *focus.* The point on the surface above the focus is called the *epicenter.* The quake sets off seismic waves, or vibrations, that move out from the focus.

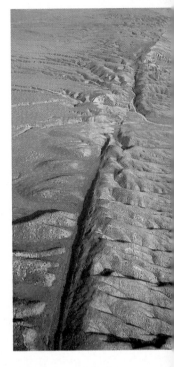
Most faults are deep underground. But sometimes, a section of a fault, such as this segment of the San Andreas Fault in California, *above,* appears as a large crack in the ground. The San Andreas is a horizontal fault.

two plates are colliding and the edge of one plate is being thrust under the edge of the other. This movement pushes rock on the surface of the subducting plate over the rock on the other plate. This process is occurring at several places along the western edge of North America. There, the Pacific Plate and two other plates are sliding beneath the North American Plate.

Although most earthquakes occur along plate boundaries, a significant number of them occur in the middle of the plates. Some of the most destructive earthquakes ever to hit the United States have been midplate quakes. An earthquake that struck New Madrid, Mo.,

Fault: A crack in Earth's outer layers.

Focus: The point on a fault where an earthquake begins.

Epicenter: The point on the surface above the focus.

Horizontal (or slip-strike) fault: A fault area where one side is moving sideways past the other.

Magnitude: A measure of the strength of an earthquake on the Richter scale.

Normal fault: A fault in which one side drops below the other during a quake.

Precursor: A physical or chemical event that may occur in the weeks, days, or hours before an earthquake strikes.

Seismic gap: A section of a fault where large earthquakes have not occurred in several decades.

Seismic waves: Vibrations, or waves through the ground, produced by earthquakes.

Seismograph: An instrument that detects earthquakes.

Seismologist: A scientist who studies earthquakes.

Thrust fault: A fault in which one side moves up and over the other side during a quake.

in December 1811—the first of three that rocked the area in late 1811 and early 1812—was so powerful that it changed the course of the Mississippi River and was felt in 27 states. Geologists believe midplate earthquakes take place along very deep faults that formed hundreds of millions of years ago because of the collision or breakup of tectonic plates. Most of these faults are normal faults.

Earthquakes may begin anywhere along a fault. The actual place where the fault begins to move is called the *focus* of an earthquake. The focus of the Loma Prieta earthquake, for example, was about 18 kilometers (11 miles) below the surface. The *epicenter* of an earthquake is the point on the surface above the focus. The epicenter of the Loma Prieta earthquake was about 97 kilometers southeast of San Francisco.

When an earthquake occurs, energy moves outward from the focus in a series of *seismic waves* that travel through the ground. There are three types of seismic waves: *primary waves*, *shear waves*, and *surface waves*. Primary waves travel the fastest. These waves cause rock to contract and expand. As the primary wave passes through, particles of rock are pressed together. After the wave has passed, the particles move apart.

Secondary waves, which travel at about half the speed of primary waves, cause the rock particles to vibrate from side to side. When secondary waves reach the surface, they create surface waves, which travel only along Earth's outer layers. Surface waves cause two types of motion—a rolling motion like that of ocean waves and a side to side motion. Surface waves are the slowest type of seismic wave and the biggest. As a result, they usually cause the most damage.

The strength of an earthquake depends mainly on the depth and size of the fault and how far the fault moves. Earthquakes with a shallow focus are more deadly than deeper quakes because more of their energy is concentrated at the surface. Also, in general, the longer the fault—and the greater the distance it moves during an earthquake—the more severe is the earthquake. During an earthquake, faults can move anywhere from a few centimeters to up to 10 meters (33 feet). Another factor determining a quake's power is the strength of the rock. Hard rock can withstand more pressure from plate movements than can soft rock and so releases more energy when it does break loose to cause an earthquake.

To measure the strength of earthquakes, seismologists use a *seismograph*, an instrument that can detect ground motion as small as 1 hundred-millionth of a centimeter. A seismograph produces wavy lines that record the varying *amplitudes* of the seismic waves passing beneath it. Like other waves, seismic waves resemble hills and valleys. Amplitude represents the distance a material—in this case the rock—rises or falls from its position at rest as a seismic wave passes through it.

Perhaps the most well-known gauge of the intensity of an

earthquake is the Richter scale, developed in 1935 by United States seismologist Charles F. Richter. The Richter scale measurement is based on the amplitude of the seismic waves. The *magnitude*, or strength, of the earthquake is calculated from the maximum amplitude—the maximum height of the wavy lines recorded by a seismograph.

The numbers on the Richter scale range from 1 to 8.9. An earthquake with a magnitude of 1 or 2 is so slight that only a seismograph can detect it. Thousands of such earthquakes occur every day. Earthquakes with a magnitude of 5 or less are generally considered minor. An earthquake registering 8.9 on the Richter scale, however, would destroy all the structures in the affected area. Theoretically, there is no upper limit to the Richter scale. That is why it is referred to as "open ended." But in reality, no type of rock is strong enough to withstand the pressure on a fault needed to produce a quake larger than 8.9.

The Richter scale is logarithmic. Each whole number represents a 10-fold increase in the motion of the ground. That means that an earthquake with a magnitude of 8, for example, is 10 times stronger than a quake registering 7, but 100 times stronger than one of magnitude 6. The 1989 Loma Prieta quake had a Richter magnitude

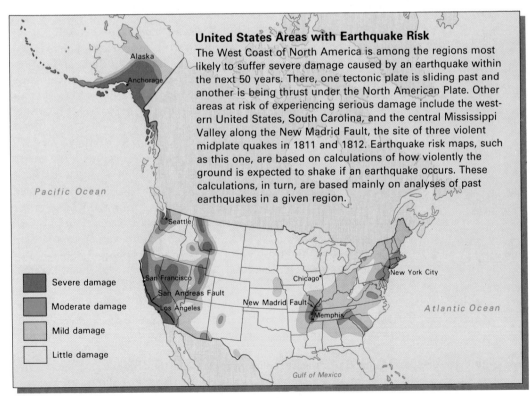

United States Areas with Earthquake Risk
The West Coast of North America is among the regions most likely to suffer severe damage caused by an earthquake within the next 50 years. There, one tectonic plate is sliding past and another is being thrust under the North American Plate. Other areas at risk of experiencing serious damage include the western United States, South Carolina, and the central Mississippi Valley along the New Madrid Fault, the site of three violent midplate quakes in 1811 and 1812. Earthquake risk maps, such as this one, are based on calculations of how violently the ground is expected to shake if an earthquake occurs. These calculations, in turn, are based mainly on analyses of past earthquakes in a given region.

Severe damage

Moderate damage

Mild damage

Little damage

Alaska

Anchorage

Pacific Ocean

Seattle

San Francisco

San Andreas Fault

Los Angeles

Chicago

New Madrid Fault

Memphis

New York City

Atlantic Ocean

Gulf of Mexico

Source: United States Geological Survey MF-2120.

of 7.1. By comparison, the San Francisco earthquake of 1906, which destroyed most of the city and which occurred before the invention of the Richter scale, had an estimated magnitude of 8.25. There have been three known earthquakes with an estimated magnitude of 8.9—one in the Pacific Ocean near the Colombia-Ecuador border in 1906, a second in Japan in 1933, and a third in Chile in 1960.

In the 1930's, seismologists began using Richter scale magnitudes to indicate the amount of energy released by an earthquake. They found that the energy released increased by a factor of about 30 with each whole number on the Richter scale. A magnitude 7 quake releases the equivalent of 180,000 tons of TNT; a magnitude 8 quake, 5.4 million tons. Thus, the 1906 San Francisco quake released more than 30 times more energy than did the Loma Prieta quake.

Another method of measuring the strength of an earthquake is by looking at its effects on people and buildings. This method is called the modified Mercalli scale. It does not have the mathematical precision of the Richter scale because the effects of an earthquake depend on local conditions such as soil type, building construction, and distance from the epicenter. Its damage categories range from I, which would be barely felt, to XII, which would be total destruction. Using the Mercalli scale and historical accounts of old earthquakes, seismologists can estimate the strength of those quakes.

Scientists who study earthquakes note that quakes themselves don't kill people. They cause death indirectly. Most earthquake-related casualties are the result of collapsing buildings, bridges, and dams.

During an earthquake, the various types of seismic waves cause these structures to contract and expand, sway from side to side, or bounce up and down. Buildings and other structures must be strong enough and flexible enough to withstand all these motions.

Engineers have developed ways to build earthquake-resistant structures. Comparing the Loma Prieta earthquake with the earthquake that rocked Armenia in December 1988 dramatically illustrates how effective earthquake-resistant construction techniques can be. The Loma Prieta earthquake measured 7.1 on the Richter scale; the Armenia earthquake measured 6.7. The Loma Prieta quake caused about 62 deaths and more than 3,700 injuries, left more than 12,000 people homeless, and caused up to $6 billion in damage. But the less powerful Armenia earthquake left 25,000 dead and 500,000 homeless and caused an estimated $20 billion in damage.

In Armenia, most of the buildings were not made to withstand powerful vibrations, so they were severely damaged or destroyed. The most common type of modern building was a nine-story structure made of prefabricated hollow concrete floors loosely fastened to concrete columns and beams. During the earthquake, the vibrations caused the floors to separate from the columns and beams.

By contrast, relatively few buildings were damaged by the Loma Prieta earthquake. The most heavily damaged buildings were

Measuring the Strength of Earthquakes

The best-known way of measuring the strength, or magnitude, of earthquakes is the Richter scale, which ranges from 1 (very slight) to 8.9 (very severe). Each whole number on the Richter scale represents a tenfold increase in strength. Thus, a magnitude 7 quake is 10 times stronger than a magnitude 6 quake and 100 times stronger than a magnitude 5 quake.

A seismologist examines the record of vibrations from an earthquake as recorded by a seismograph, an instrument that detects ground motion. A quake's magnitude on the Richter scale is determined by the height of the wavy lines registered by the seismograph. The stronger the quake, the taller are the lines.

In addition to measuring a quake's strength, the Richter scale indicates the energy released by the quake. Each whole number on the scale represents a 30-fold increase in the amount of energy released. A magnitude 7 quake releases the energy equivalent of 180,000 tons of the explosive TNT; a magnitude 8 quake, the equivalent of 5.4 million tons of TNT. Using the scale at left to indicate the energy released by a magnitude 8.9 earthquake would require a red bar about 17 meters (55 feet) long.

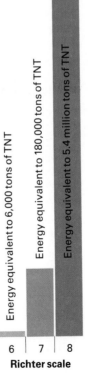

Energy equivalent to 6,000 tons of TNT

Energy equivalent to 180,000 tons of TNT

Energy equivalent to 5.4 million tons of TNT

| 6 | 7 | 8 |

Richter scale

The Magnitudes of Some Famous Earthquakes

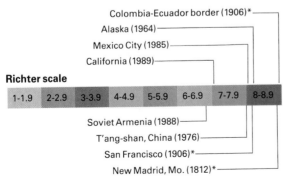

Colombia-Ecuador border (1906)*
Alaska (1964)
Mexico City (1985)
California (1989)

Richter scale

| 1-1.9 | 2-2.9 | 3-3.9 | 4-4.9 | 5-5.9 | 6-6.9 | 7-7.9 | 8-8.9 |

Soviet Armenia (1988)
T'ang-shan, China (1976)
San Francisco (1906)*
New Madrid, Mo. (1812)*

*Estimated.

unreinforced brick or stone structures built before 1933, when California instituted building codes to minimize earthquake damage. Most of these buildings near the epicenter collapsed or were heavily damaged. Many old wood-frame buildings slid off their foundations.

Earthquake-resistant building techniques range from very simple to fairly complex. Making wood-frame buildings better able to withstand earthquakes involves bolting them to their foundations and bracing their walls. Houses can be braced by installing diagonal beams in the walls, by inserting steel rods or plates within the walls, or by attaching sheets of plywood to the frame during construction. Many of San Francisco's houses and medium-sized buildings— structures of 5 to 15 stories—were protected in this way.

Another way to protect medium-sized buildings is to install devices that act like the shock absorbers in a car. These include springs and *bearings* (pads of rubber and steel wrapped around a lead core). Installed between the building and its foundation, the springs and bearings absorb some of the up-and-down and sideways movement caused by an earthquake that would otherwise damage the building. There are about 150 buildings with some type of shock-absorbing system worldwide, most of them in Japan.

These systems, however, cannot be used for skyscrapers, which must be anchored up to tens of meters in the ground to keep them from tipping over during a quake. Thanks to California's building codes, most of San Francisco's skyscrapers survived the Loma Prieta earthquake fairly well. Like those elsewhere, San Francisco's sky-scrapers have a supporting framework consisting of columns and beams made of steel or steel-reinforced concrete that are rigidly connected at their joints. Under California's building codes, however, frameworks must be strongly reinforced to withstand seismic shak-ing. For example, beams must be thicker and joints stronger than those in a normal skyscraper. A reinforced framework absorbs and distributes the energy from an earthquake throughout the building, allowing it to move as a unit without collapsing.

Engineers are looking for even better ways to design earthquake-resistant buildings. An experimental computer-controlled earth-quake-protection system for medium-sized buildings is now being tested in a six-story building in Japan. This system was developed by scientists at the National Center for Earthquake Engineering Re-search in Buffalo, N.Y., and engineers from Takenaka Corporation in Japan. The system uses two computer-controlled devices to counteract the swaying motion of the building. The first device consists of a metal block weighing 5.4 metric tons (6 short tons) suspended at the top of a building. This device is a variation of a device already used in some skyscrapers to minimize swaying caused by strong wind. The second device consists of four pistons anchored to a central column and connected to building columns. It is designed to counteract movement at the base of the building.

Before construction began in Japan, the Buffalo scientists built a model of the building and tested it on an earthquake simulator called a shaking table. This huge concrete slab is controlled by a computer that stores records of more than 1,000 earthquakes obtained from seismographs. Using the simulator, the scientists can re-create the motion of these quakes. In tests of the computer-controlled system, the scientists found that it reduced the swaying in the model normally caused by a magnitude 7 earthquake by up to 70 per cent.

Sometimes, however, no matter how well-constructed a building is, earthquakes cause serious damage. One reason is the type of soil on which a structure rests. Surface waves traveling through loosely packed soil tend to be stronger than waves moving through solid rock. As a result, they set up more powerful vibrations in sandy soil. If sandy soil is also damp, it can be very unstable. During a strong earthquake, the vibrations cause the water in the soil to surround the sand particles, temporarily turning the soil into liquid. As a result, the buildings sitting on this liquid foundation could collapse. This is what happened in October 1989 in the Marina district of San Francisco, where many buildings were seriously damaged.

Another important factor determining the extent of damage is the *natural frequency* of the building. Like a tuning fork, every material vibrates when shaken or struck. The rate at which it does so is called its natural frequency.

An especially perilous situation exists when the frequency of a building matches that of the soil on which it rests. This accounted for much of the devastation that occurred when two large earthquakes, registering 8.1 and 7.3 on the Richter scale, struck Mexico City in 1985, killing at least 7,000 people. Much of Mexico City sits on an old lake bed of loosely packed sand and clay. The natural frequency of these sediments matched those of buildings 10 to 14 stories high. As a result, the vibrations in the soil greatly amplified the vibrations in the buildings, producing violent shaking that severely damaged or destroyed the buildings. Taller and shorter buildings, which had different frequencies, generally escaped such heavy damage.

Since the 1960's, increased funding for earthquake research and technological advances in the devices used to record and measure earthquakes have spurred scientists to make great efforts to develop methods for predicting earthquakes. They are trying to forecast when earthquakes will occur with enough certainty that people and government agencies can act to minimize damage and destruction. The task is difficult, however, because geologists still don't understand all the characteristics of the forces, such as seismic waves, at work within Earth. In addition, earthquakes have occurred along any particular fault for many hundreds or thousands of years. But scientific records of earthquakes have been kept only since about 1900.

So geologists have developed some ingenious methods to make

How Earthquakes Damage Buildings

Seismic waves produced by earthquakes damage buildings and other structures by making them move in various ways. Buildings can be constructed strong enough to withstand these motions and flexible enough to move as a unit and so avoid being shaken apart.

Seismic waves can cause houses to slide off their foundations. They can also make buildings contract and expand, shake from side to side, and bounce up and down.

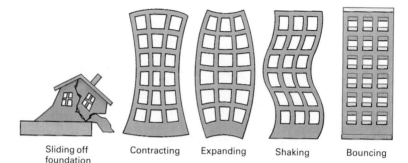

Sliding off foundation   Contracting   Expanding   Shaking   Bouncing

Building Earthquake-Resistant Structures

There are a number of ways to build earthquake-resistant structures, some of them simple, others complex. Houses can be bolted more securely to their foundation. Houses and medium-sized buildings can be strengthened with diagonal beams or cross bracing within the walls. Buildings may also have a *shear wall,* an interior support wall made of steel-reinforced concrete.

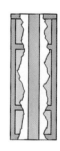

Bolt house securely to foundation   Cross bracing   Shear wall

Devices that separate a building from its foundation can absorb some of the motion from an earthquake. These devices include springs and *bearings* (pads of rubber and steel surrounding a lead core).

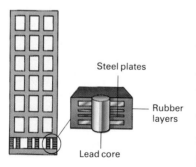

Steel plates

Rubber layers

Lead core

To counteract swaying during an earthquake, an experimental system being tested in Japan, *right,* uses two computer-controlled devices: a large metal block set on tracks at the top of the building, and a set of four giant pistons attached to a central column in the basement. If the building moves to the right, the devices pull it to the left.

Metal block

Pistons

general predictions about areas at risk for an earthquake. One such method is the so-called *seismic gap* method developed by seismologists in the 1960's. A seismic gap is a place along a fault where large earthquakes have occurred in the past but not within the last several decades. Seismologists locate seismic gaps by analyzing the number and location of earthquakes recorded by the vast system of seismographs that have been set up throughout the world, especially in earthquake-prone regions. This information is plotted on a map. Places on a fault with an unusually low number of recent earthquakes, thus, are likely candidates for future ruptures.

Using the seismic gap method, seismologists had determined that both the Loma Prieta area and Mexico City were generally at risk. For example, in May 1985, geophysicists L. Victoria LeFevre of the California Institute of Technology in Pasadena and Karen C. McNally of the University of California, Santa Cruz, predicted that an earthquake would occur in a seismic gap along the southwestern coast of Mexico and Guatemala within the near future. The earthquakes that rocked Mexico City in September of that year began along this section of the fault. In 1988, geologists at the United States Geological Survey had determined that the segment of the San Andreas Fault that ruptured during the Loma Prieta quake was more likely to rupture than any other section of the fault north of Los Angeles.

Although useful for long-term prediction, the seismic gap method cannot even come close to estimating the exact time of an earthquake.

Scientists use a variety of methods to learn how earthquakes damage structures. Huge hydraulic jacks, *above left,* exert pressure— similar to that from a large earthquake—on a section of the Nimitz Freeway still standing after the Loma Prieta quake. Engineers test a model of a building on a shaking table, *above,* a computer-controlled concrete slab that can re-create the motion of earthquakes. Information from such tests may help in designing structures that can better withstand powerful earthquakes.

In their attempts to forecast individual quakes more precisely, seismologists have experimented with several other techniques. With one method, they determine how often earthquakes occur along a particular segment of a fault in order to estimate when the next one will occur. In China and western Asia and some parts of the Mediterranean region, this involves the study of historical records.

In the United States, however, historical records do not go back far enough, so seismologists must study the faults themselves. They do this by digging trenches along a fault and examining the geologic layers in it. Normally, these are fairly regular horizontal layers, formed by sediments laid down over thousands of years. An earthquake, however, shifts and tilts the layers.

Geologist Kerry N. Sieh of the California Institute of Technology has studied geologic layers at various points along the San Andreas Fault in southern California. He found 10 major breaks in the layers that, he concluded, correspond to major earthquakes. He also found that these breaks occur at intervals that suggest major quakes happen on average every 132 years. The last major earthquake on this part of the fault was in 1857, 133 years ago. This finding has led many seismologists to predict that a major earthquake is likely in the near future. But telling the future may not be quite that easy.

According to Sieh's data, the time spans between earthquakes have not been a constant 132 years. Instead, he has found evidence of clusters of quakes—two to three quakes separated by several decades. The clusters seem to be separated from each other by quiet periods lasting two to three centuries. At present, the section of the San Andreas Fault studied by Sieh appears to be in a quiet period between clusters. So a major quake may not be imminent.

Another way of attempting to predict earthquakes is to look for *precursors*, physical or chemical events that take place just before an earthquake occurs. Since the 1960's, seismologists in the United States have rigged sections of the San Andreas Fault with an array of scientific instruments. Among these instruments are devices that can detect minute changes in the tilt or elevation of the land, note small movements on the surface or hundreds of meters below, monitor gases released from the ground, or record changes in the rock's ability to conduct electricity. After an earthquake, the seismologists examine the data from these instruments and compare them with data from other earthquakes to determine if a pattern exists.

Seismologists using this approach have discovered a number of precursors. For example, they have found that the land around the fault may tilt up or down in the weeks before a quake. Another precursor may be an increase in the number of smaller quakes, called *microearthquakes*, in the area shortly before a major tremor.

In the 1970's, several seismologists found that electricity flows more easily through the rock in a fault in the hours before an earthquake. To explain this phenomenon, the scientists developed

Predicting Earthquakes

Seismologists can make fairly accurate long-term predictions of where earthquakes are likely to occur. Their forecasts of when earthquakes will strike are much less precise, mainly because of an incomplete knowledge of the forces within Earth that cause earthquakes.

Earthquakes occurring between Jan. 1, 1969, and July 31, 1989

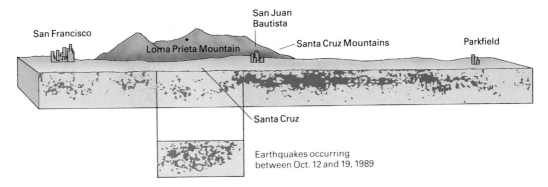

San Francisco · Loma Prieta Mountain · San Juan Bautista · Santa Cruz Mountains · Parkfield · Santa Cruz

Earthquakes occurring between Oct. 12 and 19, 1989

Seismic Gap Analysis

One way to make long-term predictions about where earthquakes will strike is to identify *seismic gaps,* areas along faults where large earthquakes have not occurred for several decades. Between 1969 and the late 1980's, few earthquakes (represented by red dots) occurred in a segment of the San Andreas Fault southeast of San Francisco. This led geologists in 1988 to conclude that this segment was highly likely to rupture within 30 years. On Oct. 17, 1989, the segment slipped, producing the Loma Prieta earthquake.

Measuring Fault Movements

Geologists also monitor the movement of faults, looking for signs of a potential earthquake. A technician fires a laser, *left,* on one side of the San Andreas Fault at a reflector on the other side. Measurements of the time it takes the beam, *below,* to return to the laser enable geologists to detect the movement of rock along the fault of less than 1 millimeter (¹⁄₂₅ inch).

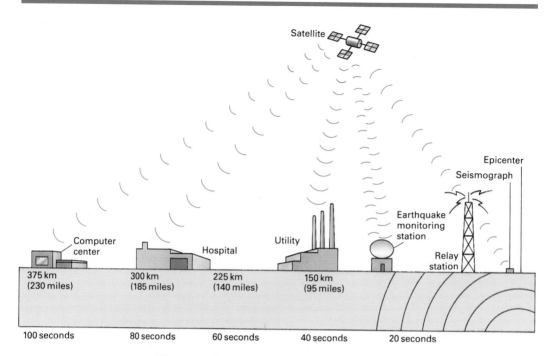

Satellite

Epicenter

Seismograph

Earthquake
monitoring
station

Computer
center

Hospital

Utility

Relay
station

| 375 km (230 miles) | 300 km (185 miles) | 225 km (140 miles) | 150 km (95 miles) | |

100 seconds   80 seconds   60 seconds   40 seconds   20 seconds

Warning of a Coming Quake

Real-time warning systems would provide a few seconds' or minutes' warning that an earthquake is occurring. Such systems are based on the fact that radio waves travel faster than seismic waves. If one or more of the seismographs positioned along various faults detected movement, this information would be transmitted to a relay station then forwarded via satellite to an earthquake-monitoring station. There, a computer would evaluate the information. If the computer determined that a serious earthquake was occurring, it would radio a warning via the satellite to utilities, computer centers, and hospitals and other emergency-response agencies. The farther from the epicenter, the greater would be the warning time.

what they call the *dilatancy theory*. According to this theory, the rocks at a fault about to rupture are under such strain that tiny cracks open up in them. As the rock expands, gases trapped in the rock escape and water flows into the cracks. The water increases the electrical conductivity of the rock. This theory may also explain why there may be an increase in the amount of radon, a naturally occurring radioactive gas, released from the ground before a quake.

Geologists have successfully used precursors to predict some earthquakes, most notably in China in 1975. In early February, Chinese scientists noticed that a number of microearthquakes were occurring in Liaoning Province in northeast China. The microquakes climaxed a series of other events, including changes in Earth's magnetic field in that region, that had occurred in the previous two or three years. These earlier events had led Chinese seismologists to predict in June 1974 that a moderate earthquake could occur in the next two years. On the morning of Feb. 4, 1975, Chinese authorities—believing the microquakes indicated a large quake was about to occur—urged the people there to get outdoors and stay there. An earthquake of magnitude 7.3 shook the region that evening. Although the earthquake caused much damage, there was little loss of life because the people were not in the collapsing buildings.

The problem with precursors is that they don't always occur. For example, Chinese scientists failed to detect any precursors before a major earthquake struck T'ang-shan, China, on July 28, 1976, causing about 250,000 deaths. There apparently were no precursors in the Loma Prieta quake either.

Given our still-imperfect ability to predict earthquakes, adequate preparation may be the most effective way of protecting ourselves against earthquake damage. One of the most promising developments in this area is the research on *real-time earthquake warning systems* being conducted by a number of scientists. These systems are based on the fact that radio waves travel faster than seismic waves, so the systems can radio a few seconds' or minutes' warning that an earthquake has occurred or is occurring—before the seismic waves arrive. The farther from the epicenter, the greater the warning time.

Information about any movement along faults recorded by seismographs would be transmitted to a central monitoring station. If the computer there determined that an earthquake greater than magnitude 6 was occurring, it would radio a warning via satellite to computers at emergency-response agencies, police and fire stations, hospitals, and other essential services. The system could also warn computers at railroads and public transportation systems to stop trains, at utility companies to shut down natural gas lines, and at computer data centers to take steps to protect the information stored there. The system could also help seismologists determine which areas were likely to have suffered the greatest damage so that emergency units could be sent there.

No matter how much we learn about earthquakes, they will always remain one of nature's most awesome phenomena. By unlocking their secrets, however, we can reduce our fear of them and help cope with their destructive power.

For further reading:

Atkinson, William. *The Next New Madrid Earthquake: A Survival Guide for the Midwest.* Southern Illinois University Press, 1989.
Bolt, Bruce A. *Earthquakes.* W. H. Freeman and Company, 1988.
Stein, Ross S., and Yeats, Robert S. "Hidden Earthquakes." *Scientific American,* June 1989.
Tator, Joel. *Surviving the Big One: How to Prepare for a Major Earthquake.* 1989. Videocassette available from KCET Video, 4401 Sunset Boulevard, Los Angeles, CA 90027.

U.S. scientists are preparing to do battle with Africanized "killer" bees, now arriving from south of the border.

Invasion of the "Killer" Bees

BY JESSICA ANN MORRISON SILVA

The biology course in a tropical rain forest was something that University of Miami graduate student Inn-Siang Ooi probably had eagerly awaited. The course, offered by the Organization for Tropical Studies, lets students study firsthand the rain forests of Costa Rica and their inhabitants. Little did Inn-Siang know that some of those forest dwellers would viciously attack and kill him.

Halfway through the course, in July 1986, Inn-Siang and a group of other graduate students hiked to a system of caves where they could observe bats roosting. Inn-Siang and a few other students went ahead of the group, climbing over expanses of jagged limestone. As they neared the mouth of one of the caves, Inn-Siang went around a rock ledge and disappeared from sight. Suddenly, he came stumbling back toward the group, his arms flailing wildly at a cloud of bees that swirled about his head. Unable to escape the bees and covered with stings, Inn-Siang lost his footing

Absconding: Departure of an entire Africanized bee colony in response to a disturbance.

African honey bees: Honey bees native to Africa; of the same species as European honey bees but of a different subspecies.

Africanized honey bees: Hybrid bees resulting from interbreeding between African and European honey bees.

Drone: A male honey bee, whose only function is to mate with the queen.

European honey bees: Honey bees native to Europe; brought to North America by colonists in the 1600's.

Queen bee: The one egg-laying female bee in a hive.

Swarming: The departure of a queen and thousands of workers from a hive to start another colony; occurs when the queen has been replaced by a new queen.

Worker bees: Female bees that perform all of a colony's labor, such as raising young, gathering food, and protecting the hive from predators.

The author:
Jessica Ann Morrison Silva is a free-lance science writer who has written extensively about Africanized bees.

on a treacherous outcrop of rock and fell into a crevice. As he lay trapped, the bees continued their attack, and when the other students tried to go to their comrade's aid, the bees turned on them and forced them to retreat. It was night before Inn-Siang's lifeless body was pulled from the fissure. An autopsy revealed that he had been stung at least 8,000 times.

Inn-Siang was the unlucky victim of *Africanized honey bees*, more commonly known as "killer bees" because of their aggressive behavior. One *entomologist* (scientist who studies insects) has called the Africanized bee "a honey bee with a personality problem." The honey bee common in the United States is the European honey bee, brought over from Europe in the 1600's. Like the European bees, Africanized bees collect pollen and nectar and produce honey. But unlike European bees, Africanized bees defend their hives fiercely. They respond more quickly to a threat, chase their victim farther, and inflict many more stings. So, even though their venom is no more potent than that of domestic bees, Africanized bees on the attack can bring quick and painful death to a hapless rabbit, bird, or human being. They have even been known to kill horses.

Although one can easily see how these insects earned the name killer bees, scientists much prefer to call them Africanized bees. The name refers to their heritage: They are descendants of a cross between African and European honey bees. The hybrids got their start in 1957 after some African bees escaped from a Brazilian laboratory and began interbreeding in the wild with the more gentle European bees. Since then, Africanized bees have spread throughout South and Central America and Mexico, invading the hives of European bees, killing as many as 1,000 people, and wreaking havoc with agriculture, beekeeping, and life in general. That's the bad news. The even worse news is that they're heading our way; U.S. agricultural officials expect the bees to enter Texas from Mexico by the end of 1990.

Most experts predict that the bees will eventually have a significant impact on agriculture and commercial honey-making operations throughout the southern part of the United States. Many beekeepers in that region may shut down, fearful that they could face lawsuits by bee-sting victims. Those that stay open may have to pay high liability insurance premiums, buy extra equipment, and hire more employees to cope with the aggressive bees. The higher costs involved will be passed on to farmers, who rent hives of bees to pollinate many of their crops. In some areas, Africanized bees may become so dominant that farmers will have to rely on them for pollination. If so, reduced crop yields are a distinct possibility because the bees are not only ferocious, they are also unreliable pollinators.

Because of the potential menace that Africanized bees pose to American agriculture, their impending arrival has been taken very seriously by the U.S. government. Scientists with the U.S. Depart-

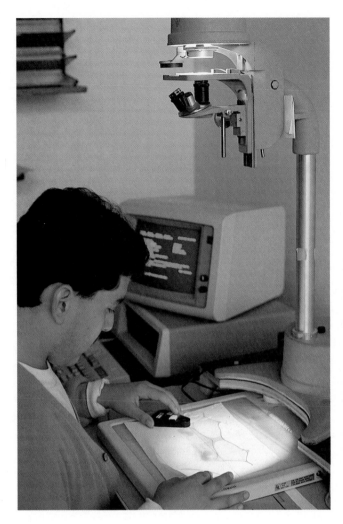

Genetic Cousins

Africanized honey bees, *bottom,* carrying loads of pollen, are almost identical to European bees, *below.* Visual and computer analysis of magnified bee body parts, *left,* is often needed to make a positive identification of Africanized bees.

ment of Agriculture (USDA) have been studying the bees and their behavior intently, searching for ways to blunt the invasion. Some USDA researchers have been working in laboratories in the United States, while others have been conducting field work in Mexico, in cooperation with Mexican agricultural officials and scientists.

Africanized bees have become such a problem because they were accidentally released from a research laboratory in Brazil. In the 1950's, Brazilian officials engaged a geneticist at the University of São Paulo, Warwick E. Kerr, to develop a new variety of bees that would be better honey producers than European bees. Although European bees flourish in Europe and the United States, they had not adapted well to the hot, humid climate of South America. With the intention of producing a hybrid bee for the tropics, Kerr imported from South Africa and Tanzania 47 African honey bee queens that were ready to lay eggs. The ferocious African bee is a subspecies of the same species

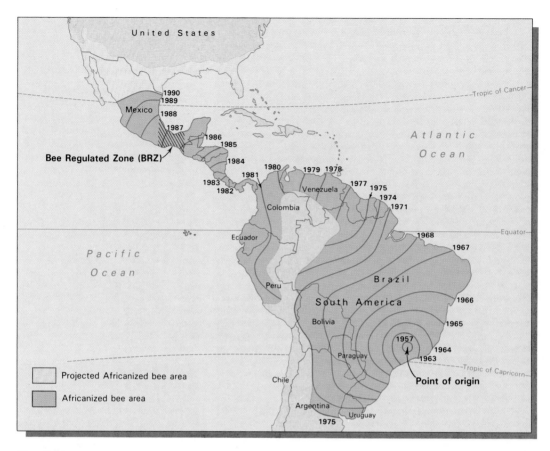

United States

1990
1989
1988
Mexico
1987
1986
1985
Bee Regulated Zone (BRZ)
1984
1983
1982
1980
1979 1978
1981
1977
1975
Venezuela
1974
1971
Colombia
Ecuador
1968
1967
Pacific
Ocean
Brazil
Peru
South America
1966
Bolivia
1965
1957
1964
Paraguay
1963
Chile
Point of origin
Argentina
Uruguay
1975

Atlantic
Ocean

Tropic of Cancer
Equator
Tropic of Capricorn

Projected Africanized bee area

Africanized bee area

The Advance of the Bees

Africanized bees originated in Brazil in 1957 and since then have spread steadily northward and southward. In 1987, U.S. and Mexican agricultural officials set up a "Bee Regulated Zone" in southern Mexico in an attempt to stop or weaken the invasion. Despite that effort, the bees continued their advance and could eventually spread through at least the lower one-third of the United States.

that includes European bees. African bees thrive in Africa's tropical climate and produce honey all year long. They evolved their highly aggressive nature as a means of protecting their nests from human honey hunters and a variety of animal predators.

Kerr's goal was to crossbreed the two kinds of bees to create an insect with the relatively gentle personality of European bees and the tolerance to heat and humidity of African bees. But, reportedly, a visitor to Kerr's laboratory in 1957 mistakenly removed special traps that had been placed over the African beehives. Soon, 26 swarms of pure-African bees had escaped the laboratory. The insects promptly began to infiltrate wild bee colonies and mate with European bees. These uncontrolled matings produced a hybrid bee, but it wasn't the hybrid that Kerr had intended. The aggressive Africanized honey bee had been born.

Except for their stinging behavior, the hybrid bees were almost indistinguishable from European bees, though they were very slightly smaller and weighed a bit less. In fact, all honey bees—African, European, or Africanized—look the same to the unaided eye and share basic biological and behavioral traits.

Honey bees are *social insects:* They live together in large groups, and each individual in a group contributes to the welfare of the whole. This cooperative behavior involves a sharp division of labor. Hives consist of 30,000 to 80,000 bees, and each has one reproducing female, the queen. The queen is larger than all the other females, which are called *workers*. Male bees, whose only purpose in life is to mate with the queen, are called *drones*.

The queen has the longest life of any of the bees in a hive. A queen typically lives for one to three years, but some bee experts have reported that life spans of four to six years for queens are not uncommon. Worker bees usually live for about 6 to 12 weeks, and most drones die within one month after hatching.

A worker bee performs a succession of specific tasks. Over the course of her life, she serves as a janitor, a nurse, a builder, a security guard, and a food collector—in that order.

The janitor bee—at 1 day old—carries out hive wastes, cleans honeycomb cells, and secretes a disinfectant into the cells to prepare them for eggs. Next, she is a nurse for a week, caring for and feeding young, developing bees—called *larvae*—which resemble worms.

When she is about 10 days old, the worker takes up the construction business. She secretes a wax (beeswax) from her abdomen to help build a honeycomb—a mass of six-sided compartments that house honey, pollen, developing eggs, and *pupae*—dormant bees that are developing into adults.

Moving on to her next chore, the worker guards the hive, attacking intruders such as birds and wasps. A worker that stings a trespasser dies, her stinger torn out and lodged in the victim's body. The worker who avoids that fate, as most do, lives out her days gathering food for the hive—pollen from flowers and sugary nectar from vegetable and fruit blossoms. In a sac just behind her mouth, she adds a chemical substance to the nectar that transforms it into honey.

Keeping the hive populated with bees is the responsibility of the queen and the drones. Leaving the nest for a short while, the queen mates in midair with up to a dozen drones. During mating, the drones die. The queen then returns to the hive to lay her eggs, many of which did not get fertilized in the mating. The unfertilized eggs, containing genes from only the queen, yield drones. Fertilized eggs, with genes from both the queen and a mate, develop into females.

Most females become workers, but several are destined for royalty. Nurse bees feed those few female larvae a substance called *royal jelly*, a mayonnaiselike food produced in special glands in the head. The royal jelly causes the larvae to develop into queens. When they emerge from their cells, the new queens fight to the death, each vying for "the throne." The old queen either dies or leaves with between 5,000 and 25,000 workers to start another colony. This phenomenon, called *swarming*, is how new colonies are formed, and it is one of the most dramatic examples of bees' social behavior.

But it is honey and the bees' nectar and pollen-gathering behavior that makes them so valuable to human society. Beekeepers in the United States sell more than $140 million worth of honey and beeswax a year. To ensure that their bees produce enough honey for consumers' breakfast tables, beekeepers place empty honeycombs into hives for the workers to fill.

Farmers rent bees to pollinate crops. Some 1,600 U.S. beekeepers truck hives thousands of kilometers each year to provide pollination services. As worker bees gather pollen and nectar in crop fields, pollen sticks to their hairy bodies and is carried from one plant to another, allowing fertilization to take place. Bees pollinate some 90 major crops, worth more than $20 billion.

When it comes to producing honey, Africanized bees do not seem to meet the standards of American agriculture. That conclusion is based in part on field research in Venezuela, where commercial honey-making operations declined dramatically after the invasion of Africanized bees in 1976. One leading bee expert, Thomas E. Rinderer of the USDA, studied the honey-producing abilities of European and Africanized bees in Venezuela. He and his colleagues found that European bees make more honey than Africanized bees when plants secrete lots of nectar; Africanized bees are the superior honey producers when relatively little nectar is available. In the United States, Rinderer says, different plants produce large quantities of nectar at specific times of the year, a situation better suited to European bees. Also, he adds, Africanized bees carry less nectar and forage farther from the hive than European bees, traits that make them less efficient honey producers.

As pollinators, Africanized bees do fairly well. With their quick, darting movements, they disperse pollen farther than the much-slower European bees do. Furthermore, Africanized bees produce more young than European bees and those young grow to adulthood faster, so an Africanized hive has more workers gathering pollen. But these positive characteristics are offset by several negative traits that could drastically hamper crop pollination on U.S. farms. Because Africanized bees produce large numbers of fast-growing young, their hives quickly become overpopulated. As a result, Africanized bees swarm up to 10 times more frequently than European bees, making them much less dependable as pollinators. Africanized bees are also prone to a type of swarming called *absconding*, in which the entire colony flies away to a new location in response to even a slight disturbance, such as a small animal passing. To beekeepers—and the farmers who depend on them—that's money literally flying away.

To most people's minds, of course, the bees' most negative trait is their aggressiveness. But whether they are all as fierce as the ones that killed Inn-Siang Ooi is a matter of some debate. Many scientists believe that in many areas the mixing of African and European genes has yielded a bee that is less aggressive in defending its hive than the pure-African varieties. This theory supports the idea of promoting

A Ferocious Nature

A researcher in Venezuela, *left,* tests the aggressiveness of Africanized bees by disturbing a hive. Hundreds of stingers left in gloves, *below,* attest to the fury of disturbed Africanized bees and make it clear how they came to be called "killer" bees.

continued interbreeding between the two kinds of bees to further dilute the African variety's undesirable characteristics. Some researchers contend that gene mixing explains the unpredictability of the Africanized bees' behavior. Some bees in what are thought to be Africanized colonies have been reported to be as mild-mannered as European bees. Such colonies might have acquired a number of genes from European bees.

But other researchers dispute that notion. One of them, entomologist Orley R. Taylor of the University of Kansas in Lawrence, argues that the genes of European bees cannot dilute the aggressiveness of Africanized bees. Taylor contends that Africanized bees in Central and South America are just as aggressive as wild bees in Africa, even though they have been interbreeding with European bees since the late 1950's. In fact, he says the bees in Latin America differ so slightly from African bees that they are in essence the same insect.

Bees in Agriculture

Bees are economically important to farming. In commercial hives, *right,* they produce honey, and rented hives are often trucked to fields so the bees can pollinate crops, *above.* Scientists fear that if Africanized bees displace European bees in many U.S. areas, they would not be as effective in doing either of these jobs.

Tests have confirmed the extreme defensiveness and ferocity of the Latin-American bees. In Venezuela and Argentina, Rinderer and USDA geneticist Anita M. Collins simulated animals intruding on Africanized and European bee colonies by waving a suede-leather target at hive entrances. The scientists found that Africanized bees had five times as many guards stationed at the hive openings— almost as if they were expecting trouble. In addition, twice as many Africanized bees responded to the disturbances, and they inflicted 8 to 10 times more stings on the target than did European bees.

Despite these findings, Rinderer disagrees with Taylor that Africanized bees cannot be "tamed." He says that in Brazil, where Africanized bees have been around for the longest time, the insects are already less aggressive than the Africanized bees one encounters in other South American countries. The reason, he explains, is that Brazilian beekeepers, who have succeeded in adapting their operations to Africanized bees, have "selected" for gentler bees. That is, they have looked for Africanized bees that are somewhat less aggressive than most and helped them to breed.

Nonetheless, reducing the aggressiveness of Africanized bees is not an easy process, and that is especially true in the wild. One problem is that in areas that have become heavily populated by Africanized bees, the invaders have a clear advantage in numbers. The hybrid bees produce more drones than their European cousins, so a queen—European or Africanized—has a greater chance of mating with an Africanized drone than a European drone. What's more, European bees quickly accept Africanized males into their colonies, making it even more likely that a queen will produce Africanized offspring. On the other hand, Africanized hives will rarely admit European males.

Africanized bees often invade European hives en masse. If the hive has no queen at the time, the newcomers quickly install one of their own. When, as is more often the case, the hive does have a queen, they kill her and replace her with an Africanized queen. A swarm of Africanized bees that cannot find an existing hive will colonize almost anywhere—on the side of a house, in a hole in the ground, in an old tire or a garbage can, or under a bridge.

Through this continual process of swarming and forming new colonies, Africanized bees have spread relentlessly northward at a rate of about 300 to 500 kilometers (200 to 300 miles) a year. By the time the bees reached Mexico, in late 1986, it was evident that unless drastic action was taken, it would only be a matter of time—three or four years—before they made it to the United States.

In September 1987, the USDA's Animal and Plant Health Inspection Service (APHIS)—an agency responsible for many pest-control programs—joined with the government of Mexico to establish an Africanized Honey Bee Cooperative Program in a "Bee Regulated Zone" (BRZ) just west of the Isthmus of Tehuantepec in southern Mexico. The isthmus, at 145 kilometers (90 miles) wide, is the narrowest part of Mexico. Two goals were set for the program: to slow the northward movement of the bees and to genetically modify the bees that make it past the BRZ.

Activities in the BRZ were concentrated in two "operational units," centered at Puerto Escondido, a town on the Pacific coast, and at the city of Veracruz, on the Gulf of Mexico. The units flanked the Sierra Madre range. The scientists thought that this mountainous area itself could be safely ignored because Africanized bees had seldom ventured into the high mountains of southern Mexico.

In both units, Mexican workers set out hives baited with natural sex attractants called *pheromones*. The hives were checked once every two weeks, and any in which Africanized bees were found were wrapped in plastic bags and filled with poisonous exhaust fumes from a truck. By late 1989, the bee hunters had destroyed nearly 14,000 Africanized swarms in this manner.

The bee-trapping teams enlisted the support of Mexican beekeepers in their efforts, training them to paint their queens with bright acrylic paint or nail polish and then check their hives at least every two months. The beekeepers assumed that any unpainted queens they found in hives were Africanized and replaced them with European queens. Beekeepers were also encouraged to equip their hives with devices that prevented queens from entering or leaving.

Some scientists believe that the cooperative program slowed the bees' migration and genetically diluted those that moved through the BRZ areas, but others disagree. What was certain was that by January 1990, the main Africanized population was less than 500 kilometers (300 miles) from the Texas border. Work continued in the BRZ, especially the Veracruz area, but it was clear by then that the bees would soon be arriving in the United States.

But Americans needn't be concerned about seeing dark clouds of killer bees moving across the Rio Grande. Scientists expect that for a while at least, only a few swarms of bees at a time will head north from Mexico—first into Texas and later into Arizona, New Mexico, and California. From the border areas of those states, the bees will slowly migrate north and east. How far they will ultimately spread is anyone's guess. Experts agree that the bees will establish themselves at least as far north as the lower third of the country—the region of warmth—in an uneven line running from the middle of California on the west to South Carolina on the east. But some scientists say the bees will eventually invade most of the United States. USDA researchers in Venezuela reported Africanized bees living in the cold environment of the high Andes mountains. When scientists translate that finding to North American latitudes, they predict that the bees will be able to survive winters as far north as Minneapolis, Minn. Some experts, though, question whether the bees observed in the Andes were really Africanized bees.

Determining with scientific certainty whether a colony of bees is indeed Africanized can be difficult. Because Africanized and European bees look so similar, bees from suspect colonies must be analyzed in the laboratory to establish their identity. That task—certain to be a common one as the bees spread through the United States—was made easier by a computer program developed in the 1980's by Rinderer. Laboratory technicians make precise measurements of a bee's body parts and enter the data into the program, which then calculates the probability that the bee is Africanized. If the computer says the bee is most likely Africanized, APHIS operating procedures call for several immediate steps: Officials are to set up traps in a 3.5-kilometer (2-mile) radius of the infestation, kill all swarms of bees in that area, and ask beekeepers in a 16-kilometer (10-mile) radius to be on the lookout for possible Africanized bees.

APHIS has already had opportunities to test its killer-bee identification and control procedures in the United States because from 1979 to 1989, Africanized bees arrived in this country no fewer than 20 times—by ship. "Stowing away" in cargo, the bees made it to several U.S. ports, only to be intercepted by APHIS inspectors. But on one occasion in the mid-1980's, some bees escaped the eye of an

Technology Against the Bees

Researchers have devised a number of techniques aimed at stopping Africanized bees or at least slowing their progress as the bees enter the southern United States.

Researchers in Arizona have been experimenting with radar in an attempt to identify areas where European drones go to mate with queens. A researcher, *above,* holds a radar "gun" to measure the speed of flying drones while, behind him, a trailer with a revolving radar dish searches for large groups of drones. On a radar screen inside the trailer, *below,* drone swarms almost a kilometer away can be pinpointed. The investigators are also testing large nets, *left,* that are suspended near the ground from balloons to trap drones. The nets, baited with scents that attract Africanized drones, will be used in mating areas to capture Africanized drones and keep them away from European queens.

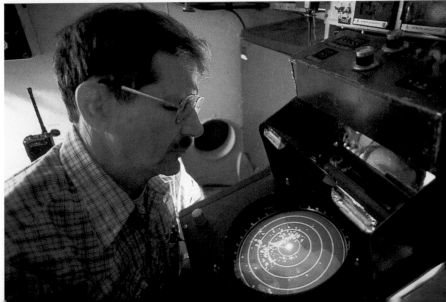

Scientists want to eliminate any Africanized bees they may find through such means as hives containing substances that attract bees or are poisonous to them. A scent-baited hive tested in Mexico's Bee Regulated Zone, *above,* traps thousands of Africanized bees, which are later killed with poisonous fumes.

inspector in Los Angeles and flew inland, establishing about a dozen colonies in Lost Hills and other nearby areas. USDA and California officials found the colonies after quarantining commercial hives for 32 kilometers (20 miles) around Lost Hills, checking them for Africanized bees. The officials also killed all wild bees within an 80-kilometer (50-mile) radius. The plan worked; no more Africanized bees were seen in the area.

When Africanized bees begin arriving in the United States in force, agricultural scientists will battle them every inch of the way. Some of the tactics that will be used to combat the Africanized-bee invasion will be the same ones employed by port officials and in the BRZ. Other measures are being developed in USDA laboratories and at several American universities.

Some researchers are working to develop faster, surer methods for identifying Africanized bees. At several laboratories, for instance, investigators are finding chemical and molecular differences between European and Africanized bees that could become the basis of new tests.

Scientists are also looking for more efficient ways to kill Africanized bees. One promising new approach utilizes the techniques of genetic engineering. USDA geneticist H. Alan Sylvester hopes to alter the genes of European bees to give them a competitive advantage. He has been investigating the possibility of inserting into European bees a gene that would enable them to tolerate *lactose*, a sugar in dairy products that is ordinarily poisonous to bees.

Lactose-laced baits could then be used against Africanized bees. All bees would eat the lure, but only Africanized ones would die; the European bees' new gene would protect them.

USDA entomologists Jon L. Williams and Robert G. Danka have developed a simple way for people to destroy wild Africanized swarms without having to track them down. The researchers suggest setting out traps baited with table sugar, which studies have shown will attract bees from 1.5 kilometers (1 mile) around. Finding 30 or more bees in the trap means that there is probably a wild swarm in the area, and if laboratory analysis indicates the bees are Africanized, then a delayed-action poison can be placed in the trap. "The bees bring it back to their colony," says Rinderer, "which eats it, and in 20 minutes you've killed the whole colony."

An alternative method for killing swarms was devised by USDA entomologist Justin O. Schmidt. Schmidt developed a bait hive using chemical substances that all types of honey bees use to communicate by smell. In tests, these "odor traps" attracted swarms of European bees looking for nesting sites. Africanized bees could be caught in the same way and then destroyed.

Another USDA scientist, plant physiologist Gerald M. Loper, has been experimenting with using radar to track swarms of European drones looking for queens. Loper and colleagues want to learn the general mating patterns of the bees, so they can teach beekeepers to anticipate how far and in what direction their queens will fly to find mates. Before allowing a queen to take a mating flight, beekeeepers would scout the area and kill any probable Africanized swarms.

Beekeepers, Rinderer says, will be the first line of defense in the United States against Africanized bees. As Brazilian beekeepers have shown, it is possible to manage Africanized bees intelligently, selecting for desirable traits and keeping European genes alive. But, Rinderer says, all concerned—beekeepers, state and federal agencies, and agricultural scientists—must do their part in dealing with the invasion. He adds that public involvement is also needed. People must learn not only to protect themselves against Africanized bees but also to resist becoming so panicked about the problem that they indiscriminately kill every bee they see. That sort of overreaction would probably result in the destruction of more European bees than Africanized bees, which obviously would not be a good thing. Rinderer and most other experts are hopeful that with a combined effort and perhaps just a bit of luck, we can guide the killer-bee story to a successful conclusion, gradually reducing the bees' aggressiveness and minimizing their impact on agriculture.

For further reading:

Camazine, Scott, and Morse, Roger A. "The Africanized Honeybee." *American Scientist*, September-October 1988.
Garelik, Glenn. "The Killers." *Discover*, October 1985.
Gould, James L., and Gould, Carol G. *The Honey Bee*. W. H. Freeman, 1988.
Kerby, Mona. *Friendly Bees, Ferocious Bees*. Franklin Watts, 1987.

Oil spills such as the *Exxon Valdez* accident in Alaska can have far-reaching effects on marine life and the environment.

Oil and Water— A Bad Mix

BY ROBERT W. HOWARTH AND ROXANNE MARINO

Every year, more than 1.5 trillion liters (400 billion gallons) of oil is transported around the world by sea in some 7,000 tankers. These huge ships—some of them longer than three football fields—are built especially to carry oil. Many of these tankers have accidents, spilling about 380 million liters (100 million gallons) of oil into the ocean each year. Although these spills can cause environmental damage, most are small and attract little public attention.

A dramatic exception was a spill that occurred in Alaska in March 1989. The tanker *Exxon Valdez* had just been filled with 200 million liters (53 million gallons) of crude oil at the terminal of the Alaska pipeline in the town of Valdez. It traveled only 40 kilometers (25 miles) before running aground on a reef in Prince William Sound. About 42 million liters (11 million gallons) poured into the biologically rich water through gashes in the ship's hull.

Although it may take scientists many years to assess the full extent of the damage, the spill clearly caused immediate widespread destruction. The oil spread over the surface of almost 7,800 square kilometers (3,000 square miles) of water. It coated at least 1,800 kilometers (1,100 miles) of beaches and shoreline, including those of five national wildlife refuges and three national parks. Cleanup workers and scientists found about 33,000 dead birds and 1,000 dead sea otters. But wildlife biologists believe this may represent only 10 to 30 per cent of the total killed because many animals may have rotted or been eaten by predators before they could be counted. In an area known for its teeming life and noisy sea birds, one naturalist

Opposite page: A rubber-suited cleanup crew use high-pressure hoses to wash oil from a beach in spring 1989 after the *Exxon Valdez* oil spill in Alaska's Prince William Sound. A dead loon held by a bird rescue worker, *inset,* was just one of thousands of birds and marine mammals killed by the oil.

The authors:
Robert W. Howarth is an associate professor in the Department of Ecology and Systematics at Cornell University in Ithaca, N.Y. Roxanne Marino is a research support specialist in that department.

said after the Exxon spill, "What surprised me most was the silence."

In addition to the Exxon spill, there were a number of smaller yet significant spills in 1989 and 1990. In January 1989, off Antarctica's northwest peninsula, an Argentine ship, the *Bahia Paraiso*, capsized after running onto rocks. Through a large gash in its hull, some 760,000 liters (200,000 gallons) of diesel and jet fuel spilled into the icy water, creating an oil slick that covered about 26 square kilometers (10 square miles). It surrounded the nesting sites of about 30,000 penguins and other shore birds.

In June, the tanker *World Prodigy* hit a reef near Newport, R.I., and spilled nearly 1.9 million liters (500,000 gallons) of home-heating oil. The largest spill of 1989 occurred in December after an explosion of unknown cause ripped the hull of an Iranian tanker, the *Kharg-5*, off the coast of Morocco, releasing about 140 million liters (37 million gallons) of crude oil into the Atlantic Ocean. And in February 1990, the *American Trader*, operated by British petroleum interests, spilled nearly 1 million liters (300,000 gallons) of Alaskan crude oil into the Pacific Ocean near Huntington Beach, Calif.

Oil spills such as these cause damage to the environment, but scientists do not yet understand all the effects of oil spills. Oil spills, in general, are very difficult to study. Because spills are accidents and are not anticipated, scientists are rarely prepared to go to the site and begin studies in the critical period right after a spill occurs. Also, scientists seldom have a complete understanding of what marine life was like in the area just before the spill. The oceans are vast and variable and have not been completely studied. For these reasons, the best-studied spills have not always been the largest or most damaging ones. Instead, they have been spills that occurred near marine laboratories and research stations, areas where scientists are readily available and where the marine life has been well studied.

To some extent, each spill is different, with its own surprises. The effects of spills, and the problems involved with cleaning them up, differ depending on the kind of oil involved, the local weather conditions, and the temperature and motion of the water.

Some oils are worse than others

There are many different types of oil, all made of complex mixtures of thousands of different chemical compounds. Some of these compounds are relatively harmless to life, but others are extremely *toxic* (poisonous). The most poisonous of these compounds belong to a group called *aromatic hydrocarbons*.

Crude oils are oils as they come out of the ground, and their chemical makeup depends on where the oil was formed. For example, crude oil from Alaska's Prudhoe Bay, the kind carried by the *Exxon Valdez*, is about 25 per cent aromatic hydrocarbons by weight. Crude oil from the Gulf of Mexico contains smaller amounts of aromatic hydrocarbons—proportions of 8 to 10 per cent—and so it is somewhat less poisonous.

Crude oils are processed at refineries into refined oils, which include gasoline, diesel fuel, jet fuel, and home-heating oils. The home-heating oil spilled by the *World Prodigy* and the diesel and jet fuels spilled in the Antarctic are somewhat more poisonous than crude oils because they contain higher percentages of aromatic hydrocarbons—up to 40 per cent.

Both crude oil and refined oil are less dense than seawater, so spilled oil floats on the surface, forming an oil slick. This slick is spread by the winds and currents. A slick of crude oil usually mixes with surface water to form a gooey brownish substance called *mousse*, because of its resemblance to the dessert chocolate mousse. With time, all oil slicks disappear as the compounds in the oil evaporate, dissolve into the water below the slick, or are broken down by bacteria in the water.

How long a slick lasts is determined to a great extent by the weather and water temperature. The warmer the water, the more quickly the oil will evaporate. The rougher the wind and waves, the more likely the oil is to mix and dissolve into the water beneath the slick. At the time of the *World Prodigy* spill in June 1989, the water was very warm, about 22°C (70°F.), and this allowed much of the oil to evaporate quickly. Also, the air was calm, so the oil did not mix with water. In contrast, at the time of the *Exxon Valdez* spill, the air and water temperatures were low. Windy weather and strong waves spread the slick. Oil mixed with water to form mousse, and the oil slick lasted for months.

How oil harms birds and mammals

Oil slicks can do immense harm to birds and marine mammals. Some birds seem to mistake oil slicks for schools of fish and actually dive into them. Marine mammals, such as seals and sea otters, that get coated with oil cannot swim as well as normal. In addition, an oil coating causes fur and feathers to lose their insulating ability. As a result, animals coated with oil rapidly lose body heat to the water and die of the cold. Oil can poison these animals if they swallow it while attempting to groom themselves to get rid of the oil. This apparently is what killed many sea otters after the *Exxon Valdez* spill.

Oil can also harm sea and shore birds by

A Massive Oil Spill
Oil spreads across the waters of Prince William Sound from a gash in the hull of the *Exxon Valdez* in March 1989. The huge tanker collided with a reef, spilling about 42 million liters (11 million gallons) of oil into the sound. The *Exxon Valdez* accident was the worst spill ever to occur in United States waters.

contaminating the fish that they eat and by altering their behavior. These effects were particularly apparent after the *Bahia Paraiso* and *Exxon Valdez* oil spills, both of which occurred in areas full of sensitive and unusual species of birds. The *Bahia Paraiso* spill occurred just as many chicks were hatching. Adult birds, including cormorants, were feeding on oil-poisoned fish and then feeding their young, which in turn were poisoned and died. Another species of bird, the skua, no longer protected its chicks from predators. Following the *Exxon Valdez* spill, cleanup workers found about 3,000 dead birds a month in the late summer, some at sites as far as 800 kilometers (500 miles) from the accident. Apparently they were also killed from eating contaminated fish.

How oil harms fish and other ocean-dwellers

After most oil spills, some of the oil dissolves in the seawater below the slick. This oil is not visible, and there are not large amounts of it. Yet oil is so poisonous—particularly the aromatic hydrocarbons—that even tiny amounts can harm some animals and plants.

Concentrations of dissolved oil as low as 2 to 10 parts per billion (ppb) can kill microscopic fish larvae. Such low concentrations are difficult to imagine. Try picturing a football field flooded with water to a depth of 3 meters (10 feet). If two tablespoons of oil were mixed evenly throughout the water, the resulting concentration of oil would be 2 ppb. Because fish larvae are microscopic in size, their death is not easily noticed, but the death of large numbers of larvae after an oil spill can result in reduced populations of adult fish in later years. Adult fish are usually much less sensitive to dissolved oil than are fish larvae. When oil concentrations reach 300 or more ppb, adult fish may die.

Fish larvae are so sensitive to oil pollution because they are growing rapidly. Similarly, some species of *attached algae*, or seaweeds, are readily poisoned by oil when they are growing rapidly in the spring but are quite resistant in the fall, their nongrowing period. So if an oil spill occurs when fish larvae are abundant or when attached algae are growing rapidly, it will cause more harm than at another season of the year. The *Exxon Valdez* spill came in the spring when fish larvae normally abound in Alaskan waters and attached algae are growing most rapidly. In 1990, it was still unclear how much those organisms were damaged, but judging from other spills, many biologists feared that a lot of damage could be expected.

One of the major processes for removing oil from seawater is chemical breakdown by bacteria that are naturally present in the water. These microorganisms are particularly active in warm water, so dissolved oil rarely lasts for more than a few weeks in waters where the temperature is about 20°C (68°F.) or higher. Conversely, in cold northern waters in winter, the breakdown of oil by bacteria is a very slow process, and high concentrations of poisonous oil compounds can last for at least five months following a spill.

Oil not only dissolves in water below a slick, it also finds its way to the sediments on the coastal sea floor. On its own, oil will not sink. But small droplets of oil—even single molecules—will stick to particles of silt, clay, and tiny pieces of organic material suspended in the water. These heavier particles then often sink with the attached oil. In addition, microscopic animals called zooplankton sometimes feed on very small globs of oil just below an oil slick, mistaking them for food. The oil then gets incorporated into the animals' waste and sinks with it to the bottom.

The oil that reaches the bottom sediments is seldom visible. Scientists use special sensitive instruments to measure the amount of oil. Although this invisible oil is poisonous to bottom-dwelling animals, life in the sediments does not cease to exist. Instead, species that are sensitive to oil die off and are replaced by ones that are better able to tolerate pollution. Bottom-dwelling worms, clams, and small crustaceans may disappear in a matter of days and be replaced by other species, such as worms that are accustomed to polluted water.

Oil that sinks into bottom sediments can take decades to disappear because little or no oxygen is available for oil-eating bacteria. And because cold slows that process even more, oil in sediments is apt to remain much longer in areas such as Alaska and Antarctica than in warmer climates.

The oil that reaches shore

Oil slicks that reach shorelines, pulled by tidal currents as well as pushed by the wind—can cause serious damage. Oil can seep several meters into beaches and marshes, killing plants and animals living there. It can also kill organisms living in the shallow waters and tide pools along the shore.

Damage can be particularly severe in saltwater marshes, coastal wetlands dominated by tall grasses. Marshes are important habitats for a variety of wildlife, including crabs, ducks, and geese. Many marine animals in their younger life stages also live in these marshes. Tidewaters carry oil from a slick into a marsh. When the tide ebbs, the oil remains, killing plants and animals. There, too, as in the sea-floor sediments, oil can remain for decades.

Many effects of oil spills are subtle and take months or years to become apparent. For example, after a small spill near Falmouth, Mass., in 1969, researchers at the Marine Biological Laboratory in nearby Woods Hole studied the consequences of the spill on small fiddler crabs that live in saltwater marshes. Most of the crabs survived the spill, but they moved more slowly than usual when threatened by birds and so were more likely to be eaten. The crabs also dug burrows that were shallower than normal, and as a result they were more likely to freeze to death in the winter. The full consequences of these behavioral changes, probably caused by nervous system damage, did not become clear until the year following the spill, when the number of crabs had dropped greatly.

How Oil Harms Plants and Animals

An oil spill can do significant damage to plants and animals. Some species are killed outright by getting coated with oil or taking it into their bodies. Other effects of oil on wildlife are less apparent but can cause serious damage for years or decades.

Birds coated with oil may die of *hypothermia* (reduced body temperature) because their feathers no longer provide protection from cold weather. In addition, birds are often poisoned by eating oil-contaminated fish.

Marine mammals, such as seals and sea otters, often get coated with oil that is floating on the surface of the water. Their fur loses its ability to insulate against cold water, and they may die of hypothermia.

Adult fish can absorb oil dissolved in water through their gills. When the level of dissolved oil is 300 parts per billion (ppb) or more, adult fish may die from poisoning. Concentrations of dissolved oil—as low as 1 ppb—can reduce the ability of fish to migrate to spawning grounds.

Bottom-dwelling animals—mainly *invertebrates* (animals without backbones) such as crustaceans, clams, and worms—are harmed by oil that settles to the sea floor. Some of the bottom dwellers disappear and are replaced by creatures more resistant to pollution, such as hardier varieties of worms.

Fish larvae—fish in their earliest growth stage—are easily poisoned by even tiny amounts of oil dissolved in water. Those that do not die often have slower rates of growth, prolonging the time that they are small and vulnerable to predators.

Marine plants, such as *attached algae* ("seaweeds"), may be killed by dissolved oil, especially when they are in a period of rapid growth. The plants may also be grazed away by marine animals whose normal predators have been killed or weakened by oil.

How Oil Settles to the Bottom

Oil by itself will not sink. It reaches the sea floor as a "passenger" on heavier types of matter. Some oil sticks to tiny particles of clay, silt, and organic material suspended in the water beneath an oil slick. The particles with the attached oil descend slowly to the bottom. Oil eaten by microscopic marine animals called *zooplankton* becomes part of their waste. This, too, sinks to the sea floor.

Oil slick on surface

Oil droplets

Zooplankton

Zooplankton waste

Clay or silt particles

Oil in sea-floor sediments

Oil's long-term effects

The effects of an oil spill last as long as toxic concentrations of oil stay in an area. Oil on beaches and in bottom sediments can continue to seep out into the water for years or decades. This is a major concern in areas affected by the *Exxon Valdez* spill. Beaches there are made up of cobble rocks roughly the size of softballs. A great deal of oil is trapped in the sand to a depth of at least 1 meter (3 feet). As the tide comes in, it washes some of this oil into the water. Many of these beaches are near streams where salmon return to spawn, or lay their eggs. One major question biologists are asking is whether the resulting low levels of oil in waters near shore will affect future migrating salmon. Some recent studies have shown that concentrations of 1 to a few ppb in seawater can cause migrating salmon to become disoriented, as if drugged. The affected salmon might not be able to reach their spawning grounds.

Oil spills can have indirect effects on plants and animals by upsetting ecological balances. Scientists are concerned, for example, that the *Exxon Valdez* oil spill may indirectly reduce the plant life at the base of the *food chain*—the phenomenon of larger organisms eating smaller organisms—by increasing the population of sea urchins in Prince William Sound. These small, spiny bottom-dwelling creatures feed on kelp, a type of seaweed, and are in turn eaten by sea otters. If too many sea otters were killed by the spill, the sea urchin population may explode out of control and eat most of the kelp. Once overgrazed, recovery of the kelp—and the marine life that depends on it—could be extremely slow.

Cleaning up oil spills

Considering the severe and long-lasting damage that an oil spill can cause, people are naturally concerned with how oil spills are cleaned up. Oil can spread very fast if the wind and currents are strong, so a rapid response is essential. Unfortunately, oil is extraordinarily difficult to clean up, and in most cases, including all of the major spills of 1989, the vast majority of spilled oil is not recovered from the environment. Rather, it remains there until natural processes remove it.

As the first line of action, emergency response teams arrive at the scene of a spill and set out floating barriers, called *booms*, around the oil to stop the spread of the slick and to concentrate the oil into thicker "pools." Spilled oil usually does not form a pool of uniform thickness on the surface of the water. Rather, the slick consists of several small pools up to 1 centimeter (0.4 inch) thick within a widespread oil layer as thin as 0.001 centimeter (0.0004 inch). The booms, some of which look something like giant strings of sausages, are sometimes made of plastic mesh filled with an oil-absorbent material, such as spun wool or synthetic foam. Other booms are made of rigid plastic and look like long floating fences.

Why Some Oil Spills Are Worse Than Others

No two oil spills are exactly alike. Some spills cause more damage than others, depending on such factors as the kind of oil involved, the weather, and water conditions.

Type of oil		Wind conditions		Water conditions	
Crude oil	• Thicker than most refined oils. More likely to form "mousse" • Often lower in poisonous compounds than refined oils	**Calm**	• Oil slick spreads more slowly • Containment of the slick may be possible	**Warm water**	• Speeds breakdown of oil by bacteria • Speeds evaporation of oil
				Calm seas	• Oil slick spreads more slowly • Less oil mixes with water • Slick more easily contained by booms and collected
Refined oil (heating oil, jet fuel, kerosene, gasoline)	• Often thinner than crude oil • Usually evaporates more easily • May be highly poisonous • Thicker fuel oils slow to evaporate	**Windy**	• Oil slick spreads rapidly • Waves stirred up, which mix oil into water • Containment of the slick difficult or impossible	**Cold water**	• Slows action of oil-eating bacteria • Slows evaporation
				Rough seas	• Churns up oil, forming mousse • Oil in slick escapes under booms • Skimmers and other cleanup equipment are ineffective • Strong currents spread slick rapidly

The most common method of picking up oil within the boom is the use of motorized boats or barges called *skimmers*. Some skimmers have a ramp at the front that scoops up oil and deposits it in a holding tank. Others are fitted with vacuum machinery and large suction hoses. The thicker the oil pool, the better a skimmer works. But the effectiveness of booms and skimmers is limited by weather conditions. If the strength of the water current beneath the oil increases, the oil pool corralled by a boom is broken into small droplets that are pushed under the boom. Booms and skimmers can be used effectively only in currents of less than 2 kilometers (1¼ miles) per hour and in calm weather. After most oil spills, including the *Exxon Valdez* spill, winds, currents, and choppy water greatly reduce the effectiveness of booms and skimmers.

Chemicals called *dispersants* can be used to break up an oil slick and prevent the fouling of beaches. They are sprayed from boats or

Cleaning Up the Mess

A variety of methods and equipment are used in efforts to clean up an oil spill. Motorized barges called *skimmers, right,* scoop oil off the surface of the water. Floating barriers called *booms, right bottom,* are set out to contain the oil slick and keep it from spreading. Oiled beaches are often cleaned by hand, one rock at a time. Oil-contaminated sand and soil is usually just shoveled into plastic bags, *below,* and carted away to a landfill.

aircraft. Dispersants are essentially strong detergents that dissolve oil into the water. The oil is then out of sight, and so perhaps out of mind. Although this reduces the direct threat to birds and mammals, it increases the risk of poisoning fish and other animals living in the water. This is especially a problem if dispersants are used in small bodies of water or in shallow, protected areas where water circulation is slow. Another problem with using dispersants is that the longer the oil floats, the more it gets churned into mousse, and the more difficult it then is to disperse. Dispersants must be applied to a slick within hours in order to be highly effective. The equipment for this type of rapid response is rarely on hand near the site of a spill.

Once an oil slick reaches the shoreline, one cleanup approach is to spray beaches with high-pressure jets of hot water. The spraying pushes the oil back into the water, where boats try to vacuum it up. In addition to being very expensive, this method removes only surface oil, and it can push oil that is beneath the surface even deeper into the underlying sand and rocks. Some federal scientists speculated that this cleanup activity after the *Exxon Valdez* spill actually did more harm than good.

A promising new cleanup method was tested on some beaches in Prince William Sound during the summer of 1989 by the U.S. Environmental Protection Agency (EPA). The new method involved speeding the growth of natural oil-eating bacteria. These bacteria need additional nutrients to use the oil as food just as agricultural plants need fertilizer to grow well. So EPA scientists sprayed the beaches with a bacteria fertilizer designed to stick to oily surfaces. The fertilizer additions seemed to speed the decomposition of oil on the surface of the beach, but much oil remained. Also, the fertilizer can cause excessive growth of one-celled marine plants called phytoplankton.

The cleanup of a major oil spill leads to yet another environmental problem: what to do with the immense quantities of oily wastes that result from the cleanup operation. After the Alaskan spill, some 45 million kilograms (100 million pounds) of oiled wastes had to be burned or buried. This included oil-saturated booms, rags, clothing, and dead animals.

Preventing oil spills

It is clear that transporting large quantities of oil poses a danger to the environment. But oil is a vital resource for our society, so we will not stop shipping it. Because oil spills cannot be completely prevented, and since oil is so difficult to clean up, the best thing we as a society can do is work to minimize the odds of spills occurring.

The vast majority of oil spills result from human error. So an important first step would be to reduce the seriousness of such errors by incorporating more checks and balances into tanker operations. For example, the use of tanker "traffic lanes" could be strictly enforced. Tugboat escorts should be required for tankers maneuver-

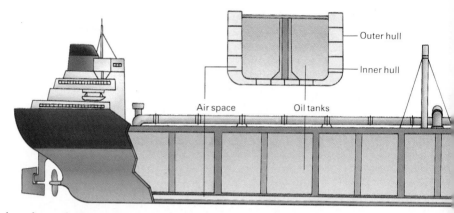

Preventing Oil Spills
Because oil spills can be so damaging to the environment and so difficult to clean up, many scientists and other experts think more effort should be put into preventing spills from happening. Some experts say that all oil tankers should be constructed with double hulls, *right,* two walls of metal separated by an air space. Both walls must be punctured before oil will escape from the ship. As of 1990, only 16 per cent of the world's tankers were double-hulled.

Outer hull

Inner hull

Air space   Oil tanks

ing through dangerous or environmentally sensitive areas. Controllers could use radar more fully to monitor the movement of tankers the way air traffic controllers monitor aircraft. Such radar exists for the tanker traffic around the port of Valdez, but in response to budget cuts, the U.S. Coast Guard had cut back the staff of this facility before the *Exxon Valdez* accident. In addition, oil companies could ensure that their crews are well trained and supervised, not overworked, and not pushed to cut corners to save time.

Tanker maintenance should be improved and aging tankers retired before they are likely to develop cracks in their hulls. A study reported in April 1988 by the Coast Guard found that metal cracks and other structural failures among the Alaskan tanker fleet were unusually high, probably from the stresses of navigating through rough northern seas.

Hull design is another important factor. Most oil tankers have a single hull—that is, the oil within the ship is separated from the water outside by just one layer of metal plating. When an accident occurs and the hull is punctured or torn, the oil pours out. Some tankers have double hulls—two walls of metal separated by an air space. With this design, both hulls must be punctured or torn before oil can escape from the ship. Double-hull construction has been proven effective at preventing oil spills in at least two tanker accidents in recent years. Double-hulled tankers have been in use for some 20 years, yet only 16 per cent of the world's tankers currently are of this design. Before the Alaska pipeline was built, the Department of the Interior assured Congress that only double-hulled tankers would be used to haul oil from the port of Valdez. This requirement was later dropped, and the *Exxon Valdez* had only a single hull.

As another safeguard, oil loading and refining facilities could be built in the least fragile environments. For example, many environmentalists had argued against putting a port at Valdez in the environmentally sensitive waters of Prince William Sound.

When oil loading and refining facilities are built, state-of-the-art cleanup equipment should be required at the site to ensure rapid response to any spill that might occur. Government agencies, along

with the operators of facilities, should develop detailed plans for dealing with oil spills. For the *Exxon Valdez* spill, such plans existed, but the necessary equipment was not ready for use.

There are no easy answers to issues surrounding oil spills. The deaths of birds and mammals are the most obvious consequences of a spill, but there are many other types of damage, such as alterations in food chains, that are difficult to detect. To understand such effects requires very detailed study over long periods of time, and this has not often been done. Scientists do know enough at this point, however, to say that damage can be quite serious and long lasting.

Sometimes, as luck would have it, wind and water conditions are such that an oil spill will do little damage. In the case of the *Exxon Valdez*, our luck ran out. The spill occurred in a highly sensitive area at a bad time of the year. Society should not leave so much to luck in the future. While better cleanup techniques undoubtedly could and should be developed, cleaning up after a spill is generally ineffective due to fundamental constraints such as wind and currents. Thus, preventing oil spills remains our most effective means of protecting the environment.

Mandatory tugboat escorts through environmentally sensitive areas such as Prince William Sound, *above,* could help keep tankers on a safe course. Other measures, such as greater use of radar and better-trained crews, could also help reduce the incidence of oil spills.

For further reading:

Cook, David. *Ocean Life*. Brown, 1985.
Howarth, Robert. "Fish vs. Fuel: A Slippery Quandary." *Technology Review,* November 1981.
"Wreck of the *Exxon Valdez*" (special section). *Audubon*, September 1989.

Editor's Note: This article had to be printed before the full extent of the *Hubble Space Telescope's* mechanical problems was known. For later information, see *Space Technology* in the Science News Update section.

The *Hubble Space Telescope* will allow astronomers to see stars forming, look for other planets, and better understand the birth of the universe.

An Orbiting Eye on the Universe

BY C. R. O'DELL

When the space shuttle *Discovery* roared off its launching pad in Cape Canaveral, Fla., in April 1990, it carried in its cargo bay the most precise optical telescope ever to observe the heavens. While I and other scientists watched the shuttle ascend, it occurred to me that we were witnessing the biggest single leap in the history of observational astronomy since the Italian astronomer Galileo built his first telescope in 1609 and began to observe the sky. This leap was the launch of the *Hubble Space Telescope*, named for American astronomer Edwin P. Hubble. And it has opened the possibility of answering some of the most profound questions about the nature of the universe: How old and how vast is our universe? When did the vast collections of stars known as *galaxies* begin to form? And are there planets around other stars, just as there are around our sun?

The day after liftoff, the crew of *Discovery* used the shuttle's Remote Manipulator Arm to lift the telescope—which is 13 meters (43 feet) long—from the cargo bay and launch it into orbit 610 kilometers (379 miles) above Earth. Although the deployment encountered some initial difficulties, the launch of the *Space Telescope* gave me particular satisfaction because I have been involved in its making since 1971, longer than any other scientist associated with the project. I was involved in the preliminary design work, and I was the telescope's "project scientist" with the National Aeronautics and Space Administration (NASA), for a total of 11 years.

Our original goal had been to launch the telescope in early 1982. But technical problems forced delays of the launch date to October 1986. Then tragedy struck. In January 1986, the space shuttle *Challenger* exploded, killing all seven crew members. The shuttle fleet was grounded for two years. Finally, more than seven years later than originally planned, the *Space Telescope* is in orbit.

The *Space Telescope* is the realization of dreams that began long before my involvement with it. In 1923, German rocket scientist Hermann Oberth proposed that rockets could be used to lift telescopes into space. At that time, Oberth's speculation seemed wild. But in 1946, after World War II, the United States military asked a group of scientists for opinions on possible uses of V-2 military rockets captured from Germany. Astronomer Lyman Spitzer, Jr., then an assistant professor at Yale University in New Haven, Conn., suggested using the rockets to lift astronomical observatories into space. After NASA was formed in 1958, the construction and operation of a large space observatory was quickly identified as one of the natural goals for NASA to pursue.

The author:
C. R. O'Dell is professor
of space physics and
astronomy at Rice Uni-
versity in Houston.

In the 1960's and 1970's, NASA launched a series of satellites known as *Orbiting Astronomical Observatories*. These observatories were used mainly for studying ultraviolet light from stars. The mirrors used in these satellites to focus the starlight were of low quality, however, and so did not form very sharp images. Nevertheless, the technical challenges in making these satellites helped pave the way for the *Hubble Space Telescope*.

Why all of the effort to place an observatory in space? There are three major reasons, and all have to do with the kinds of radiation given off by celestial objects and how Earth's atmosphere interferes with that radiation. First, Earth's atmosphere blocks much of the radiation given off by stars and other celestial objects, allowing us to see those objects only in visible light and radio waves, which are a limited portion of the *electromagnetic spectrum*. The electromagnetic spectrum consists of radiation at different wavelengths. In the order of increasing wavelength, these are gamma rays, X rays, ultraviolet light, visible light, infrared rays, microwaves, and radio waves. Many of the most interesting astronomical objects give off much of their radiation in the form of ultraviolet and infrared rays, which are blocked by the atmosphere and therefore cannot be seen with ground-based telescopes. The *Space Telescope* was built to view the universe in visible light and also in ultraviolet and infrared light.

Second, the atmosphere blurs the visible light images of stars and galaxies. Small differences in air temperature in the lower atmosphere create turbulent pockets of warm and cool air that bend light rays from celestial objects. This turbulence is what makes stars appear to twinkle when viewed with the unaided eye, and it blurs a star's image when viewed through a ground-based telescope. Only a telescope orbiting above the atmosphere can escape this blurring.

Third, Earth's atmosphere itself radiates and reflects light, making the sky brighter—even at night—from the surface of Earth than from space. An orbiting telescope in the inky black sky of space is unaffected by the natural glow of the atmosphere.

B y orbiting above Earth's atmosphere, the *Space Telescope*'s *resolving power* (ability to see fine detail) is much greater than that of ground-based telescopes. Not only are astronomers able to see celestial objects in sharper focus with the *Space Telescope*, but they also are able to detect the faint images of objects too far away to be seen from the ground. The telescope's resolving power concentrates the light from a celestial object onto an extremely small area of the telescope's *focal plane*—the place where light collected by the telescope's *primary mirror* (its principal light-gathering mirror) is focused. This area is about 100 times smaller than the comparable area on a ground-based telescope. Concentrating the light onto an extremely small area allows the telescope to detect the light from an extremely faint and distant object. This light would otherwise be overwhelmed by the more powerful light of a foreground object or by the diffuse glow of sunlight that pervades our solar system. This glow is created when sunlight is scattered by small dust particles in space, and though quite faint itself, it is bright enough to overpower light from very faint objects, if that light is not concentrated.

Because of the resolving power of the *Space Telescope*'s primary mirror, it does not require a large light-gathering area in order to detect extremely faint and distant objects. For ground-based telescopes, the larger the light-gathering surface of the mirror, the more

Glossary

Charge-coupled devices: Light-sensitive silicon chips that convert light to electronic signals.

Electromagnetic spectrum: The range of electromagnetic waves from the short gamma rays and X rays to the long microwaves and radio waves.

Focal plane: The area in a telescope where the image of an object is formed.

Photometer: A scientific instrument that measures the brightness of an object.

Primary mirror: The principal light-gathering mirror of a telescope.

Resolving power: A telescope's ability to see objects in fine detail.

Secondary mirror: A mirror smaller than the primary mirror, used to redirect light onto scientific instruments.

photons (particles of light) can be collected, and so, fainter, more distant objects can be detected. But due to its superior resolving power, the *Space Telescope* can detect objects about 50 times fainter and about 7 times more distant than those that can be detected by the 5-meter (200-inch) Hale telescope mirror atop Palomar Mountain near San Diego, which has a light-collecting area 4 times greater than the *Space Telescope*'s 2.4-meter (95-inch) mirror.

Building an instrument of this kind to operate in the extreme hot and cold conditions of space was a stunning engineering achievement. The core of the observatory is the telescope itself, which is housed in a cylindrical tube and consists of the primary mirror, a secondary mirror, a support system that holds the mirrors in place, and an array of scientific instruments. Outside the tube are two radio antennas and two solar panels. The antennas transmit data to a satellite, which transmits it to Earth, and the antennas also receive

Making the Space Telescope

The telescope and its scientific instruments are housed in a cylindrical tube 13 meters (43 feet) long and covered with a protective foil.

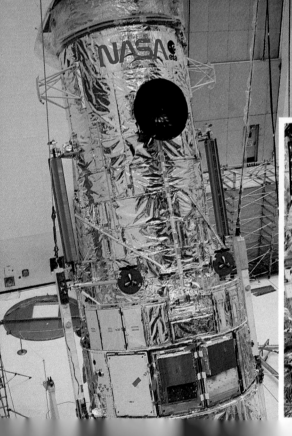

Engineers at Lockheed Missiles and Space Company in Sunnyvale, Calif., assemble some of the thousands of components that will operate the *Space Telescope*.

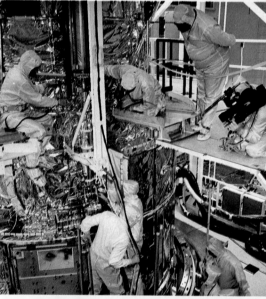

radio instructions from Earth-based astronomers. The solar panels provide power by converting sunlight into electricity.

The 2.4-meter primary mirror, the largest size that would allow the observatory to fit in the shuttle's cargo bay, represents the "eye" of the *Space Telescope*. The big difference between this mirror and other telescope mirrors is the accuracy to which its surface has been shaped. All telescope mirrors undergo a laborious process in which technicians grind away glass until the mirror achieves the proper concave shape and smoothness to focus light without distortions. For ground-based telescopes, there has never been any necessity to achieve an extremely high degree of smoothness, because the mirror's ability to focus sharp images is limited by the blurring effect of the atmosphere. But the *Space Telescope*'s mirror, made by Hughes-Danbury Optical Systems Incorporated of Danbury, Conn., was ground so smooth over a two-year period from 1979 to 1981 that the highest ripple on its surface is no more than eleven-billionths of a meter. If the mirror were to be scaled up so that its diameter stretched from New York City to Los Angeles, its concave shape would mean that the edge of the mirror would be about 125 kilometers (78 miles) higher than the center of the mirror, but the tallest ripple on its surface would be only 25 millimeters (1 inch) high. The telescope's smaller secondary mirror is also very smooth.

Technicians at Hughes Danbury Optical Systems, Incorporated, in Danbury, Conn., inspect the 2.4-meter (95-inch) primary mirror. It is the most perfect mirror of its size ever made, and it took workers two years to grind the surface of the glass to its ultrasmooth finish.

Beaming the results

The *Space Telescope* radios data to a *Tracking and Data Relay Satellite*, which relays the data to a ground station at White Sands, N. Mex. From there, the data go, via a communications satellite, to NASA's Goddard Space Flight Center in Greenbelt, Md. The data are then transmitted along ground lines to computers at the Space Telescope Science Institute in Baltimore.

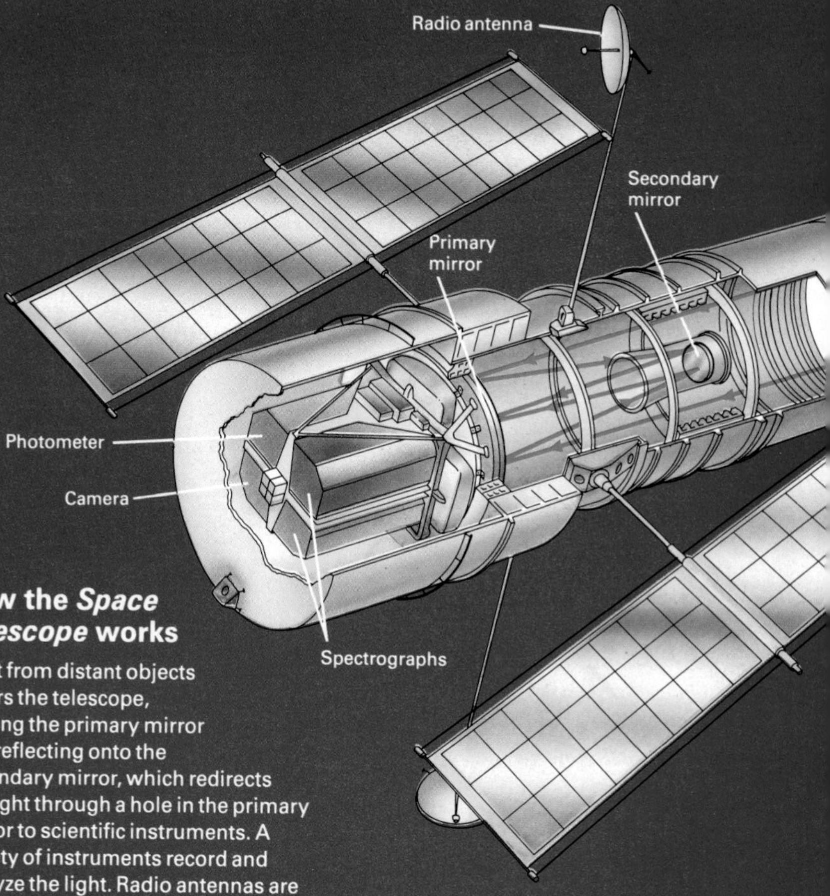

Radio antenna

Secondary mirror

Primary mirror

Photometer

Camera

Spectrographs

How the *Space Telescope* works

Light from distant objects enters the telescope, striking the primary mirror and reflecting onto the secondary mirror, which redirects the light through a hole in the primary mirror to scientific instruments. A variety of instruments record and analyze the light. Radio antennas are used to send data to Earth and receive programming instructions for the telescope. Two solar panels power the observatory.

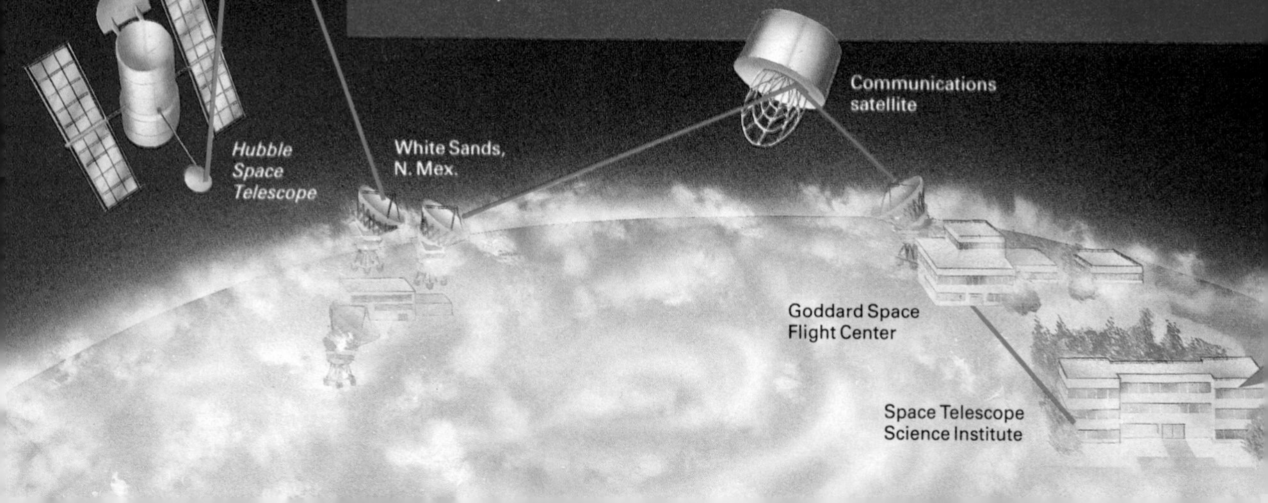

Tracking and Data Relay Satellite

Hubble Space Telescope

White Sands, N. Mex.

Communications satellite

Goddard Space Flight Center

Space Telescope Science Institute

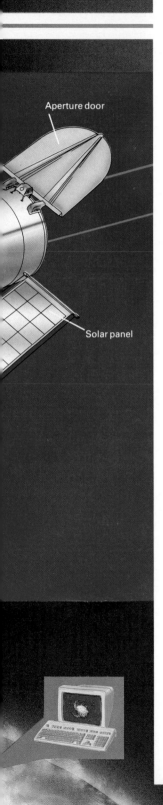

Aperture door

Solar panel

As light enters the telescope's cylindrical tube, it strikes the primary mirror and is reflected onto the secondary mirror. The light then bounces back and is focused through a hole in the primary mirror onto scientific instruments. The primary and secondary mirrors must be kept in perfect position to maintain this focus. The separation of the two mirrors—they are 4.9 meters (16 feet, 1 inch) apart—must not be altered by more than 0.0025 of a millimeter (0.0001 of an inch). Finding a way to keep the mirrors in perfect alignment under the extreme temperature conditions of space was a major challenge for the scientists and engineers at NASA's Marshall Space Flight Center in Huntsville, Ala., where the *Space Telescope* was developed.

The telescope orbits Earth once every 95 minutes, continually traveling from the hot sunlit side to the cold night side and then back into heat. In doing so, it encounters extreme changes in temperature, which would cause most materials to expand and contract. The designers had to find a material for the mirrors and for the mirrors' support structure that would be unaffected by temperature changes. For the mirrors, they chose Corning Glass Works's Ultra Low Expansion glass. For the support structure, they settled on a material made of carbon fibers imbedded in plastic. Both materials expand and contract very little as temperatures change.

Another problem was how to point the telescope at a particular star or galaxy and keep it accurately trained on that object for the duration of its observations. We also needed to make sure the telescope would not wobble or make any other movement that could blur the image. As it turned out, this was the biggest single technical problem that we encountered, and it was the most important of several factors that caused us to postpone our original launch date from 1982 to 1986.

The solution was the development of *fine guidance sensors*, scientific instruments that identify "guide stars" by their known brightness. When an astronomer selects a certain object for study by the *Space Telescope*, a computer program selects two nearby "guide stars" from a specially assembled catalog of about 19 million known star positions. The fine guidance sensors lock onto these guide stars and position the telescope so that the target object is in the center of the telescope's field of view. If the guide stars start to drift out of the sensors' field of view, the sensors send electrical signals to the spacecraft's controls so that the telescope adjusts its position. This system also keeps the telescope from wobbling. The pointing system, which was developed by the Lockheed Missiles and Space Company of Sunnyvale, Calif., is so accurate and stable that it is equivalent to keeping a beam of light trained on a dime 640 kilometers (400 miles) away for several hours.

Once pointed at the target, the telescope's mirrors focus light on an array of scientific instruments positioned behind the telescope's primary mirror. These instruments have three main functions: to record an image of the object, to analyze the light from that object, and to measure the brightness of the object.

The instruments that record images are two electronic cameras, one of which uses light-sensitive silicon chips called *charge-coupled devices* (CCD's). The other is a television camera that records photons one at a time. Both turn light into electronic signals. This information then is radioed to Earth, where it is converted into pictures by computers. CCD's are extremely sensitive to light and record between 70 and 100 per cent of the photons that strike a mirror.

The instruments that help scientists analyze light are called *spectrographs* because they break up light into the spectrum of different colors that comprise it. When astronomers study light from a distant star, they find dark and bright lines in the spectrum, which are known as *spectral lines*. The lines found in an object's spectrum are a result of the object's chemical makeup and temperature. By comparing spectral lines found in stars or other objects with those of known chemical elements, astronomers can obtain detailed information about the star's chemical composition and temperature.

The instrument that measures the brightness of stars with extremely high accuracy is called a *photometer*. The *Space Telescope*'s photometer can measure changes in brightness that occur over periods as brief as a few millionths of a second, making it ideal for the study of *pulsars* (rapidly rotating, extremely dense stars). Some pulsars give off visible light beams as they rotate, and some complete a single rotation in a time as brief as a few thousandths of a second.

The *Space Telescope* is a remotely operated, unmanned observatory. On-board computers receive instructions from ground controllers telling the telescope what to observe and when. Radio antennas on the spacecraft transmit the data the telescope gathers to a *Tracking and Data Relay Satellite* (*TDRS*), which is in an orbit far above the telescope. The *TDRS* sends the data to a ground station in White Sands, N. Mex., which, in turn, relays it to a communications satellite. This satellite sends the data to NASA's Goddard Space Flight Center in Greenbelt, Md. From the Goddard center, the data travel along ground lines to astronomers at the Space Telescope Science Institute on the campus of Johns Hopkins University in Baltimore.

Any astronomer in the world can ask to use the *Space Telescope* for observations. He or she submits an observing proposal to the Science Institute in Baltimore. A review committee then selects the best proposals. NASA and the Science Institute work with the astronomer to schedule the observations and generate the computer commands that will actually carry them out.

What are the questions that astronomers hope the *Space Telescope* will answer? They range from questions about the early universe, such as when did galaxies form and how did they evolve, to questions about our own galaxy and whether a *black hole* lies at its center. (A black hole is an object so dense that not even light can escape its

Viewing the Heavens

Orbiting above Earth's atmosphere, the *Space Telescope* is able to produce much sharper, more finely detailed images than any ground-based telescope ever could. The image of a distant star cluster viewed through a telescope on Earth, *below*, would be blurred as light from the star was distorted by the atmosphere. But in an image produced by the *Space Telescope, right*, free from such distortion, each star in a cluster would be distinct.

Waiting to be Found

With the *Space Telescope*, astronomers expect to see stars in the process of forming from clouds of dust and gas, *right*, galaxies on the far edges of the universe, *below*, and perhaps some surprises that they cannot yet even imagine.

gravitational field.) Astronomers also intend to probe the nature of *quasars* (the most energetic and distant objects in the universe) and to make more accurate calculations about distances to objects in the universe and the rate at which the universe is expanding.

Astronomers also hope to learn more about how stars form and whether it is typical for planetary systems to form around stars like our sun. We already know that new stars are continuously being formed in our galaxy, the Milky Way, but we haven't been able to trace the process to its very beginnings.

An equally exciting prospect will be the search for planets around stars similar to our sun and at distances up to about 25 *light-years* from Earth. (A light-year is the distance light travels in a year, about 9.46 trillion kilometers [5.88 trillion miles].) We don't know whether such planets exist, or how big they might be. The *Space Telescope*, however, should be able to detect planets the size of Jupiter—the largest

planet in our solar system, with a diameter of 142,700 kilometers (88,700 miles)—if they are at least about 778 million kilometers (483 million miles) from any of 50 nearby stars—about the distance that separates Saturn and Earth. Even with the *Space Telescope*'s great resolving power, any planets closer than that to a star would be too near for the telescope to resolve into separate images.

Several of the most important questions the *Space Telescope* is expected to help solve were raised by the work of the astronomer after whom the telescope is named. Hubble found in 1924 that there are other galaxies in the universe. He calculated that the distance to an object then known as the Andromeda Nebula was so great that the "nebula" could not possibly be part of the Milky Way. Hubble later showed that there are a vast number of galaxies in the universe and

Future Great Observatories

The *Space Telescope* is only the first in NASA's Great Observatories Program. In the 1990's, three more orbiting telescopes will be launched.

The *Advanced X-Ray Astronomy Facility* will study objects, such as *supernovas* (exploding stars) that give off much of their radiation in the form of X rays.

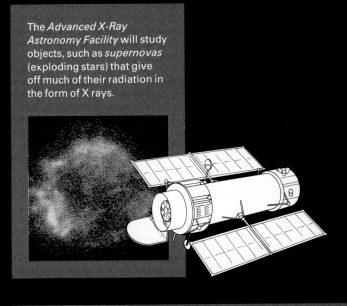

The *Space Infrared Telescope Facility* will examine more closely some interesting infrared-radiating objects that appear on an infrared map of the sky made by an earlier infrared telescope.

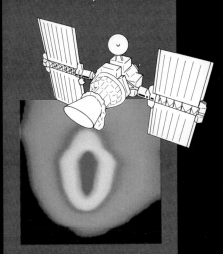

The *Gamma Ray Observatory* will survey the entire sky and produce a map of objects that give off high-energy gamma rays.

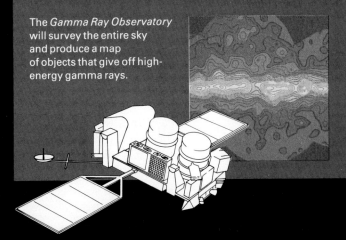

that galaxies are receding from each other at a speed proportional to their distance from Earth. The farther away a galaxy is, the faster it is receding. Thus, Hubble demonstrated that the universe is expanding in all directions and that the rate of this expansion can be calculated if one knows the constant value of the proportion between speed and distance. This value is called the *Hubble constant*. The Hubble constant, however, is uncertain because we cannot accurately measure distances to remote galaxies. But the *Space Telescope* will help us measure those distances.

The chief method for finding the distance to another star, the method Hubble used, is to measure the star's brightness. An astronomer knows that if two stars have about the same mass and are of the same age, they will give off equal amounts of energy and thus will have the same brightness, called *absolute brightness*. Their *apparent brightness* in the sky, however, may differ. If one appears brighter than the other, then the fainter star is more distant. For example, if it is 100 times fainter than its counterpart, it is 10 times farther away. The difficulty is to find stars about which enough is known to deduce their absolute brightness and so to allow this comparison. There is a type of star in our Galaxy suited for this—the *Cepheid variables*. Cepheids are stars that vary in brightness at regular intervals, and there is a direct relationship between this regular variation and the star's absolute brightness. Hubble used the 2.5-meter (100-inch) telescope at the Mount Wilson Observatory near Pasadena, Calif., to find Cepheid variables in the Andromeda galaxy. These Cepheids were thousands of times fainter than comparable Cepheids in our Galaxy. Hence, Hubble was able to calculate the distance to the Andromeda galaxy.

Ground-based telescopes are not able to resolve Cepheids in more distant galaxies, and so astronomers have not been able to calculate accurately the distances to those galaxies. The *Space Telescope* is expected to find Cepheids in galaxies as far away as the Virgo cluster of galaxies, which is about 50 million light-years from Earth.

If they can determine accurately how far away the Virgo cluster is, astronomers will be able to determine the value of the Hubble constant more precisely. This will allow them to calculate more accurately the rate at which the universe is expanding. By knowing the rate at which the universe is expanding, we can calculate backward in time to when the universe came into being and so determine its age. Because the expansion rate is now uncertain, astronomers can say only that the universe began between 10 billion and 20 billion years ago.

The *Space Telescope* is expected to add greatly to our knowledge of the early universe. It will be able to see the most distant light-emitting objects in the universe. The light the telescope receives from a distant object had to travel across space. So the light was given off when that object was much younger than it is now. For example, if the light takes 1 billion years to reach Earth, then the image we see is that of the object 1 billion years ago. As we probe the farthest objects with the *Space Telescope*, we will be studying the universe in its earliest stages, which could help us understand how galaxies formed.

Another important area of astronomical research concerns quasars, which appear as simple points of light through ground-based telescopes. Astronomers suspect that quasars are the cores of galaxies, probably fueled by gaseous material falling into a super-massive black hole. But where is the fuel coming from? Quasars are so bright that light from any nearby material cannot be seen by ground-based telescopes. The *Space Telescope*'s great resolving power will allow us to see whether quasars are more than simple points of light—whether they are indeed surrounded by galaxies.

These are the questions we now know how to ask. But astronomers discovered many times in the past that the universe contained objects they had not previously imagined. Those discoveries raised new questions about the nature of our universe. The questions that the *Space Telescope* will be remembered for answering have probably not yet been asked.

The *Space Telescope* is the first of a series of major space observatories—known collectively as the Great Observatories Program—to be built and launched by NASA in the 1990's. Like the *Space Telescope*, these other observatories will observe portions of the electromagnetic spectrum that are blocked by Earth's atmosphere.

The *Gamma Ray Observatory* will study sources of high-energy gamma rays, such as black holes and *neutron stars*, extremely small but incredibly dense stars. Although gamma-ray detectors on high-altitude balloons and on satellites have recorded individual sources of gamma rays, this observatory will be the first to survey the entire sky and produce a map of all the gamma-ray sources that can be detected.

The *Advanced X-ray Astronomy Facility* will study selected parts of the sky for objects that give off X rays. Some of the least-understood objects in the universe, such as black holes and neutron stars, give off most of their energy in the form of X rays. The *Space Infrared Telescope Facility* will detect *infrared* (heat) radiation from relatively cool objects. Such objects include unusually cool stars, certain kinds of galaxies, and invisible objects shrouded in dust.

The *Space Telescope* and the observatories to come promise to usher in a new era in astronomy, one that will widen our horizon beyond anything we can presently foresee. It will be an era of discovery and exploration that will undoubtedly solve many of the mysteries we currently contemplate while raising new ones for us to ponder.

For further reading:

Bahcall, John N., and Spitzer, Lyman, Jr. "The Space Telescope." *Scientific American*, July 1982.

Longair, Malcolm. *Alice and the Space Telescope*. Johns Hopkins, 1990.

Smith, Robert W. *The Space Telescope*. Cambridge University Press, 1989.

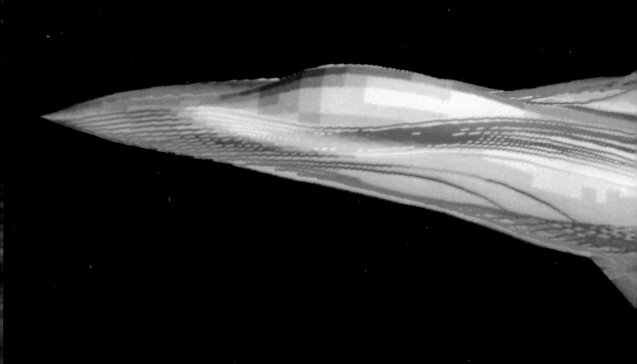

BY JAY MYERS

Science by Supercomputer

Pictures produced by supercomputers
enable scientists to "observe" problems and
processes that are extremely difficult—or
even impossible—to see in any other way.

The author:
Jay Myers is a senior editor of *Science Year.*

The airplane looks like an ice sculpture suspended in the blackness of space. What seem to be brightly colored strands of yarn sweep back gracefully from its nose and wings.

Suddenly, the shape of the plane's nose changes and some of the strands creep down the side of the craft. An engineer watching this intently jots down a few notes.

Now, the wings become longer. Again, the strands move. What's happening? How are these changes taking place?

The "airplane" is a model. But the model is not a solid piece of material and there are no strings attached. Rather, the engineer is working with an image displayed on a televisionlike screen that is controlled by an extremely powerful computer—a supercomputer—at the National Aeronautics and Space Administration's Ames Research Center near Moffett Field, Calif. The model represents the United States Air Force's F-16A jet fighter. The engineer is looking at ways to streamline the aircraft to decrease its air resistance.

As the engineer types out commands to change the shape of the model, the supercomputer calculates how this will affect the speed and direction of the wind streaming over the craft as it flies through the air. The supercomputer then "redraws" the model and the colored strands that show airflow. The engineer can see immediately what effect the changes will have on the airplane as it flies.

In the past, aeronautical engineers had to test their models in wind tunnels with streams of colored smoke to show the airflow, an expensive and time-consuming process. Now supercomputers can do most of this work for them. And these powerful computers are helping scientists and engineers in many other fields as well. There are more than 400 supercomputers at work throughout the world, allowing researchers to tackle problems that once were extremely difficult—or even impossible—to do.

Supercomputers are expensive—prices range from about $2-million to $25 million. But some supercomputers serve more than 1,000 researchers in a single year, and so their cost is shared.

A supercomputer works like other computers but has much greater speed and a far larger memory. And, like other computers, supercomputers have grown more powerful with each succeeding generation. Many industry experts regard the Cray-1, introduced in 1976 by Cray Research, Incorporated, of Minneapolis, Minn., as the first commercially available supercomputer. It could perform 100 million basic arithmetic tasks—such as multiplication—per second. By 1990, the fastest supercomputers could perform more than 2 billion basic arithmetic tasks per second.

A supercomputer's speed and memory allow it to rapidly search through and use enormous amounts of information in computations. Supercomputers also have powerful "brain centers," or central processing units (CPU's). Some supercomputers—like most personal computers—have one CPU to control the computer's arithmetic and logic operations. These computers process data one step at a time, a procedure called *serial processing*. Other supercomputers have two or more CPU's, enabling them to work on different parts of a problem simultaneously. This is called *parallel processing*.

The difference between serial and parallel processing is easy to understand if we think in terms of waiting in line for some kind of service. Imagine that your local bank has only one teller. But this teller is an amazing individual named Sam Series, who works so rapidly that he can handle all the deposits and withdrawals of 100 customers per minute, taking them one at a time.

The bank in the next town, however, can handle 200 customers per minute, even though it has no teller who even comes close to Sam's speed. This bank has four tellers, the Parallel family—Patty, Penny, Paul, and Peter—each of whom can process 50 customers per minute. Customers waiting in line go to whichever teller is available.

Sam's bank is like a supercomputer with one CPU doing serial processing, one customer—or piece of data—at a time. The bank with four tellers is like a computer with four CPU's doing parallel processing. They share the workload.

One of the most powerful supercomputers in the world is housed in what looks like an ultramodern bench. The Y-MP8, made by Cray Research, Incorporated, of Minneapolis, Minn., can have up to eight central processing units—the "brain centers" of computers—to perform more than 2 billion basic arithmetic tasks per second.

All early computers and the first supercomputers were serial-processing machines. The use of parallel processing in supercomputers, however, increased sharply in the 1980's as CPU's became more reliable and less costly and as better software was developed. International Business Machines Corporation makes supercomputers with six CPU's and in 1989 announced a way of putting two of them together to act like a supercomputer with 12 CPU's. Cray planned to introduce a supercomputer with 16 CPU's.

Other machines are "massively parallel," with hundreds—and even thousands—of processors. As more software is developed for these machines, they may become a major force in supercomputing.

The use of supercomputers to "draw" pictures is revolutionizing the way scientists and engineers work. A researcher uses a supercomputer to build a precise electronic model of a certain phenomenon, such as the flight of a supersonic fighter. The researcher can then instruct the computer to *simulate* (represent in an image) various realistic situations.

A geologist can "watch" in just a few seconds great continental shifts that take nature millions of years to accomplish—and can try to predict future movements of Earth's land masses. Biologists can use supercomputer simulation to determine how certain molecules fit together—valuable information in the development of new medicines. Astronomers can investigate the behavior of black holes, distant galaxies, and other objects in deep space billions of kilometers away. Mathematicians can use supercomputers to "draw" geometric structures that are actually graphs of equations.

Some scientists call simulation a third way of doing science—in addition to the traditional techniques of developing theories and doing experiments. With the advent of supercomputer simulation, science will never be the same.

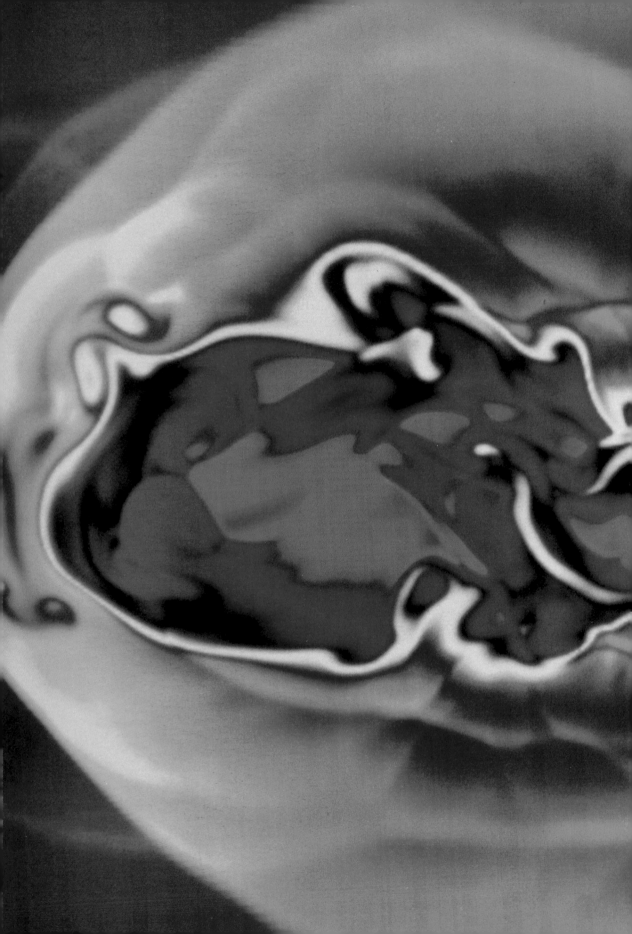

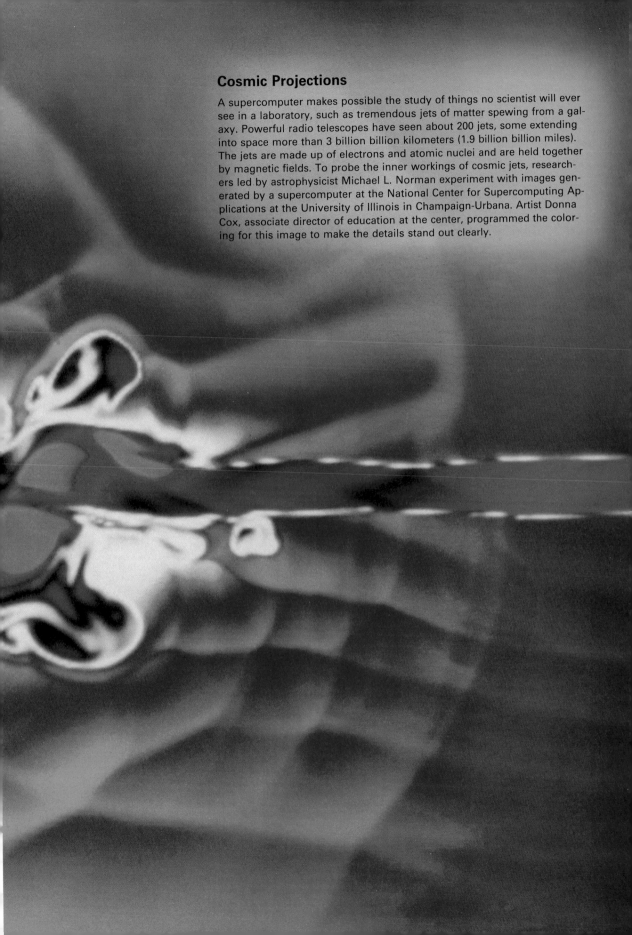

Cosmic Projections

A supercomputer makes possible the study of things no scientist will ever see in a laboratory, such as tremendous jets of matter spewing from a galaxy. Powerful radio telescopes have seen about 200 jets, some extending into space more than 3 billion billion kilometers (1.9 billion billion miles). The jets are made up of electrons and atomic nuclei and are held together by magnetic fields. To probe the inner workings of cosmic jets, researchers led by astrophysicist Michael L. Norman experiment with images generated by a supercomputer at the National Center for Supercomputing Applications at the University of Illinois in Champaign-Urbana. Artist Donna Cox, associate director of education at the center, programmed the coloring for this image to make the details stand out clearly.

Worlds in Collision

Supercomputer simulations enable scientists to examine events that occur over millions of years, such as the collision of two galaxies. Astrophysicist Joshua Barnes of the Canadian Institute for Theoretical Astrophysics in Toronto created a model at the John von Neumann National Supercomputer Center in Princeton, N.J., to determine what would happen if two galaxies collided. In this simulation, mysterious and invisible material called *dark matter* appears as red dots, stars in the galactic disks are blue, and stars in the centers of the galaxies are white.

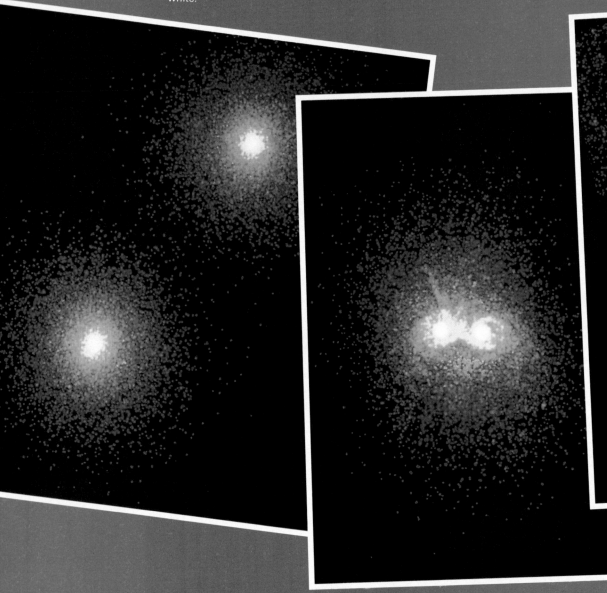

The two galaxies move toward each other, *above left,* and 250 million years later, come together, *above right.*

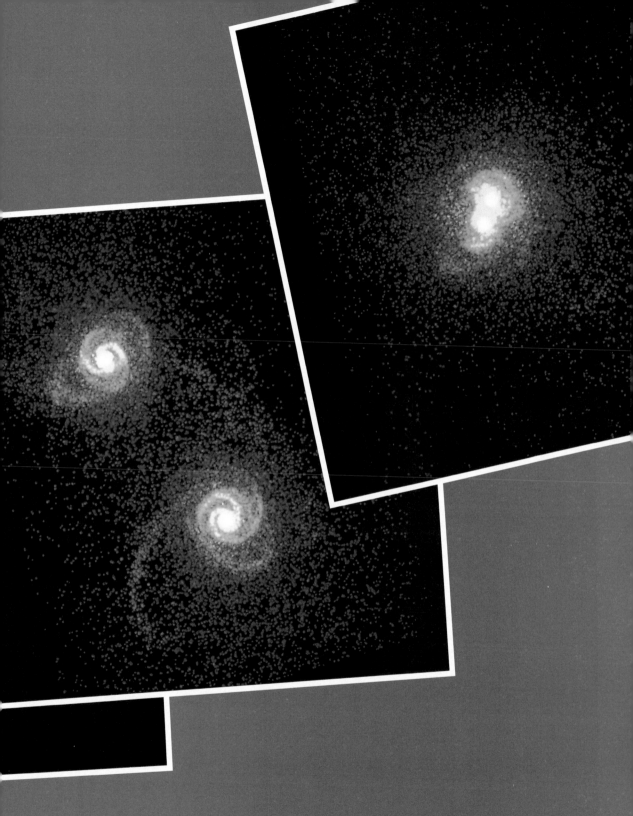

Momentum then reseparates the galaxies 375 million years later, *above left*, but 500 million years after that, gravity forces them to merge, *above right*.

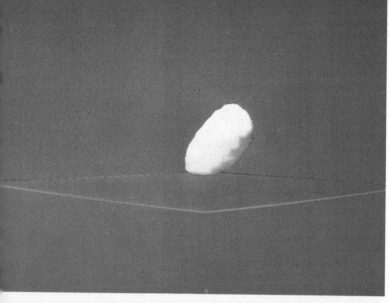

The Evolution of a Storm

A simulation of how a tornado-spawning thunderstorm forms, produced on a supercomputer at the National Center for Atmospheric Research in Boulder, Colo., may lead to improved weather predictions.

Fed by moist, warm air, a small cloud, *top,* begins to grow. Wind speed is fastest at the top of the cloud, and this forms it into an anvil shape, which is clearly evident at 60 minutes, *center.*

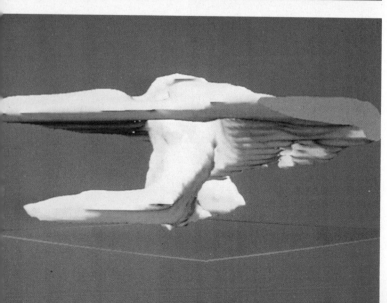

As the storm matures, it begins to rain heavily and the cloud rotates faster and faster. This rotation becomes very rapid under the cloud, and, 60 minutes later, *bottom,* a small, wedge-shaped piece of the cloud, called the wall cloud, approaches the ground, setting up the conditions in which the funnel cloud of a tornado can form.

Seeing Sound

Traditionally, designers of concert halls have tried to determine how music played there will sound by reflecting a light beam representing a sound wave off the surfaces of a scale model. A designer can work with only one beam at a time. But a computer program traces the paths of thousands of sound waves in a model of a concert hall. The program, developed by graphics researcher Donald Greenberg and graduate student Adam Stettner at Cornell University in Ithaca, N.Y., produces symbols to represent the sound. The sizes and shapes of cones, for example, indicate percentages of the sound reaching a listener from various angles. When the designer changes the model—by raising the ceiling, for example—the symbols change to indicate the new sound. The program runs on several Hewlett-Packard 835 workstations connected in parallel to act as one machine.

77

Models for Medicine

A supercomputer model helps to diagnose and treat tumors of the eye with *ultrasound* (sound whose waves vibrate so rapidly that human beings cannot hear them). Ophthalmologist D. Jackson Coleman and physicist Mark J. Rondeau of the Cornell University Medical College in New York City use a supercomputer to produce a 3-dimensional image of the patient's eye. Doctors can then "rehearse" the ultrasound surgery, determining where to direct the beam and how much ultrasound energy will be needed to destroy the tumor. The large blue cone represents a beam of ultrasound entering the eye, what looks like an egg yolk is a tumor, and what appears to be a long strip of paper is a detached *retina* (the layer of light-sensitive cells that transmit visual information to the brain). The small cone leaving the eye represents ultrasound that has not been absorbed.

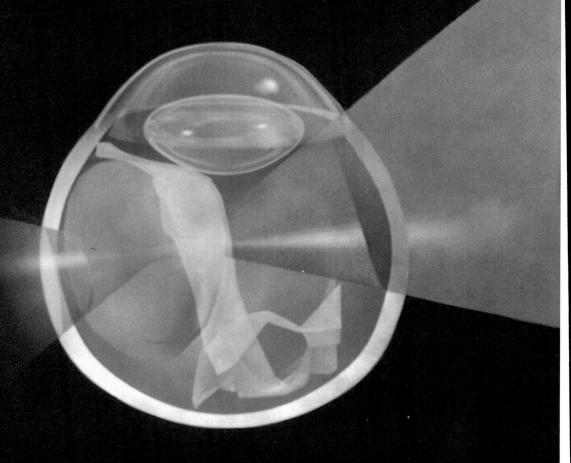

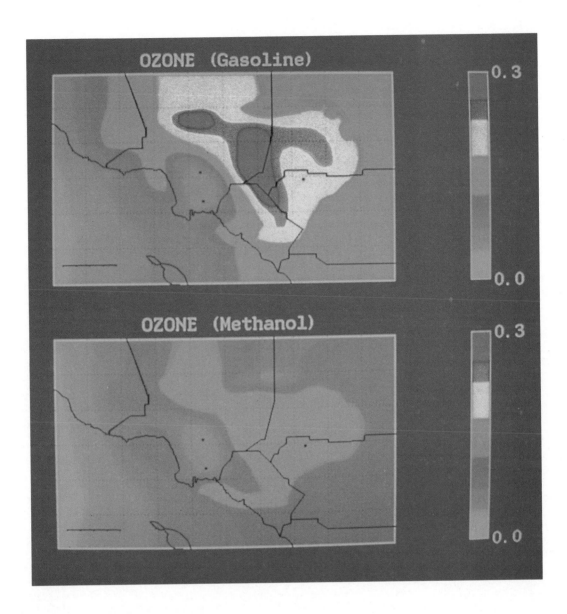

OZONE (Gasoline)

0.3

0.0

OZONE (Methanol)

0.3

0.0

Auto Fuels and Air Pollution

A supercomputer simulation of ozone concentrations in the Los Angeles
Basin answered an urgent environmental question: Would changing the
main fuel for motor vehicles from gasoline to *methanol* (wood alcohol)
significantly decrease air pollution? The model, created by chemical engineer Gregory McRae and mechanical engineer A. G. Russell of Carnegie
Mellon University in Pittsburgh, Pa., compared the effect on the air of gasoline and ethanol. Different colors represented various degrees of ozone
concentration ranging from very low (blue) to high (red and purple). When
motor vehicles continued to be powered by gasoline, *top,* ozone concentration reached highs of 0.3 parts per million. Had there been a complete
changeover to methanol, *bottom,* the ozone concentration would have
been reduced by nearly 50 per cent.

Math Made Visible

A colorful and complex branching pattern is actually a visual representation of a simple mathematical equation generated at Cornell Theory Center in Ithaca, N.Y. The same equation is solved over and over, adding successive branches as each succeeding solution is put back into the equation. This kind of image is called a *fractal* and is characterized by *self-similarity,* a repetition of certain geometrical patterns in various sizes.

Researchers have designed many fractals that bear an uncanny resemblance to natural objects, such as a maple leaf. Marc Berger, a mathematician at Carnegie Mellon University in Pittsburgh, created this image using a machine at Pittsburgh Supercomputer Center.

A fractal with the branching patterns of a human lung was produced by computer graphics specialist Yoichiro Kawakuchi of Nippon Electronics College in Japan.

The Hill Ruin

The Hill Ruin, with its maze of tall granite walls, overlooks the wooded territory once controlled by the rulers of Great Zimbab-we. Although the purpose of the Hill Ruin remains a mystery, archaeologists believe it was probably a sacred site where spirit mediums and priests lived and conducted religious ceremonies.

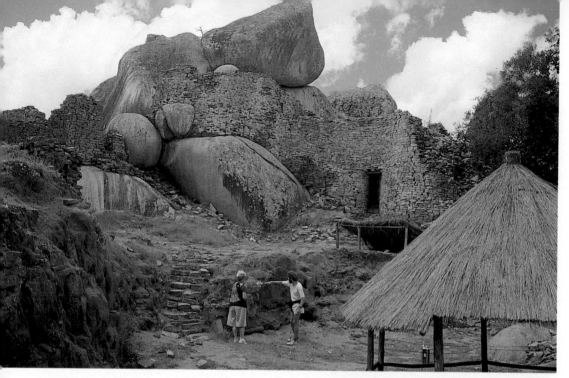

An imposing retaining
wall winds over and
around massive boul-
ders at the western end
of the Hill Ruin, *above.*
The opening in the wall
is one of only two en-
trances to the Hill Ruin.
A narrow passage be-
tween a stone wall and a
boulder, *right,* is one of
many that link numerous
small enclosures within
the Hill Ruin.

radioactive carbon decays, or changes into another form, at a known rate after a plant or animal dies, this analysis allows archaeologists to determine the actual age of an object to within several hundred years. Summers and his team concluded that Great Zimbabwe was built in the A.D. 300's and abandoned in the 1500's.

All the archaeologists who conducted scientific excavations were faced with two major problems. First, the inhabitants of Great Zimbabwe left no written records that could guide archaeologists in their digging and help them interpret their finds. Second, the excavations by Bent and, especially, Hall were so destructive that they could almost be described as vandalism. In their search for artifacts, the two men had stripped off large areas of soil, especially in the Great Enclosure. In doing so, they had hopelessly churned the site's archaeological layers.

As in the layers of rock laid down over time in a geologic formation, the deeper you go, the older the archaeological layers are. As a result, they provide archaeologists with a way of establishing the *relative age* of the bones, artifacts, and other deposits in the layers—that is, their age in relation to each other. Unfortunately, Hall and Bent's careless digging had destroyed this means of dating artifacts in many areas of Great Zimbabwe.

To deal with the problem, the archaeologists dug small trenches in areas where they thought there was a chance of finding undisturbed layers. Each layer of each trench was carefully exposed, studied, and recorded, either in drawings or in photographs. In addition, the archaeologists noted precisely the location of all features, such as building foundations and artifacts, within each layer.

The complicated story of Great Zimbabwe emerges from the mosaic of carefully excavated trenches dug in and around the site by MacIver, Caton-Thompson, and Summers. The first inhabitants of Great Zimbabwe, who arrived in about A.D. 300, left little more than a scattering of clay potsherds behind them. At this time, the interior plateau of southern Africa between the Zambezi and Limpopo rivers—roughly what is now modern Zimbabwe—was populated with many cattle-herding and farming communities inhabited by people whose identity is lost to history. The first "Zimbabweans" were probably members of this group, judging from their pottery, which is similar in shape and design to the pottery archaeologists have found elsewhere in the region. As far as we know from the archaeological record, these people built no stone walls. In fact, it may not even be accurate to refer to them as inhabitants; they may only have grazed their cattle nearby.

There is no evidence that anyone lived at Great Zimbabwe for the next 700 years. Then in about 1000, the Shona arrived. Although archaeologists do not know exactly where the Shona people came from, oral histories and folk legends say they were migrants from the north who had begun to dominate the eastern part of the plateau by about the 900's. The people who settled at Great Zimbabwe were members of a branch of the Shona called the Karanga, the direct ancestors of the present-day inhabitants of the Zimbabwe area.

Like Great Zimbabwe's first inhabitants, the newcomers farmed millet and sorghum and herded cattle, goats, and sheep. At first, perhaps no more than a few dozen families lived at the site. Archaeologists have found the remains of the foundations of the huts they built both on the hill and in the valley below. The huts were almost certainly like the huts common among the Shona until recent times—circular structures made of mud and sticks with cone-shaped roofs made of thatch.

At first, the newcomers built no stone walls, except, perhaps, for simple cattle corrals. By the late 1000's, however, they had begun constructing the first of the many stone enclosures whose ruins dot the site today. The Summers team concluded that the first stone walls were built to reinforce the walls of the more substantial mud huts being constructed in the Hill Ruin. Eventually, stone walls connected most of the boulders on the summit of the hill, creating many narrow passageways and small enclosures.

Between the 1100's and 1300's, Great Zimbabwe grew in size and importance. At that time, it was one of several such developing settlements on the eastern edge of the plateau.

These settlements reaped the many benefits of their location. One of the most important was being beyond the range of the dreaded tsetse fly, which lives at lower altitudes and carries the parasites that cause African sleeping sickness in both people and cattle. In addition, compared with the lowlands, the plateau had a milder climate, more abundant water, and somewhat more fertile soil. It was also richer in game and in minerals, such as gold. The settlements were also near the Sabi River Valley, a major pathway to the Indian Ocean coast.

Like other Shona settlements, Great Zimbabwe was most certainly ruled by a headman or chief. Such chiefs were believed to have unusual spiritual powers that enabled them to communicate with tribal ancestors, whom the Shona revered, by means of spirit mediums. This link with the spirit world was the source of the chiefs' power. It enabled them to exact tribute from their people and to control the two pillars on which the settlements' political and economic power rested—cattle and trade.

Until the late 1800's, cattle were the base of the Shona economy as well as a source of prestige and social influence. It was this wealth-on-the-hoof that enabled the chiefs to gain and maintain control of their territory.

According to the archaeological record, imported glass beads and other exotic baubles first appeared at Great Zimbabwe sometime before 1100. They are a sign that the tentacles of the Indian Ocean gold and ivory trade had finally reached the interior of south-central Africa.

Opposite page: The oval-shaped Great Enclosure dominates the valley at Great Zimbabwe. Its free-standing outer wall, made of granite blocks fitted together without mortar, is more than 250 meters (820 feet) long and 7 meters (23 feet) tall. Within and around the Great Enclosure are many smaller enclosure walls that once surrounded huts.

The Great Enclosure

The Conical Tower, *above,* in
the Great Enclosure is one of
the most mysterious structures
at Great Zimbabwe. Made of
solid stone, the tower may
have been a symbolic storage
bin or a symbol of the chief's
authority. A chevron pattern of
blocks, *right,* decorates the top
of the wall behind the tower.
The pattern may have been a
symbol of the chief's clan.

This commerce was founded on the insatiable demand for African gold and ivory in Arabia and India, and on the monsoon winds that enabled a ship to sail from India to Africa and back within a year. The Africa-bound ships carried cheap cotton cloth, strings of glass beads, Chinese and Indian porcelain and glass, and other cheap baubles. These goods were exchanged for gold, copper ingots, elephant ivory, iron, slaves, and other commodities.

The chiefs of Great Zimbabwe almost certainly maintained a monopoly over the gold trade in their territory. Archaeologists believe this gold was mined in the hill country southwest of the settlement by other groups of Shona. The miners extracted the gold by digging small shafts along mineral veins with picks and hoes. Then smiths turned the gold into beads or stored gold dust in porcupine quills for easy transport. Evidently, the chiefs at Great Zimbabwe acted as middlemen in the system.

A narrow passageway winds between the outer wall of the Great Enclosure and an inner wall that parallels it for about one-half of its length. Near the southern end of the Great Enclosure, the inner wall widens out to pass the Conical Tower.

Archaeologists have tried to piece together the story of Great Zimbabwe through excavations and by examining accounts of the way the Shona lived until recent times. Stone blocks line the excavated foundation of a hut at Great Zimbabwe, *top*. Archaeologists believe the circular huts had thatched roofs and looked similar to those common among the Shona in rural areas, *above*.

By the 1400's, Great Zimbabwe may have been the most powerful of 10 or so regional chiefdoms. Based on the spacing of the ruins of various settlements, archaeologists believe each chiefdom controlled a territory about 160 kilometers (100 miles) in diameter, sufficient land to allow large-scale seasonal movement of cattle.

Great Zimbabwe reached the height of its power in the late 1400's, judging from the abundance of trade goods found in layers dated to this period. At that time, it was an imposing place. The frequent mists and rain that blew—and still blow—up the valley from the Indian Ocean kept the countryside around the settlement green for much of the year. Then, as today, the enormous weathered boulders on the Hill Ruin were frequently mantled in swirls of gray clouds.

From the valley, the most noticeable feature of the Hill Ruin would have been the stout granite retaining wall that protected the western end of the hill. We know that some people lived in a large enclosure, now called the Western Enclosure, behind this wall. Zimbabwean archaeologist Keith Robinson of the 1958 team discovered the foundations of huts and grain storage bins there. What the site was used for, however, is still a mystery. The most commonly accepted theory is that the Hill Ruin was an intensely sacred place where spirit mediums or priests lived. If so, these priests, like Shona priests in historical times, probably presided over rainmaking ceremonies and rites honoring tribal ancestors.

One reason for believing in the Hill Ruin's spiritual importance is Bent's discovery of eight mysterious soapstone birds in the Western Enclosure. Each bird is part of a column about 1.5 meters (5 feet) high. Most of the birds, which probably represent crowned hornbills, have long necks, a horizontal beak, and feathered legs. The columns bear different symbols, such as *chevron* (V-shaped) patterns. The column of the most elaborately carved bird has a crocodile crawling upward. Even today, archaeologists don't know the significance of the birds. Perhaps they were symbols associated with different kin groups among the Shona.

Another clue to the importance of the Hill Ruin

is the difficulty in getting there. The Zimbabweans could reach the summit by following a narrow stepped entrance on the north slope. Or they could follow a narrow pass that wound its way up to the Western Enclosure between huge boulders. But access was clearly limited.

The final clue is the attitude of the Shona toward the Hill Ruin in historical times. Karl Mauch found that the Shona still revered the site for its associations with ancestral spirits and avoided it.

Archaeologists have speculated that the Shona elite, such as chiefs and priests, were buried in the Hill Ruin. Legend has it that European excavators in the early 1800's found skeletons ornamented with gold. But there is no evidence of this. And modern archaeologists have found no skeletons at all at the site.

To modern visitors, the most visible symbol of power at Great Zimbabwe is the Great Enclosure. The Zimbabweans started work on the Great Enclosure in about 1450. The Summers team found traces of the first structure on the site, a simple enclosure—perhaps a mud hut—and a storage pit. Soon afterward, the ancient builders pulled everything down and started work on an inner wall that curves about halfway around the site and an outer wall that surrounds the site completely. By this time, the Zimbabweans were expert stoneworkers and could take full advantage of the special properties of the local granite. They would search for natural granite outcrops, where the rock fractured naturally into rectangular blocks that needed little trimming. Experiments have shown that setting fires against the rock fractures it, producing dozens of suitable blocks with relatively little effort.

The builders' finest work is evident in the outer wall, which is more than 240 meters (800 feet) long. There they enclosed a central core of untrimmed blocks in neat outer skins of evenly laid stonework. Its granite blocks were fitted together in two parallel rows without mortar. The space between the rows was filled with rubble and untrimmed granite blocks. Summers and his team concluded that the builders began the wall on the eastern side of the North Entrance,

Artifacts discovered at Great Zimbabwe have also provided clues about how its inhabitants lived. A soapstone bird, *below*—probably representing a hornbill— is one of eight such sculptures unearthed in the Hill Ruin. The birds may have been symbols of various Shona kin groups. Beads and other gold artifacts found at Great Zimbabwe, *below left,* are evidence of the thriving trade that took place long ago in this ancient African settlement.

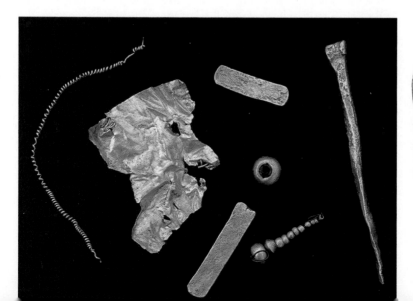

one of three openings in the wall. Evidently, they worked clockwise from there. The Summers team based this conclusion on the height of the wall, which gradually slopes downward from the North Entrance. Its average height is 7 meters (23 feet), but in some places it rises to 10 meters (33 feet).

The different architectural styles evident in the wall also led the archaeologists to conclude that work on the wall proceeded gradually, perhaps over a period of 50 years or so. For example, the blocks grow smaller and the rows more regular over the length of the wall. In addition, the wall grows increasingly refined farther away from the North Entrance.

One of the most interesting features of the wall is a double-chevron pattern of inclined blocks that adorn a 52-meter (170-foot) length of the southern end of the wall. The chevron pattern, similar to that on one of the soapstone bird columns, may have been the symbol of the chief.

From the North Entrance, an inner wall parallels the outer wall for about half its length. Near the southern end of the Great Enclosure, this inner wall widens out to pass what may be the most mysterious stone structure at Great Zimbabwe—the Conical Tower. This symmetrical structure is 10 meters across at the base and tapers gradually to a flattened top higher than the outer wall. It is solid, not hollow, so it was not a storage bin. There are no footholds or handholds on the sides for climbing, so it probably was not used as an astronomical observatory or as an observation or signal tower. Some archaeologists speculate that it was a symbolic grain bin or a symbol of the chief's authority.

Within the Great Enclosure, archaeologists have found the remains of the substantial huts that once nestled within the stone-walled enclosures. Although they have no solid evidence, they believe that these huts housed Great Zimbabwe's chiefs and their immediate families. Members of the Shona elite—perhaps relatives of the chief—may have dwelled in the mud-and-thatch houses that clustered within and around other stone-walled enclosures close by in the valley. Unfortunately, we know little of these huts or their occupants, because few have been thoroughly excavated.

Because early excavators dug over the interior of the Great Enclosure so carelessly, we have no way of knowing for certain what activities took place there. Archaeologists speculate, however, that the Great Enclosure was probably a busy place, for it was here that the chief likely conducted most of his business, administered justice, received tribute, and met with traders.

Even at the height of Great Zimbabwe's power, however, the population probably never numbered more than a few hundred people. The local soils, never very fertile, simply would not have supported large numbers of people. Most of the chief's subjects probably lived in small hamlets scattered over the surrounding countryside. Judging from modern Shona custom, Great Zimbabwe probably attracted crowds for rainmaking ceremonies and other seasonal gatherings, but even then these crowds were relatively small.

Great Zimbabwe flourished until the early 1500's, when the site was abandoned. A few Shona may have lived at the site late into the 1500's; the archaeological evidence is confusing. The Zimbabweans may have left because the focus of the gold trade shifted north to the Zambezi River. It is more likely, however, that a series of complicated environmental factors were responsible. Oral histories speak of a shortage of salt, a vital commodity for cattle herders. Centuries of farming may have exhausted soils that were only moderately fertile to begin with. Or there may have been a drought that killed off the cattle and with them the power of the chief.

While no one now doubts that Great Zimbabwe was built by Africans, many intriguing mysteries still await future excavators. Who were the powerful chiefs who once lived here? What was the significance of the layout of the Great Enclosure and exactly who lived in the Hill Ruin? Why did Great Zimbabwe achieve such prominence, and why was it abandoned? And perhaps most important of all, what were the beliefs of the people who built this remarkable place, whose design seems to have been shaped by religion.

While many questions about Great Zimbabwe remain, the most pressing problem at the site is preservation. Although much has been done over the years, many walls in the Hill Ruin and in the valley are collapsing under the weight of rubble and densely packed ash from ancient hearths. The Zimbabwean government's long-term plan is to produce computerized maps of the precise locations of all unstable stone blocks as a first step for any future restoration work. But such ambitious schemes are currently beyond its limited resources. For the moment, archaeologists must be content with monitoring the movement of the blocks with data from old photographs and with fine wires. Some of the blocks have moved as much as 2.5 centimeters (1 inch) in a year.

Great Zimbabwe is far more than tropical Africa's most spectacular archaeological site. It is a compelling symbol of nationalist pride and of the deep ties between the Shona and their ancestral homeland. While it exists, the Shona know that the *vadzimu*, the tribal ancestors, still watch over the land. To Westerners, Great Zimbabwe serves as a powerful reminder that sub-Saharan Africa enjoyed a colorful and eventful past, a past that teaches us much about the great cultural diversity of humankind.

For further reading:

Garlake, Peter. *Great Zimbabwe*. Thames and Hudson, 1973.
Oliver, Roland, and Fagan, Brian. *Africa in the Iron Age*. Cambridge University Press, 1967.
Phillipson, David. *African Archaeology*. Cambridge University Press, 1984.

More than 90 years after they became extinct in their native China, a rare species of deer is back home.

Père David's Deer Return to China

BY MARIA M. BOYD

The mud sucked at my boots as I tramped through the marshland along the Yangtze River. Off to my right, through the dry, brown stalks of tall reeds, I could see China's longest river, more than half a kilometer (one-third mile) wide. It was November 1989, and huge flocks of geese, ducks, and herons rested here on their journey south for the winter. In my mind, I could also see Père David's deer, treading with sure feet in the marshy ground, nibbling on the reeds.

I was studying this area in Hubei Province in southern China to determine its suitability as a second reserve for this rare species of Chinese deer that became extinct in its native land 90 years ago. As I walked, I thought back to another November day, in 1985, when my Chinese colleagues and I released the first of these deer as part of a program to reintroduce them to China.

The Marquess of Tavistock, an English nobleman, had given the Chinese 20 Père David's deer from his private herd. We released them into a reserve created especially for them outside Beijing, and they had thrived. By late 1989, the herd numbered 76. Now we were moving into stage two of our plan—establishing a second reserve 10 times larger.

The reintroduction of Père David's deer to China is one of a number of such programs in progress around the world. Their purpose is to return to their native habitats animal species that have disappeared from the wild, usually because of the relentless encroachment of people into their habitat. One of the most notable reintroduction projects was the successful return in 1982 of Arabian oryxes to Oman, one of the countries on the Arabian Peninsula where the once-common antelope had been hunted to the edge of extinction. Scientists are now trying to return such species as black-footed ferrets to Wyoming, red wolves to North Carolina, and swift foxes to western Canada.

Preceding pages: Père David's deer, also known as Milu, stand in a lake at Nan Haizi, the reserve created for them near Beijing, China.

Human pressures on wildlife habitat have been particularly acute in China, the world's most populous country. There is no question that China's wildlife is fast disappearing. With more than 1 billion people to feed and shelter, China finds that reserving land for wildlife is a difficult proposition. In some parts of the country, nearly every piece of available land is used for farming. Nevertheless, since 1949, when the Communists won control of China, the government has been creating wildlife reserves where endangered species—most notably the panda, but also the Manchurian tiger, golden monkey, and elephant—live under strict government protection. Today, China has more than 400 wildlife reserves. The Père David's deer reserve, however, is the only refuge where a native Chinese species eliminated from the wild is making a comeback. For the Chinese, who have long regarded the deer as part of their country's natural and cultural heritage, the return of the deer has been an emotional homecoming.

The Chinese have two names for Père David's deer. One is *ssu-bu-xiang*, which means "the four unalikes." To the Chinese, the deer appeared to have the neck of a camel, the hoofs of a cow, the tail of a donkey, and the antlers of a deer. The deer's more common name, however, is *Milu*, which means "marshland animal."

The Milu is one of the larger species of deer. Males can grow up to 1.3 meters (4 feet 3 inches) tall at the shoulders and can weigh as much as 250 kilograms (550 pounds). Females can reach 1.2 meters (4 feet) and weigh as much as 150 kilograms (330 pounds).

From studying ancient Chinese records and fossils of Milu antlers and bones, we know that the deer once commonly ranged throughout the marshy lowlands of northeastern and north-central China. The earliest known record of Milu in China is found in manuscripts from the Shang dynasty, which arose during the 1700's B.C. Filled with drawings of the deer, the manuscripts indicate that the Milu were important quarry in imperial hunts.

The author:
Maria B. Boyd is a zoologist and the codirector of the Milu Ecological Research Centre at Nan Haizi.

100

An ink and water-color drawing of Milu antlers rendered by the Chinese Emperor Ch'ien-lung in 1767 includes Chinese characters (vertical column, upper right) that identify the antlers as having come from the imperial hunting grounds at Nan Haizi. The Milu survived at Nan Haizi for about 1,500 years after they became extinct in the wild.

The first Westerner known to have seen the Milu was a French missionary to China named Père (Father) Armand David. Père David became more famous as a naturalist than as a man of God. His discoveries for the Western world included 58 species of birds, about 100 kinds of insects, and numerous species of plants and mammals, among them the giant panda.

In 1865, on one of his many trips on horseback exploring the countryside around Beijing, Père David came upon Nan Haizi, a large imperial hunting park south of the city. The park, which covered about 370 square kilometers (140 square miles), was surrounded by a brick wall 3 meters (10 feet) high. Père David peered over the wall and saw a herd of about 120 deer, which, he said, appeared to be "some kind of reindeer."

Unfortunately for Père David, who wanted a closer look at the deer, Nan Haizi was forbidden to foreigners. And when efforts by French and British diplomats in China to legally obtain some specimens of the deer for him failed, Père David resorted to unofficial means—bribes. At a late-night meeting, Père David gave several of the park's guards hats, mittens, and 20 pieces of silver in exchange for some skins and fragments of antlers and bones from the deer. He sent the specimens to Alphonse Milne-Edwards, the director of the Museum of Natural History in Paris, who announced the discovery of a new species of deer and named it Père David's deer, or *Elaphurus davidianus*, in honor of the missionary.

After the deer became extinct in China, a herd was preserved at Woburn Abbey Park in England, *above,* by the Duke of Bedford, who began collecting these animals in the late 1800's. The Milu reintroduced to China were donated from this herd. All the Milu alive today are descended from Woburn Abbey's original herd of 18 deer.

According to ancient Chinese writings, by the time Père David came upon the deer in the imperial preserve, the animals had been extinct in the wild for about 1,500 years. The most likely reason for their disappearance was overhunting, because the deer inhabited the same swampy lowlands used for growing crops, especially rice. Ironically, the deer had survived in what could be considered China's first wildlife reserve only because of their popularity as game for Chinese emperors. No one but the emperor was permitted to hunt the Milu at Nan Haizi. But, in fact, emperors rarely did because they believed the animals brought good luck.

In the late 1800's, the Chinese finally sent a number of Milu to European zoos and private parks to satisfy the passion wealthy Europeans of the time had for collecting unusual plants and animals. Few of the Milu flourished in their new homes, however, because the conditions in the zoos were so unlike those of the animal's natural habitat and because their small numbers made breeding difficult. In addition, little was known about the diseases that affected the deer or about their nutritional requirements.

In 1894, an English collector, Herbrand, the 11th Duke of Bedford, acquired his first pair of Milu from a zoo in Paris for Woburn Abbey, his vast estate in Bedfordshire. In 1896, the Woburn Abbey herd produced its first fawn. Aware that the Milu elsewhere were not thriving, the duke told his animal buyer to collect all the

Père David's deer he could. By 1901, the duke owned all the Milu in the world—a total of 18 deer.

Today, there are about 1,600 Père David's deer throughout the world, all descended from the 18 deer collected by the Duke of Bedford. About 700 of them live at Woburn Abbey Park, a 1,200-hectare (3,000-acre) estate where they range freely. The Woburn Abbey herd is, in fact, the largest free-ranging herd of Milu. A smaller herd of about 60 animals live at Front Royal, Va., at a breeding center maintained by the Smithsonian Institution in Washington, D.C. The rest live in private parks and zoos around the world.

I first learned about the Milu in 1961 while I was still a zoology student at Komensky University in my native Czechoslovakia. I wanted to know more about these mysterious creatures from an even more mysterious land, but very little had been written about them.

In 1965, I married an American zoologist who was, by coincidence, a friend of Lord Tavistock, the Duke of Bedford's great-grandson and the current owner of Woburn Abbey and its Milu herd. Lord Tavistock was delighted by my interest in the deer and in 1978 invited me to study them at Woburn Abbey. In 1980, I enrolled at Oxford University and began doing my thesis on the deer. By carefully observing them, I learned a great deal about their behavior.

The Milu are marshland animals. In China, they lived in swampy areas, mostly lowland plains crisscrossed by many rivers. At Woburn Abbey, located in forested English countryside, the Milu frequently spend long periods in the park's seven lakes, cooling themselves, swimming, and playing.

Unlike most species of deer, the Milu are social animals that live in one large herd for much of the year. Also unlike most deer, which graze on grass and browse on leaves, the Milu are grazers only. They also eat water plants.

The deers' mating season, announced by the bellowing of the *stags* (male deer), lasts for about six weeks beginning in June. As part of the mating ritual, the stags engage in a complex set of actions, the most interesting of which is decorating their antlers with grass. All male deer decorate their antlers during the mating season, but the Milu seem to do a more splendid job of it.

The herd's dominant stag—who may have to fight other stags to win his first-place status—takes control of the *hinds* (females) and prevents all the other males from getting near them. For about three weeks, this stag mates repeatedly with the hinds. During this time, he does not eat and rarely sleeps. As a result, by the end of the three weeks, he has lost up to one-fourth of his body weight. In this weakened state, he is easily ousted by the second-ranking stag, who then mates with the hinds for several weeks.

From about the end of November to mid-January, the stags shed their antlers. During this period, they live apart from the hinds. Once

The Life Cycle of the Milu

The Milu, unlike most species of deer, are social animals that live in one herd for most of the year. The *stags* (male deer) leave the herd in November, when they begin to shed their antlers. When the antlers begin to grow again in January, the stags rejoin the *hinds* (females).

Two stags prepare to fight at the beginning of the spring mating season, *above.* The victor in a series of battles with other stags wins the right to mate with the females. As part of the mating ritual, the stags decorate their antlers with grass, *right,* often creating spectacular displays.

A newborn fawn joins the herd, *above*. After giving birth, the hinds hide their fawns in tall grass or shrubs for several days.

The Milu are marshland animals who spend many hours in the water, swimming, playing, and cooling themselves, especially in the summer, *right*.

the antlers start growing again, however, the males rejoin the females. The stags and hinds live together until the stags start to lose the *velvet* on their antlers in April and May. The velvet is a furry skin that protects and nourishes the antler while it is growing. Once the antler is fully grown, blood vessels in the velvet dry up. The stags then rub their antlers against trees, scraping off the velvet and exposing the bone beneath. The exposed antlers make formidable weapons during the mating season.

The fawns at Woburn Abbey, I found, are usually born between the middle of April and June, about 10 months after the previous mating season. The hinds move away from the main herd to give birth. Unlike many other species of deer, which may have twins or even triplets, the Milu female always gives birth to only one fawn. After the fawn is born, the mother hides it in tall grass or beneath trees and shrubs for three to five days. During this "lying-out" period, the mother grazes with the rest of the herd, but returns twice a day to nurse her fawn. Finally, the fawns are introduced to the herd.

The fawns generally spend most of their time together within the herd, under the watchful eyes of several adult hinds. They usually join their mothers only to eat.

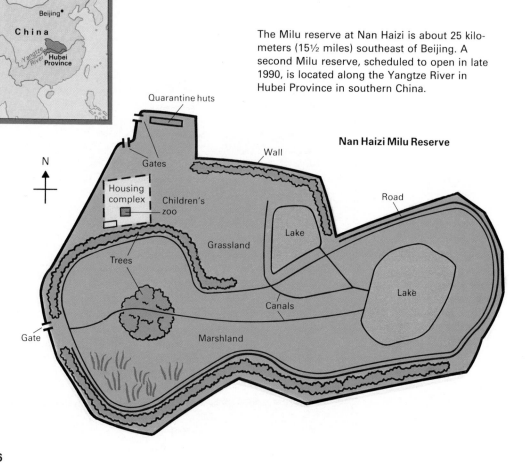

The Milu reserve at Nan Haizi is about 25 kilometers (15½ miles) southeast of Beijing. A second Milu reserve, scheduled to open in late 1990, is located along the Yangtze River in Hubei Province in southern China.

My research at Woburn Abbey assumed a new significance in 1981, when a delegation of Chinese scientists arrived to see the deer and learn about the habitat they require. Over the years, Lord Tavistock repeatedly had let the international scientific community know of his wish to reestablish the deer in China. More than 80 years after the last Milu had disappeared from China, the Chinese had decided that it was time for the deer to return home.

To oversee the project, the Chinese established the Milu Reintroduction Group of the People's Republic of China, made up of scientists and officials from a variety of organizations and agencies. I became the codirector of the project on the English side. My Chinese counterpart is zoology professor Wang Zongyi, formerly curator of mammals at the Museum of Natural History in Beijing.

Reintroducing an animal to its native habitat is a complicated process. It was clear we would have to conduct a study in China to determine whether it would be possible to bring the deer back. But before we could go even that far, I had a lot of work to do in England. First, I had to learn as much as I could about the range of conditions the deer could survive in. I knew they would thrive in a mild environment like that at Woburn Abbey, but we were unlikely to find an identical habitat in China. We needed to know conditions that were crucial to their survival. For example, what temperature changes could they tolerate? What vegetation did they need for food

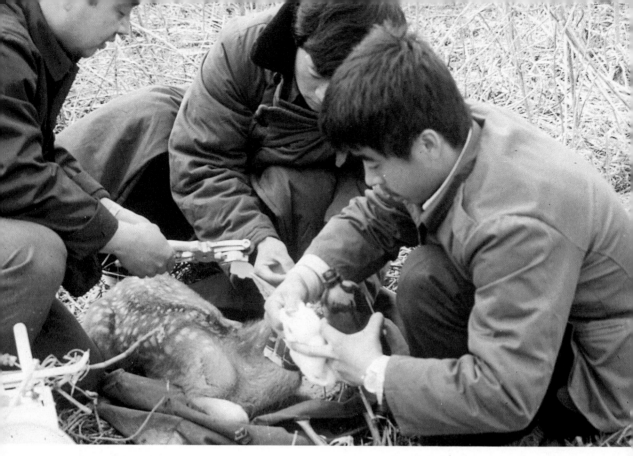

Research workers at Nan Haizi attach an identification tag to the ear of a newborn fawn. Such tags enable the researchers to record the activities of individual Milu as the study of these animals continues in their native land.

and concealment? We needed to know if the Milu had changed since they disappeared from China and if so, how. For example, they might have become accustomed to different weather and food. I contacted all the zoos and reserves throughout the world that had Milu to learn about the deer's living conditions there.

Second, I had to learn as much as I could about the deer's behavior. Building on my previous research, I spent days charting the deer's daily activities. For example, I noted how much time they spent grazing, sleeping, and resting. I also needed to know how the deer's activities changed with the seasons of the year.

It was also essential to discover exactly what factors affected the deer's ability to reproduce. For example, did the weather affect the timing of the mating and calving seasons? What factors affected the fawns' ability to survive? I was particularly interested in the behavior of the hinds before and after they gave birth. Before we could move the Milu to a different environment, we had to make sure they would be able to reproduce there.

To observe the deer during the mating season, I used as a blind a horse trailer lent to me by Lady Tavistock. The trailer was moved into position two weeks before the mating season began so the animals could get used to its presence and my comings and goings. Knowing I was watching might have caused them to behave in unusual ways, giving me a false picture. In the trailer, armed with good binoculars, a stop watch, a camera or two, and a notebook, I could observe the deer for hours at a time without frightening them. Sometimes I even slept there.

In 1984, I began studying how to reintroduce the Milu into China. The most important goal of this study was to determine where the deer should be reintroduced. Also important was determining how large a reserve they should have. Previous research on other deer had revealed that a healthy herd needs about 2 hectares (1 acre) per animal.

In March of that year, I flew to China. My first stop was the place where the Milu had last lived in China—Nan Haizi, which at that time was a tree nursery. From there, I traveled to Shanghai, where I met with Cao Keqing, a paleontologist at the Natural History Museum there who has discovered Milu fossils at a number of sites in China. For weeks we poured over the records of his excavations and visited other Chinese museums that have Milu fossils. We also studied Chinese writings about the distribution of the deer in the wild.

Finally, we reviewed Chinese meteorological records for ancient and modern times and compared them with records for the region around Woburn Abbey. The final site, we decided, had to have not only a temperate climate and plentiful grass but also roads good enough to permit scientists to get there easily. In many places in China, the roads make travel difficult. We also knew that whatever site we chose, we had to have the support of the local people and government.

Using these criteria, we drew up a list of five possible reintroduction sites within the deer's original range—including Nan Haizi—and began visiting them to determine their suitability. After about four months, we decided that Nan Haizi was probably the best site for the project. Although there were other sites that offered a better habitat, we had three main reasons for recommending the former imperial park. The first was Nan Haizi's historical significance as a place where the deer had lived for so long. Second, the site is close to the Chinese capital, where we could go to enlist the support of major governmental organizations and officials for solving any practical problems we encountered. Third, Beijing is also the seat of China's most important universities and scientific institutions, whose scientists we were relying on to help with our research.

Another of Nan Haizi's advantages was that, because the site was a tree nursery, no people would be displaced. In addition, it already had a 34-hectare (84-acre) lake, an essential requirement for marshland animals.

Our recommendation was quickly accepted by the Chinese government. Nan Yuan township, which was in control of Nan Haizi, donated about 100 hectares (250 acres) of the tree nursery to the project, and this became the reserve.

We began constructing the reserve in September 1984 using a plan devised by a number of scientists, including Wang Zongyi and myself. First, we surrounded the entire area with a brick wall 2.5 meters (8 feet) high. Nearly 400 people—including local residents and soldiers from the army—worked for 100 days to build it. The workers also dug several freshwater wells and diverted a stream, polluted by waste from nearby factories, to prevent it from running through the reserve. Next, we built quarantine huts for the deer.

To our delight, our hard work began paying off even before the Milu arrived. Species of birds rarely seen in the area were drawn to the reserve by its open spaces, clean water, and undisturbed environment. We were particularly surprised to see water birds, such as herons, spoonbills, and black storks.

While we were constructing the reserve, extensive preparations were taking place in England. The 20 Milu—5 males and 15 females—that would make the trip to China were caught in April 1985 and taken to a quarantine center in England. Veterinarians checked each deer for such diseases as tuberculosis and foot-and-mouth disease to ensure that the Milu would not carry new strains of these diseases to China. Only when we were sure that the deer were healthy were they approved for the trip.

The Milu were flown into Beijing on Aug. 24, 1985. Despite heavy rain, hundreds of people gathered at the airport to welcome them. The enthusiasm was so great that, as the deer were being unloaded, I feared that the excited Chinese handlers would drop the heavy cages and the deer would have their first taste of freedom in their ancestral homeland on the runways of Beijing airport.

The deer were immediately trucked to Nan Haizi, where they were placed in quarantine and once again tested for disease. During this period, we tried to keep the environment in the quarantine huts as stress-free as possible. Chiefly, that meant limiting the contact between the deer and the people at the reserve. We had constructed the feeding troughs in the quarantine huts so that the keepers could fill them without being seen by the deer. When contact was necessary—for example, when the huts were being cleaned—the keepers were instructed to speak softly. Thankfully, all went well, and after three months, the deer were released amid much celebration. In March and April 1987, 14 fawns were born. In September, Lord Tavistock sent another 18 females. By spring 1990, there were more than 100 Milu at the reserve.

In the five years since the Milu returned to China, the project at Nan Haizi has grown beyond our wildest imaginings. Observing the deer and recording their behavior with still and video cameras remains our primary activity. These photographs and films serve as a record of the deer's behavior and, eventually, will form the basis of a comprehensive study of the deer. To discover whether the different environmental conditions in China have caused significant behavioral changes, we have undertaken a number of studies at Nan

Haizi on courtship and mating, maternal care, nutrition, and juvenile behavior, to list a few.

Our findings are serving as the foundation for herd management practices at the reserve. For example, they help us determine how much supplemental food the deer need in the winter and how to spot signs of disease. In addition, by comparing these findings with research done at Woburn Abbey, we are learning more about the deer and their behavior in general. So far, the main differences we have found involve the timing of different seasons in the deer's life cycle, probably because of climate differences. At Woburn Abbey, for example, the first fawns of the year are born around April 15. At Nan Haizi, the earliest recorded birth is March 2.

We also hope the Nan Haizi Milu herd will be a model for the development of breeding programs for other endangered species. Because the world's entire Milu population is descended from 18 animals, we take extreme care when breeding the deer. *Inbreeding* (mating closely related animals) can make hereditary diseases more widespread or lead to *infertility* (the inability to reproduce). The main way we prevent inbreeding is by keeping the dominant stag from breeding for more than two years in a row. After the second year, we isolate him from the herd during the mating season. This helps ensure that the stag will not mate with one of his daughters soon after she becomes mature, an event that occurs at age 2.

The knowledge we have gained at Nan Haizi is proving vital in efforts to proceed to the next stage in our program—the creation of the reserve in Hubei Province. This reserve, scheduled to open in late 1990, will have about 50 deer to begin with.

Originally, we thought we might be able to establish a herd of Milu in the wild somewhere within the deer's original habitat in northern or north-central China. But this would be impossible. Released into the wild, the Milu would be inhabiting the same lowland fields now used for growing rice. Such competition would, as it has in the distant past, surely prove fatal to the deer.

We hope that the Nan Haizi Milu Reserve and the new reserve on the Yangtze River will become world famous not only because of the Milu but also as symbols of China's commitment to conservation. In the world's most populous country, where open land is more precious than most Westerners can imagine, two magnificent areas have been set aside for the Milu. In doing so, the Chinese have ensured that these deer are home to stay.

For further reading:

Banks, Vic. "The red wolf gets a second chance to live by its wits," *Smithsonian,* March 1988.
Grodinsky, Caroline, and Stüwe, Michael. "With lots of help, alpine ibex return to their mountains," *Smithsonian,* December 1987.
Crump, Donald J., ed. *Wildlife: Making a Comeback.* National Geographic, 1987.

An interview with Bob Ballard,
conducted by Darlene R. Stille

Explorer of
the Deep Seas

The discoverer of the *Titanic* discusses the highlights
of his career and shares his thoughts on how to take
students on an epic journey into the world of science.

An artist's painting shows the *Titanic* resting
at the bottom of the North Atlantic Ocean.

. . . one of my idols was a fictitious person, Captain Nemo of Jules Verne's novel Twenty Thousand Leagues Under the Sea. *Captain Nemo was a technologist and an explorer, which is exactly what I am . . . he would go around and explore the world in his submarine. . . . I think, in a sense, I'm trying to be Captain Nemo. I really do.*

The interviewer:
Darlene R. Stille is the associate editor of *Science Year*.

Science Year: Dr. Ballard, you grew up on the California coast and so you were always able to enjoy the ocean, to swim in it, to walk the beaches. Your friends probably did the same thing. Did you regard the ocean any differently at that time than your friends did?

Ballard: I can't remember talking to my friends about the ocean. I went to the ocean to be alone. The beach was where I went and thought about everything kids think of: Why am I here? What am I supposed to do? Some kids had a dog to rely upon, I had the ocean. Also, I always knew that I could go down to the ocean and find an adventure waiting for me.

SY: What sort of adventure?

Ballard: In tidal pools. I loved tidal pools, still do. They form in holes in a stony or rocky area. When the tide's in, the area is underwater. And if an animal in a hole isn't paying attention when the tide goes out, all of a sudden it finds that the rest of the ocean has vanished for a few hours and it's sort of trapped. Then the tide comes back and it escapes and new guys get in—little fish, little crabs, sea anemones. So it was like a window into the sea. I had my own aquarium, and it changed daily. Also, I used to collect things that the tide brought in. The biggest thrill would be to get a fishing float. Once I found one that had come all the way from Japan, a third of the way around the planet. It had barnacles on it because it had been drifting for so long. I used to collect all that stuff and drag it home and smell up the house. And when it rotted, my mother would throw it out.

SY: Obviously, you grew up loving the sea. But was there any particular experience in your early life that you can identify as having set you on the career path toward being an oceanographer?

Ballard: I think it was just being in such close proximity to the sea. And there was always this sort of mystery for me about things that came out of the sea. I loved to fish off the pier, to throw a line in and have some monster come out of the sea on my hook. Maybe it was only 3 inches long. But there it would be from under the water. If it was a pretty fish, it was a mermaid. If it was an ugly fish, it was a creature from the black lagoon.

SY: Who were the two or three most influential people in your life, in terms of your science career?

Ballard: Well, there were my teachers, of course, and my family—my father was an engineer—and my sister. I have a retarded sister, and she has really been an inspiration to me. I used to look at her across the breakfast table and think, it's not fair. And I also understood that by the flip of a coin, that could have been me. I was just lucky to be healthy and smart. And I thought, I'm not going to waste that.

Also, one of my idols was a fictitious person, Captain Nemo of Jules Verne's novel *20,000 Leagues Under the Sea*. Captain Nemo was a technologist and an explorer, which is exactly what I am. He built this submarine, and he had a loyal team of troops who followed him around the world. Unfortunately, he was a little strange, too. But, he would go around and explore the world in his submarine. I think, in a sense, I'm trying to be Captain Nemo. I really do.

Robert D. Ballard

He is most famous for discovering legendary shipwrecks—the luxury liner *Titanic* and the German battleship *Bismarck*. But Bob Ballard is also a distinguished scientist who has made many important findings about the ocean floor.

Robert Duane Ballard was born on June 30, 1942, in Wichita, Kans., but grew up in southern California. Even as a high school student, Ballard knew he wanted a career in oceanography, and he made his first research cruise at the age of 17.

Ballard earned his B.S. degree from the University of California at Santa Barbara in 1965. He had been in the university's ROTC program and upon his graduation was commissioned a lieutenant in Army Intelligence. He then went on reserve status while attending the graduate schools of marine geology at the University of Hawaii and the University of Southern California. In 1967, he was transferred into the Navy and went on active duty as liaison officer to the Woods Hole Oceanographic Institution on Cape Cod, Massachusetts.

When he was discharged from the Navy in 1969, he stayed on at Woods Hole as a research associate and completed his graduate studies in marine geology and geophysics at the University of Rhode Island, receiving his Ph.D. in 1974.

Meanwhile, Ballard had become involved in the design and use of underwater research vehicles. He worked with other Woods Hole scientists using a small research submersible called *Alvin* for deep-sea exploration and research. Over the course of his career, Ballard has made more than 200 dives in *Alvin* and other submersibles.

His first major expedition was Project FAMOUS (French-American Mid-Ocean Undersea Study) in 1973 and 1974. *Alvin*, two French submersibles, and *Angus*, a camera sled that Ballard had designed to be towed by a surface ship, were used to map the Mid-Atlantic Ridge, an area of the ocean floor where two of the great plates that make up Earth's crust are separating.

In 1977, Ballard was part of a team of scientists who discovered strange life forms around hot water vents on the ocean floor off Ecuador. Ballard attached to *Angus* a temperature-sensing device that triggered cameras when the water grew hotter. The pictures revealed worms and clams and other forms of life that scientists later learned live off chemicals in the hot water.

"Black smokers," tall "chimneys" created by minerals spewing out of hot water vents off the coast of Baja California, were discovered by Ballard in 1979. Coming from these chimneys were clouds of dark water that looked like smoke, and again, strange life forms nearby. In the Special Reports section, see LIFE AT THE VENTS.

Then he turned his attention to developing remote-controlled robot subs and in 1981 set up the Deep Submergence Laboratory within Woods Hole's Department of Ocean Engineering. With funding from the Navy and the National Science Foundation, he developed the *Argo/Jason* system, named after Jason and the Argonauts of Greek mythology, adventurers who set off in search of the Golden Fleece.

Argo, like *Angus*, is a camera sled that is towed by a research ship. But instead of *Angus'* 35-millimeter still cameras, *Argo* carries video cameras that "see" extremely well in the darkness of the deep. Guided by sonar, *Argo* scans the sea floor and transmits video images live to the ship above. *Argo* also carries a smaller self-propelled robot sub named *Jason*. When *Argo* sees something that needs closer investigation, *Jason* is sent out, under remote control, equipped with video cameras and an arm for collecting samples.

Ballard discovered the *Titanic* (which struck an iceberg and sank in 1912) on Sept. 1, 1985, as part of a test of *Argo* conducted for the Navy. He returned to explore the *Titanic* in 1986 using *Alvin* and a smaller version of *Jason* called *Jason Jr.*, or *J.J.* In June 1989, he found the German battleship *Bismarck*, sunk in the Atlantic Ocean during World War II.

Ballard next put the *Argo/Jason* system—with another camera sled called *Medea*—to work in the service of science education. He established the Jason Foundation for Education in 1985, and in May 1989 he conducted the first Project Jason expedition to explore hydrothermal vents and Roman shipwrecks in the Mediterranean Sea. To create what Ballard calls "telepresence," images from *Jason* are sent to the ship via optical fiber cables. From the ship, TV pictures are relayed to museums in the United States and Canada. There, students can watch as the scientists are making their discoveries. In 1990, the second Project Jason expedition examined ships sunk during the War of 1812 at the bottom of Lake Ontario.

Ballard is a senior scientist in the Department of Ocean Engineering and director of the Center for Marine Exploration at the Woods Hole Oceanographic Institution. He also serves on the board of the Jason Foundation for Education. He has written several books and magazine articles and hosts the weekly "National Geographic Explorer" series on the Turner Broadcasting System. He lives in an old farmhouse near Woods Hole.

SY: There are many specialties that an ocean scientist can pursue, and one that comes to mind right away is marine biology. You were always fascinated by the life in the oceans, yet you chose marine geology over biology. Why was that?

Ballard: When I was in high school, I thought I would be a marine biologist. But when I was a senior, I had an experience that changed my mind. I wrote a letter to Scripps Institute of Oceanography saying I love oceanography and I want to be an oceanographer. What do I do? Signed, me. Fortunately, the letter crossed the desk of a person with a soul who was in charge of a National Science Foundation summer training program specifically designed for high school kids. He sent me an application, I filled it out, and I was chosen to go to sea on a research cruise. What an adventure! We got in this big storm and our little boat almost sank. We had to be rescued by the Coast Guard. It was an incredible experience for a 17-year-old kid. Well, on that cruise was a freshly minted marine biologist, who had just finished his Ph.D. I probably annoyed the heck out of him with a million questions. He said, "If you're interested in the ocean and want to go into this field, don't become a marine biologist. There are no jobs. We're overpopulated with marine biologists." It was like someone took a big pin to my balloon. Plus, my brother was studying to be a particle physicist and my father's an engineer, and they wanted me to be a physicist. What should I become?

SY: And how did you resolve this conflict?

Ballard: The next year, I went off to college at the University of California at Santa Barbara. My adviser was a marine geologist. I didn't know what to do. So I took physics, chemistry, math, I took it all. I majored in something called the physical science degree. Think that sounds easy? Wrong. Instead of four years, it takes five. You have to major in two physical sciences and minor in two. So I majored in chemistry and geology and I minored in physics and math. What an education! And then I did my graduate work in marine geology.

SY: One of your life's most meaningful relationships has been with a little submarine named *Alvin*. Do you remember the first time you met *Alvin*?

Ballard: I first met *Alvin* on paper, actually, when I was in college. My father was head of the Minuteman missile program at North American Aviation. I asked my dad if he could help me get a summer job there. Well, North American Aviation, like a lot of other corporations back in the late 1950's and early 1960's was wondering whether the oceans were going to be like space. Was there going to be a conquest of inner space? North American Aviation had set up an ocean systems operation to build specialized little submarines for deep-sea explorations. I got a summer job with the ocean systems group, and they were bidding on a contract to build *Alvin*. I was just a "gofer" working in the research library. But here I am, a freshman in college helping in a very minor way on the plans for this submarine. I worked for two summers at North American on this project, but they didn't get the bid, and I lost track of *Alvin*.

I first met Alvin *on paper. . . . I got a summer job with the [North American Aviation] ocean systems group, and they were bidding on a contract to build* Alvin. *. . . but, they didn't get the bid, and I lost track of* Alvin.

SY: How did you happen to meet up with *Alvin* again, Dr. Ballard?

Ballard: When I came to Woods Hole. And I wasn't especially happy about coming here at the time. I had just switched graduate schools and moved from the University of Hawaii to the University of Southern California, because I had been offered a well-paying job on the design of submarines at North American Aviation. I was at USC pursuing my doctorate in marine geology, which was being paid for by my company. I had a car and a great apartment on the beach. I was doing just great until this guy knocked on my door and said, "You're in the Navy. You've got six days to report to active duty." I was sent to Woods Hole to be the Navy representative of oceanography in all of New England. It turned out to be the greatest accident that's ever happened to me. But at the time, I was furious. I knew nothing about Woods Hole, and I came here with a real chip on my shoulder. They ruined my graduate school career. My salary dropped catastrophically. I grew up in sunny California, and I didn't want to be in New England with the cold weather and grumpy people. I wanted out of here.

But then I found out they had *Alvin*. They were the only place that had a deep-diving submarine. Plus, the head of earth sciences here had set up the marine geology graduate school at USC, and he was working with *Alvin*. When he found out that the new young naval officer had been a marine geology graduate student at USC, he treated me like a son. He said welcome aboard, and I began working with the *Alvin* group. Off I went to sea and began doing science and diving—it just was perfect.

Eventually, I fell in love with the Woods Hole Oceanographic Institution. When I got out of the Navy, in 1969, I stayed on with the *Alvin* group and went back to graduate school. And again I was lucky. I happened to be a graduate student during the most exciting period in earth sciences history.

SY: What was going on then?

Ballard: The theory of plate tectonics was just exploding on the earth science scene. The theory holds that Earth's crust is made up of about 12 gigantic plates that move around on the hot mantle below. The continents and the sea floor ride on these plates. At first, it seemed just bizarre, the idea of the continents plowing around. But the idea finally made sense to me. The movement of the plates could account for many geological processes—mountain building, volcanism, earthquakes. And the beauty of plate tectonics is that it's easily understood. You don't have to go off on a mountain with some guru for nine years and say, "Please go over this again." It's very simple. Truth tends to be simple. When an answer is real complex, it's probably wrong. Anyway, when I was working on my doctorate, that was an incredible period in earth science. Every day there were new discoveries, reinterpretations. There's nothing like that in geology now.

SY: You've made more than 200 dives in your career. Is there any dive in particular that's especially memorable to you?

I happened to be in graduate school during the most exciting period in earth science history. . . . The theory of plate tectonics was just exploding on the earth science scene. . . . At first, it seemed just bizarre, the idea of the continents plowing around. But the idea finally made sense to me.

Discovering Mysteries of the Deep

With more than 200 dives to the bottom of the sea, Bob Ballard has made major contributions to ocean science. His most personally gratifying dives were made during Project FAMOUS, a U.S.-French expedition to the Mid-Atlantic Ridge in 1973 and 1974. During those dives in the research submarine *Alvin,* he was one of the first people to see the great cracks in the sea floor (as shown in this artist's conception) where two of the giant plates that make up Earth's crust are moving apart. He also led a 1977 expedition that discovered strange life forms around hot-water vents in the Galapagos Rift off Ecuador.

Ballard sips a hot drink in the cramped crew quarters of *Alvin* as the submersible descends to investigate unusual life forms at hot-water vents in the Galapagos Rift. He regards his role in discovering these vents and the life around them as his most important contribution to science.

After coming up from a dive to the Mid-Atlantic Ridge, *Alvin* is guided by divers back to its support ship, the catamaran *Lulu*.

Landing Alvin *on the deck of the* Titanic *was . . . just awe inspiring. . . . What we came in on was the razor edge of the ship's bow. It was sort of like staring at the slab in the movie* 2001. *I just stared at this thing and thought, guess what, that's the* Titanic.

Ballard: One that I almost got killed on pops into my mind. It was in a French bathyscaph in 1973. Fortunately, they're not used anymore. They're all in museums. A bathyscaph is a balloon in reverse. A balloon is a bag filled with helium, which is lighter than air. A bathyscaph is a metal balloon filled with gasoline, which is lighter than seawater. It was also filled with beebee shot to make it sink. It had these little valves, and you let out some shot when you wanted to go up; let out some gasoline when you wanted to go down. It was a monstrous thing, more than 100 feet long, a giant bomb.

They towed it out in the ocean and we got in. I'd never been in the thing before. And down we go to explore a canyon 9,000 feet below. It's totally dark down there except for the lights from the submarine. And I'm looking out the window when all of a sudden, an electrical fire breaks out. Well, the Frenchmen stop speaking English and they start speaking French. They're all upset. Things are getting dark. Emergency lights are going on, just little pin lights. They turned off the oxygen to kill the fire, and so there's almost no air in there. What little that's left tastes like burnt rubber, smells awful, and it's burning my eyes. I see the Frenchmen putting on their emergency breathing systems. They're very preoccupied. Well, where is mine? I reach under my seat and I bring out this thing that looks like a gas mask. I put it on, and it's not working! I take it off and look for the instructions. It's all in French. I'm coughing and I can't breathe. The Frenchmen think I'm panicking and they try to keep this thing on my face. It feels like they're smothering me with a pillow, so I try to get the thing off. We're struggling, and I'm dying. I get dizzy. And then one of the Frenchmen says, "Oh, pardon." And he reaches over and turns on my emergency oxygen supply—which happened to be turned off.

SY: What dive was the most exciting for you?

Ballard: Landing *Alvin* on the deck of the *Titanic* in 1986. It was majestic, just awe inspiring. We came down and landed in front of the ship. But at first, we couldn't see it in the darkness. We knew where it was because our tracking system told us. I'm at the mud line tooling along in this little submarine, and it was like coming in on a giant. What we came in on was the razor edge of the ship's bow. It was sort of like staring at the slab in the movie *2001*. I just stared at this thing and thought, guess what, that's the *Titanic*.

We then rose up to its deck and saw these things that looked like icicles, but they were made of rust. So I called them rusticles. The ship's covered with these rusticles. We came up over the rail, and the deck came slowly into view through the particulate matter floating in the water, as though veils were parting. Then the final veil was open, and I was looking at the deck of the *Titanic*. I had thought it still would have a wooden deck, but it didn't. The wood was all gone, eaten by marine worms. I'm looking at the underlying metal.

SY: Why were you so interested in the condition of the *Titanic*'s deck?

Ballard: We couldn't get the robot sub *Jason* out unless we landed *Alvin* on the deck. And I didn't know how strong the deck was. I didn't know if it could support us. So I figured out a couple of safe places and I picked a spot right up in the bow where there was probably a big strong piece of deck. Landing was extremely dangerous. We had to maneuver between the railing and a big bollard, used for securing lines. And there were capstans and other protrusions that weren't on the blueprints. When we came down, we were worried about falling inside the ship. If the deck collapsed, down we'd go. It really would have been pretty bad. We had our hands on the weights. If something went wrong, we'd pop our weights and we'd go home. Finally, we set down on the deck and started pumping ballast, getting heavier and heavier, listening for creaks. And then I looked up and right in my face was this capstan for winding the ship's anchor chain. I could see an inscription on the top, "Napier brothers, Glasgow," an incredible piece of frozen history. Up to that point, the *Titanic* had been in the history books, it wasn't real.

From then on our exploration of the *Titanic* felt a bit like going around in grandma's attic when you're not supposed to go up there. Gosh, look at this silly thing over here. And we just wandered around looking at these old things.

We did all of our looking inside the ship through *Jason*'s TV cameras. When we sent *J.J.* down the grand staircase, we were glued to the tube in *Alvin*. We'd become *J.J.*. We were inside *J.J.*, and we were scared. *J.J.* came to the edge of the grand staircase, now a big gaping hole in the ship, and we felt disoriented. We said, let's follow the wall down and keep the wall in front of us. Going down that wall became sort of like holding onto someone's hand as you went through the spook house at the county fair. We'd say let's turn and look over there. Then we'd say, oh my gosh, let's go back to the wall because I'm getting lost. Finally we got to the bottom of the staircase and we were saying to each other, do you want to go in that dark room over there? What's in there? Now that was exciting.

When we sent J.J. *down the grand staircase, we were glued to the tube in* Alvin. *We'd become* J.J. *We were inside* J.J., *and we were scared. . . . Finally, we got to the bottom of the staircase and we were saying to each other, do you want to go in that dark room over there? What's in there? Now, that was exciting.*

SY: Your discovery of the *Titanic* and all the excitement surrounding this event is, no doubt, what you are best known for. But, you have been on many other fascinating expeditions. Of all your undersea discoveries to date, which was the most personally gratifying to you?

Ballard: I would say the first dives to the mid-Atlantic Ridge in 1973 and 1974. It took so much effort and training because no one had ever been there before. It was like preparing a group of astronauts to go to the moon. It was really an overkill. But that was the way it was done back then. And it was very gratifying to be selected for this mission and then to do well, to go down there and explore and be at the cutting edge of science.

SY: In the mid-Atlantic Ridge, you found the place where two tectonic plates are spreading apart. How did you feel when you first saw plate tectonics in action?

Ballard: You know, you can ultimately reduce the concept of plate tectonics to a crack where the ocean floor splits open. Half is going one way and half is going the other way. I remember going down and

Exploring the *Titanic*
An artist's painting shows *Alvin* on the deck of the legendary passenger liner *Titanic,* which sank in the North Atlantic Ocean in 1912. The robot sub *J.J.,* equipped with a TV-camera "eye," begins its explorations of the ship, while inside *Alvin,* Ballard and his crew control *J.J.,* watching its progress on a TV screen as it makes its way down the hole that was once the grand staircase.

J.J.'s lights stare back from the razor edge of the *Titanic's* bow, resting in the mud on the sea floor *below, left.* Huge "rusticles," iciclelike formations of rust, hang down the sides of the ship, *below, right.*

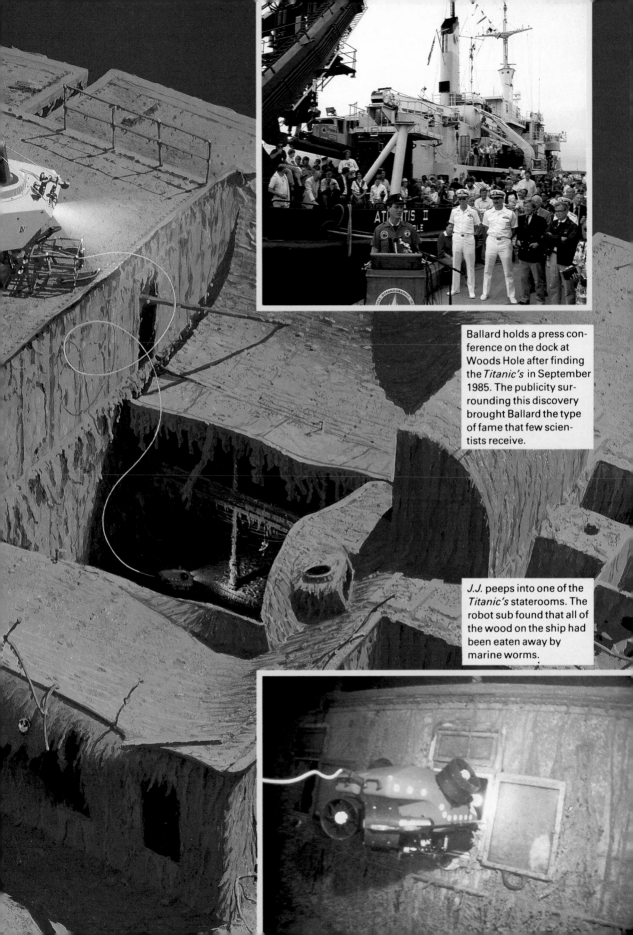

Ballard holds a press conference on the dock at Woods Hole after finding the *Titanic's* in September 1985. The publicity surrounding this discovery brought Ballard the type of fame that few scientists receive.

J.J. peeps into one of the *Titanic's* staterooms. The robot sub found that all of the wood on the ship had been eaten away by marine worms.

being part of the first group of humans to look at one of those cracks. And I can remember it vividly. We came upon it in total darkness. Imagine coming to the edge of the Grand Canyon at night—and not knowing it's there. All of a sudden, we came across a crack where the world had been wrenched open by a great force, just torn apart. You see something like that and you immediately understand plate tectonics. As geologists, we wrote up a description: "Looks like it's 15 meters across, there's no dipslip movement, appears to be tension, and so on." That took about 30 seconds, and we went on. We got a couple hundred yards and I said, "Let's go back. Let's go back there and eat. We've got to eat lunch somewhere." So we went back and perched on the edge of this great plate at the bottom of the ocean, and we ate lunch.

SY: Which of your discoveries to date do you believe has made the greatest contribution to science?

Ballard: Absolutely, without a shadow of a doubt, it was the discovery of the hydrothermal vents in 1977 in the Galapagos Islands. Nothing came close to that. I, personally, did not find the hydrothermal vents. It was a group effort. Science is a group effort. I helped find the hydrothermal vents, and I'm very proud of my contribution. But, there was intellect along that was very crucial—Jack Corliss, Jack Diamond, John Edmund, Tjeerd van Andel. Those were the real intellects behind it. I was asked to be the chief scientist of the cruise because I was technically, logistically, good at leading expeditions. I'm a mapper. All explorers are mappers. And I'm fortunate to have developed a key piece of technology that found the vents. I just happened to find them with *Angus*. And we then went down with the submarines and actually saw the hot water spewing out of the vents and the tubeworms and clams all around them.

SY: You frequently refer to yourself as an explorer. Is this how you basically see yourself?

Ballard: Exploring is my heritage. Ballard is a Norman name, and Normans traditionally have been explorers. It's in my blood. I'm a 13th generation American. My family came over here from England in 1665 and landed in Virginia. My family was a family of pioneers. My grandfather was killed in a gunfight in Wichita, Kans. He was a U.S. marshal. Bat Masterson was a cousin. My dad once was a cowboy. My family literally, physically, walked across America. My father was the first one to reach the other side; and I just kept on walking.

SY: People are worried about the quality of science education in the United States, not only in terms of educating future scientists but also in creating an acceptable level of scientific literacy among ordinary people. As a high-visibility scientist, how do you see your role in making science more meaningful to the general public?

Ballard: I've literally stopped my career as a research scientist and said what's going on here? It's as if an accident occurred. You start to investigate this accident, and what you find out is just appalling. America's 17th in scientific literacy right now, behind Hungary. How

Imagine coming to the edge of the Grand Canyon at night—and not knowing it's there. All of a sudden we came across a crack where the world had been wrenched open by a great force, just torn apart. You see something like that and you immediately understand plate tectonics.

did that happen? I began investigating, and it's appalling what I've found out.

To begin with, we have gotten very commercial, very materialistic, and very shortsighted. Twenty-five years ago, 75 per cent of the kids who went to college stated their reason for going was to learn. Now 75 per cent of the people say they go to college to make money—go to college and you're guaranteed some sort of income.

But, the problem is not in the colleges. It begins in our elementary schools. Do you know that 80 per cent of the classes between the 4th and 12th grade are being taught by teachers who don't hold degrees in the discipline they're teaching? They're amateurs. They don't have a degree in math and they're teaching math. They barely know physics, but the superintendent of schools says, you're going to teach physics. I've gone and met these teachers. They're completely demoralized. And they have the future of America in their hands.

I've literally stopped my career as a research scientist and said, "What's going on here?" . . . America's 17th in scientific literacy right now, behind Hungary. How did that happen? I began investigating, and it's appalling what I've found out.

Then what happens to the kids? In the 4th grade, a kid's favorite class is math. Can you imagine that? By the 10th grade, it's the least favorite. What happened to these minds? What ruined them? We don't have to come up with a way of getting kids interested in science and math. They start out interested. We force it out of them. How do we do that in the 5th, 6th, 7th, and 8th grades? Are they being tortured? Are they being punished? The answer is, to some degree, yes. They're being bored by the way science and math are being taught. But these subjects are not boring. Science is the greatest adventure of all. It's the pursuit of truth. I think that kids need to get that message, the true message of science: that it's an adventure, a very exciting adventure.

SY: How do you see our educational process being fixed so that we do not turn children off to science and math?

Ballard: By relating science and math to real-life experiences. One of the interesting things that came out of the *Titanic* project was the tremendous fascination children showed in it. This was unexpected. After all, the *Titanic* sank three-quarters of a century ago. We thought older people would be interested in it and they were, but there was overwhelming interest among youngsters. Why were they so interested? Because of *J.J.*, the robot submarine. Kids had been exposed to science-fiction adventure by films like *Star Wars* and *E.T.* That was a fantasy to them. Then all of a sudden, you had real robots, and they were smart, they had personalities, they investigated, and they took risks. The kids saw this as an adventure. I saw it as an opportunity to excite kids.

When we were sitting in *Alvin* on the deck of the *Titanic*, we sent *J.J.* into one of the rooms inside the ship. Can you imagine yourself in this situation? You're scared and all wound up. Suddenly, in the middle of the blackness you see a chandelier hanging from the ceiling. This ship broke up, went vertical, fell over, sank more than 12,000 feet in 1912, and here you are inside it looking at a chandelier. Wow! What a feeling of excitement, and there were only three of us to share it. There could have been 3 million.

SY: How could that be?

Ballard: Through something I call telepresence. It's a technology that involves computers, robots with TV cameras, and satellite communications systems. I take an expedition out to explore a particular site on the sea floor. When we get over the site, we send *Argo* and *Jason*—the robot subs—down. We control them from aboard the ship. What their TV cameras see is sent up to the ship, from there to a satellite, and the satellite sends the picture to various museums around the country. Kids in auditoriums at these museums get to be there live even as the discoveries are being made, and to ask the scientists questions. In May 1989, we "took" 225,000 students down to the floor of the Mediterranean Sea. We discovered hydrothermal vents. We explored an ancient Roman shipwreck. They were right there with me, with the scientists making these discoveries.

SY: Were any students on the actual expedition?

Ballard: Yes. We had several students with us aboard the ship.

SY: How were the students selected to go?

Ballard: By different processes at the various sites. I've been trying to encourage them to have science fairs and the winner goes. In that way they create a hero. I want the science fair winner to be a hero among his or her peers. "Gee, why did you get to go on that great adventure?" "Well I won the science fair." "Is that what it takes?" "Yes." "I want to go, too." It's equating hard work to reward. It's the old classic techniques, just some of those old-fashioned ways of working. No secret to it.

SY: How do you see telepresence being integrated into school curriculums?

Ballard: For Project Jason, I've built 13 simulation rooms that are identical to the one I'm in at sea. You walk into that room and you walk aboard my ship. I see you; you see me. I hear you; you hear me. Let's say that you're a 12-year-old in Sarasota, Fla. And you've been told we're going on this expedition to explore one of two warships from the War of 1812. They're on the bottom of Lake Ontario, but they're in mint condition. You look through a TV screen "window" and you see live what *Jason* is seeing. Now I want you to come down to the front of the room in Sarasota and sit in the same seat that I'm in aboard the ship in Lake Ontario. This is the control room. It looks like a NASA control center with all sorts of instruments and monitors. There's a joy stick we use to control the robot, and we're going to give you certain control functions. I don't know how good a driver you are, but if you're good at video games, you're set. So if you push this joy stick forward, the vehicle will go forward. Pull back, the vehicle will go backward, and so on. Now, the amount you push controls how fast it goes. Then I let you control the sub for a while. By the way, all the other children at all the other sites are watching you. They're right with you by satellite. What's happening in your mind? In the 225,000 minds watching you?

Now, what I want you to do is to crash the vehicle. I want you to shove the joy stick forward as hard as you can and crash the sub into

. . . what happens to the kids? . . . They start out interested [in math and science]. We force it out of them. How do we do that? . . . Are they being tortured? Are they being punished? The answer is, to some degree, yes.

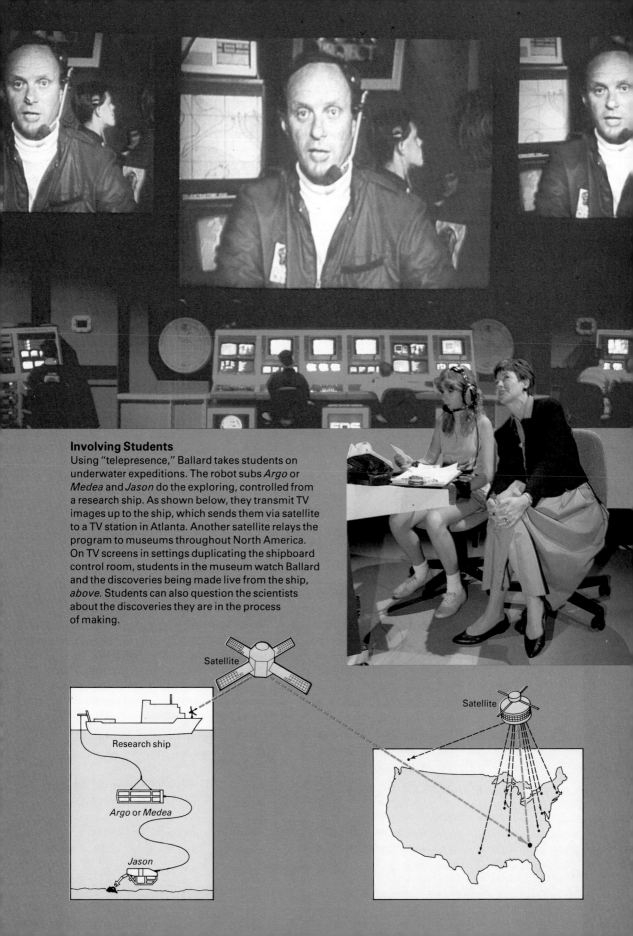

Involving Students

Using "telepresence," Ballard takes students on underwater expeditions. The robot subs *Argo* or *Medea* and *Jason* do the exploring, controlled from a research ship. As shown below, they transmit TV images up to the ship, which sends them via satellite to a TV station in Atlanta. Another satellite relays the program to museums throughout North America. On TV screens in settings duplicating the shipboard control room, students in the museum watch Ballard and the discoveries being made live from the ship, *above.* Students can also question the scientists about the discoveries they are in the process of making.

Satellite

Research ship

Argo or *Medea*

Jason

Satellite

the shipwreck. Oh, no, you say. And what are all the other kids going to be doing? They'll be screaming. But you go ahead, you follow orders. You send the sub crashing toward the shipwreck. And everyone is screaming, but all of a sudden the sub stops.

Why is that? Because it has a force field around it. And everyone says force fields? I mean they have them in "Star Trek" to keep Klingons from attacking. But are there really force fields? I thought that was all make-believe. No, it's a force field, and tomorrow in science class the teacher will explain.

The next day in class, you find out it's trigonometry. What we've done is build a software envelope of mathematics around the sub that won't permit it to crash into anything. We're tracking the vehicle 10 times a second to a centimeter of accuracy and we've told it not to enter this envelope of mathematics. The kid will say, I never thought I liked math, but I like force fields.

SY: Are you switching careers now? Are you giving up research to become a science educator?

Ballard: Yes. But what I'm trying to do is what a coach does. That's why I wear a baseball hat, why I wear jump suits, and aboard ship we look like a sports team. Suppose you get done with softball or basketball practice, and the coach says give me 21 sprints. That's not fun, you say. What if I don't do the 21 sprints? Well, the coach says, I guess you're not going to play tomorrow. So, if you want to play, you'll do the 21 sprints. As a science coach, I say I want you to do your math. No, you say, I don't like math. Well, then you can't play. Play what? The game of science. If you do your math, you can play in the game of science, and science is a game that you can play all your life.

SY: What advice would you give a young person today who is interested in becoming an oceanographer or any other kind of scientist?

Ballard: Dream, plan, and organize yourself. Learn teamwork. Learn how to get along with people. Go camping. Go hiking. Play sports. Think of yourself as getting ready for an epic journey—like Jason and the Argonauts in ancient Greek mythology getting ready to search for the Golden Fleece. And then go for it. If you're going to go on this journey, go for broke. Remember, it's just as hard to do a simple thing as it is to do a hard thing. Just the same process. I think people underestimate their ability to succeed through sheer determination. I'm not that smart, I'm just determined. It took me a long time to get my Ph.D., but I was determined to get it. A Ph.D. is not so much a measure of intelligence as a measure of determination.

SY: Is there any advice that you give young people in terms of what they should study?

Ballard: Physics. When you learn physics, you learn the fundamental laws of the universe. They are applicable anywhere. You go to Mars and there's no government, no religion, but there's physics. Even on Mars, $E = mc^2$, and for every action there's an equal and opposite reaction. Physics is the universal language, the great secret code.

. . . what I'm trying to do is what a coach does. . . . As a science coach, I say I want you to do your math. . . . If you do your math, you can play in the game of science, and science is a game that you can play all your life.

SY: We've talked quite a bit about your accomplishments. Have you had any frustrating experiences, any disappointments?

Ballard: Trying to get people interested in helping educate kids is the most frustrating thing I've ever done. It was a lot easier to find the *Titanic*. This is hard. Do you know what it costs for a child to go into one of the Jason Project simulation rooms for an hour? They get in free, but the cost to make it happen is $4.50 a child. You know what it costs to see a first-run movie? At least $5. A real, live underwater adventure costs less than most movies, but people aren't doing a thing about it. You wouldn't believe what I have to go through to get people to put that money in. They'll listen and say isn't that nice and walk away. I have spent the last five months on the road talking to museums and community leaders and educators. I am so discouraged. We don't care about science education anymore.

SY: Why do you think that is?

Ballard: Because it seems OK. It's like smoking cigarettes. The doctor says you don't have lung cancer yet, so you go on smoking. One day you get cancer, and you say "I better quit smoking," but it's a little late. We're 17th in scientific literacy and declining. We're not training scientists, not training skilled workers. We've stopped investing in the future.

SY: Do you see yourself ever going back to research projects?

Ballard: I don't think that's important to me right now. I've just put together a proposal called "Living Habitats of the World." I'm trying to convince the Osaka aquarium—in Japan—to have a room with television screens that would allow people to see live, through telepresence, different parts of the world. Suppose you're in Japan and you want to see what's going on in Monterey Bay, California. You tune in that channel, and poof! You're there at the speed of light. It's a sunny morning and you're 50 feet underwater in a beautiful kelp forest. I'm trying to put robot cameras in a tropical rain forest—one in the tree canopy and the other on the forest floor. You'd be able to see and hear the rain forest, the insects and the monkeys.

Then if someone says there's a big problem in Monterey Bay, you'll want to know about it because you've been there. If someone tries to chop down the rain forest tree where your camera is, you'll get mad. You won't want that tree chopped down.

SY: What do you see as the next step in your career?

Ballard: I want to be a part of global awareness. I think informed people are enlightened people. I want to bring the globe to everybody so they're aware, and that's what I'm going to do. That's my job.

I want to be part of global awareness. I think informed people are enlightened people. I want to bring the globe to everybody [through remote TV] so they're aware, and that's what I'm going to do. That's my job.

For further reading:

Ballard, Robert D. *The Discovery of the Titanic*. Madison Press Books, 1987.
Exploring the Titanic. Madison Press Books, 1988.

How a Vent Forms

1. As two plates pull apart, this creates a deep gap on the sea floor. *Magma* (molten rock) from deep within Earth wells up to the surface as lava, filling the gap.

2. When the lava hits the frigid seawater, it hardens, but it also cracks. Plate movements and a swelling and shrinking of molten rock far under the sea floor fracture the lava rock further.

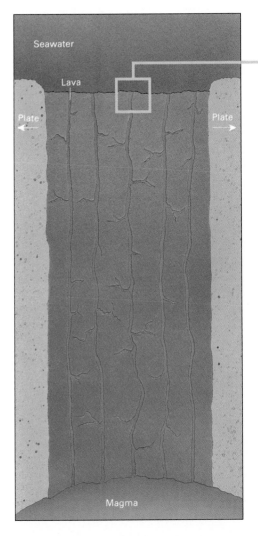

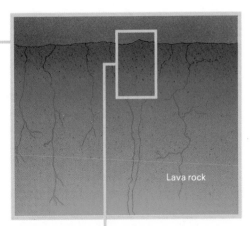

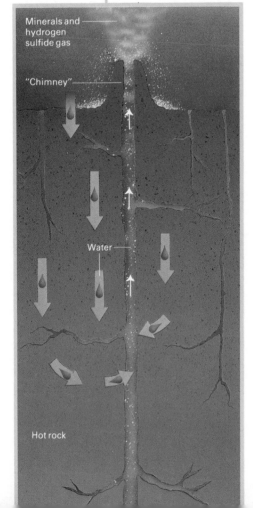

3. Seawater seeps down into the cracks in the lava and "percolates" through the hot rocks below. This heated water dissolves minerals from the rocks; chemical reactions produce hydrogen sulfide gas. Eventually, the hot water returns to the surface and spews out of a fissure, carrying minerals and gas with it. When this water hits the cold water, dissolved minerals solidify, forming particles that slowly build up a "chimney" around the outlet.

vents, where cold seawater cools the hot vent water to room temperature (20°C or 68°F.). Most of the cool-water bacteria are very similar to "sulfur-eating" bacteria found in marshes, mudflats, and the upper layers of the sea.

Chemosynthetic bacteria are among the oldest forms of life, and judging from fossil evidence, life at the vents began hundreds of millions of years ago. Fossilized vents have been found on ancient sea bottoms that are now dry land on the Mediterranean island of Cyprus and in Oman, a country on the Arabian Peninsula.

According to one theory, the ancestors of present-day vent animals began by colonizing hot springs that had formed in shallow water. When sea levels rose, they adapted as their homes went deeper underwater. About 600 million years ago, larvae of the ancestors of tubeworms and other creatures must have found their way to vents, adapted to conditions there, and evolved to their present forms. Mussels appeared at vents about 225 million years ago. The clams appeared 25 million years ago.

Animals of the vents apparently travel from a dying vent field to a new one in the egg or larval stage—swept along by ocean currents. Those that reach a favorable environment establish a new colony.

As for the bacteria, they can come from anywhere. There are bacteria in every drop of seawater, mostly in a state of suspended animation. They rain down from the surface, and deep-sea currents carry them along.

The creatures that settled around the vents long ago evolved into new species—often strange and bizarre ones. At the deep-sea oases, scientists have identified about 100 new species. They have found that there are relatively few species of animal at any one vent, but there is considerable variation from vent to vent. Scientists believe this variation is a result of what they call the "founder effect." The first large animal species to arrive at a vent founds a community that quickly takes over the entire food supply. There is no room and no food for another large species.

One animal, found only at the Galapagos Rift, is a peculiar flowerlike organism about 5 centimeters (2 inches) in diameter, which the scientists aboard *Alvin* in 1977 called the "dandelion animal." It turned out to be a cluster of separate animals with different functions. Some of the animals in the cluster capture food, using tentacles armed with stinging, poisonous cells; others digest the food; and still others move the cluster along through the water.

Spaghetti worms drape the rocks at a number of vents. This worm is believed to be a *suspension feeder*, a creature that catches bacteria with mucus that covers an organ located on the tip of the front end of its body, just above the mouth. Movements of this organ propel bacteria to the creature's mouth. It may also absorb from the water organic compounds released by dead bacteria.

Strangest of all are the giant tubeworms that live at the Galapagos

Rift and the East Pacific Rise an area just south of the tip of Baja California. They attach themselves to rock by their rear ends and sway in the currents. They have no mouth to take in food and no gut to digest it, so scientists were perplexed about how they could live—until they dissected some. The researchers found that the worms house their own food supply. A special part of their body is made up of "sulfur-eating" bacteria. In fact, the bacteria make up half the body weight of a tubeworm.

The worm does not, however, eat the bacteria. Rather, it feeds the bacteria, which, in turn, make food for the worm. Apparently, the worm absorbs hydrogen sulfide and everything else the bacteria need through its crimson head plumes, which contain about 300,000 tiny filaments. A set of blood vessels conveys these chemicals to the bacteria, which combine them and release sugars, fats, and other nutrients that the worm uses as food.

Like the tubeworms, the giant clams have bacteria living in their tissues—in this case, their gills. Studies indicate that clams may live up to 25 years, but observers in *Alvin* have noted the strange fact that the clams at any one vent all seem to be the same age. There does not appear to be a younger generation of clams. Scientists speculate that clam larvae float to a new vent site and establish themselves. Some time later, crabs arrive. The crabs have no special adaptations for living at the vents. They are simply drawn there by the presence of an abundant supply of food.

At the Mid-Atlantic Ridge vents, scientists have found eyeless shrimps that apparently scrape loose sulfide particles off the surfaces of black smoker chimneys. Researchers believe that the shrimps digest bacteria that grow in a thin film on the sulfide particles. Scientists have counted as many as 1,500 shrimp per square meter (140 per square foot).

The eyeless shrimps bear a large, reflective spot on their dull, gray backs. This spot is made up of two large lobes connected by nerves to the shrimp's brain. Cindy Van Dover, a graduate student working at Woods Hole, wondered if they could be some kind of eye. She tested the tissue and found the lobes contain rhodopsin, a light-sensitive chemical found in all known kinds of eye. But what possible use could this have in the pitch-black depths? She speculated that vents off Vancouver Island, where the shrimps she tested came from, might actually glow. She asked scientists diving in the area with *Alvin* in July 1988 to look for some kind of light at the vents. To do this, they turned off *Alvin*'s powerful outside lights, and the pilot of the submersible held the sub still against a rock while a special sensitive camera snapped pictures. The pictures showed that the vents actually did glow. Most of the glow was made up of *infrared* (heat) rays, but there was also a small amount of visible light. The shrimps may use their visual sensors to home in on the vents—their source of food—and to avoid the deadly hot water that pours out.

Life at the Vents

Bacteria that obtain their vital energy from hydrogen sulfide gas emitted by deep-sea vents support communities of strange creatures. At some vents, there are blind shrimp; at others, giant clams, or worms that look like spaghetti.

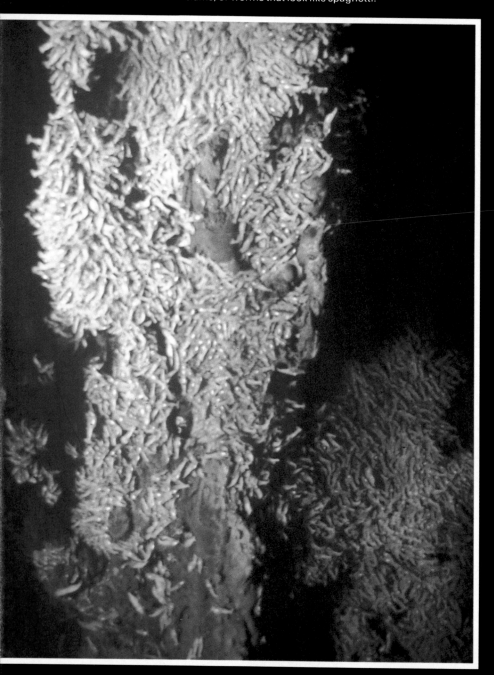

Eyeless shrimp cling to craggy chimneys of a vent. These creatures apparently scrape sulfide particles off the chimneys and digest bacteria that grow on the particles.

Blind crabs are attracted to the vents by other creatures living there. Crab larvae, bacteria, and dead animals provide the crabs with a plentiful food supply.

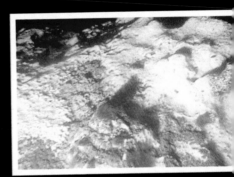

Sulfur-eating bacteria form fluffy mats, *above,* on rocks and sediment at the vents. Giant clams 30 centimeters (1 foot) or more in length, *above left,* obtain food from bacteria living in their gills.

Spaghetti worms drape themselves over rocks at the vents, *left.*

Chains of Life

Human beings and most other creatures are part of a complex chain of life that depends upon the energy of sunlight for food production. But sunlight cannot reach a hot-water vent 2,500 meters (8,200 feet) beneath the sea. To sustain life in that environment, nature has developed a chain based on hydrogen sulfide gas emitted by the vents.

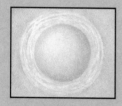

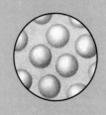

Life in Darkness

Hydrogen sulfide from a deep-sea vent, *above left,* drives the chain of life in the darkness at the bottom of the sea in a process called *chemosynthesis.* Bacteria, *above right,* combine hydrogen sulfide, carbon dioxide, and other substances in seawater to produce sugars that serve as their food.

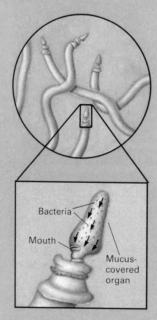

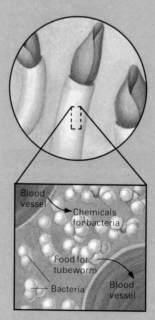

Bacteria

Mouth

Mucus-covered organ

Blood vessel

Chemicals for bacteria

Food for tubeworm

Bacteria

Blood vessel

Life in Sunlight

Sunlight provides energy for the chain of ordinary life, in a process called *photosynthesis.* Plants such as corn use sunlight to drive chemical reactions that combine carbon dioxide gas from the air with water and nutrients drawn up through roots to make food. The plants, in turn, are used as food by other creatures, including human beings.

Other creatures live off these sulfur-eating bacteria in two major ways. Some, such as the spaghetti worm, *above left,* eat the bacteria. This worm catches bacteria on a mucus-covered organ near its mouth. Others, such as the tubeworm, *above right,* live in a food-producing partnership with the bacteria. The bacteria live in a part of the tubeworm's body. The worm's red plume absorbs from the water everything the bacteria need to live. Blood vessels carry these nutrients to the bacteria, which, in turn, release sugars, fats, and amino acids that serve as the tubeworm's food.

There are many other kinds of animals at the vents—some at only one site. Limpets archaic enough to be living fossils, plus about 40 other kinds of snails, graze the bacterial lawns. Tiny crustaceans called copepods devour protozoans that eat bacteria. Small bristle-worms live in mussels and nibble on their gills.

The discovery of hot-water vents may seem to be of little practical importance to people. But "sulfur-eating" bacteria might be put to use cleaning up factory wastes and mine runoff, according to microbiologist Holger Jannasch of the Woods Hole Oceanographic Institution. All that is needed is a steady source of sulfide and a location close to the sea. The bacteria might be used as food for mussel "farms." Jannasch has eaten mussels raised on sulfur-eating bacteria and says they taste fine.

Meanwhile, the discovery of life at the vents has opened up so many questions in biology that their study will keep researchers busy for years to come. And scientists almost certainly will find many more vents. The midocean rift that spawns vents extends some 64,000 kilometers (40,000 miles), beneath the Atlantic, Indian, and Pacific oceans. By the summer of 1990, only 1 per cent or less of its awesome length had been explored.

In March 1984, scientists in *Alvin* found a different kind of deep-sea oasis on the Florida Escarpment, where the continental shelf drops off like a steep underwater cliff into the Gulf of Mexico. Water containing methane gas seeps out from springs in the escarpment. The life at this oasis was similar to that of the Pacific vents—tubeworms, mussels, clams, tiny snails, and crabs—but based on bacteria that eat methane, rather than hydrogen sulfide.

Researchers have also found flourishing oases that are based on petroleum coming up through the ocean floor. Various species of bacteria derive energy by "eating" this substance.

The discovery of life at the vents revealed that nature is more versatile than previously thought. Where simple organisms such as bacteria can establish themselves, entire communities of more complex creatures can evolve and thrive. Life without light turns out to be common; what is a forbidding environment for one chain of life is an ideal setting for another. There may well be similar surprises in store as scientists continue to probe the ocean depths and other remote areas of Earth and push ahead into outer space.

For further reading:

Ballard, Robert D., and Grassle, J. Frederick. "Return to Oases of the Deep." *National Geographic*, November 1979.
Childress, James J., and others. "Symbiosis in the Deep Sea." *Scientific American*, May 1987.
Monastersky, Joseph. "Deep-Sea Shrimp." *Science News*, Feb. 11, 1989.
Wallace, Joseph. *The Deep Sea*. Smith, 1987.

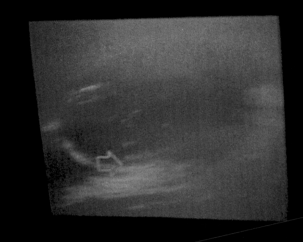

TRACK CON 2

236200728   237050128   237140128   UC 237030728   048142356   000045410

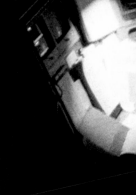

048142354

Ground controllers at NASA's Jet Propulsion Laboratory in Pasadena, Calif., *left,* track the *Voyager 2* spacecraft and watch a live image of Neptune transmitted from the craft. A photo from *Voyager 2, above,* taken with special filters enables astronomers to study details of Neptune's atmosphere.

Voyager 2's visit to the giant planet Neptune in August 1989 ended a 12-year journey of discovery across the solar system.

Neptune: Last Stop on a Grand Tour

BY JONATHAN I. LUNINE

143

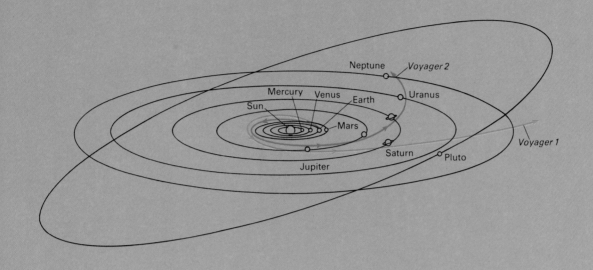

Neptune · Voyager 2 · Mercury · Venus · Earth · Uranus · Sun · Mars · Saturn · Voyager 1 · Pluto · Jupiter

Journey Through the Solar System

Launched in 1977, *Voyager 2* flew by Jupiter in 1979, Saturn in 1981, Uranus in 1986, and Neptune in August 1989. *Voyager 1,* also launched in 1977, flew by Jupiter in 1979 and Saturn in 1980. Both *Voyagers* now are on courses that will take them out of the solar system.

The author:

Jonathan I. Lunine is associate professor of planetary science at the University of Arizona in Tucson.

The air was misty and cool at 4 a.m. on Aug. 25, 1989, when I walked from my temporary office space at the Jet Propulsion Laboratory (JPL) in Pasadena, Calif., over to JPL's imaging science area. The previous day, the *Voyager 2* spacecraft had returned detailed photographs of Neptune and the powerful storm systems in its atmosphere. Now, the best pictures of the planet's largest satellite, Triton, were just starting to come in. No human being had ever seen the face of this distant moon. But during the next hour it revealed itself to the cameras of *Voyager 2* as a geologically active world with a giant polar cap, large curving valleys, ancient basins flooded with icy lavas, and strange dark patches and streaks that turned out to be the signs of active geysers.

During the fly-by of Neptune and Triton, my colleagues and I watched with fascination as *Voyager 2* observed these intriguing worlds, which were much more complex than we had expected. We also watched with a touch of sadness, because we were witnessing *Voyager 2*'s last stop on its "Grand Tour" of four outer planets, a journey that began in 1977 and spanned a course of more than 6.4 billion kilometers (4 billion miles).

The idea of a Grand Tour arose in the mid-1960's when space scientists realized that the giant outer planets—Jupiter, Saturn, Uranus, and Neptune—would be aligned on one side of the solar system during the 1980's, an event that occurs once every 175 years. This "grand alignment" would allow a spacecraft to use the gravitational field of one outer planet to speed it on its way to the next planet in a kind of slingshot effect. Thus, one spacecraft would be able to fly by all of the outer planets with the exception of Pluto, which was not in the proper alignment.

In the early 1970's, the National Aeronautics and Space Adminis-

Facts About Neptune

Distance from the sun: Average—4.5 billion kilometers (2.8 billion miles).

Distance from Earth: Closest—4.3 billion kilometers (2.7 billion miles).

Diameter: 49,500 kilometers (30,800 miles).

Length of year: About 165 Earth-years.

Length of day: About 16 hours.

Minimum temperature of upper atmosphere: −220° C (−370° F.).

Atmospheric gases: Hydrogen (75%), helium (24%), methane (1%), trace amounts of ammonia.

Number of moons: Eight.

Number of rings: Four.

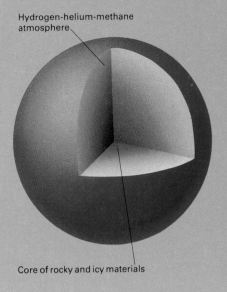

Hydrogen-helium-methane atmosphere

Core of rocky and icy materials

tration (NASA) proposed using two newly designed unmanned probes, later named *Voyager 1* and *2*, to make the Grand Tour. Scientists and engineers at JPL, which the California Institute of Technology operates for NASA, would oversee the mission. The United States Congress, however, approved only a scaled-down mission to Jupiter and Saturn.

The two spacecraft were launched from Earth in 1977, and both *Voyagers* reached Jupiter in 1979. *Voyager 1* reached Saturn in 1980 and then was sent on a course that will eventually take it out of our solar system. As *Voyager 2* was approaching Saturn, however, JPL

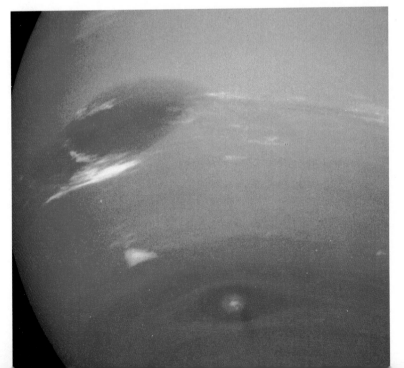

A giant storm system in Neptune's atmosphere—dubbed the Great Dark Spot—is the size of Earth. Swirling clouds (white areas) indicate that winds in the storm system are twice as fast as hurricane winds on Earth.

145

engineers knew that by altering the path of the spacecraft they could make it pass close enough to Saturn to get a gravitational boost that would send it on to Uranus. This maneuver was successful, and *Voyager 2* arrived at Uranus in 1986. There, the spacecraft got another boost from the gravitational field of Uranus. This boost sent it on to Neptune to fulfill the goals of the originally planned Grand Tour and to return the best views we have ever seen of Neptune.

The first recorded human sighting of Neptune apparently was made by the Italian astronomer Galileo in 1613. Galileo reported seeing through his telescope an object close in position to Jupiter. By calculating how the orbits of the planets would have looked at that time, present-day astronomers make a strong case that Galileo was looking at Neptune. But Galileo did not recognize it to be a planet and so is not credited with its discovery.

That honor goes jointly to English astronomer John C. Adams, French astronomer Urbain J. J. Leverrier, and German astronomer Johann G. Galle and his assistant Heinrich L. d'Arrest. In the 1840's, Adams and Leverrier independently studied the movement of Uranus in its orbit around the sun and deduced that the planet's orbit was being slightly disturbed by the gravitational influence of another, unseen planet. In 1845, using calculations based on the gravitational laws formulated in the 1600's by English mathematician and

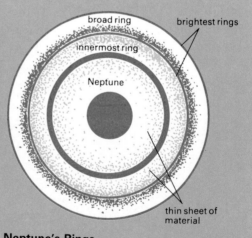

Neptune's Rings
Data from *Voyager 2* showed that Neptune is surrounded by four rings, *above,* made of rock, dust, and ice. An image from *Voyager 2, left,* clearly shows the two brightest rings, reflecting sunlight. The innermost ring (arrow) is also faintly visible. Not visible in the photograph because its particles are so small and sparse is a broad ring (shaded area in artist's sketch above). A thin sheet of material may extend inward almost to the planet.

astronomer Sir Isaac Newton, Adams predicted the location of this unseen planet with remarkable accuracy. Perhaps because he was then young and relatively unknown, Adams was unable to persuade astronomers to look for the planet at that location through their telescopes. In 1846, Leverrier sent his prediction of the unseen planet's location to Galle, director of the Urania Observatory in Berlin, Germany. On September 23, Galle and d'Arrest found the planet—later named Neptune—near the position predicted by Leverrier's mathematical calculations. Thus, Neptune was the first planet "discovered" as a result of the precise mathematical application of Newton's gravitational laws.

Three weeks after Neptune was found, English astronomer William Lassell sighted a large moon orbiting Neptune. This moon was named Triton; astronomers soon found that Triton has a *retrograde orbit*—that is, it orbits and rotates in a clockwise direction opposite to that of most objects in the solar system. Ordinarily, the planets and moons orbit the sun and spin on their *rotational axes* in a counterclockwise direction, as viewed from above their north poles. (An axis of rotation is an imaginary line drawn through the center of a moon or planet around which the object spins.)

Because Neptune is so far from Earth—about 4.3 billion kilometers (2.7 billion miles) at its closest point—nothing more was discovered about the Neptune system for more than 100 years. Astronomers were occupied with other questions, such as the nature of stars and galaxies. But in 1948, American astronomer Gerard P. Kuiper, at Yerkes Observatory in Lake Geneva, Wis., decided to take a close look at Neptune and discovered another moon orbiting in a highly *elliptical* (oval-shaped) path. This small moon was named Nereid, after Greek sea nymphs, in keeping with astronomers' tradition of naming many objects in the solar system after figures from Greek and Roman mythology.

After Nereid was discovered, our knowledge of Neptune did not advance again until the late 1970's, when astronomers used a technique called *speckle interferometry* to obtain crude images of Neptune's atmosphere. This technique involves taking a large number of photographs very rapidly to correct for turbulence in Earth's atmosphere, which smears the images. These images showed bright clouds against a blue background. Then, in the mid-1980's, taking advantage of a rare alignment in which Neptune passed in front of a star, astronomers detected evidence for fragments of rings (called *ring arcs*). The light of the star dimmed just before and after Neptune passed in front of it. This dimming indicated the presence of some kind of ring material around the planet.

Until the *Voyager 2* encounter of August 1989, the planetary world of Neptune was the least known of the planets visited on the Grand Tour. *Voyager 2* gave us a wealth of new information: It discovered huge storm systems in Neptune's atmosphere, four rings that

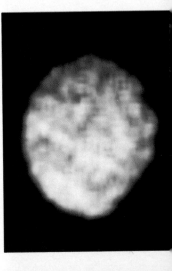
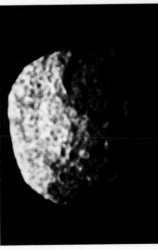

Two of the six moons discovered from *Voyager 2*'s images are irregularly shaped, heavily cratered lumps that scientists believe represent debris left over from the formation of Neptune.

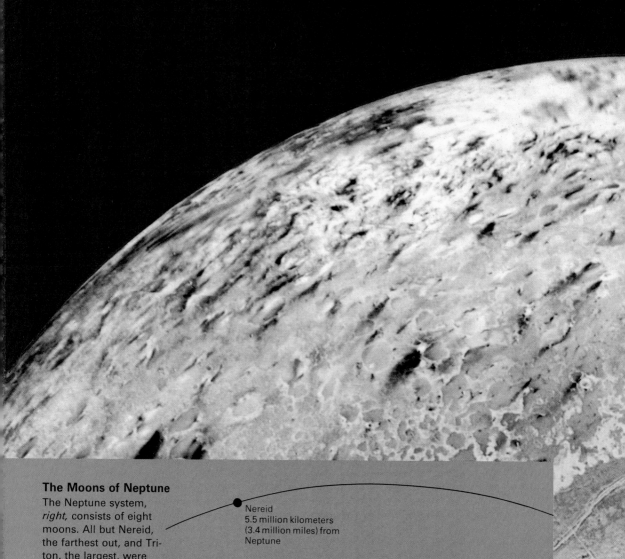

The Moons of Neptune

The Neptune system, *right,* consists of eight moons. All but Nereid, the farthest out, and Triton, the largest, were discovered by *Voyager 2.* The spacecraft returned detailed images of Triton, *above* and *opposite page,* revealing a complex geology with extensive fault lines, or cracks, and evidence of ice volcanism.

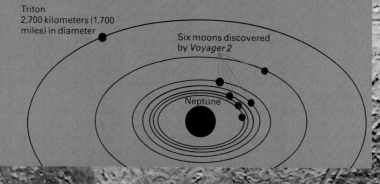

Nereid
5.5 million kilometers
(3.4 million miles) from
Neptune

Triton
2,700 kilometers (1,700
miles) in diameter

Six moons discovered
by *Voyager 2*

Neptune

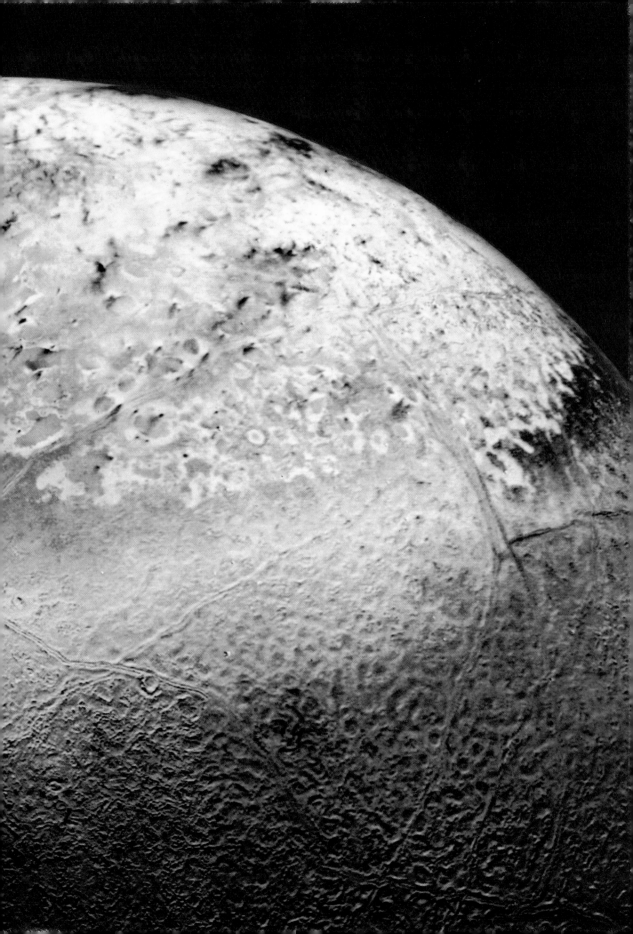

completely encircle the planet, and six new moons. In addition, the spacecraft's scientific instruments detected a bizarre magnetic field around Neptune, and its cameras photographed unusual surface features on Triton, indicating that the moon was geologically active in the relatively recent past.

Images of Neptune's atmosphere were the first delightful surprise. Neptune appears blue, due to the presence of methane gas, which absorbs and scatters red light, leaving blue light. The most abundant gases in Neptune's atmosphere are hydrogen and helium. *Voyager*'s images also revealed cloud patterns as varied as those of Jupiter and Saturn. Most prominent was a feature with a diameter as large as Earth and eye-shaped like a similar feature in the atmosphere of Jupiter called the Great Red Spot. Scientists at JPL dubbed this gray-colored feature on Neptune the Great Dark Spot. A smaller dark spot—about one-third the diameter of Earth—was also observed. Both of these spots are most likely storm systems with spiraling winds like those found in hurricanes on Earth. The existence of these storm systems indicates that Neptune's atmosphere is extremely energetic and turbulent.

A blue haze forms the lower part of Neptune's observable atmosphere and prevented *Voyager 2* from seeing any farther down. The dark spots are located within this haze. There were darker clouds in the spots themselves. These dark clouds, as well as the blue haze, may be composed of ammonium hydrosulfide. Bright white clouds, which resemble cumulus clouds that form thunderstorms on Earth but are composed of frozen methane, are part of the upper atmosphere, about 100 kilometers (60 miles) above the blue haze.

By making time-lapse images of the high methane clouds and the lower dark clouds, astronomers were able to measure changes in wind speed and direction in the dark spots. They found that winds at the top move in one direction, while winds at the bottom of the spot move in another direction. The entire storm system is rotating with a speed of about 390 kilometers (240 miles) per hour, about twice as fast as the winds in a hurricane on Earth. This indicated that the dark spots are extremely turbulent. If you could fly an airplane into the Great Dark Spot, you would be in for a very bumpy ride.

The dark spots wander across the surface of Neptune, changing position in latitude and longitude, and vary in appearance in a cyclic fashion about once every 21 Neptune days. A Neptune day is 16.11 hours, the time it takes the interior of the planet to complete one rotation. Because Neptune is a ball of gas without a solid surface, astronomers determined the rotation speed of its interior by measuring the rotation of its magnetic field. They found that the magnetic field rotates once every 16.11 hours.

The storm systems and numerous cloud patterns on Neptune took scientists by surprise. Scientists had expected to see more features in the atmosphere of Neptune than in that of Uranus, since cloud

patterns on Neptune had been detected in the late 1970's. But no one had expected the amount of atmospheric activity that *Voyager* found.

The atmosphere of Uranus is bland and almost cloudless as revealed by photographs from *Voyager 2* in 1986. If there was any turbulence in Uranus' atmosphere, it was hidden below a thick haze. An instrument on board *Voyager 2* that measures heat radiation—known as an *infrared spectrometer*—found that the amount of heat energy given off by Uranus' atmosphere was roughly equal to the amount of sunlight the planet receives. In other words, Uranus gets essentially all of its energy from sunlight.

The same instrument on *Voyager 2* showed that Neptune's atmosphere gives off about the same amount of heat energy as Uranus does, even though the more distant Neptune receives less than one-half the amount of sunlight that Uranus receives. To give off the same amount of heat energy as Uranus, Neptune must have an additional energy source deep in its interior. Why Uranus and Neptune have such apparently different interiors is a mystery, especially because the planets are nearly the same in size and density.

The strong turbulence created as Neptune's internal heat rises through the atmosphere must cause columns of gas to rise, which aids in forming clouds well above any obscuring haze. Thus, in contrast to Uranus, Neptune's atmosphere is a great seething cauldron of energy made visible in the motions of its clouds.

Although Uranus and Neptune have strikingly different atmos-

A dark plume (black spot) rising 8 kilometers (5 miles) above Triton's surface may be a geyser. Geysers on Earth spew out hot water, but scientists believe that Triton's geysers consist of nitrogen and perhaps methane with some unknown dark material that makes the plumes visible.

pheres, *Voyager 2* found that the two planets have magnetic fields of roughly the same strength. Scientists think that a planet's magnetic field is caused by the rotation of electrically conducting material in its interior. For example, they believe that iron and nickel are the electrically conducting materials in Earth's interior. Like all magnets, the one created by the rotating iron and nickel core has two poles, north and south. Earth's magnetic field is only slightly tilted from its rotational polar regions. The north magnetic pole is near the north rotational pole, so a compass needle on Earth points northward.

The orientation of Neptune's magnetic field, however, is greatly tilted from its rotational polar regions. A compass needle on Neptune would point to a "north magnetic pole" at a location corresponding to a point as far south on Earth as Boston. Also, *Voyager* found that the magnetic field of Neptune is not "centered" in the planet but is shifted from the center. Uranus' magnetic field is also "off center." This means that activity in the electrically conducting materials in the interior does not occur at the very core of these planets, as it does on Earth, Jupiter, and Saturn. But scientists do not yet understand how this type of magnetic field is generated.

Voyager 2 also returned new and valuable information about the rings that surround Neptune. To the surprise of scientists, *Voyager*'s cameras showed that the ring "arcs" observed from Earth were not fragments but complete rings that extend all the way around Neptune. The rings vary greatly in brightness at different locations, apparently because of differing amounts of material in the rings. The brightest parts of the rings apparently have the greatest amounts of material, and these were the "arcs" detected by astronomers using telescopes on Earth.

Voyager detected four major rings and also transmitted evidence for a very thin sheet of material beginning midway between the two outer rings and possibly extending down to the planet. Neptune's rings contain much less material than the rings of Uranus, which in turn contain very much less material than the rings of Saturn. Astronomers think the ring systems of all three planets are composed of water ice and some other darker materials ranging in size from dust particles to boulders. Scientists who have analyzed *Voyager*'s data think that the source of the material in the ring systems may be debris that resulted from collisions between small moons.

Voyager discovered six new moons around Neptune, ranging in diameter from about 54 kilometers (34 miles) to about 400 kilometers (250 miles)—all much smaller than Triton. Some of these moons orbit within the ring system and may be what scientists call *shepherding moons* because their gravitational forces help keep the ring material organized in a narrow ring. *Voyager*'s cameras showed that two of the moons are irregularly shaped, cratered lumps—probably pieces of debris left over from the formation of Neptune.

Voyager's richest findings occurred at Triton. The spacecraft's instruments recorded a temperature on Triton of $-235°C$ ($-391°F$.), making it the coldest object we have ever studied in the solar system. Triton has a diameter of about 2,700 kilometers (1,700 miles), making it about four-fifths as large as Earth's moon and one-fifth bigger than the planet Pluto. By measuring how much Triton's gravitational pull bent *Voyager*'s *trajectory* (path) as it passed just 40,000 kilometers (25,000 miles) above Triton's surface, JPL scientists were able to determine the density of the material that makes up Triton. The degree of the bending of the spacecraft's trajectory indicated the strength of Triton's gravity. Knowing the strength of its gravity, scientists could calculate the moon's mass, and knowing the size of the moon, they could then determine its density by a simple mathematical formula—mass divided by volume equals density. They determined that Triton's density was slightly more than twice that of liquid water, which indicates that the moon is probably made up of about 60 per cent rock and 40 per cent water ice.

Triton is one of only a few moons in the solar system that has an atmosphere. *Voyager*'s instruments detected both methane and nitrogen gases in Triton's atmosphere, and images of the surface showed that the hemisphere facing the sun in August 1989 (the southern hemisphere) is covered with a thick deposit of frost called a *polar cap*.

Triton's polar cap is very bright, reflecting almost all the sunlight it receives, and is probably composed largely of pure nitrogen. As Triton orbits about Neptune and as Neptune orbits about the sun, the complex ballet of their orbital motions must give Triton periods of "mild" and "extreme" seasons, comparable to, but more variable than, summer and winter seasons on planets. But astronomers do not yet know how much the temperatures vary from season to season. At the time of *Voyager 2*'s encounter, Triton was approaching extreme summer in the southern hemisphere. Data from the encounter indicated that sunlight warming the southern polar cap was causing the nitrogen ice to *sublime* (pass directly from a solid to a gas). This nitrogen gas forms an atmosphere, and atmospheric pressure creates a wind that causes the gas to move to the northern hemisphere, where it is winter. At the north pole, the extreme cold temperatures and absence of sunlight during winter cause the nitrogen gas to condense as an ice. The polar cap in the southern hemisphere then is shrinking while the polar cap in the northern hemisphere grows larger. Astronomers have observed that polar caps on Mars shrink and expand with the seasons in much the same way.

Triton's southern polar cap, however, has something that the Martian caps do not: geysers. Careful analysis of photographs made by *Voyager 2*'s cameras revealed two distinct plumes rising from the surface. These plumes rise to an altitude of about 8 kilometers (5 miles). On Earth, geysers spew out water heated by hot rocks deep in Earth and held under pressure by rock formations near the surface; on Triton, nitrogen is most likely the pressurized material blown out,

with perhaps some methane as well. The released gases dislodge
small dark particles that make the plumes visible.

What powers the geysers on Triton? We don't know for sure, but
the fact that the geysers seemed to be clustered in a region on
Triton's surface where the sun was directly overhead and solar
heating was strongest suggested one possible explanation. From
laboratory studies, we know that nitrogen ice reflects or scatters
almost all the light that strikes it, absorbing very little sunlight. So it
does not warm up. But the dark particles in the geyser plumes seem
to originate from below the nitrogen ice surface and would easily
absorb sunlight. As a result, the ice below the surface would become
warmer than the ice layer on the surface. This below-surface ice
could be heated to temperatures more than five degrees above the
−235°C surface temperature. Such heating would cause the below-
surface nitrogen ice to sublime to gas, thus creating strong pressure.
This pressure would eventually become too great for the surface
layer of ice to withstand, and gas would blow out as a geyser.

Scientists examining the DNA molecule
have found the abnormal gene that
causes the fatal disease cystic fibrosis.
Better treatments may result.

Tracking Down a Deadly Gene

BY BEVERLY MERZ

"Jason tastes funny—sort of like pretzels or potato chips," Susanna said after kissing her 1-year-old brother on the cheek. Mrs. Brandt had to admit that her daughter was right. Lately when she kissed her infant son, she too had noticed that his skin had a salty taste to it. She made a mental note to ask the doctor about it.

The mention of Jason's salty skin sounded an alarm with the family's pediatrician. When considered with several other symptoms that the doctor had noted, including below-normal weight gain and recurrent lung congestion, the saltiness could mean that Jason was suffering from a serious and—so far—fatal disease, cystic fibrosis.

Cystic fibrosis is a disease that affects the *exocrine glands*, glands that secrete sweat, tears, saliva, mucus, digestive juices, and other substances through tiny tubes called ducts. In people with cystic fibrosis, these substances are different than in normal people. Mucus is thicker and stickier, and tears and sweat are saltier. The thick mucus can form plugs that block the lungs' air passages. It can also clog the pancreatic ducts, causing problems with digestion.

Jason's doctor knew that excessive salt in sweat was a symptom of cystic fibrosis, so he ordered a simple test. Laboratory technicians taped a gauze pad to the baby's arm to collect perspiration. When they analyzed the sample a few minutes later, they found it contained several times the normal amount of salt. The doctor called in Mr. and Mrs. Brandt and told them that Jason indeed had cystic fibrosis. When the Brandts received that unhappy news, they realized that their son would need special care throughout his life.

The author:
Beverly Merz is national editor for science and technology for the *American Medical News.*

Cystic fibrosis is a hereditary disease caused by a defect in a gene—a piece of *deoxyribonucleic acid* (DNA), the master molecule of heredity. The defective gene is present in every cell in the body. Because of the gene, Jason's lungs would often be clogged with mucus, making it difficult for him to breathe and trapping disease-causing viruses and bacteria. The disorder would also cause him to lose salt more rapidly when he perspired heavily, so that he would have to take care to eat extra salt on hot days and avoid becoming overheated. Jason's condition might also disrupt the functioning of his digestive system, leading to intestinal problems and possible undernourishment.

Yet, the outlook for Jason and the 30,000 other Americans with cystic fibrosis may soon be much better. In September 1989, research teams in the United States and Canada reported that they had discovered the gene responsible for cystic fibrosis. Their achievement has brought a bonanza of new knowledge about the disease that may lead to new diagnostic tests and treatments.

Cystic fibrosis is one of the most common inherited diseases among white people. The disorder occurs in 1 of every 2,000 white babies; only 1 in 17,000 black babies has the disease; and it is hardly ever found in Asians or Native Americans.

It is hard to predict when the symptoms of cystic fibrosis will appear or how severe they will be. Some babies develop breathing difficulties or digestive disturbances early in life; others develop those problems later in childhood. Not all patients suffer digestive problems, and those who do can usually be treated with medications and special diets. On the other hand, lung complications are virtually universal and are the most serious problem.

Children with cystic fibrosis have chronic coughs caused by mucus build-up. The children are cautioned not to take cough suppressants or to try to stifle their coughs, because coughing loosens mucus. They can, however, use antihistamines and decongestants to open their air passages. And many children with cystic fibrosis must take antibiotics frequently to fight recurrent bacterial infections in their lungs.

To aid breathing and slow down the deterioration of the lungs, physicians and physical therapists have developed a treatment to clear mucus from the lungs. The patient sits or lies in a series of positions that allow different portions of the lungs to drain. At the same time, another person claps or vibrates the patient's chest and back to help dislodge the mucus so that it can be coughed up and expelled. The treatment can take 30 minutes or more and may need to be repeated several times a day.

Unfortunately, even regular therapy and medication cannot stop the ravages of the disease. In some cystic fibrosis sufferers, the right side of the heart becomes enlarged from overwork. This condition is a direct result of lung damage, which reduces the amount of oxygen that passes into the blood flowing through the lungs. To compensate

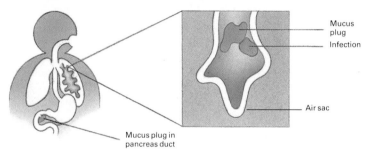

Mucus plug

Infection

Air sac

Mucus plug in
pancreas duct

What Is Cystic Fibrosis?

Cystic fibrosis is a fatal disease that involves thick mucus secretions. Clapping the patient's back, *left,* loosens mucus in the lungs so it can be coughed up and expelled to help prevent the formation of mucus plugs in the air sacs of the lungs. Such plugs, *bottom,* at right, make breathing difficult and trap infection-causing bacteria. Mucus also forms plugs that can block a duct between the pancreas and the small intestine, *bottom,* at left, causing digestive problems.

for the lack of oxygen, the heart pumps harder to step up the flow of blood and thus increase the body's oxygen supply.

Another complication of cystic fibrosis is a small tear in one of the lungs, caused by the deterioration of the lung tissue. This allows air to leak into the chest cavity. Occasionally, the tear heals uneventfully, but more often the pressure of the escaped air collapses the lung, requiring an operation to repair the lung and reinflate it.

Some people with cystic fibrosis die of severe lung or heart damage in the first few years of life, though others with mild cases may live into their 40's or 50's with the feeling that they have little more than a continual bad cold. More than half of all cystic fibrosis patients survive beyond their mid-20's.

A small number of older cystic fibrosis patients have undergone lung or heart-lung transplant operations aimed at prolonging their lives. But this is a drastic approach, too costly and difficult to be a practical treatment for the thousands of people with cystic fibrosis.

Cystic fibrosis has undoubtedly been killing children throughout human history, but the first descriptions of symptoms suggestive of the disease were recorded in the early 1700's. Folk tales of that period alluded to the "salty brow" as signaling an early death.

Cystic fibrosis was first identified as an actual disease in 1936, when

Swiss physician Guido Fanconi and two of his colleagues published a paper describing links among all of the major symptoms—lung congestion, intestinal disorders, and a malfunctioning pancreas. Two years later, an American pediatrician, Dorothy Andersen, described 49 babies and children with what she called "cystic fibrosis of the pancreas." She reported that those with serious digestive disorders died shortly after birth from intestinal obstructions or in early childhood of malnutrition. The rest of the children eventually all died from respiratory infections.

Andersen and other doctors treating cystic fibrosis noticed that some couples had more than one child with the disease. This observation led them to believe that the children inherited the disease from their healthy parents. Andersen also noted that about one-fourth of all the children in the families she studied had the disease, which also indicated that the disorder had a genetic cause.

By the 1930's, much had been learned about how physical characteristics are inherited. Research had shown that all inherited traits, from hair color to blood type to various abnormalities, are determined by genes. Scientists also knew that at conception the fertilized egg receives two copies of every gene, one from each parent. Furthermore, each gene is either *dominant* or *recessive*. For example, the gene for brown eyes is dominant, while the gene for blue eyes is recessive. This means that if an individual inherits both those genes, the brown-eye gene will "overpower" the blue-eye gene and he or she will have brown eyes. If two parents with brown eyes carry the recessive blue-eye gene in their cells, they can produce a child with blue eyes. But this will happen only if the child inherits two blue-eye genes, one from each parent. (In actuality, several genes are involved in eye color and most other physical features. But the principle is the same for each of the genes responsible for any given characteristic.)

In light of this knowledge, Andersen hypothesized that cystic fibrosis is caused by a recessive gene. In that case, parents in a family afflicted with cystic fibrosis would each carry one recessive copy of the gene, which does them no harm. But any of their children who inherit two recessive genes—one from each parent—will develop the disease.

Children born to parents who carry a recessive gene for a disease have a 1-in-4 chance of inheriting two normal genes—one from each parent. They have 2 chances in 4 of inheriting one copy of the disease gene from either parent, thereby becoming a carrier of the gene but not developing the disease. And they have 1 chance in 4 of inheriting both copies of the abnormal gene—and with them the disease. Although Andersen had no way of telling how many of the children in the families she studied were carriers, her observation that about one-fourth of the children had cystic fibrosis supported her theory.

Other physicians studying the family histories of cystic fibrosis

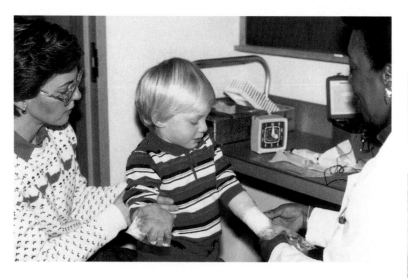

Diagnosing Cystic Fibrosis

Cystic fibrosis symptoms can start in infancy, *above,* or be delayed until later in childhood. A commonly used method of diagnosing the disease is the sweat test, *above left.* In this procedure, a gauze pad is taped to an arm to collect perspiration. A higher-than-normal amount of salt in the perspiration indicates that the child has cystic fibrosis.

patients soon came to the same conclusion that Andersen had reached. By the early 1950's, cystic fibrosis was universally understood to be a recessive genetic disease. Scientists estimated that 1 white person in about 20 was a carrier of the gene.

But understanding how the disease was transmitted did not help doctors treat patients. Although new products, such as artificial enzymes to improve digestion and antibiotics to counteract lung infections, eased the symptoms of cystic fibrosis, medical researchers realized that there was little chance of curing the disease until they tracked down the faulty gene and learned how to correct its effects. Because there was no way at that time to identify carriers of the gene, doctors could not tell if a couple might have a child with cystic fibrosis. The best they could do was to counsel parents who had already produced a baby with cystic fibrosis that there was a 1-in-4 chance of their having another child with the disorder.

In the early 1970's, a diagnostic test called *amniocentesis* became available as a means of detecting many genetic diseases early in pregnancy. In this procedure, the doctor uses a long, thin needle to extract a small amount of *amniotic fluid* from the sac surrounding the fetus. The fluid contains many cells from the fetus that can be examined in the laboratory for abnormalities. But researchers could not find an abnormality that signaled cystic fibrosis.

Then, in 1980, molecular biologist David Botstein and his colleagues at the Massachusetts Institute of Technology (MIT) in Cambridge developed a laboratory procedure that ultimately was helpful in detecting the presence of many disease genes, including the gene that causes cystic fibrosis. They did this by looking for tiny differences in the DNA that makes up genes.

DNA is similar in structure to a twisted ladder. Its "rungs" are made of molecules called *bases*. There are four types of bases— adenine (A), cytosine (C), guanine (G), and thymine (T). Two bases make up each rung; A always pairs with T, and C with G. The order of the bases in genes—segments of the ladder—makes up the code for the DNA molecule's genetic information.

Between genes, and within them as well, there are lengthy stretches of DNA that have no known purpose. The MIT researchers discovered that the order of bases within these noncoding sections often varies from one person to another. For example, where A is found in one person's DNA, C may appear in another person's. The scientists reasoned, therefore, that these variations, which occur randomly along the DNA molecule, could serve as molecular signposts—or *markers*—providing reference points for geneticists trying to locate particular genes.

In the early 1980's, several groups of researchers began to look for markers that were located close enough to a disease gene to be inherited with the gene most of the time. If they found the marker, they would know that the individual also had the gene, even if the gene itself could not be pinpointed.

But finding markers for a given disease gene is no easy matter. It involves taking blood samples from members of families with a history of the disease and extracting the DNA from white blood cells. The DNA is then cut into thousands of fragments with *restriction enzymes*, "biochemical scissors," each of which cuts the DNA molecule at a specific sequence of bases. The fragments are then exposed to an electric field, which causes them to separate by size.

Because a restriction enzyme cuts at a particular base sequence, one person's DNA containing that sequence would be cut into different-sized pieces than would another individual's DNA that does not have the sequence. These longer and shorter fragments distinguish one person's DNA from another's.

In the Brandt family, these telltale fragments from the vicinity of the cystic fibrosis gene might be of four different sizes, which the researchers could call W, X, Y, and Z. Jason and Susanna would each have inherited two fragments, one from each parent. To determine which fragment sizes are inherited with the disease-causing gene, researchers would need only to look at Jason's cut-up DNA. If, for example, they found that he had W and Y fragments, they could predict that any other Brandt child with that unfortunate combination of fragments would be likely to develop the disease. But children with any other combination, such as W and X, would probably be safe because they would have just one copy of the defective gene.

By 1981, several teams of geneticists in the United States, Canada, and Europe had set out to find the fragments that would enable them to do that kind of diagnostic work—and, they felt sure, to home in on the cystic fibrosis gene itself. The task they faced was daunting. Genes are arranged on tiny structures called *chromosomes*. Human beings have as many as 100,000 genes on 46 chromosomes in the nucleus of each body cell. Chromosomes vary greatly in size, but the DNA

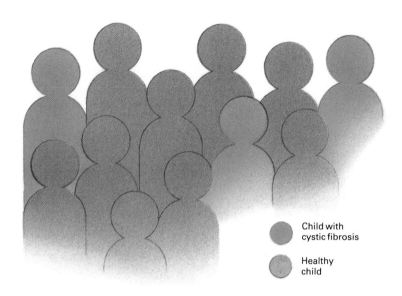

Child with
cystic fibrosis

Healthy
child

Doctors noticed that in families afflicted with cystic fibrosis, about 1 out of 4 children had the disease. This was a sign that the disease is caused by a *recessive* gene, a gene that does not by itself pass on a physical trait or a disease. If a child has cystic fibrosis, he or she must have inherited two copies of this recessive gene, one from each parent.

Cystic Fibrosis Runs in Families

Good medical detective work led doctors in the 1930's to discover that cystic fibrosis is an inherited disease. Like all inherited characteristics, this disease is passed from parents to children through genes. Children inherit two sets of genes, one set from each parent.

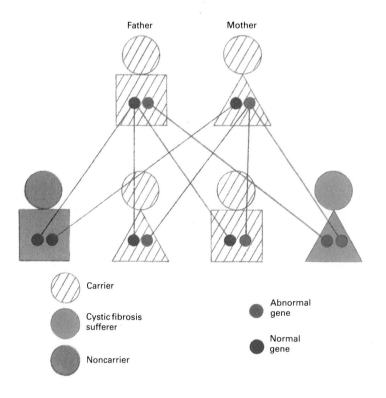

Father   Mother

Carrier

Cystic fibrosis
sufferer

Noncarrier

Abnormal
gene

Normal
gene

The normal version of the cystic fibrosis gene is *dominant*—that is, it "overrules" the recessive, disease-causing gene. Each parent has one dominant and one recessive version of the gene, so neither of them has cystic fibrosis. But because of the way genes pair up at conception, each of their children will have a 1-in-4 chance of inheriting both recessive genes and getting the disease. There is a 1-in-2 chance that a child will inherit one copy of each gene and, like the parents, become a carrier of the recessive gene. The children also have a 1-in-4 chance of inheriting two normal genes.

165

How Genes Can Cause Disease

Genes are located in the nucleus of cells. They are arranged on structures called chromosomes, of which there are 23 pairs in every cell. Genes are sections of a molecule called *deoxyribonucleic acid* (DNA).

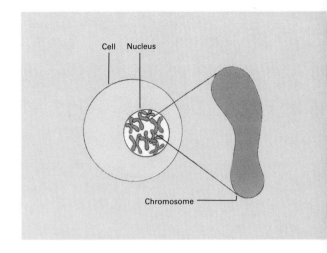

Cell   Nucleus

Chromosome

strand on any given chromosome contains well over 1,000 genes. The researchers did not even know which chromosome to begin with.

The quest for the cystic fibrosis gene among the 100,000 human genes could be compared to looking for the house of an old friend, whose address you do not know and whose telephone number is unlisted, in an unfamiliar city. If you were to learn from a mutual acquaintance that your friend lives in a particular neighborhood, your search would be narrowed to a single sector of the city. Similarly, the researchers needed to get to the right genetic "neighborhood"—the chromosome containing the cystic fibrosis gene. To find it, they had to discover at least one section of DNA that would serve as a "marker."

In November 1985, geneticist Lap-Chee Tsui at the University of Toronto in Canada, after studying DNA taken from more than 50 families, reported that he had found a marker for the gene and had traced it to chromosome 7. That same month, two other researchers—Ray White of the University of Utah in Salt Lake City and Robert Williamson of St. Mary's Hospital in London—announced that they had found other markers, which also turned out to be on chromosome 7. Moreover, White and Williamson determined that those markers were closer to the cystic fibrosis gene than Tsui's marker and were on opposite sides of the DNA region containing the cystic fibrosis gene, like bookends on the two ends of a row of books.

This discovery was like stumbling upon a couple of popular hangouts—say, an outdoor cafe and a drugstore—as you drive around the neighborhood, and then recalling that your friend had said he lived somewhere between those very places. But where? There are about 20 city blocks, all crowded with buildings, between them. You might then decide to park your car and walk the streets between the two places, hoping to spot another familiar landmark.

For the next three years, geneticists followed much the same tack. With painstaking care, they "walked" up and down the lengthy

How Optical Microscopes Work

Optical microscopes use lenses to bend light rays from a *specimen* (an object being viewed) to fool the eye into "seeing" a magnified image. There are two kinds of optical microscopes—*simple,* which have only one lens; and *compound,* with two or more lenses mounted in a tube.

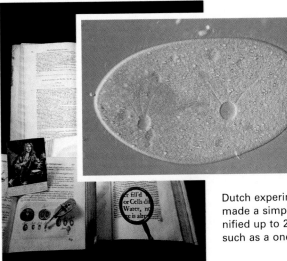

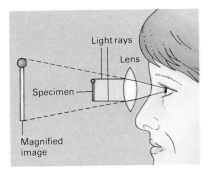

Dutch experimenter Anton van Leeuwenhoek in 1674 made a simple microscope, *left* and *above right,* that magnified up to 275 times, enabling him to see "animalcules" such as a one-celled paramecium, *above left.*

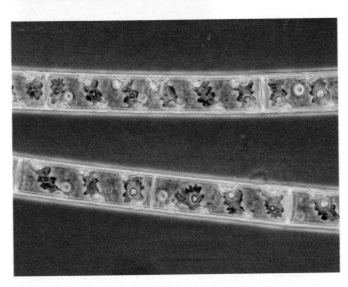

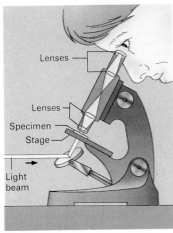

English scientist Robert Hooke built a compound microscope in the 1670's, *above right,* that he used to discover plant cells, *above* (shown 230 times actual size). This microscope used a mirror to reflect light from an oil lamp off the specimen. Today's compound microscope, *right,* reflects natural or artificial light through a specimen on an elevated stage and can magnify up to 2,000 times.

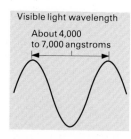

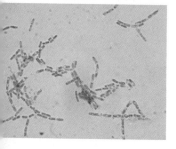

Limits of Light

An ordinary optical microscope cannot "see" clearly two points that are closer together than about half the wavelength of light, *top.* Details inside soil bacteria, *above* (shown 500 times their thickness of 10,000 angstroms), are close to the limit of what this type of microscope can "see" clearly.

Because this type of microscope was so difficult and uncomfortable to use, it gave way to another instrument that had existed since about 1590—the *compound microscope*—one with a lens at each end of a tube. Neither of these lenses alone could magnify as well as Leeuwenhoek's, but they could when working together. The lens nearer the specimen produced an enlarged image. The lens nearer the eye further magnified that image. These less-powerful lenses had a much longer focal length than did Leeuwenhoek's, so the compound microscope was easier to use. Indeed, the evolution of the modern scientific microscope began with the invention of the compound microscope—generally credited to spectacles makers Hans and Zacharias Janssen of the Netherlands.

In the 1670's, English scientist Robert Hooke designed a compound microscope that he used to make a number of discoveries, including the finding that plants are made up of cells. In fact, he coined the biological term *cell* because the "chambers" he saw in a magnified piece of cork reminded him of monks' cells in a monastery. Hooke also verified the existence of creatures like those Leeuwenhoek had seen.

Developing the modern optical microscope

The advances that led to today's scientific optical microscopes involved overcoming two types of distortion. One type was caused by the breaking up of sunlight and other forms of white light, which is made up of all the colors of the rainbow. Lenses in early microscopes broke up white light used to illuminate specimens and focused the various colors differently, producing colored fringes around the magnified image. In about 1830, microscope makers learned to minimize this distortion by adding specially shaped lenses to their instruments.

The other type of distortion was a blurring that stems from the inability of an ordinary lens to focus the entire image at a single point. In about 1886, German physicist Ernst Abbe, working with microscope maker Carl Zeiss, developed correction lenses to counteract this effect. Abbe and Zeiss had a practical reason for using correction lenses, rather than trying to produce a distortion-free lens. An ideal lens, very nearly spherical, would be extremely difficult to produce.

By the late 1800's, the compound microscope had evolved into a shape that is still commonly used. The tube containing the lenses is mounted vertically on a body that has a horseshoe-shaped base. Mounted directly beneath the tube is a horizontal stage with a small hole in the middle. The specimen is mounted on a separate glass slide that clips to the stage so that the specimen is positioned over the hole. Underneath the hole is a mirror that reflects sunlight or light from a microscope lamp up through the specimen and into the tube.

The advanced optical microscope, with a magnification of about 1,000X, brought great benefits. Foremost was the help in establishing the germ theory of disease. In 1882, for example, German physician Robert Koch discovered the bacillus that causes tuberculosis. In addition, researchers observed previously unknown workings of the body, such as white blood cells destroying bacteria.

Many of today's advanced optical microscopes have a magnification of 2,000X and a *resolution* (ability to produce separate images of closely spaced points within a specimen) of about 2,000 *angstroms*. (One angstrom equals 1 ten-millionth of 1 millimeter.) These microscopes can see any plant, bacterial, or animal cell, but viruses are so small that some of them cannot be seen through such instruments. The virus that causes polio, for example, is only about 300 angstroms across.

It turns out that these organisms can never be studied through an ordinary optical microscope, no matter how advanced. Certain laws of physics limit the resolution of any lens or combination of lenses that could possibly be developed. These laws relate resolution to the wavelength of the light that illuminates the specimen. The *wavelength* (distance between successive wave crests) of the colors that make up white light ranges from about 4,000 to 7,000 angstroms. According to the physical laws, no ordinary optical microscope could resolve distances smaller than about 2,000 angstroms.

To resolve smaller objects requires light with a shorter wavelength. So researchers developed microscopes that use ultraviolet light, which has wavelengths shorter than those of visible light. This development extended resolution down to about 1,000 angstroms.

Seeing with electron waves

A way to obtain even more resolution was developed with a beam not of light but of *electrons*—tiny, negatively charged particles that orbit the nuclei of atoms. Electrons have a dual nature—they have properties of both particles and waves.

The wave character of electrons was proposed by French physicist Louis de Broglie, and for this he received the 1929 Nobel Prize for physics. De Broglie said that an electron's wavelength depends upon its energy—the higher the energy, the shorter the wavelength. Devices that were available

"Seeing" with Electrons

An electron microscope, *bottom* (inset), focuses a beam of electrons with magnets just as an optical microscope focuses a light beam with glass lenses. Electrons have a shorter wavelength than do waves of light, so they can "see" smaller objects. In a scanning electron microscope, the beam hits the specimen to produce three-dimensional images, such as the blood clot *below,* formed of red blood cells (shown 6,500 times actual diameter of 0.007 millimeter) and sticky fibers.

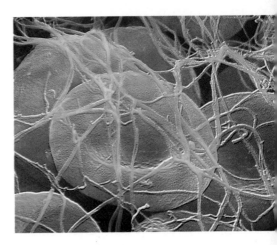

In a transmission electron microscope, the beam passes through specimens, such as the polio viruses *below* (shown 135,000 times their actual diameter of 300 angstroms and artificially colored).

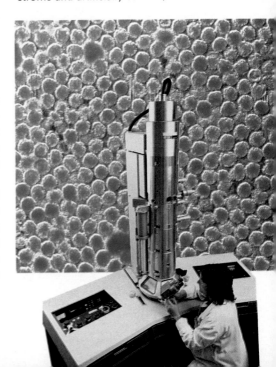

when de Broglie made his proposal could produce a beam of electrons with a wavelength of about 0.05 angstrom.

In 1933, the first *transmission electron microscope* (TEM) appeared, a device that uses electron waves instead of light waves to illuminate the specimen. In a TEM, the electron beam originates in a filament that is similar to the one in an ordinary light bulb and is accelerated by an electric field. The "lenses" of the TEM are magnetic coils, which can focus an electron beam just as glass lenses focus light in the optical microscope—though with much more distortion. The electron beam travels through a thin slice of the specimen and produces an image on the same type of screen used in a television set.

Because magnetic lenses produce so much distortion, a TEM cannot resolve distances that might be expected with a wavelength of 0.05 angstrom. Nevertheless, the resolution of the best TEM's—about 2 angstroms—represented a tremendous improvement over the compound optical microscope.

The TEM showed the exact shape and size of previously unseen viruses and revealed the internal structure of plant, bacterial, and animal cells. With the TEM, scientists were even able to view strands of *deoxyribonucleic acid* (DNA), an extremely complex molecule whose structure looks like a twisted ladder. DNA is the substance that makes up genes, by which all inherited information is passed from one generation to the next in virtually all forms of life—from pine trees to professors.

One drawback of a TEM is that it cannot "see" anything that is alive, because almost all the air is pumped out of the microscope,

Feeling Atoms

A scanning tunneling microscope, *above,* uses electric current to "feel" atoms on a surface such as benzene, *below, right* (molecules shown 35 million times their actual diameter of 2.78 angstroms). This current jumps from the atoms to a very fine needle that almost touches the surface, *below.* The needle scans the surface and, to keep current constant, moves up and down. A computer translates the motions into a picture.

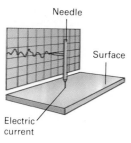

Needle

Surface

Electric current

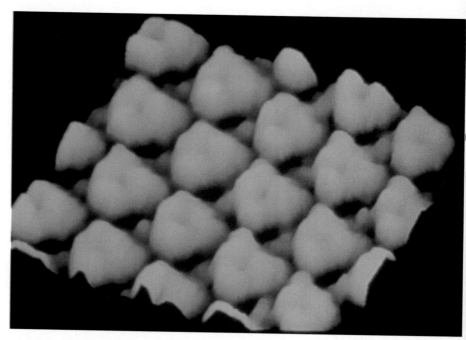

creating a deadly vacuum. This is done to prevent matter in the air from scattering the electron beam. Furthermore, even if some organisms in the specimen survived the vacuum, the high-energy electron beam would kill them. Also, some biological specimens are so transparent to electrons that they are "stained" with a heavy metal such as gold to provide enough contrast to produce an image.

Other specimens receive a thin coating of a metal such as platinum, which is deposited at an angle so that raised areas of the specimen "cast a shadow" of metal across low areas. A researcher then uses a TEM to produce an image of the "shadow," thereby obtaining an indirect view of the surface of the specimen.

3-D views of tiny worlds

Scientists were first able to produce highly magnified, direct image of surfaces in the 1960's, when Cambridge Instruments of Cambridge, England, began to manufacture *scanning electron microscopes* (SEM's). A SEM uses magnetic lenses to focus the electrons into a very narrow stream that sweeps across the surface of the specimen. This intense, narrow beam kicks out electrons from the surface of the specimen, and the pattern produced by them corresponds to the surface features of the specimen. The resulting image is sent to a televisionlike screen for viewing.

For the first time, the world of the previously invisible could be seen in 3-D. The stunning pictures that came from the SEM revolutionized microscopy, revealing, for example, tiny surface details of brain cells, a fly's eye, and the crystal structure in rocks.

A microscope that "feels"

Of all the advances in microscopy that have taken place since the 1600's, however, perhaps none is more stunning than the *scanning tunneling microscope* (STM), which was invented in 1981 by two physicists at the Zurich, Switzerland, research laboratory of International Business Machines Corporation (IBM). The physicists, Gerd Binnig of West Germany and Heinrich Rohrer of Switzerland, won two of three shares of the 1986 Nobel Prize for physics for their design. The third share went to Ernst Ruska of the Fritz Haber Institute in West Berlin, West Germany, for designing the first TEM in the 1930's.

In 1979, Rohrer and Binnig submitted their first patent disclosure on a scanning tunneling microscope. In 1981, they achieved their first real success, images that revealed "bumps" only one atom high on the surface of a crystal made up of calcium, iridium, and tin. An even more important success came in 1982, when they clarified for the first time the complex atomic structure of the silicon crystal—the basic material for almost all computer chips. "I could not stop looking at the images," said Binnig in his Nobel acceptance speech. "It was like entering a new world."

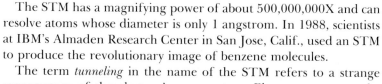

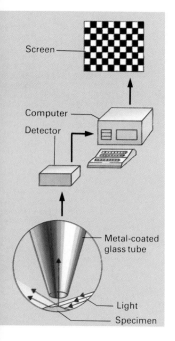

Screen

Computer

Detector

Metal-coated
glass tube

Light

Specimen

Squeezing Light

The superoptical micro-
scope, *above,* uses visible light to resolve ob-
jects much smaller than
the wavelength of the
light. Light reflected off
a specimen squeezes
through a tiny hole in a
glass tube. The distance
from the specimen to
the tube is less than the
diameter of the hole. So
the diameter, rather
than light's wavelength,
determines the resolu-
tion. A detector trans-
lates the light into electric signals that a
computer uses to
"draw" an image on a
televisionlike screen.

The STM has a magnifying power of about 500,000,000X and can resolve atoms whose diameter is only 1 angstrom. In 1988, scientists at IBM's Almaden Research Center in San Jose, Calif., used an STM to produce the revolutionary image of benzene molecules.

The term *tunneling* in the name of the STM refers to a strange consequence of the electron's wave nature. Electron waves can be thought of as "clouds" surrounding the nuclei of atoms. So the atoms that form a material's surface have an "atmosphere" made up of the parts of the clouds that extend beyond the surface. When two such surfaces are brought very close together, their atmospheres overlap. When a small voltage is applied between the surfaces, electrons "tunnel" through the atmosphere from one surface to the other.

The STM applies this tunneling phenomenon to "feel" surfaces the way you might feel the texture of a fabric such as corduroy by rubbing your finger across the fabric. In the STM, the "finger" is a very sharp needle, usually made of tungsten, whose tip can be as tiny as just one atom wide.

This tip is lowered to within about 10 angstroms of the specimen's surface. A small voltage is applied to the needle, causing electrons to tunnel between the needle tip and the surface. This sets up a tiny electric current that varies with the distance between the tip and the specimen. The smaller the distance, the greater the current.

Atoms on a surface stick out like bumps. To detect these atoms, the STM changes the distance between tip and surface to maintain the tunneling current at a constant level as the tip is drawn across the surface. The tip traces out the topography of the surface, rising where there is a "bump" and falling where there is a depression. Repeated, side-by-side scans by the tip produce information that a computer uses to create a picture of the atomic landscape on a televisionlike screen.

STM's are now available from a number of manufacturers, and more than 100 have been installed in laboratories around the world. The imaging of the benzene molecule is just one of the STM's stunning achievements. Another is an image of individual lengths of DNA that revealed DNA's twisted-ladder structure in detail. That image was made in 1988 by a team of scientists from Lawrence Berkeley Laboratory in Berkeley, Calif., and Lawrence Livermore National Laboratory in Livermore, Calif.

Researchers at Ford Scientific Laboratories in Dearborn, Mich., have used the STM to view atoms on metal surfaces. In 1988, biologists at the University of California in Santa Barbara used an STM to make an image of the wavy surface of a membrane that lines the human lung. The researchers say that the membrane's waves enable the lungs to expand with each breath.

A superoptical microscope image shows aluminum "posts" (white squares) on a silicon surface 14,000 times their width of about 1,000 angstroms, *left.*

In spite of the many contributions of the STM, this instrument has a major limitation: Because it relies on electron tunneling, which occurs only between two electrical conductors, the STM does not work easily or well with materials that do not conduct electricity. Biological specimens, which normally are nonconducting, must therefore be specially treated to make them suitable for STM imaging. The DNA, for example, had to be attached—in a very elaborate procedure—to a sheet of mica, which is a good conductor.

Tracing atoms with diamonds

This limitation of the STM was overcome by the next great advance in microscopy, the *atomic force microscope* (AFM), which was developed in 1985 and 1986 by Gerd Binnig and Christoph Gerber of IBM's Zurich laboratory, in collaboration with physicist Calvin Quate of Stanford University in Stanford, Calif. Like the STM, the AFM trails a fine tip along a surface one line at a time. The AFM's tip, however, is mounted on a metal cantilever spring and actually touches the specimen, detecting the tiny forces that exist between atoms.

The tip is made of diamond, silicon, or tungsten and, like the stylus in a phonograph cartridge, is kept in contact with the surface by a slight force. When the tip senses an atomic bump, it jumps upward; when it senses a depression, it moves downward. The AFM does not require a conducting surface, but it does need a way to measure the tiny ups and downs. So the researchers used an STM to sense the movements of the AFM's spring. When the AFM senses a bump, for example, the spring moves closer to the STM's tip, increasing the tunneling current between spring and tip.

The AFM has already scored a number of impressive achievements in biological research—many of them in the laboratory of physicist Paul Hansma and his colleagues at the University of California in Santa Barbara. In early 1989, for example, a team of scientists from Hansma's group made the first motion picture of the process that causes blood to clot. To film the clotting, the AFM scanned the surface every 10 seconds. The researchers then strung the resulting images together to form a movie that lasts 33 minutes.

The team conducted this experiment with an AFM that uses a laser beam instead of an STM to measure the movement of the tip—a technique developed by scientists at IBM's Thomas J. Watson Research Center in Yorktown Heights, N.Y. The beam bounces off the spring and strikes a light detector that senses the position of the reflected beam. The detector translates the beam position into electric signals that a computer uses to construct an image of the specimen.

Bioengineers at the University of Utah in Salt Lake City are using the AFM to study proteins, large molecules ranging in size from 20 to perhaps 500 angstroms. Proteins are responsible for most of what goes on in biology, and the biological activity of protein molecules

What Various Microscopes Can "See"

Optical microscopes can produce images of objects that vary tremendously in size—from enlarged views of mites that are 0.6 millimeter long—just visible with the naked eye—down to microorganisms 0.0002 millimeter across. Beyond the limits of ordinary light, electron beams can see objects as small as 2 angstroms. (One angstrom equals 1 ten-millionth of 1 millimeter.) The new scanning tunneling microscope can even "feel" atoms that measure only 1 angstrom across.

A mite viewed through a low-powered optical microscope; 73 times its actual length of 0.6 millimeter.

Streptococcus bacteria that cause meningitis viewed through a high-powered optical microscope; 1,000 times their actual diameter of about 10,000 angstroms.

Human T-cells, a type of white blood cell (artificially colored), viewed through a scanning electron microscope; 2,400 times their actual diameter of 0.006 millimeter.

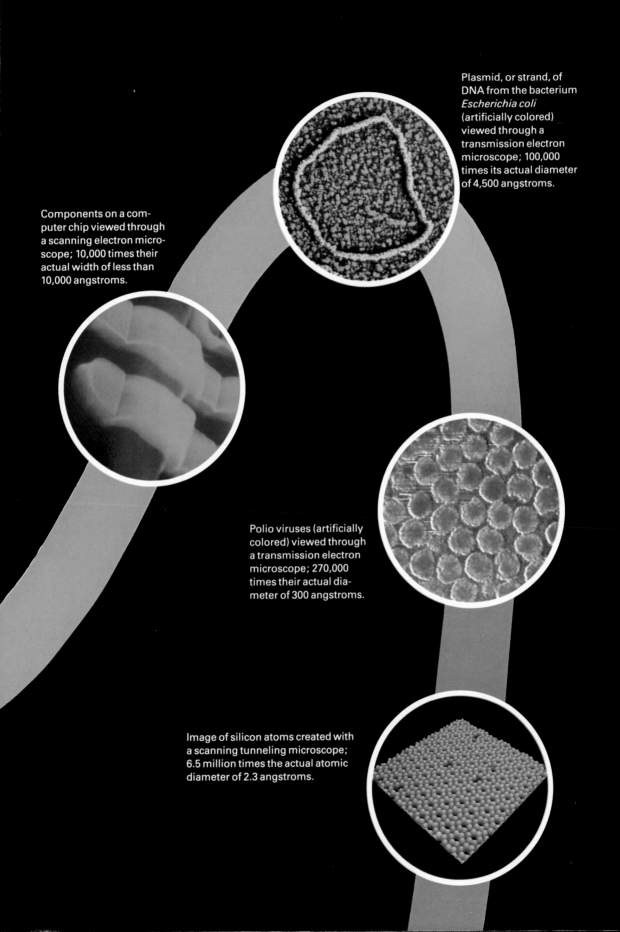

Plasmid, or strand, of DNA from the bacterium *Escherichia coli* (artificially colored) viewed through a transmission electron microscope; 100,000 times its actual diameter of 4,500 angstroms.

Components on a computer chip viewed through a scanning electron microscope; 10,000 times their actual width of less than 10,000 angstroms.

Polio viruses (artificially colored) viewed through a transmission electron microscope; 270,000 times their actual diameter of 300 angstroms.

Image of silicon atoms created with a scanning tunneling microscope; 6.5 million times the actual atomic diameter of 2.3 angstroms.

depends upon their shape. Because proteins are floppy molecules, they are easily distorted. The AFM's delicate touch enables researchers to study proteins with a minimum of distortion—even in liquids.

Seeing with salt

The *scanning ion-conductance microscope* (SICM) is another adaptation of the STM. Instead of a needle, the SICM uses a tiny glass tube—a "miniature eyedropper"—whose inside diameter is 500 to 1,000 angstroms. In a typical experiment with the SICM, scientists first glue the specimen to a glass plate and place the plate in a shallow glass tray. Next, they cover the specimen with salt water and put salt water in the tube. The researchers then place an electric terminal in the tray and put another terminal in the tube. Finally, they apply a voltage across the terminals. The salt in salt water is made up of sodium and chloride *ions* (charged atoms), which—because of their electric charge—flow between the terminals as an electric current.

The SICM then brings the tip of the tube closer and closer to the surface of the specimen. When the tip gets extremely close to the surface, the specimen begins to block the opening of the tip, retarding ion flow and thereby decreasing the current. The current therefore becomes a measure of the distance from tip to surface.

This microscope, invented by Hansma, can thus not only "see" the surface of a living cell but can also trace the movement of ions into and out of the cell through pores in the cell membrane. This passage of ions is of enormous interest to biologists because by opening and closing pores, the cell regulates the supply of ions it needs to perform its function—the firing of a nerve cell, for example, or controlling the amount of water in a cell. (In the Special Reports section, see TRACKING DOWN A DEADLY GENE.)

Squeezing more magnification from light

Biological research will also benefit from another recent—and surprising—advance in microscopy, the so-called *superoptical microscope*, developed by Michael Isaacson, an applied and engineering physicist at Cornell University in Ithaca, N.Y., and other researchers. This microscope uses light to achieve a resolution about one-tenth the wavelength of visible light, or 500 angstroms.

This seems to fly in the face of the law that limits resolution in optical microscopes. The explanation is that this law applies to microscopes that use lenses to focus light—but the superoptical microscope, whose formal name is *near field scanning optical microscope*, has no lenses. One version of this instrument consists of a thin aluminum-coated glass tube, with an opening at the tip that is only 500 angstroms wide. The tube contains an optical fiber, a strand of glass that conducts light extremely well. The stage on which the specimen sits is so close to the tip that the light beam enters the hole in the tip before the beam has a chance to spread out. The resolution is defined not by the light's wavelength but by the size of the hole, which is much smaller than the wavelength. The light that squeezes through the opening in the tip of the tube travels along the optical fiber to detectors and other devices that produce a picture on a televisionlike screen.

Because this instrument does not use electron beams, which can damage some objects, scientists could use it to inspect computer chips and to study living cells. Medical researchers, for example, could use it to locate places on a living cell's surface where such proteins as insulin and other hormones attach themselves.

A microscope that "hears"

Scientists have even turned to high-frequency sound waves to produce the *acoustic microscope*. An acoustic microscope at the University of California at Irvine bombards biological specimens with sound waves vibrating at rates as high as 1 billion cycles per second. This is a thousand times higher than the 1 million cycles generated by conventional ultrasound machines used, for example, to examine the fetus in a pregnant woman. Like a conventional machine, the ultrasound microscope detects echoes that bounce off the specimen. A computer uses information carried by these echoes to construct an image on a televisionlike screen.

The sound waves generated by the acoustic microscope do not damage tissue, so researchers can use this instrument to examine living cells. A physician could even perform a harmless biopsy by examining cells on a patient's skin without removing any tissue.

With the very atoms that make up matter now in view, where the evolution of the microscope will lead is anybody's guess. Perhaps one of the new microscopes will soon evolve into an instrument capable of probing the inner workings of deadly "little animalcules" such as the virus that causes AIDS. Or perhaps tomorrow's biologists will use a microscope to "see" or "feel" or "hear" the specific parts of the DNA molecule that make up individual genes. By revealing differences between normal and abnormal genes, this advanced instrument could help unravel many of the secrets of health and disease. Clearly, for the evolution of the microscope, the end is not in sight.

For further reading:

Ford, Brian J. *Single Lens: The Story of the Simple Microscope.* Harper & Row, 1985.
Hilton, Jim. *All You Ever Wanted to Know About Microscopy and Were Afraid to Ask.* Altitude, 1984.
Taylor, Ron. *Through the Microscope.* Facts on File, 1985.

Space Camp and the Alabama Space & Rocket Center share a site in Huntsville, Ala. Youngsters attending Space Camp get the feel of astronaut life by learning to use a maneuvering unit, *opposite page,* and other devices that real astronauts use in space.

SPACE CAMP

EARTH'S LARGEST SPACE MUSEUM

ALABAMA
SPACE & ROCKET
CENTER
HUNTSVILLE, ALABAMA

At Space Camp, students and teachers alike learn firsthand the science and technology behind the U.S. space program.

A Camp for Space Science

BY PETER COBUN

Training Center
Classes are held in the cavernous Space Camp Training Center, which contains astronaut training devices and mock-ups of space shuttle cockpits.

The author:
Peter Cobun is associate editor of *The Huntsville* (Ala.) *Times*.

Eerie, flickering computer monitors glow in the nearly darkened room, softly illuminating the young men and women huddled intensely behind the banks of control panels. These are the people of mission control, preparing for launch of a space shuttle on a mission set to capture and repair a damaged weather satellite and dock with the United States space station. Countdown is approaching a critical stage.

"T minus 9 minutes and holding," booms an efficient voice through the headsets of the control room specialists. "This is a planned 10-minute hold. The next major event in the countdown will be a launch status verification check of all the flight controllers in mission control."

"PROP?" the flight director calls briskly to the propulsion system engineer. "Launch status verification?"

"It's a go," responds PROP, scanning his instrument panel monitoring all shuttle engines.

"INCO?" the flight director asks.

"All go," reports the instrumentation and communications officer, monitoring her hydraulics, guidance, and navigation computers.

"SCIENCE?"

"Go!" calls the mission scientist and flight surgeon, who sees that both the conditions inside the shuttle and the crew's health are all go for launch.

"CDR?"

The calm voice of the shuttle commander gives an "A-OK for launch."

A scene at the Kennedy Space Center at Cape Canaveral, Fla.? No, this is the United States Space Camp/Space Academy in Huntsville, Ala., where high school juniors and seniors are taking part in a simulated 24-hour "shuttle mission," marking the culmination of an eight-day stay that mixed experiments, lectures, studies, and simple, unabashed fun.

Since 1982, more than 90,000 young people from all 50 states and an ever-growing number of nations have been introduced to the programs of Space Camp/Space Academy. The young people who come to this northern Alabama city — where scientists and engineers dreamed, designed, built, and tested the rockets that sent astronauts to the moon — learn how they can become involved in science and technology. They, too, dream. Some will be pilots, some aerospace engineers, they say. Others insist — with youthful determination and conviction — that they will be the first to go to Mars and beyond.

For the temporarily Earthbound dreamer, Space Camp/Space Academy provides opportunities for students in fourth grade through high school to explore all fields of space science and engineering, from designing rockets to building a space station. They participate in simulated space activities, using space shuttle orbiter

Space-Style Dorm
Based on design concepts for the proposed U.S. space station, Space Habitat, *below,* houses trainees and counselors in dormitory-style rooms, *below left,* during their stay at Space Camp.

Rocket Launch
Everyone who attends
Space Camp/Space
Academy learns how to
build and launch a
rocket.

and mission control mock-ups specially designed for each age group. Some "fly" the orbiter. Some don space suits and walk in "space." Others direct and monitor a flight from mission control. They learn not only the basics of shuttle operation and the science and history of the space program, but also the importance of teamwork and the responsibilities of leadership.

Space Camp/Space Academy features educational programs, using the excitement of space exploration to inspire young people to study math, science, and high-technology subjects. It takes more than 20,000 students from their classrooms each year—at the current rate of admission—and hurls them into "space." By the time they "land" at week's end, many have a new or renewed interest in mathematics, science, and technology.

"Coming to Space Camp has definitely made me a lot more interested in school and really changed my interests completely," according to 15-year-old Brenda Arnett, of Elkins, W. Va., a sophomore at Elkins High School, who in February 1990 was making her third trip to Space Camp. "Now I love biology and chemistry. Space Camp has a way of making you understand things. It helps in your learning." Equally important, Space Camp/Space Academy exposes teachers to the latest information on space science subjects, as well as making available a number of resources for classroom use.

Space Camp was the dream of German-born rocket scientist Wernher von Braun, who arrived at Huntsville in the 1950's to develop the first U.S. ballistic missile at the Redstone Arsenal. In 1960, having been named director of the National Aeronautics and Space Administration's (NASA's) George C. Marshall Space Flight Center in Huntsville, von Braun went before a joint session of the Alabama legislature to sell his idea of a space science museum in Huntsville. A brilliant scientist and visionary, von Braun was a superb salesman as well. The state's lawmakers and citizens bought his idea, voting nearly $2 million for the museum's construction. Today, the Space and Rocket Center is one of Alabama's most popular attractions, with more than 600,000 visitors annually and a total of more than 6 million visitors since its opening in 1970.

Von Braun left Huntsville in 1970 for an administrative post at NASA headquarters in Washington, D.C., but he often returned, stopping in to visit the Space and Rocket Center. With center director Edward O. Buckbee in tow, von Braun would walk through the museum and the adjacent Rocket Park—with its models of powerful rockets—asking questions and testing ideas. During one of these strolls on a warm, summer afternoon in 1975, von Braun noticed a group of about 40 students diligently taking notes as their teacher described the rockets.

"Do you have many of these types of visitors?" von Braun asked Buckbee. "A large percentage of our visitors," said Buckbee, "are student groups visiting for the day. It's very popular."

Von Braun turned to Buckbee. "We ought to have some kind of program where there is a continuing educational experience. Like a camp. We have band camps, cheerleading camps, football camps, scout camps. Why can't we have science camp?"

Thus was born Space Camp. A department of the nonprofit Space and Rocket Center, owned and operated by the state of Alabama, Space Camp/Space Academy receives the cooperation of NASA and the sponsorship of several aerospace and computer companies and other large corporations. Its programs are open to students for more than 11 months of the year and to adults and teachers for part of the year. Another Space Camp facility is located at Titusville, Fla., adjacent to the Kennedy Space Center, though it is open only to students in grades four through seven. Students must have a teacher's recommendation and parental permission to attend Space Camp/Space Academy, and everyone must fill out a health form. But there are no course prerequisites or grade requirements.

Because of age differences, Space Camp/Space Academy is divided into several different programs. Space Camp in Huntsville is a five-day program for students in grades four through six. In 1990, the program cost between $425 and $550. Space Camp in Titusville is also a five-day program, but it includes seventh-graders as well.

Space Academy Level I in Huntsville is a five-day program for grades seven through nine, costing from $475 to $600 in 1990. Space Academy Level II in Huntsville is an eight-day program, costing $675, for high school sophomores, juniors, and seniors. Scholarships are available and are based on scholastic achievement, ethnic background, and financial need. Also located in Huntsville are Adult Space Camp, a three-day session for adults costing $450, and Teacher Space Orientation, a five-day program for teachers operated jointly by Space Academy and the University of Alabama. In 1990, the teachers' session cost $750, which included registration at the university.

Everyone who participates in Space Camp/Space Academy learns how to build and launch a small rocket. In addition, everyone becomes familiar with equipment used to train astronauts, and everyone takes part in a simulated space mission. There are also films and lectures in the history of the space program, future space projects, and career paths in the fields of space science, space engineering, and space flight. All of these common activities, however, are geared to the various age groups and therefore differ somewhat in their complexity and variety.

For those who take part in Space Camp and Space Academy Level I, all five days are needed to cover those activities. The longer, eight-day program of Space Academy Level II offers a greater variety of activity. Space Academy Level II has been accredited and approved for up to three hours of general science college credit by the University of Alabama in Huntsville. This program emphasizes the academic foundation needed for space-related careers. Its curriculum, patterned after NASA crew-training manuals, offers three "tracks" of study—technology, engineering, and aerospace.

Technology track students design and conduct space shuttle experiments and receive instruction in solar and plasma physics, space biology, astrophysics, remote sensing, optics, and computers. For example, in the field of space biology, students study *phototropism*, (the tendency of plants to grow in a certain direction in response to light). They conduct an experiment in which seedlings are set up to receive light from different sources and different angles. The students then chart the inclination of the plant toward the light and compare the results of their experiment with a similar experiment that astronauts performed in space.

In the engineering track, students study robotics, optics, materials science, and thermodynamics. They train in scuba-diving techniques and conduct experiments in Space Academy's 462,000-liter (122,000-gallon) underwater astronaut trainer. Some experiments involve connecting pieces of tubing while floating underwater to simulate building structures in the near weightlessness of space. In another experiment, students design and build a container to withstand a fall of 14 meters (45 feet)—with an egg inside. Students are graded on how close the container comes to its targeted landing site, how well it survives the fall, and how well the egg survives.

Training Devices
A student gets acquainted with the Multi-axis Training Simulator, a device that simulates a spacecraft tumbling out of control. Students learn how to orient themselves in the spinning simulator and then bring it under control.

The aerospace track—for potential aerospace engineers or shuttle or airplane pilots—includes studies in celestial navigation, meteorology, orbital mechanics, and space piloting. For example, in studying celestial navigation, students learn how to take star sightings with a *sextant* (an optical instrument once commonly used by navigators on ships and aircraft to plot their position).

But Space Camp is not just for young people. Adult Space Academy offers three-day sessions from September to December of each year. The sessions include training with equipment like that used to train astronauts and performing a simulated space shuttle mission. The Adult Space Camp attracts people from many different professions and backgrounds who have an interest in the space program and astronaut training and enjoy spending their leisure learning about both. In addition, a number of foreign dignitaries have visited Space Camp, including space scientists and engineers from the Soviet Union and even cosmonauts.

Space Camp never lets participants forget—not for a moment—that what they are experiencing is based on NASA's astronaut training program. A total, controlled environment has been created to immerse each trainee in a world that is, for the most part, foreign to them. Many trainees choose the option of discarding their "civies" for a week to purchase and don sky-blue Space Camp flight suits. But regardless, the "civvy" mind-set is left at the door.

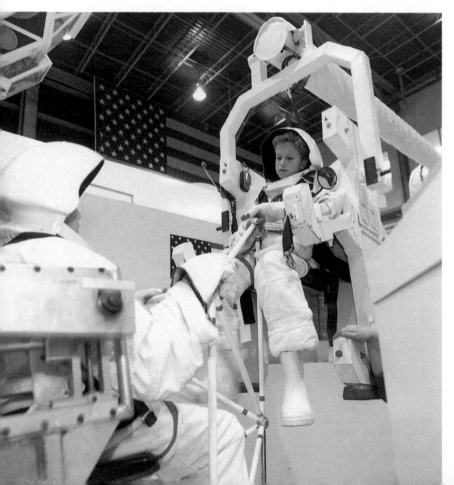

Space Campers learn how to operate a mock-up of the manned maneuvering unit that astronauts use to walk in space.

You know this when you're shown your quarters in the Space Habitat, the dormitory where up to 762 Space Camp and Space Academy trainees, as well as team leaders, can bunk. Inspired by space station and space shuttle design concepts, the habitat is designed to enhance each trainee's understanding of what it is like to live and work in space.

Four stories tall, the complex features an exterior molded by curved metal panels, giving the structure a cylinderlike appearance. Six horizontal "tubes"—each longer than a football field—are divided into six-person "sleep stations." The facility also includes counselors' rooms, a nurses' station, and a rooftop observation deck for telescopic viewing.

Space Camp trainees quickly learn astronaut jargon out of simple necessity. Bathrooms are labeled "waste management," and the doors to the heating and air conditioning system are affixed with a "life support system" sign. There's a sick bay and even a branch of the First Interplanetary Bank where trainees exchange their "green-backs" for the "shuttle bucks" used throughout the camp. If you've got a problem, see the "station commander," or resident manager.

The day begins early—usually the breakfast call comes at 6 a.m.—and though bed check is 10:30 p.m., excitement often keeps adrenaline flowing and lights on until midnight. Three meals are served daily in the "galley," where snacks are also available. And

Mission Control
Students learn to play the important roles of ground controllers at a mock-up of mission control. Using computers and video monitors, they duplicate the duties of the tracking officer, the launch/landing director, the flight director, the computer systems officer, and the mission scientist, among others.

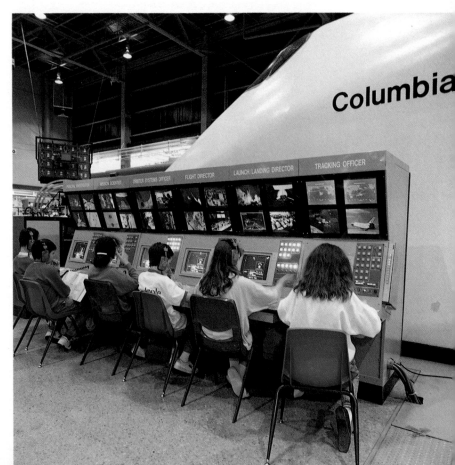

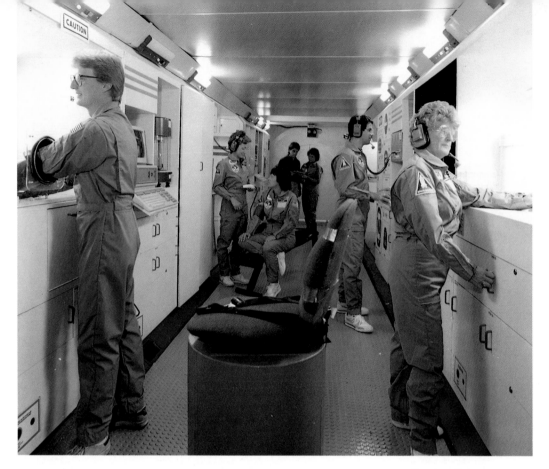

being introduced to a variety of space science subjects, including astronomy, holography and optics, principles of rocketry and propulsion, and space physiology. Teachers learn more than a dozen innovative activities and experiments to use in their classrooms. Leading experts in the fields of space science and technology and space history offer nearly a dozen lectures. The entire course provides about 40 hours of intensive classroom, laboratory, and training time, and teachers earn three hours of credit from the University of Alabama in Huntsville.

Only a small percentage of the young Space Camp graduates, if any, will become astronauts. The administrators and educators who planned the programs for Space Camp/Space Academy—a committee that included NASA representatives, classroom teachers, and veteran astronauts—know that. "But we also know," says Buckbee, "that if they are given the proper motivation and learn why they must have science and math, they can use that foundation and let it take them into a field of their choice."

Teachers Program

Space Camp is not just for youngsters. Teachers attending Space Camp learn a variety of experiments in a mock-up of Spacelab. The Space Camp teachers program provides educators with over 40 hours of classroom, laboratory, and training time to help them discover new ways of teaching science and math.

For further information:

United States Space Camp/Space Academy, The Space and Rocket Center, 1 Tranquility Base, Huntsville, AL 35807.

By inserting genes for desirable new traits into crop plants and farm animals, genetic engineers hope to improve the foods we all eat.

Genetics Heads for the Supermarket

BY BEN PATRUSKY

"Are these real tomatoes?" the supermarket customer asks. "The sign here says they're 'genetically engineered.' What does that mean?"

The produce manager smiles and holds up a plump, red tomato. "It means that scientists put new stuff in them—new kinds of genes—to make them better."

Don't be surprised if some day soon, maybe within just a few years, you hear conversations like that when you drop into the supermarket to shop. And people won't be talking about just better tomatoes, but about better fruits and vegetables of all kinds: potatoes, corn, soybeans, rice—almost any important crop you can think of. Nor will discussions of new and improved foods be confined to the produce department. Scientists are also busily at work these days developing genetically engineered cattle, pigs, poultry, and even fish to make them "better."

"Better" can mean any number of things. It can mean tastier, or crunchier, or more visually appealing, or more nutritious. It can mean a longer "shelf life," the time that food can stay in the store before it spoils and has to be thrown out. Better can mean leaner beef or pork, or cows that produce more—and more healthful—milk.

Glossary

Agrobacterium tumefaciens: A soil bacterium that researchers use to transfer new genes into plant cells.

Cotyledon: An embryo leaf in the seed of a plant.

Deoxyribonucleic acid (DNA): The molecule of which genes are made.

Dicotyledon (dicot): A plant with two cotyledons in each seed.

Electroporation: The use of electricity to open pores in plant cell membranes to admit new genes.

Gene: A segment of DNA; the unit of heredity in both plants and animals.

Hybrid: A new breed of plant or animal produced by the mating of two different breeds.

Microinjection: The use of an extremely fine needle to inject DNA into fertilized animal egg cells.

Monocotyledon (monocot): A plant with just one cotyledon in each seed. Monocots include most grain crops.

The author:
Ben Patrusky is a free-lance science writer and a media consultant to several scientific institutions.

Better can also mean plants that are more resistant to disease and insects.

Clearly, we are on the threshold of a new era in agriculture, an era made possible by a number of dazzling advances in molecular biology and genetic engineering. Scientists are now able to *clone* (make copies of) just about any gene—the basic unit of heredity—from any organism and splice it into the cells of another species of plant or animal. This technology enables researchers to give plants and animals a variety of desirable new characteristics. Those new traits will then be passed on to the organism's offspring and to all later generations.

Revolutionary as these advances are, they represent merely the latest chapter in the continually unfolding saga of agriculture. The same basic principles now being applied to the genetic engineering of foods have been used since people first began to cultivate fields and domesticate livestock more than 10,000 years ago. Always, the aim has been to create crops and animals that are tastier, hardier, more nutritious, or more useful.

In the beginning, ancient farmers selected, for example, the strongest and most disease-resistant plants in their fields and saved the seeds from those plants for the next growing season. In much the same way, they improved their livestock, each year mating the largest and healthiest male in their herds with the most productive female. By this process of breeding through selection, which slowly created new combinations of genes in their crops and animals, the ancient farmers were practicing an elementary form of genetic engineering.

From the 1500's through the 1700's, agricultural methods in Europe and North America underwent great change as farmers began to intervene even more directly in the improvement of their crops. In one field, a farmer might have cultivated a strain of wheat especially rich in grain while, in an adjacent field, he identified wild relatives of wheat that could withstand destructive pests. The sturdiness of the wild plant could then be bred into the cultivated plant to produce a new, combined strain, or *hybrid*.

Whatever the type of plant, and whatever the desired characteristic, the basic strategy was the same: The farmer took pollen from a wild plant with the needed trait and crossbred it with a crop plant to be endowed with that trait to create a new hybrid plant. Of course, that was often more easily said than done. Usually, this mixing-and-matching gave rise to offspring with not only the desired trait but also a large number of unwanted characteristics that had to be genetically "weeded" out before the hybrid seeds could be used for cultivation. Savvy breeders learned to "backcross," to use pollen to cross the hybrid strain with the original crop plant, and to repeat that process through several generations, always selecting for the trait they wanted. Finally, the farmer would have, for example, a wheat crop that was rich in grain and resistant to pests.

Foods of the Future

Scientists are trying to improve crop plants and farm animals by giving them genes for desirable new traits. The added genes could result in pest-resistant crop plants, thus cutting down on the need for chemical pesticides; animals that produce meat with less fat; and other foods that are tastier and more nutritious.

Food or Food Source	New Characteristics
Grains	Pest- and drought-resistant, higher yields, more and higher-quality protein
Fruits and Vegetables	Pest-resistant, more flavorful, higher in nutrition
Chickens	Disease-resistant, faster-growing, lay more eggs
Hogs	Disease-resistant, larger and faster-growing, leaner meat
Beef cattle	Disease-resistant, faster-growing, leaner meat
Dairy cows	More—and more nutritious—milk
Sheep	Disease-resistant, larger and faster-growing, leaner meat
Fish	Larger, faster-growing, disease-resistant

The next major step in the march of agricultural progress was a series of famous experiments on garden peas conducted by the Austrian botanist and monk Gregor Johann Mendel in the mid-1800's. Mendel's work revealed the scientific rules governing the inheritance of genetic characteristics and spearheaded further, dramatic improvements in plant and animal breeding. Through rigorously controlled pollination, painstaking backcrossing, and careful statistical analysis of results, Mendel was able to show that an inherited trait is determined by the combination of two hereditary units, which he called *elementes*. One of these units—which we now call *genes*—comes from the male parent and the other from the female parent.

At the time, Mendel's findings were all but ignored. Not until the early 1900's did scientists come to realize the full impact of Mendel's observations. In the following decades, "plant explorers" searched the world for wild species with desirable traits that could be crossed with crop plants. Far more substantial gains were achieved in the so-called Green Revolution of the 1960's and 1970's. Refinements in conventional mix-and-match breeding methods led to the development of new high-yield grains that enabled the crowded countries of the Third World to increase their food supplies. The Green Revolution was also aided by the increased use of tractors and other mechanical equipment and the abundant—though controversial—application of chemicals, such as insecticides, *herbicides* (weed killers), and fertilizers.

Breeding the Old-Fashioned Way

People have been improving crops and animals for thousands of years. But traditional breeding methods are based on trial and error, and it usually takes many generations, over a period of years, to develop a new strain of plant or breed of livestock.

To combine the best traits of two strains of corn plants—one with big ears and one with sweet ears—the farmer cross-pollinates the two over a dozen or more growing seasons.

Continued cross-mating between sheep with more meat and sheep with thicker wool will eventually produce meatier, woollier sheep.

The advent of genetic engineering technology in the 1970's has opened an entirely new avenue for agriculture, with several potential advantages over traditional breeding methods. For one thing, gene splicing takes the trial-and-error testing out of crossbreeding, greatly shortening the time required to develop new varieties of plants and animals. Rather than randomly mixing tens of thousands of genes—some of which produce undesirable characteristics—and then backcrossing through at least eight generations, gene splicing lets scientists introduce specific desired genes directly, with little or no need for backcrossing. On average, it takes about 12 years to develop a new strain of plant with traditional breeding methods but only 2 years with genetic engineering.

Another benefit that genetic engineering promises for agriculture is reduced impact on the environment. Scientists might, for example, give crops new genes that would enable the plants to manufacture their own pest-killing proteins. Farmers could then cut down on their use of chemical pesticides, which are polluting water underground and in rivers and lakes.

Beyond that, the new technology allows scientists to transfer genes between altogether different species—from, say, a potato to a tomato or a mouse to a cow. Such a feat was previously impossible because different species cannot mate.

Three key discoveries helped set the stage for the genetic engineering revolution in agriculture, beginning in 1953, when biologists James D. Watson and Francis Crick worked out the structure of *deoxyribonucleic acid* (DNA). DNA is the master molecule of heredity and the stuff that genes are made of. Genes, organized on *chromosomes*, tiny threadlike structures in the nucleus of a cell, carry coded instructions for making proteins from building blocks called *amino acids*. Proteins lend shape to cells, help carry out basic chemical processes of life, and ultimately account for such individual differences as hair and eye color, as well as differences between species. Each gene codes for just one protein.

Watson and Crick discovered that DNA is shaped like a spiral staircase, a structure that explained how the molecule functions. The "steps" of the staircase are formed by just four chemicals, called *bases*, with two paired bases to each step. It is the step-by-step sequence of the bases that creates the blueprint for a protein.

The other two key events that gave birth to genetic engineering came in the early 1970's as the result of research on *Escherichia coli*, a common intestinal bacterium. One development was the discovery of *plasmids*—small, free-floating rings of DNA that are separate from the bacterium's lone chromosome. Researchers found that when *E. coli* bacteria reproduce, copies of both the chromosome and the plasmids are passed on to the "daughter" cells. Another important discovery was the detection in bacteria of two previously unknown groups of substances, called *restriction enzymes* and *ligases*. Restriction enzymes serve as "biochemical scissors" that cut the DNA molecule at specific sites. Ligases act like glue to rejoin DNA fragments into a continuous strand.

It didn't take long for researchers to combine these discoveries. They used restriction enzymes to cut a gene out of a human or animal chromosome and to open up a plasmid, and they called on the ligases to glue the new gene into the plasmid. When these engineered rings of DNA were mixed together with bacteria in a test tube, the plasmids readily gained entrance into the cells. The bacteria then produced the protein encoded by the added gene.

These techniques had obvious commercial applications. Today, in huge vats at bioengineering companies, bacteria and other cells, most notably yeast, are churning out an abundance of important proteins. Among those of value to agriculture are cow and pig *somatotropin*, a growth hormone produced naturally—but in very tiny amounts—by the pituitary gland. Daily doses of the engineered cow hormone have been found to increase milk yield. Pig somatotropin given to hogs during the last six to eight weeks before they are marketed causes the animals to grow faster and larger and increases the ratio of lean meat to fat.

The engineered hormones are of exceptional purity, but because they are considered drugs, the proteins must be approved by the Food and Drug Administration (FDA) before they can be used legally by farmers in the United States. Although sanction of the two hormones was still pending in 1990, the FDA in March 1990 gave the nod to another genetically engineered protein, rennin. Rennin, which is normally extracted from calves' stomachs, makes milk curdle and has long been used in the making of cheese. The bacterially produced rennin was the first engineered food product to be approved for sale in the United States.

Their success with genetically altered microorganisms led scientists in the 1980's to think they could also give new genes to plants and animals. The big stumbling block was in finding ways of getting the genes into plant and animal cells.

For plants, researchers enlisted the help of a common soil

Genetic Engineering:
A Short-Cut to Better Foods

Genetic engineering enables scientists to create improved breeds of plants and animals in much less time. Researchers have devised several ways to insert new genes into plant cells. Plants grown from cells that receive new genes will have the traits specified by those genes.

Ferrying Genes in Bacteria

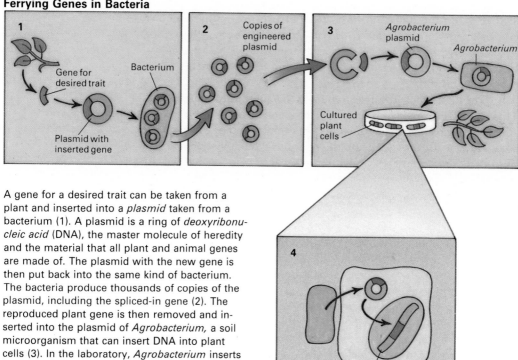

A gene for a desired trait can be taken from a plant and inserted into a *plasmid* taken from a bacterium (1). A plasmid is a ring of *deoxyribonucleic acid* (DNA), the master molecule of heredity and the material that all plant and animal genes are made of. The plasmid with the new gene is then put back into the same kind of bacterium. The bacteria produce thousands of copies of the plasmid, including the spliced-in gene (2). The reproduced plant gene is then removed and inserted into the plasmid of *Agrobacterium,* a soil microorganism that can insert DNA into plant cells (3). In the laboratory, *Agrobacterium* inserts the engineered plasmid into cultured plant cells, and the "foreign" plant gene is then incorporated into the cell's DNA (4). Plants grown from those cells will have the trait specified by the new gene.

Opening Plant Pores with Electricity

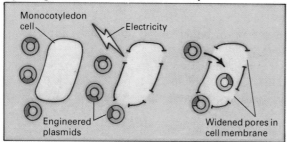

The *Agrobacterium* technique does not work with plants called *monocotyledons.* The cells of these plants, which include most grain crops, have a chemistry that prevents *Agrobacterium* from inserting its plasmid into the cell. But using a small jolt of electricity widens the pores in the cell membrane so a plasmid can enter.

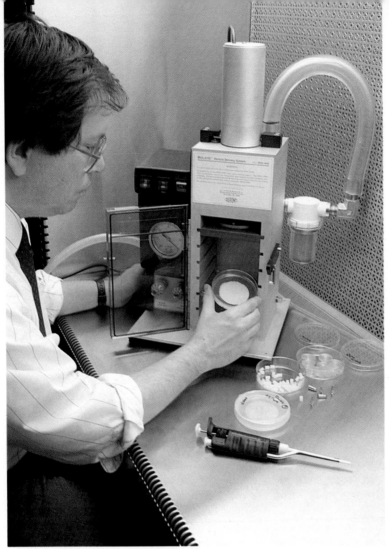

Blasting Genes into Plant Cells

A researcher at the Du Pont Company in Wilmington, Del., puts a cell culture into a "gene gun," *left*. The instrument, developed jointly by Du Pont and Cornell University in Ithaca, N.Y., can shoot genes into the cells of both dicots and monocots.

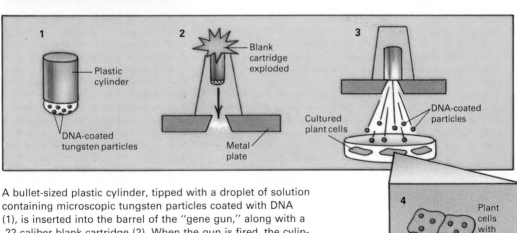

A bullet-sized plastic cylinder, tipped with a droplet of solution containing microscopic tungsten particles coated with DNA (1), is inserted into the barrel of the "gene gun," along with a .22-caliber blank cartridge (2). When the gun is fired, the cylinder is propelled into a plate, which stops it. The tungsten particles spray through a hole in the plate (3) and into a culture dish below. The particles pierce plant cells in the culture dish, and the cells take up the DNA (4).

Putting New Genes into Animals

Animals are given new genes through a technique called *microinjection*. This allows genes from one species to be added directly to the fertilized egg of another species.

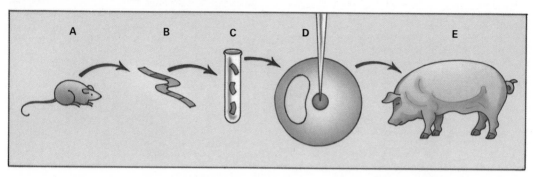

A gene for the desired trait—rapid growth, for example—is taken from an animal, in this case a mouse (A). Copies of the gene (B) are put into a solution (C). An extremely fine needle is dipped into the solution, then inserted into the nucleus of a fertilized swine egg (D). The egg is then implanted in a "foster mother" (E). If the genes are taken up by the DNA in the egg, the pig that develops from the egg will grow faster than normally.

microorganism, *Agrobacterium tumefaciens*, which causes a cancerlike growth called crown gall disease on plant stems. Like *E. coli*, *Agrobacterium* houses a plasmid, which contains the tumor-causing genes. Upon entering a plant, the bacterium produces a duplicate copy of its plasmid DNA and transfers it into a plant cell. The genes in the plasmid then take up residence in the plant's DNA and set off the disease process that results in the tumor on the stem.

Investigators at several U.S. laboratories removed the tumor-producing genes from the *Agrobacterium* plasmid and replaced them with other kinds of genes. In this way, the bacterium was converted into a gene-ferrying system. When mixed with plant cells grown in laboratory cultures, the engineered bacterium transferred new genes into the plants' chromosomes. In 1983, scientists at the Monsanto Company in St. Louis, Mo., showed for the first time that a "foreign" gene could and would function in plant cells.

The *Agrobacterium* technique has its limitations, however. For one thing, it is often a tedious and time-consuming process to grow an entire fertile plant from a single cell or bit of tissue. Although each cell of a plant contains all the genetic information it needs to become a whole plant, once a cell has become part of a particular plant structure, such as a stem, many of its genes are shut off. The key is to make plant cells return to an "undifferentiated" state so their genes can be turned on and off in the proper sequence to allow the organized development of a complete plant.

Researchers accomplish this by growing the engineered plant cells or tissues in laboratory dishes containing special hormones and nutrients that prompt the formation of a *callus*, a disorganized mass of undifferentiated cells. Then they treat the callus with other kinds of hormones, which induce the formation of leaves and roots to form a plantlet. The tiny plant is raised to maturity in a greenhouse, and its seeds are planted to produce a second generation of plants so the scientists can see if the trait specified by the new gene is retained. If it is, that means the gene has become a permanent member of the

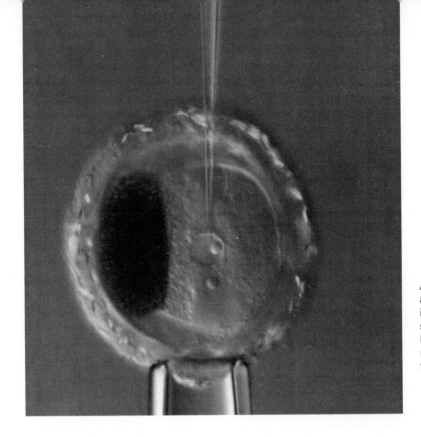

A fertilized swine egg atop a tiny *pipette* (tube) is held in place with a slight vacuum while DNA is injected into the nucleus through an ultrafine needle.

plant's chromosomes and will be passed on to all later generations.

Another drawback to the use of *Agrobacterium* is that it infects only a small number of important plants, primarily of the broadleaf variety. These plants are called *dicotyledons* or *dicots* because they have two *cotyledons*, or embryonic leaves, within each seed. Dicots include such crops as tomatoes, lettuce, tobacco, potatoes, sugar beets, and cucumbers. But another major class of plants, the *monocotyledons* or *monocots*—with just one cotyledon in their seeds—have a different cell makeup that protects them against infection by *Agrobacterium*. Hence, there has been no sure way to deliver new genes to these important crop plants, which include sugar cane and such cereal grains as rice, wheat, and corn.

Recently, scientists in the United States did succeed in using *Agrobacterium* to introduce new genes into rice, the primary food crop for much of the world. Other vital grain-producing plants and soybeans, however, continue to resist the *Agrobacterium* delivery system, so scientists have been searching for new ways of getting DNA into the cells of monocots. One procedure being studied is called *electroporation*. With this technique, a small jolt of electricity applied to plant cells temporarily enlarges pores in the cell membrane, allowing engineered plasmids to gain entrance. The main drawback with electroporation—and it is a big one—is that scientists have yet to learn how to induce single cells or tissue cultures of most cereal plants to develop into normal adult plants.

But there may at last be a solution both to that problem and to the

Some Plant Successes

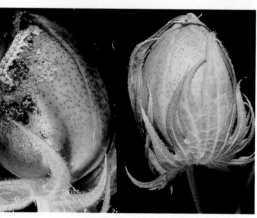

Genetic engineering has already been used to improve a number of plants, though none are yet on the market. A plant breeder at Cornell University, *top,* holds a squash engineered to resist squash-boring insects. A cotton plant engineered by the Monsanto Company in St. Louis, Mo., to resist boll worms, *above,* at right, is free of the pests, while a regular cotton plant, at the left, is infested with the tiny worms.

still-tricky matter of getting DNA into plant chromosomes in the first place. Researchers at Cornell University in Ithaca, N.Y., and at Agracetus, a biotechnology company in Madison, Wis., have developed high-velocity "guns" that shoot genes into plant cells. The operation of these laboratory devices is quite simple. In the Cornell version, for example, a droplet of a solution containing microscopic tungsten particles coated with DNA is placed on the tip of a plastic cylinder the size of a bullet and inserted into the "barrel" of the gene gun. A blank .22 caliber cartridge is fired above the plastic cylinder, and the force of the explosion propels the cylinder down the gun barrel and into a metal plate with a small hole at its center. The plate stops the cylinder, but the tungsten particles spray through the hole and pepper a culture dish full of plant tissue. The particles pierce many of the cells, delivering their cargo of genes, and a number of those genes become incorporated into the plant chromosomes.

A particular advantage of the gene-gun technology is that DNA can be delivered directly into *meristem* tissues, undifferentiated cells at the tip of stems that can be grown into whole plants without going through the tissue culture-to-callus-to-plantlet cycle. As a result, it takes much less time for researchers to learn whether they have developed a new strain of plant possessing the traits specified by the added genes. So far, the gene gun has enabled scientists to produce new lines of soybeans and tobacco. They have been unsuccessful with corn because the meristem tissues of corn plants do not utilize genes that are fired into them. In an alternative approach with corn, researchers are experimenting with using pollen—the plant equivalent of sperm—as the target. They use the bombarded corn pollen to fertilize corn plants and later examine the seeds of those plants in search of ones carrying the desired traits.

The genetic engineering of animals relies for the most part on *microinjection*, the use of a tiny needle to inject DNA into fertilized egg cells. This technique, first developed in experiments with mice, begins with the removal of eggs from the female immediately after fertilization. At that stage, the *pronuclei*—the nuclei of the egg and sperm cells—

have not yet fused to form a single nucleus. An extremely fine needle is used to inject the new DNA into one of the pronuclei, generally that from the male because it is bigger than the female pronucleus and therefore easier to target. The eggs are then implanted in the uterus of a "foster mother"—a female animal different from the one that donated the eggs but of the same species. By mid-1990, this procedure had been used to produce genetically engineered pigs, cattle, sheep, goats, chickens, and fish, though all were experimental animals that were not due for market anytime soon.

Microinjection has one persistent shortcoming: a low success rate. In mice, only about 10 to 15 per cent of microinjected eggs develop into newborn animals, and of that proportion only about 25 per cent have the desired trait and will pass the new gene on to the next generation. In pigs, the success rate is even lower; only about 8 per cent of injected eggs develop to birth, of which perhaps 7 per cent have the new trait. Thus, only 2 to 6 mice eggs per hundred, and just 1 in about 150 swine eggs, successfully incorporate injected DNA.

But even when microinjection succeeds, the results can be disappointing. For example, pigs with new genes coding for growth hormone, despite growing faster and having leaner bodies, are not normal animals; they suffer from lack of energy, lameness, stomach ulcers, and severe arthritis. As a result, U.S. agricultural researchers have stopped producing genetically engineered pigs and have gone back to mouse studies in an effort to learn the cause of these problems and how to correct them.

Because of such problems with animals, plant products will almost certainly be the first genetically engineered foods to show up in supermarkets—perhaps as early as 1993. Before receiving approval from the FDA and other regulatory agencies, engineered crops have to undergo extensive field tests over several growing seasons. From 1986 to early 1990, there were about a dozen field trials of engineered crops in different parts of the United States, and by the end of 1990 that number will have risen to at least 40. Crops now in the testing stage, or close to it, include new strains of potatoes, alfalfa, soybeans, and tomatoes. For the most part, the plants have been endowed with a gene for resistance to herbicides, insects, or viral diseases.

One series of trials, for example, involves the powerful and widely used herbicide glyphosate. Because weeds crowd out crop plants, destroying weeds provides more growing room for crops and hence produces a much larger harvest. But glyphosate kills all green plants, crops included, so farmers must be very selective about when they use it. They usually spray before the crop plants poke their heads above the ground, and in later months they weed their fields mechanically. With plants resistant to glyphosate and other herbicides, farmers will be free to apply the agents more frequently so as to all but eliminate the necessity of mechanical weeding.

Such a use of genetic engineering, however, is strongly opposed by many environmentalists and other critics. They contend that with herbicide-resistant crops, farmers would use more weedkillers than ever, greatly increasing the contamination of ground water and the poison hazard to human beings and animals. Those critics think that farmers should concentrate instead on so-called alternative agriculture, a more traditional approach to farming that relies on crop rotation and soil-tilling to control weeds (in the Science News Update section, see AGRICULTURE [Close-Up]).

For insect resistance, scientists have turned to a gene derived from *Bacillus thuringiensis*, a naturally occurring soil bacterium that has long been sprayed on plants by farmers and gardeners. The microorganism generates a protein that is toxic to a variety of caterpillars—which are responsible for much of the insect-caused crop damage in the United States—but harmless to people and animals. One problem with spraying the bacteria, though, is that they are readily destroyed by sunlight or washed away by rain, so they must be applied several times. Inserting the bacterial gene into plant cells and letting the plants themselves produce the toxic protein promises to make control of caterpillars far more efficient and less costly, and it should certainly cut down on the use of synthetic chemicals to fight these pests.

In an ingenious variation on this approach, the *B. thuringiensis* gene is spliced not into plants directly but into other kinds of bacteria that live inside plants. In 1989, scientists at Crop Genetics, a biotechnology company in Hanover, Md., reported that a plant bacterium engineered with the *B. thuringiensis* gene was effective in killing the corn borer. Every year in the United States, according to the U.S. Department of Agriculture, this pesky insect destroys an estimated 200 million bushels of corn. Scientists say that using the engineered microorganism, which dies with the plant, would prevent most of that loss while posing no threat to people, animals, or the soil.

Researchers have also learned to protect plants against disease-causing viruses, such as the tobacco mosaic virus (TMV), which attacks a variety of important crops. Like other viruses, TMV consists of little more than a few genes surrounded by a protein coat. In 1987, scientists in the United States showed that plants engineered with the gene coding for the coat protein resisted infection by TMV. For reasons not yet entirely understood, the protein, when produced by the plant, prevents the virus from reproducing itself in plant cells. This same general approach has been found to work against many other plant viruses.

For all the agricultural promise of genetic engineering, there remains the question of just how accepting the public will be of its products. Not everyone is thrilled about the prospect of genetically engineered foods. Critics contend that changing the genetic makeup of plants and animals could have unforeseen consequences. They fear that new and potentially harmful genes could be released into nature or that foods could be changed in subtle ways to endanger human health.

Most scientists involved in genetic-engineering research discount such worries. But federal regulatory agencies favor a go-slow approach and are proceeding with caution before allowing engineered produce, meats, and other products to take their place on dinner tables.

Consider the FDA's dilemma on the issue of somatotropin produced by genetically engineered bacteria. Large dairy concerns propose giving their cows a daily dose of the hormone to increase milk output. Opponents claim that the drug's safety has yet to be adequately demonstrated and that even trace amounts of this protein in milk could pose a risk to human health. The manufacturers of somatotropin argue otherwise. They point out that the protein is the same as the cow's own hormone, which is naturally present in milk. Moreover, the makers argue, because somatotropin is a protein, it is rapidly digested and never gets into the bloodstream. For many farmers, however, the debate may actually hinge less on uncertainties about genetically engineered products and more on economics—the fear that the widespread use of somatotropin to increase milk production will result in a milk surplus that could put many small dairy farmers out of business.

The debate over genetically engineered foods is bound to continue for some time to come as opponents of the new technology demand their day in court. But according to genetic researchers, one thing is certain: Sooner or later, the agriculture of tomorrow will be upon us. It may begin with just a trickle of new products. But then the floodgates will open, and supermarkets will be brimming with genetically engineered foods. Genetics, in the view of many experts, is where the future of agriculture lies, and they predict that there will be no holding back that future. The money and research time that have been invested are too great, they say, and so is the need—to produce more, better, and healthier foods to satisfy consumer tastes and to increase the efficiency of agriculture to feed Earth's rapidly growing population.

For further reading:

Arnold, Caroline. *Genetics: From Mendel to Gene Splicing*. Franklin Watts, 1986.
Bains, William. *Genetic Engineering for Almost Everybody*. Penguin, 1988.
Lewis, Ricki. "Building a Better Tomato." *High Technology*, May 1986.
"The New Harvest: Genetically Engineered Species" (special section). *Science*, June 16, 1989.
Siwolop, Sana. "Sowing the Seeds of Super Plants." *Discover*, December 1983.

Although oxygen is essential to life, certain oxygen compounds may contribute to the aging process and to disease.

Two Sides to the Oxygen Story

BY PETER J. ANDREWS

Oxygen is essential to most life on Earth, including human life. When we inhale, oxygen gas in the air enters our lungs and travels through the bloodstream to our cells, where it helps to convert food into energy. Oxygen is the major component of water, which makes up 60 per cent of our bodies.

But oxygen also has a destructive side to its character. Oxygen causes metals to rust and food to go rancid. Oxygen is necessary for fire that can help us by providing warmth and energy but can also harm us by destroying homes and other property. And now scientists suspect that oxygen also may play a role in the aging process and may contribute to several major diseases, including cancer.

To increase their understanding of the destructive side of oxygen, researchers are exploring its role in the chemistry of the cell. *Biochemists* (scientists who study the chemistry of living things) have already discovered that the body produces several substances to prevent oxygen from damaging the cell. Some scientists are attempting to learn whether laboratory-produced versions of some of these materials might protect cells against the destructive side of oxygen.

The author:
Peter J. Andrews is a chemist and a free-lance writer.

Oxygen (O) is a *chemical element*—a substance that is made of only one kind of atom. But oxygen almost never exists as single atoms. The oxygen gas we breathe in the air, for example, is made up of two oxygen atoms bound together as a molecule of oxygen. The chemical formula for a molecule of oxygen is O_2. An atom of oxygen combined with two atoms of hydrogen (H) creates a molecule of water (H_2O).

Oxygen when Earth was young

At the dawn of Earth's history about 4½ billion years ago, almost all the oxygen was chemically bound up in rocks. Heat in Earth's interior caused oxygen and other chemicals to rise to the surface and react to form such substances as carbon dioxide gas and water.

Gradually, ultraviolet light from the sun produced small amounts of free oxygen by breaking up molecules of water vapor in the atmosphere. It took the first living things, however, to pry significant amounts of oxygen loose from its bound state. Three billion years ago, tiny organisms floating in the water began to absorb carbon dioxide dissolved in water and give off oxygen gas, as a product of a reaction known as *photosynthesis*. This is the chemical process by which green plants—descendants of the floating organisms—use sunlight, water, and carbon dioxide to make food.

Today, Earth's atmosphere is 23 per cent oxygen, and this high level of oxygen is maintained by the constant photosynthesis reactions of plants in the water and on land. Plants absorb carbon dioxide and release oxygen, while animals absorb oxygen and release carbon dioxide. Even today, however, almost half the weight of Earth's crust is due to the tremendous mass of oxygen still bound up in solid materials called *oxides*. Silicon dioxide, or sand, is probably the most familiar of these materials. In addition, a whopping 86 per cent of the mass of seawater is oxygen.

Early research on oxygen

Scientific discoveries about oxygen are some of the most important in the history of chemistry. These discoveries began in the 1700's. Until that time, people believed that only four "elements" made up all matter. These had been defined by philosophers in ancient Greece as earth, air, fire, and water. In the late 1700's, however, investigators determined that one of these, air, actually consisted of a number of different gases. The leader in the study of gases was English clergyman and chemist Joseph Priestley. He and Carl Wilhelm Scheele of Sweden share credit for discovering oxygen. Priestley and Scheele, working separately in the 1770's, prepared pure oxygen by heating several substances that we now know to be oxides and collecting the gas they emitted.

Priestley and Scheele both realized that the gas they had isolated was a component of air. And they found that nothing would burn unless this gas was present. Priestley also noted that "plants reverse the process of breathing. They take in foul air [carbon dioxide] and give off good air [oxygen]."

Neither scientist realized, however, that he had discovered a new element. Both were ardent followers of the *phlogiston theory* and believed that they had prepared "dephlogisticated air." This theory held that every combustible substance was partially composed of a "principle" of fire called phlogiston. Wood, for example, was thought to be composed of ash plus phlogiston. When wood lost its phlogiston, it turned to ash. Metals were thought to corrode as their phlogiston was lost. Rust, for instance, was believed to be iron that had lost its phlogiston.

There were many problems with this theory, not the least of which was that iron gained weight as it "lost phlogiston." French chemist Antoine Lavoisier debunked the phlogiston theory in 1776. He recognized that oxygen is an element, and he provided the first accurate explanation of what fire is—a rapid combining of oxygen with other materials. Since then, chemists have learned a lot more about oxygen and why it plays such a vital role in so many important chemical reactions.

Oxygen and ozone in the air

Oxygen gas that is made up of O_2 molecules is colorless and odorless. It becomes a liquid at temperatures below $-183°C$ $(-297°F.)$, and it becomes a solid at temperatures below $-218°C$ $(-360°F.)$.

Ozone (O_3) is made up of three oxygen atoms. It is a pale blue gas. It has a smell—the familiar sharp odor experienced after a thunderstorm or near an electric generator. Ozone is explosive and poisonous, even in low concentrations. It is also much more reactive than molecular oxygen.

Although ozone is less common than O_2 oxygen, it also plays an important role in maintaining life on Earth. About 23 kilometers (14 miles) up in the atmosphere, a layer of ozone screens out the sun's high-energy ultraviolet radiation. Without this protection, life as we know it on Earth's surface would not be possible.

This vital layer is considered to be at risk. Scientists have found that a "hole" in the ozone layer appears each year over Antarctica. Many blame the production of artificial chemicals called *chlorofluorocarbons* (CFC's) for this ozone hole. There is reason to believe that almost every molecule of these chemicals, used in refrigeration, foamed plastics, and certain cleaning solvents, sets off reactions that consume thousands of ozone molecules. Worldwide concern about the ozone hole has led to plans for stopping production and use of many CFC's and for recycling air conditioners and refrigerators.

At the ground level, however, ozone is a major air pollutant. It can injure lungs and damage plants. Most ground-level ozone comes from automobile exhausts.

A Hungry Atom

An atom of oxygen, like all atoms, is made up of a nucleus surrounded by electrons orbiting in specific "shells." The oxygen atom has two electrons in its inner shell and six in its outer one. But the outer shell can hold up to eight electrons, so this makes oxygen "hungry" for two more electrons. Because of this, oxygen readily combines with one or more other atoms by capturing or sharing their electrons. (Diagram is not to scale.)

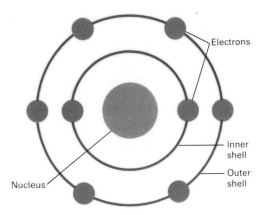

Electrons

Inner shell

Outer shell

Nucleus

How oxygen forms chemical bonds

What oxygen does—whether helpful or harmful to human beings—depends upon what it is bound to chemically. And oxygen atoms "want" to bind with other atoms to form molecules. This tendency to bind is a result of oxygen's atomic structure. The oxygen atom—like all other atoms—is made up of a nucleus orbited by electrons, often represented as being similar to the solar system, with the sun orbited by planets.

The key to how an atom forms chemical bonds is in the number and location of its electrons. Chemists think of these electrons as being in very specific orbits, or *shells*. An atom can have up to seven shells, and there is a maximum number of electrons that each shell can hold.

Atoms whose outer shells are not completely filled with the maximum number of electrons "try" to fill them by acquiring more electrons. This is how chemical bonds are formed and why chemical reactions take place.

For example, the oxygen atom has two shells with two electrons in the inner shell and six in the outer shell. But its outer shell can hold eight electrons, so the atom "wants" to add two electrons. In other words, oxygen is "hungry" for two electrons, and this hunger makes oxygen a highly reactive element.

To complete its outer shell, an oxygen atom can share electrons with one or more other atoms. This is precisely what happens when two oxygen atoms combine to form an oxygen molecule. Each atom shares two of its electrons with the other atom.

If exposed to enough chemical, heat, or electric energy, the two oxygen atoms in an O_2 molecule will break apart and react with most of the other elements. Oxygen molecules that are dissolved in water, for example, break apart easily if the water happens to be in contact with a metal. The oxygen atoms will react with the metal to form an

How Oxygen Satisfies Its Electron Hunger

Two oxygen atoms can satisfy their "hunger" for electrons by combining to form an oxygen molecule, the normal form of oxygen gas in the air. Each atom shares two of its outer-shell electrons with the other so that both atoms' outer shells contain eight electrons.

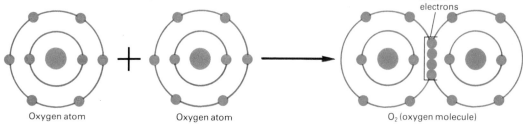

Oxygen atom   Oxygen atom O_2 (oxygen molecule)

Shared electrons

An oxygen atom can satisfy its "hunger" for electrons by sharing the electrons of two hydrogen atoms to form a molecule of water. Each hydrogen atom has one electron, so two hydrogen atoms are needed to boost the number of electrons in the oxygen atom's outer shell to eight.

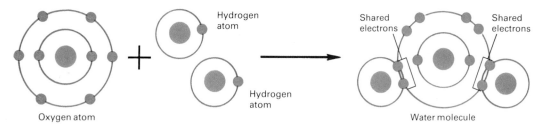

Oxygen atom

Hydrogen atom

Hydrogen atom

Shared electrons   Shared electrons

Water molecule

If there is enough energy present, an O_2 molecule will break apart and oxygen atoms will combine with other substances in a reaction called *oxidation*. Oxygen molecules dissolved in water break apart easily due to chemical energy if the water is in contact with iron. Oxygen atoms then slowly oxidize iron atoms to produce iron oxide, or *rust*.

Oxygen in the presence of water

Iron

Rust

Materials that combine very rapidly with oxygen burn. Wood oxidizes rapidly provided there is enough energy to heat it to its *kindling point* (the temperature at which a substance bursts into flame in the presence of oxygen). Kindling points for different woods range from 190° to 266°C (375° to 510°F.).

Oxygen

Wood heated to its kindling temperature

Fire

Oxygen's "Good" and "Bad" Sides

Depending on what atoms it combines with, oxygen plays either a life-sustaining role or a harmful role in the cells of the body.

Oxygen is carried to body cells by the blood. Oxygen from the air is inhaled into the lungs, where it passes into the bloodstream. Most of the oxygen *forms chemical bonds* (shares electrons) with iron atoms in a molecule called *hemoglobin* in the blood, which delivers the oxygen to the cells.

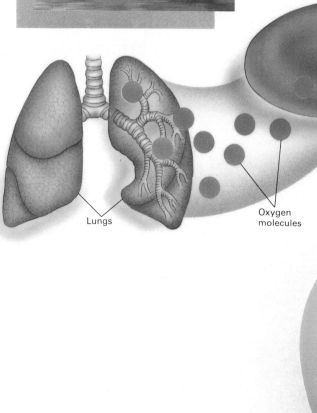

Hemoglobin

Lungs

Oxygen molecules

Cell

Adenosine triphosphate (ATP)

ATP

Oxygen performs a vital role inside a cell by taking part in chemical reactions that produce an energy-packed substance called *adenosine triphosphate* (ATP). Molecules of ATP are "batteries" for individual cells and therefore supply energy for the entire body.

Reactions in the cell also produce *free radicals* that contain oxygen. In these compounds, an oxygen atom's outer shell has either more or fewer than eight electrons. Because an oxygen atom "wants" eight electrons in its outer shell, these free radicals will react rapidly with any atom or molecule that happens to be nearby. As a result of reactions with fats, proteins, or the DNA molecule of which our genes are made, these radicals may play a role in many diseases—and perhaps even in aging.

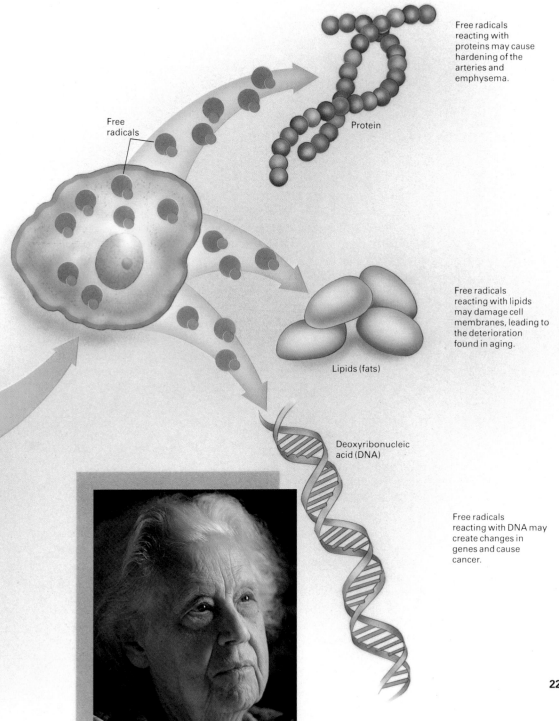

Free radicals reacting with proteins may cause hardening of the arteries and emphysema.

Protein

Free radicals

Free radicals reacting with lipids may damage cell membranes, leading to the deterioration found in aging.

Lipids (fats)

Deoxyribonucleic acid (DNA)

Free radicals reacting with DNA may create changes in genes and cause cancer.

oxide. Rusting, for instance, is the joining of oxygen and iron to form iron oxide.

Another way to break up an O_2 molecule is to heat it. When you heat a material such as wood to a temperature called its kindling temperature, O_2 molecules in contact with the material break up and react with chemicals in the material, resulting in fire.

A fast or a slow burn

The basic chemical reaction of oxygen, whether in the cell of a human being, the wood of a roaring fire, or a rust spot on the family automobile, is called an *oxidation-reduction* reaction. Oxygen picks up, or gains a share of, another element's electrons. Oxygen is said to be *reduced*, and the other chemical is *oxidized*. Chemical compounds, including gigantic molecules such as proteins, also participate in oxidation-reduction reactions.

Different oxidation-reduction reactions can occur at vastly different rates. The rusting of iron is slow oxidation, and the burning of wood is fast oxidation.

Oxidation-reduction reactions are also involved in providing energy for animal cells. In a human being, oxygen from the air is taken into the lungs. In small air sacs in the lungs, iron atoms within the blood's *hemoglobin*, a large protein located in the red blood cells, take on oxygen. The blood then travels to the heart, which pumps it to the cells throughout the body. When the blood reaches the cells, it exchanges oxygen for carbon dioxide, which is carried back to the lungs, released, and exhaled.

Within the cells, the oxygen participates in an oxidation-reduction reaction—the last step in a long, complex chemical process that produces a substance called *adenosine triphosphate* (ATP). Molecules of ATP are like batteries for the cell. Virtually all processes in a cell that require energy for operation obtain it directly from ATP.

The dark side of oxygen

Many scientists believe that, ironically, the very process by which a cell uses oxygen to produce useful ATP also produces potentially harmful compounds called *free radicals*. A free radical is made up of two or more atoms, one of which has either one too many or one too few electrons in its outer shell. Two kinds of free radicals are especially harmful. One is called superoxide; the other, the hydroxyl radical. Superoxide does most of its damage indirectly by taking part in reactions that produce the hydroxyl radical, which is an extremely electron-hungry compound.

Hydroxyl radicals react rapidly with whatever happens to be nearby. Substances they will bond with include *lipids* (fats), proteins, and deoxyribonucleic acid (DNA)—the substance of which genes are made. These chemical reactions can damage body cells or cause changes in genes.

Fortunately, the body has a defense against free radicals. This consists of compounds called *antioxidants* (substances that prevent radicals from oxidizing other substances). Some of these antioxidants are produced by the body. Two others are vitamins C and E, and these must be provided in the diet. Antioxidants donate electrons to the free radicals, thus satisfying their electron hunger.

Oxygen and the aging process

Free radicals that pierce the antioxidant line of defense, however, are free to wreak havoc with the body by oxidizing virtually any part of any cell. Biochemist Denham Harman of the University of Nebraska's Omaha Medical School suggested in 1956 that all parts of the body constantly experience chemical change as the result of free radicals. Harman theorized that the net effect of all these changes is what seems to be a fundamental life process—the decline of the adult human body with age.

Harman reasoned that when cells use oxygen to *metabolize* food (turn it into energy and living tissue) they produce large amounts of radicals. And, in general, the higher the metabolic rate of a species, the shorter the life span of the species. A mouse, for example, consumes oxygen about 4½ times as rapidly per gram of body weight as does a human being. A mouse dies of old age when it is about 2 years old, compared with about 90 years for a human being. In addition, species of animals that produce larger amounts of a biochemical that defends against free radicals have longer life spans than do species that produce less.

But other investigators have pointed out that the evidence linking free radicals and the aging process is not so cut and dried. For example, there are genetic diseases that resemble rapid aging, but these do not seem to involve an increase in tissue breakdown caused by free radicals. And, people with defective defenses against radicals, such as a reduced ability to absorb vitamin E, do not have shorter life spans. In addition, feeding antioxidants to animals or placing antioxidants in laboratory cultured cells does not enable them to live beyond the maximum life span of the species. This was demonstrated in 1984 by chemist Richard G. Cutler of the National Institute on Aging in Baltimore.

There is also inconclusive evidence about the roles of metabolism, free-radical production, and aging. Animals on calorie-restricted diets generally have extended life spans. As long ago as 1930, biologist Clive McCay of Cornell University in Ithaca, N.Y., showed that rats fed very limited amounts of food lived almost twice as long as rats that ate normal quantities. Since then, other researchers have carried out similar experiments. But these rats do not necessarily have lower metabolisms than do animals on normal diets. Roy L. Walford, a physician at the University of California at Los Angeles, showed in 1988 that calorie restriction did not lower the metabolism of rats.

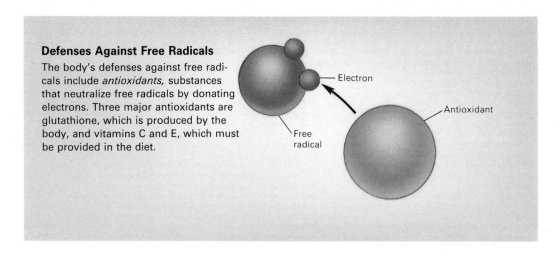

Defenses Against Free Radicals
The body's defenses against free radicals include *antioxidants,* substances that neutralize free radicals by donating electrons. Three major antioxidants are glutathione, which is produced by the body, and vitamins C and E, which must be provided in the diet.

Electron

Antioxidant

Free radical

Oxygen's role in disease

Even if free radicals are not the cause of aging, however, they probably play a role in the diseases of old age, including emphysema, arthritis, a form of hardening of the arteries known as *atherosclerosis,* and some forms of cancer.

■ **Emphysema.** This disease destroys the walls of the tiny air sacs in the lungs, resulting in the formation of large spaces that trap carbon dioxide and obstruct the flow of oxygen. The overwhelming majority of emphysema victims are older smokers. In 1983, biologist Aaron Janoff of State University of New York in Stony Brook proposed a theory that explains why older smokers are at risk for this disease, and experiments reported in 1986 proved him correct. Certain naturally occurring enzymes called *proteases* break down proteins. These enzymes are normally held in check by other enzymes called *antiproteases.* If antiproteases are somehow inactivated, the proteases are no longer controlled, and they can destroy the air sac walls. This loss of control over proteases is exactly what happens in the case of smokers. William A. Pryor of Louisiana State University in New Orleans found in 1986 that smoke-related oxygen radicals attack a major antiprotease and inactivate it.

■ **Arthritis.** One role of oxygen radicals in aggravating the inflammation associated with rheumatoid arthritis was suggested in a 1980 study by R. A. Greenwald of the Hospital for Special Surgery in New York City. Within the joints of the body is a fluid that acts as a lubricant because it contains a syrupy substance. Greenwald showed that free radicals break down this substance, causing the fluid to lose its ability to lubricate. This could allow the bones to rub together, adding to inflammation of the joint.

■ **Heart disease.** A connection between atherosclerosis and free radicals was discovered in 1984 by Haruhiko Yagi of the National

Institutes of Health in Bethesda, Md. He determined that the blood of heart attack and stroke victims has twice the normal amount of certain oxidized fats. In atherosclerosis, certain fatty substances in the bloodstream—particularly cholesterol—form deposits that damage the inner lining of blood vessels. Eventually the build-up of deposits narrows the inside of blood vessels, slowing blood flow. Yagi found that free radicals may contribute to this process by attacking the lining of the blood vessels.

■ **Cancer.** This disease is a result of an abnormally rapid reproduction of cells. Cells reproduce under the control of genes. Biochemist Bruce N. Ames of the University of California at Berkeley showed in 1984 that free radicals can damage the DNA of which genes are made. Because free radicals react at random, they can damage *any* DNA—including genes that control cell growth. If cell growth genes are damaged, the cell could reproduce itself wildly, producing a malignant tumor.

Protecting against free-radical damage

What can scientists do to help control the damaging effects of free radicals? One approach is to learn more details about the workings of known antioxidants and to determine whether other substances produced by the body are antioxidants.

By testing various substances, Ames has discovered that *bilirubin*, a reddish-yellow pigment secreted by the liver, can act as an antioxidant in cell membranes. Ames found three other substances that are strong antioxidants. Large quantities of these substances are found in certain cells of the brain and the skeletal muscle—the two types of cells with the highest metabolic rates in the body.

One result of this type of research might be to determine how much of the various antioxidants would be needed to prevent free radicals from damaging cells. Drug companies might then manufacture medicinal versions of these antioxidants, and physicians could prescribe them.

But what is antioxidants' potential for extending the life span of healthy individuals? Experiments by Cutler and other researchers on feeding antioxidants to animals may provide a clue. Animals that received antioxidants did not set records for old age. They did, however, live healthier lives than did animals that were not fed antioxidants. And more of them approached the maximum life span characteristic of their species. So blocking the destructive action of free radicals is not likely to increase the maximum lifetime of our species—but it could help individuals lead longer, healthier lives.

For further reading:

Adler, Irving. *How Life Began.* Harper, 1977.
Asimov, Isaac. *How Did We Find Out About Blood?* Walker, 1986.
Fichter, George S. *Cells.* Watts, 1986.

Science News Update

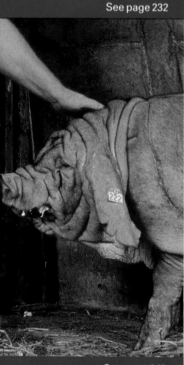

See page 232

See page 248

Science Year contributors report on the year's major developments in their respective fields. The articles in this section are arranged alphabetically.

See page 262

See page 297

See page 316

Agriculture

Ground water in the United States is not being widely contaminated by agricultural chemicals such as fertilizers and pesticides, contrary to the fears of many environmentalists. That conclusion was announced in summer 1989 by agricultural scientists who had been studying the possibility that farmers were seriously polluting the nation's water supply.

One of the researchers, *agronomist* (soil scientist) Ron Turco of Purdue University in West Lafayette, Ind., reported that there are some localized farming-related water pollution problems in various parts of the United States. But the real problem, he said, is the contamination of farmers' wells.

Turco explained that on some farms, wells were not built properly or are not being adequately maintained. In some such cases, he said, chemicals in the soil seep into the well and pollute the water. In addition, he said, wells that are near livestock pens are liable to become contaminated by nitrates from the animals' wastes. In areas where ground water has been found to contain pesticides, Turco noted, the problem was usually caused by the mishandling of those chemicals.

Turco said the fact that researchers have not found widespread groundwater contamination in farming areas speaks well of agricultural chemicals. The newer chemicals, he said, are designed to kill a target pest and then break down to harmless compounds.

Cold-resistant fruit. What makes one fruit tree more resistant to freezing than another? Plant physiologist Michael Wisniewski of the U.S. Agricultural Research Service's (ARS) Appalachian Fruit Research Station in Kearneysville, W. Va., announced in November 1989 that he had found part of the answer to that question.

Using an electron microscope, Wisniewski examined peach-tree stem tissues that had been exposed to freezing temperatures. He found that the size of the pores in the *pit membranes* determines the temperature at which the tissues freeze. The pit membranes are not part of the peach pit but rather are tiny openings in the walls between cells—much like doors between adjoining rooms. Pit membranes are found in the cells of many kinds of plants.

Wisniewski discovered that the smaller the pit-membrane pores in a plant, the lower the temperature the plant can withstand before water in the cells starts to freeze. The reason has to do with the fact that water confined to very small spaces freezes at a lower temperature than water in larger areas.

Wisniewski said the discovery may lead to the development of fruit trees that are more resistant to cold. Such trees would be bred to have cells with smaller pit membranes.

Acid rain tolerance. Many farm crops, such as lettuce and winter wheat, do not appear to suffer much damage from acid rain conditions, according to a report released in November 1989 by ARS scientists in Raleigh, N.C. Acid rain—precipitation of higher than normal acidity—is the result of airborne pollutants, mainly sulfur dioxide and nitrogen oxides. Those pollutants are converted to acids in the atmosphere and carried back to the ground in rain and snow.

The researchers watered 216 varieties of 18 test crops with simulated acid rain that was about half as acidic as lemon juice. That level of acidity is much higher than that of most acid rain. The simulated acid rain caused no significant injuries to any of the plants, nor did it reduce growth in most of the species.

The scientists first tested the plants' response to a short, one-time exposure to acid rain—a one-hour watering. In that test, the crops that proved most sensitive were tomatoes, eggplants, snap beans, cotton, peanuts, and soybeans. About 5 per cent of the leaves of those crops suffered damage. The injured leaves had small bleached or burned spots, usually where water droplets had remained for an extended time or where a large volume of water had flowed over the surface.

The least sensitive crops included potatoes, corn, lettuce, winter wheat, melons, cucumbers, alfalfa, and squash. These crops all had less than 2 per cent leaf damage.

Next, the researchers looked at whether continuous exposure to acid rain —for up to 15 days at a time— would cause more serious harm to crops. Lettuce, tomatoes, soybeans, and winter wheat were selected for that test

Learning How to Farm in Outer Space

Scientists with the United States Agricultural Research Service are developing methods for growing crops on extended space flights. The researchers hope to learn how to raise healthy plants in an environment of artificial light, little or no gravity, and perhaps the absence of soil. Plants in a spaceship will have to recycle air, water, and waste, so in a project aimed at devising such a system, plants are being grown in an enclosed chamber at the Kennedy Space Center in Florida, *below left.*

A researcher at the Climate Stress Laboratory in Beltsville, Md., *above,* studies the effect that restricted root volume has on *hydroponic* (growing in water) tomato plants. The goal is to find out how much space the plants need to remain healthy and produce tomatoes.

At the Plant Photobiology Laboratory in Beltsville, *above,* a scientist checks root growth in hydroponic soybean plants being exposed to varying kinds of light. Cutting down the blue content of light causes the edible parts of the plant to grow more than the roots.

Alternative Ways of Farming

A report that focused national attention on "alternative agriculture" was issued in September 1989 by the National Academy of Sciences (NAS) in Washington, D.C., an advisory body to the United States government. The report summed up an NAS study of this new wave in farming, which emphasizes a return to more natural growing methods and the reduced use of chemical fertilizers and pesticides. The NAS's conclusion—applauded by some in the agricultural industry and criticized by others—was that the adoption of alternative agricultural techniques by U.S. farmers "would result in even greater economic benefits to farms and environmental gains to the nation."

Agriculture is a major industry in the United States. Although 87 per cent of American farms are still family operations, most of them are run like modern businesses. The typical farm in the United States is highly mechanized, with sophisticated tractors and combines, and it makes heavy use of chemicals—mainly fertilizers and pesticides. This extensive use of machinery and chemicals, which has been the standard way of farming in the United States since the late 1940's, has been strongly encouraged by the U.S. Department of Agriculture. The primary objective of U.S. farm policy has been to increase crop yields, and in that it has been spectacularly successful; American farmers have consistently produced crop surpluses.

By the late 1980's, however, society had become less interested in producing ever-greater quantities of food. Attention turned instead to the questions of how food is produced and how those production methods may affect human health and the environment. Opponents of conventional agriculture charged that farmers were polluting water supplies with chemicals that drained into streams and rivers or sank deep into the ground. In addition, the critics said, conventional methods of cultivation, which involve extensive tilling of the soil, were causing much of the nation's farmland to erode. The issue of pesticide residues in food was another concern.

Some of the critics were themselves farmers, and they became the nucleus of the alternative agriculture movement. Alternative agriculture is still practiced on only a minority of farms, though there are no reliable figures on just how many. But the idea is catching on with a growing number of farmers across the United States.

Most proponents of alternative agriculture advocate greater use of natural fertilizers and nonchemical pest-control methods. For example, they suggest using livestock manure for fertilizer and clearing weeds mechanically instead of applying *herbicides* (chemical weedkillers).

Although some farmers who have taken up alternative agriculture shun all chemicals, most continue to use them—but in much smaller amounts. Insecticides and herbicides are applied at certain specific times when they will have the most effect. This conservative use of chemicals is part of an approach called *integrated pest management* (IPM). IPM also includes natural pest controls, such as the growing of pest-resistant plants and the increased rotation of crops to disrupt the life cycles of insects.

Alternative methods of cultivation also make it hard for weeds and insects to thrive. *Ridge tillage*, for instance—the planting of crops on small, unplowed ridges of earth—leaves weed seeds buried in the soil and covered with residues from the previous growing season. Weed growth is thereby hindered, so there is little or no need for herbicides. Ridge tillage has the added benefit of reducing soil erosion.

Cutting down on erosion is one of the main goals of alternative cultivation methods, referred to collectively as *conservation tillage*. The most extreme of these is *no-till* farming, in which the soil is left undisturbed except for the digging of a narrow slot in which the crop seeds are planted.

Alternative agriculture also includes different ways of raising livestock. In conventional farming, antibiotics are often added to animals' feed on a routine basis as a preventive measure against disease. This creates antibiotic residues in meats and can lead to drug-resistant bacteria. Farmers practicing alternative agriculture use the drugs only to treat a specific disease.

Despite the growing enthusiasm for alternative agriculture, many farmers and agricultural experts are critical of it. Their opposition is mainly economic. They believe that alternative farming methods, and particularly a drastic move away from the use of chemicals, would reduce crop yields and raise food prices.

This view has been bolstered by a study conducted at Texas A&M University in College Station. In a study reported in June 1990, agricultural economists at the university estimated that removing all chemicals from U.S. farming would hike the average family grocery bill by $20 a month. They concluded that the increase would make it difficult for some lower-income families to eat a proper diet.

Even some farmers practicing alternative agriculture say their methods might not work for everyone. Dick Thompson, who has used no

Farmer Dick Thompson, a proponent of *ridge tillage*—the growing of crops on small ridges of earth—cultivates a field on his Iowa farm, *above*. The rotary disks of the ridge-tilling machine, *left*, build up the ridges and destroy whatever weeds may have sprouted in the furrows between the ridges. This cultivation method is one of several kinds of *conservation tillage*, which emphasizes disturbing the soil as little as possible in order to reduce erosion and discourage weed growth.

pesticides or commercial fertilizers on his Iowa farm since 1967, comments that farmers without their own livestock might not be able to get enough manure to fertilize their fields. Furthermore, alternative agriculture often requires added labor—on some farms, for example, weeds are pulled manually—and many farmers cannot afford to hire additional help.

In the end, the buying public and the federal government will determine what kind of agriculture is adopted in the United States. If consumers demand a reduction in the use of agricultural chemicals, and if U.S. farm policy supports that demand, most farmers will have little choice but to go along. But experts caution that there will be trade-offs between food purity and environmental protection on the one hand and food quantity and price on the other. [Steve Cain]

A Meishan boar, *right,* is one of 140 pigs imported into the United States from China in 1989. The Chinese pigs produce larger litters than American breeds do and are also said to be more resistant to disease. Researchers will determine whether crossing Chinese and U.S. pigs would result in hybrids with the traits of the Chinese swine but the lean meat of U.S. pigs.

Agriculture

Continued

because they were among both the most sensitive and the most tolerant crops in the first experiment.

The investigators found that long-term exposure to acid rain can stunt the growth of some plants. The two crops most injured by the one-hour spraying—tomatoes and soybeans—also suffered the greatest growth reductions in the long-term-exposure test. Winter wheat and lettuce, the two crops least injured in the earlier test, showed little reduction in growth.

The scientists also found, in both tests, that different varieties of each kind of crop suffered varying degrees of damage from acid rain. They said it may be possible to take genes from acid-resistant varieties and insert them into the more vulnerable plants, thereby increasing those plants' tolerance of acidity.

Helpful fungi. Microorganisms called *mycorhizal fungi,* common in the soil, are beneficial to plants and should be protected, agricultural scientists at the Plant Development Productivity Research Unit in Albany, Calif., reported

in October 1989. They said that growers who want to get the most results out of the fungi should be careful when applying fungicides, fertilizers, or other chemicals that make life harder for these soil dwellers.

Fungi are a group of nongreen plants, which also includes mushrooms and yeasts. Mycorhizal fungi live in the roots of most crop plants, sending out threadlike filaments called *hyphae.* The hyphae act as miniature pipelines, drawing nutrients from the soil into the plant. The network of hyphae around a plant, by penetrating spaces that even the finest plant roots do not reach, may also help hold the soil together and reduce erosion.

The researchers said that mycorhizal fungi may also make it possible for farmers to cut back on the use of fertilizers that contain phosphorus. They explained that the fungi act as microscopic shuttles, bringing phosphorus—as well as zinc and copper—from the soil to plants.

Pig breeding by computer. On Feb. 1, 1990, U.S. researchers completed a computer system that makes it easier for swine breeders to select parental lines of hogs. The quality of such selections determines the quality of offspring—and, ultimately, the grade of meat that shows up in supermarkets.

The computer system, developed by agricultural researchers at Purdue University, is based on *across-herd* genetic evaluations of swine. Across-herd means that pork producers can compare animals from herds throughout the United States, looking for specific genetic characteristics, such as fast growth and the tendency to produce numerous and healthy offspring. They can also look for and purchase pigs from lines that produce leaner meat.

Safer milk supplies. Researchers in Texas announced in February 1990 that they had found a compound that, when added to grain tainted with *aflatoxin*, prevents dairy cows from producing contaminated milk. Aflatoxin is a natural poison produced by a grain-infecting fungus.

High levels of aflatoxin can cause fatal poisoning in human beings and in some animals, such as pigs. Small amounts may cause liver cancer.

The tests were conducted by scientists at Texas A&M University and the ARS, both in College Station, and at Prairie View A&M University. They added the compound, called hydrated sodium calcium aluminosilicate (HSCAS), to aflatoxin-contaminated feed given to dairy cows. Although cows are not harmed by aflatoxin, it can get into their milk.

The milk of the cows receiving HSCAS did contain a measurable amount of aflatoxin. But, depending on the dose-size of HSCAS, it was 20 to 60 per cent less than the level of aflatoxin in the milk of cows fed the same diet but not given the protective compound. Furthermore, the amount of aflatoxin in milk from cows given the largest doses of HSCAS was well within the 0.5 parts per billion limit set by the United States Food and Drug Administration.   [Steve Cain]

In the Special Reports section, see GENETICS HEADS FOR THE SUPERMARKET. In WORLD BOOK, see AGRICULTURE.

Anthropology

A comprehensive analysis of 1.7-million-year-old *Australopithecus robustus* fossils—along with stone and bone tools—found in South Africa suggests, contrary to common belief, that these ruggedly built early *hominids* were capable of making tools. (Hominids by the narrowest definition include modern human beings and our closest human and prehuman ancestors.) The research was reported in August 1989 by physical anthropologist Fred Grine and anatomist Randall L. Susman of the State University of New York at Stony Brook.

Australopithecus robustus, which became extinct about 1 million years ago, existed at the same time as other hominid species, including species of *Homo*, the genus to which modern human beings belong.

Prehistoric toolmakers. The *A. robustus* fossils were unearthed in a cave at Swartkrans, near Pretoria, along with fossils belonging to the genus *Homo* and stone and bone tools. Anthropologists had thought that the tools found in the oldest levels at Swartkrans, dating to about 1.7 million years ago, had been made by a species of *Homo*.

Fossils of *A. robustus* are much more common at these oldest levels, however. In addition, Grine and Susman's analysis of *A. robustus* hand bones suggests that this species was anatomically capable of making tools. For example, the scientists reported *A. robustus* thumbs showed signs of a muscle used for grasping objects with precision. This muscle is found in modern human beings.

Prehuman vegetarians. Susman's analysis of the tools found with the *A. robustus* fossils provides evidence supporting the theory that this hominid was a vegetarian. Wear patterns on the tools suggest that they were used for digging rather than for butchering animals.

Brain impressions. New studies of *Australopithecus africanus* suggest that this hominid, which lived about 2 million to 3 million years ago in southern Africa, may have been both more apelike and humanlike than previously believed. Most anthropologists con-

A Controversy over Remains

The painstaking work of archaeologists has contributed much to what is known about the original Native American inhabitants of North America. From archaeological sites scattered across the continent have come pottery, jewelry, tools, and human bones from the richly varied societies that lived, fought, and intermingled for thousands of years before Europeans ever set eyes on their land.

To archaeologists, these objects are the source of invaluable and irreplaceable scientific information. The skeletal remains, in particular, have enabled scientists to study the diseases and diets of ancient Native Americans, trace the biological relationships among different groups, and even chart their migration patterns.

But the objects archaeologists call scientific artifacts are, to Native Americans, the sacred relics of their ancestors. And they contend the removal of these remains from tribal lands was not only illegal and morally offensive but also an act of profound desecration. For more than a decade, they have argued that the skeletal remains should be removed from museum collections and reburied.

For years, most museums in the United States have had a policy of returning skeletal remains to modern Native Americans if a direct link to a particular tribe could be proved. In 1988, for example, the Smithsonian Institution in Washington, D.C., returned to the Blackfeet Indians of Montana bones that were dug up in 1892 from a tribal grave site by collectors working for the Army Medical Museum. But such cases were rare because the required proof of kinship was so rigorous.

In recent years, pressure from Native American groups and scientists' increasing appreciation of the achievements of Native Americans have led to a greater sensitivity toward the skeletal remains. Several states, including California and Massachusetts, have passed laws giv-

Native Americans dig a grave for Seminole Indian remains returned for reburial by the University of South Dakota at the newly established National Indian Cemetery near Wounded Knee, S. Dak., in August 1989.

ing Native Americans some say in the disposition of newly discovered remains.

Native Americans and a number of universities and scientific institutions negotiated settlements that represented significant progress in 1989 toward ending their often-bitter debate. Under these pacts, the institutions agreed to turn over large parts of their Indian collections, especially skeletal remains, to Native Americans for reburial.

In 1989, the Field Museum of Natural History in Chicago and the University of Minnesota, among other institutions, adopted more liberal policies on returning remains. In June, Stanford University in Palo Alto, Calif., decided to give to the modern Ohlone Indians of northern California an archaeological collection that had been recovered in the 1950's and 1960's from two sites in the San Francisco Bay area. Some of the items are 6,000 years old.

Perhaps the most significant agreement was that adopted in September by the Smithsonian Institution, which has the largest collection of Native American skeletons in the United States. The museum announced that instead of requiring proof of a direct hereditary link to some living person, it would, in the future, return skeletal remains and other objects to a modern tribe if there is a "preponderance of evidence" connecting the ancient and modern tribal groups.

In May 1990, as part of the agreement, the Smithsonian appointed five people to a committee that will evaluate the evidence and decide whether the remains should be returned or retained by the Smithsonian. The Smithsonian speculated that under the new policy, 5 to 10 per cent of the museum's collection of some 18,500 skeletons may be returned.

Part of the reason for the Smithsonian's change of heart appeared to be political. The museum planned to build a new National Museum of the American Indian in Washington. But Native Americans insisted that the remains issue be settled first. To win approval—and funding—for the new museum from Congress, the Smithsonian agreed to the compromise.

But there was more to it than that. Robert McCormick Adams, secretary of the Smithsonian and himself an anthropologist, had, after careful thought, concluded that the "anguish" of the Native American community was "a weight one ultimately cannot carry." He also argued that the religious feelings of Native Americans could be as important as the demands of science.

Native American groups applauded the shift in attitude, saying that the new policies would help make amends for the disrespect they believe archaeologists have shown for their religious beliefs by digging up and displaying the remains of their ancestors.

But not everyone feels the same way. Many scientists adamantly oppose the new policies. They argue that in many cases the remains have no real connection with modern American Indians. In some parts of the United States, especially the Southwest, tribes were rooted in one area for long periods. But, the scientists point out, before the European conquest of North America, most Native Americans, especially those living in the Great Plains region, ranged far and wide. And in some cases, the modern tribes to which Native Americans claim allegiance are somewhat artificial groupings that arose only when European settlers confined tribes to reservations. As a result, in the case of skeletal remains older than a few hundred years, it is usually impossible to establish any direct link with modern descendants.

Archaeologist Bert Gerow, now retired from Stanford University, who unearthed most of the Ohlone bones in the university's collection, criticized Stanford's decision on these grounds. He argued that the connection between the archaeological remains and modern Ohlones is too weak to justify the wholesale return of the collection. And he said the decision would result in a loss of knowledge of the way of life and cultural sophistication of the Ohlones.

Archaeologist John Rick, the curator of the Stanford University Museum, defended the decision, however. He argued that the California sites had been continuously inhabited for thousands of years and were in the middle of a region in which only one language was spoken. Although this does not prove that only one tribal group inhabited the two sites continuously from 6,000 years ago until comparatively recent times, Rick says that the Ohlone were the only plausible modern descendants.

Although Stanford, the Smithsonian, and other institutions have embarked on a new attempt to balance the scientific and cultural value of archaeological remains with the religious feelings of Native Americans, many hard decisions lie ahead. At Stanford, for example, Rick and others are still negotiating with Native American groups to determine what remains should be returned and whether any additional research may be carried out on those parts of the collection deemed particularly important.

Despite the new agreements, there are still those who think that nothing should be returned unless there is a direct link to a living person; and there are those who think every Native American skeleton deserves a proper religious burial. Few believe that the debate between the two sides is over.   [David Lindley]

Anthropology

Continued

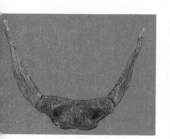

A fossilized bone found in a cave in Israel, *below,* suggests that Neanderthals may have been capable of speech. The fossil, which is 6,000 years old, is a U-shaped bone called a hyoid. The Neanderthal hyoid is nearly identical to modern hyoids. In modern human beings, the hyoid is connected by muscles to parts of the *larynx* (voice box), *below right,* and is instrumental in producing speech.

sider *A. africanus* a close relative or, possibly, a direct human ancestor.

In August 1989, a team of scientists led by Dean Falk of the State University of New York at Albany reported on their analysis of grooves in the *brain cast* of the Taung skull, an *A. africanus* fossil found in South Africa in 1924. A brain cast is a fossilized impression of the brain imprinted on the inside of the skull. The grooves in the brain cast represent folds in the surface of the brain. The pattern of these grooves varies in different species, depending on the number of folds and their location on the brain's surface. The scientists concluded that the pattern of grooves in the Taung brain cast more closely resembles the pattern found in apes than that in human beings.

Some anthropologists, however, argued that simply looking at the pattern of grooves may not be an accurate way of determining how complex *A. africanus*'s brain was and, thus, how intelligent this species was. They noted that the extent of folding in the brain is more closely related to expansion of

the brain's outer layers. And they pointed out that 2 million to 3 million years ago, the brains of hominids had not become, relative to body size, larger than those of apes. That does not necessarily mean, however, that *A. africanus*'s brain had not grown more complex than apes' brains.

Brain size. The brain of *A. africanus* was smaller on average than scientists have thought, according to research reported in February 1990 by scientists led by physical anthropologist Glenn C. Conroy of Washington University Medical School in St. Louis, Mo. To determine brain size, anthropologists measure the volume of the *braincase,* the part of the skull that houses the brain. But the scarcity of *A. africanus* skulls—only six reasonably complete skulls have been found—has made it difficult for anthropologists to determine accurately the average size of this hominid species' brain. In addition, one of the skulls is so clogged with stone that scientists have been unable to measure the braincase directly.

Conroy and his colleagues used com-

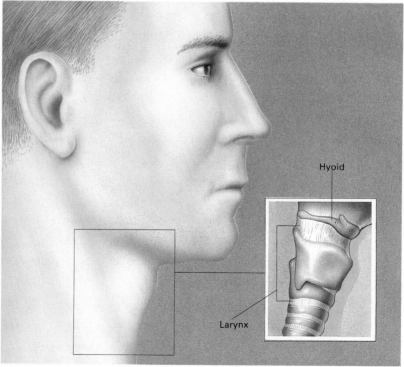

Hyoid

Larynx

Archaeology, Old World

Continued

in Canberra discovered that blood residues on a stone slab from an ancient village in eastern Turkey belonged to an extinct species of cattle that lived about 9,000 years ago.

The village, Çayönü Tepesi, is one of the earliest known farming villages. The stone slab was found in a building where archaeologists have discovered more than 90 human skulls and several human skeletons. The archaeologists speculate that the stone slab may have been used in rituals, perhaps even in human sacrifice.

To identify the blood on the slab, Wood and Loy first extracted and then crystallized the *hemoglobin* in the residues. Hemoglobin is an oxygen-carrying molecule that gives red blood cells their color. The hemoglobin crystals of different animal species vary in size and shape. As a result, the scientists were able to identify the blood as that of human beings, sheep, and an unidentified third animal species.

Later at the site, Wood and Loy found blood residues in the bones of a now-extinct form of cattle. The hemo-

globin in these residues matched that of the unidentified species.

Language and farming. Contrary to common belief, the spread of Indo-European languages—which are spoken today by about half the world's population—was peaceful and accompanied the spread of agriculture. That conclusion was reported in October 1989 by archaeologist Colin Renfrew of Cambridge University in England. The Indo-European language family includes dozens of languages, including English, Spanish, Russian, and Hindi.

Renfew's research challenges the traditional view that the parent Indo-European language was spread by nomadic warriors from the region north of the Black Sea in what is now the western Soviet Union. According to this theory, beginning about 2000 B.C., these nomads, who spoke a language known to modern scholars as proto-Indo-European, began to move out from their homeland. As they conquered most of the peoples of western Asia and Europe, they imposed their language on their subjects. Over the

A diver uses a new ultrasound system rather than an underwater drawing board to record the location of a clay pot among the wreckage of an ancient ship found off the Greek island of Dokos in the Aegean Sea. Receivers on the sea floor relay the signals to a nearby ship. There a computer converts the signals into a three-dimensional map of the site, which may be the world's oldest known shipwreck. More than 500 pots and other artifacts found there were dated to about 2250 B.C.

Treasures of Nimrud

Among the newly found treasures unearthed at the ancient Assyrian city of Nimrud (also called Kalhu) in northern Iraq, *above,* were, *below and clockwise from left,* gold earrings with dangling conical bells, a gold mesh crown, and heavy gold cuffs studded with semiprecious stones. Iraqi archaeologists, who announced the discovery in October 1989, found more than 57 kilograms (125 pounds) of beautifully crafted gold jewelry in previously unexcavated tombs at least 2,400 years old. Archaeologists have been digging at the site since the mid-1800's.

Archaeology, Old World

Continued

centuries, this language evolved into the languages spoken in these areas today.

By studying the similarities and differences in various Indo-European languages, scholars have constructed models that trace the spread of proto-Indo-European through Europe. According to some models, however, proto-Indo-European did not originate in the western Soviet Union but in what is now Turkey.

Some archaeologists also argue that Turkey was the birthplace of a form of farming that became common in Europe in the 7000's B.C. This type of farming involved growing wheat and barley and raising sheep and goats. The archaeologists note that the wild species of wheat and barley from which domesticated versions of these crops developed are native to eastern Turkey. Some of the oldest known farming villages have also been found in this region.

One theory explaining how agriculture spread to Europe focuses on the population growth that accompanied the rise of farming and the availability of a more abundant food supply. According to this theory, agriculture was spread by succeeding generations of farmers moving out from their parents' farms in search of land for their own fields and flocks. By this peaceful process, farming could have spread from Turkey to northern Europe in just 1,500 years.

Renfrew suggests that the spread of proto-Indo-European accompanied the spread of farming. He also argues that a variation of this process may explain the continued existence in Europe of some non-Indo-European languages. Among these are Basque (spoken in northeastern Spain and southern France), Finnish, Estonian, and Hungarian. He speculates that while newcomers may have brought farming to some areas, hunters and gatherers in other areas may have adopted the practice from their neighbors. As a result, the languages spoken by local people may have survived.

Medieval Russian city. A report on archaeological excavations at Novgorod, one of the oldest cities in Russia, was issued in February 1990 by Russian historian Valentin L. Yanin of Moscow State University in the Soviet Union. Novgorod is about 150 kilometers (90 miles) south of Leningrad. In medieval times, it was one of the most important cities in eastern Europe.

Novgorod was founded in the 800's A.D. Until the late 1400's, its commercial and political power extended from Estonia in the west to beyond the Ural Mountains in the east, and from the Arctic Ocean in the north to the upper Volga River in the south.

Excavations at Novgorod have revealed an abundance of wooden structures and more than 130,000 household items, religious objects, and other artifacts. Most are in a nearly perfect state of preservation because underlying the soil is a thick layer of dense clay that prevents the drainage of rain water and floodwater. As a result, the soil is saturated with moisture, which has preserved the buried material.

Yanin and his team found the lower parts of numerous wooden buildings that survived the many fires that periodically swept the city. They also unearthed many wooden streets, some of them 30 layers thick.

One of the most significant discoveries was 700 letters written on birchbark. The letters, which date from the mid-1000's to the early 1400's, include lawsuits, orders for commercial goods, and personal correspondence.

An abundance of goods found in the Novgorod excavations challenges the theory that medieval Russian cities lacked skilled craftworkers and imported their manufactured goods. Novgorod's artisans produced high-quality leather products, wooden combs, metal locks, jewelry, iron knives, glassware, and many other products. Imported items, which came from as far away as Iran and England, seem to have consisted chiefly of raw materials unavailable locally.

Yanin also reported that Novgorod's ancient books and artifacts indicate that many elements of Russian law and government were developed by the inhabitants of Novgorod themselves, not brought in by Western Europeans, as some scholars had previously thought.   [Robert J. Wenke]

In the Special Reports section, see THE MYSTERIES OF GREAT ZIMBABWE. In WORLD BOOK, see ARCHAEOLOGY.

Astronomy, Extragalactic

Several reports on telescopic observations of how galaxies are distributed in the universe were released in 1989 and 1990. The observations revealed that the galaxies are part of vast structures extending for hundreds of millions of *light-years*. (A light-year is the distance light travels in one year, about 9.5 trillion kilometers [5.9 trillion miles].) The existence of these huge structures puzzled *cosmologists* (scientists who study the early universe). They wondered how matter came to be "clumped" so unevenly when the distribution of matter was perfectly smooth soon after the *big bang*—the explosive event that astronomers believe created the universe.

Great Wall. Among the newly found extragalactic structures was one named the Great Wall. Its discovery was made in November 1989 by astronomers Margaret Geller and John P. Huchra of the Harvard-Smithsonian Center for Astrophysics in Cambridge, Mass., as part of a survey of galaxy positions and distances in the northern sky. So far, 10,000 galaxies have been measured in the survey.

The Great Wall, an extremely long chain of clusters of galaxies, may be the largest cosmic structure ever found, about 550 million light-years long and 200 million light-years wide but only about 15 million light-years thick. It is located about 200 million to 300 million light-years from Earth.

More walls. Cosmologists trying to explain the Great Wall could not dismiss it as a one-of-a-kind formation, because further evidence soon showed that such structures appear to be commonplace. In February 1990, British, United States, and Hungarian astronomers led by Thomas J. Broadhurst of the University of Durham in England announced the results of a survey of galaxies in the directions of the *galactic poles*. (The galactic poles are part of a system of coordinates that astronomers use to describe the directions of celestial objects as seen from Earth in relation to the direction to the center of the Milky Way.) Our view of distant space is least obscured by interstellar clouds when we look toward the galactic poles.

This survey revealed the presence of 13 similar "walls," roughly spaced at intervals of several hundred million light-years along a line of sight that extended 7 billion light-years from Earth. The Broadhurst team's survey is different from that of the Center for Astrophysics, which is a wide-angle mapping project that locates galaxies across a great area of the sky but does not extend very far into space. In contrast, the Broadhurst team termed theirs a "pencil-beam survey" because it examined a small area of the sky but looked out extremely far.

Great Attractor. The existence of a huge concentration of mass known as the Great Attractor was confirmed in January 1990 by astronomers Alan Dressler of The Observatories of the Carnegie Institution of Washington in Pasadena, Calif., and Sandra Faber of the University of California at Santa Cruz. The Great Attractor's existence had been suspected since 1987. The Great Attractor may be a group of *superclusters*—clusters of clusters of galaxies—located about 150 million light-years from Earth. The Great Attractor has a gravitational force so powerful that it is pulling the entire Milky Way and thousands of other nearby galaxies in its direction. According to Dressler and Faber, the Great Attractor appears to have a mass 30,000 trillion times greater than the mass of the sun.

The evidence that seemed to confirm its existence involved observations of galaxies located beyond the Great Attractor. Those galaxies appeared to be flowing toward the Milky Way as our Galaxy streams toward them. All of the motions involved are measured with respect to the so-called Hubble flow—that is, the general expansion of the universe. In the Hubble flow, galaxies recede from each other, and the farther apart they are, the faster they are moving apart. The Great Attractor apparently lies between the Milky Way and these galaxies flowing toward it. Independent observations of about 50 spiral galaxies—reported in January 1990 by astronomers under Robert A. Schommer of Rutgers University in New Brunswick, N.J.—also showed clear evidence that galaxies behind the Great Attractor are moving toward the Attractor and the Milky Way.

Explanation needed. Theories of galaxy formation in the early universe were seemingly unable to account for

Astronomy, Extragalactic

Continued

A blur of light far out in the universe was revealed by a sensitive electronic camera to be two quasars (arrows), *below*, about 100,000 light-years apart, close enough to be parts of colliding galaxies. Quasars are powerful energy sources at the center of some distant galaxies, and the close pair, discovered in January 1990, lends support to the theory, depicted in an artist's illustration, *below right*, that quasars can form when galaxies collide. The collision may concentrate enough gas and stars at the galactic center to create a black hole, which powers the quasar.

structures as large as the Great Wall or for flowing motions like that caused by the Great Attractor. The estimated 15-billion- to 24-billion-year age of the universe was not deemed long enough to allow for structures and flow patterns to grow to the scales of the two "Greats."

An alternative possibility was that the distribution of hot gas that filled the universe in the immediate aftermath of the big bang was not entirely uniform. At least some regions of space might have been filled by slightly denser gas than other regions. Such structures might then have evolved into such formations as the Great Wall and the Great Attractor. But the first results from the *Cosmic Background Explorer* (*COBE*) satellite, reported in January 1990, seem to have eliminated this possiblity.

COBE's findings. The National Aeronautics and Space Administration (NASA) launched *COBE* into polar orbit above Earth on Nov. 18, 1989. The spacecraft carried three instruments, two of them devoted to studying

the microwave background radiation. The microwave background was emitted by hot gas that formed in the aftermath of the big bang. On Jan. 13, 1990, a team led by astronomer George Smoot of the University of California at Berkeley reported that one COBE instrument showed that the radiation is the same strength, to within 1 part in 10,000, in all directions.

Another instrument, monitored by astronomer John C. Mather of NASA's Goddard Space Flight Center in Greenbelt, Md., found that the spectrum of the microwave background radiation was identical to that expected from a theoretical *black body* at a temperature of 2.735 Kelvins (-270°C or -455°F.). (A black body is an object that absorbs all radiation that falls on it, reflecting none; the energy it gives off depends on its temperature.) This *COBE* finding confirmed that the universe, about 100,000 years after the big bang, had the properties of an opaque hot gas, as predicted by the big bang theory. It also disproved a measurement made by instruments on a rocket

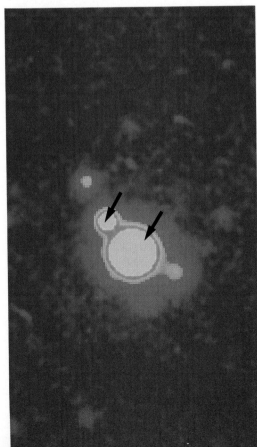

Astronomy, Extragalactic

Continued

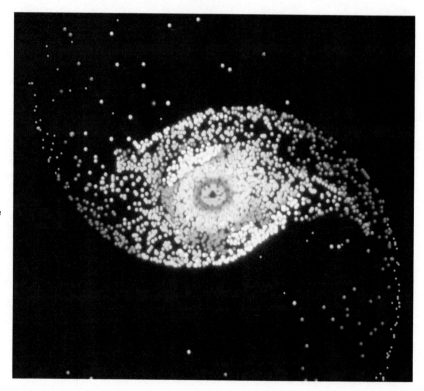

A computer simulation shows that an "eyeball" galaxy can form when one galaxy collides with another. After creating the simulations, astronomers reported in January 1990 that they found more than two dozen real examples of eyeball-shaped galaxies, apparently formed by colliding galaxies.

launched from Japan, which had suggested that at some wavelengths the microwave background's spectrum was different from that of a black body.

The findings from the two *COBE* instruments showed that shortly after the big bang, the universe was in apparent conformity with the *cosmological principle*—a widely held assumption among astronomers that the universe, when considered on very large scales, is *homogeneous* (having the same properties in all locations, when averaged over great volumes) and *isotropic* (the same in all directions). How the universe evolved from this state to form clusters of galaxies in huge structures, such as the Great Wall and the Great Attractor, has emerged as the most puzzling problem cosmologists face.

Faraway quasar. The most distant object ever found was reported in December 1989 by astronomers Donald P. Schneider of the Institute for Advanced Study in Princeton, N.J.; Maarten Schmidt of the California Institute of Technology in Pasadena; and James E. Gunn of the Princeton University Observatory in New Jersey. The distant object—a *quasar* (a term given to certain of the most energetic objects in the universe)—was detected and studied with the 5-meter (200-inch) Hale Telescope at the Palomar Observatory near San Diego.

The distance to faraway objects is measured according to their *red shift*—a shift in the wavelength of light given off by the object toward the longer, or red, wavelengths of the object's spectrum. This shift occurs when the light source is moving away from an observer. In this phenomenon, called the *Doppler effect*, the length of a traveling wave increases when the distance between the source of the wave and the observer increases. The newly discovered quasar—called PC 1158 + 4635—has the largest reliably measured red shift ever reported: 4.73. This means that the wavelength of its light has been shifted by 473 per cent when compared with the spectrum of an object at rest.

The greater the red shift, the faster the object is moving, and the faster the object is moving, the farther away it is. This quasar is so far away that the light detected at Palomar, traveling at 299,792 kilometers (186,282 miles) per second, began its journey through space when the universe was very young, only about one-fourteenth of its present age of 15 billion to 24 billion years. So when we see this light, we are looking back in time to about 1 billion to 2 billion years after the big bang.

According to the leading theory of how the universe has evolved since the big bang—called the *cold dark matter theory*—few if any galaxies should have formed so early in the universe that we will observe them with red shifts larger than 4. The cold dark matter theory holds that galaxy formation took place at a later period in the universe's evolution, and quasars are believed to be the bright centers of galaxies. So the discovery of a quasar at a red shift of 4.73 is causing cosmologists to revise this theory.

Microlensing. A new type of gravitational lensing was reported in December 1989 by British astronomers under

Michael J. Irwin of the Institute of Astronomy at Cambridge, England. Gravitational lensing is the bending of light by gravity. Previously known cases of gravitational lensing include those in which the light from a single distant quasar has been bent to form two or more images, so that there appear to be two, three, or even four quasars. The gravity at work in these cases is due to an intervening galaxy or cluster located roughly midway between Earth and the distant quasar.

In the new-found form of gravitational lensing, known as *microlensing*, a relatively small object, such as a star, is responsible for the bending of light. Microlensing causes the image of a distant quasar to brighten and fade as its light rays are bent toward or away from Earth. Irwin's team found that one of the four images of a lensed quasar had brightened significantly since the lensed quasar was discovered in 1987. [Stephen P. Maran]

In the Special Reports section, see AN ORBITING EYE ON THE UNIVERSE. In WORLD BOOK, see ASTRONOMY.

Astronomy, Galactic

Mysterious activity at the core of our Milky Way Galaxy continued to attract the attention of astronomers during 1989 and 1990. In May 1989, a group of scientists headed by Marvin Levanthal of Bell Laboratories in Murray Hill, N.J., detected gamma rays from a region of the galactic center. Because gamma rays do not penetrate Earth's atmosphere, the measurements had to be made by a high-altitude, balloon-borne instrument.

Gamma rays are a form of electromagnetic radiation that have the shortest wavelengths and require the highest energy to be produced. Thus, when gamma rays are detected from space, astronomers know that their source must involve very high-energy processes, such as gas or other matter falling into a *black hole* (an object so dense not even light can escape its gravitational field).

Astronomers believe that black holes evolve from two different processes. *Stellar black holes* form when very large, massive stars exhaust all of their internal energy sources and collapse. *Super-*

massive black holes may result from the merger of two or more galaxies or during the process of a galaxy's formation. Supermassive black holes may contain a million to a hundred million times the mass of an ordinary star.

Stellar black hole. An analysis of the gamma rays that were observed in May was reported in August 1989 by astronomers Richard E. Lingenfelter of the University of California at San Diego and Reuven Ramaty of the National Aeronautics and Space Administration's (NASA's) Goddard Space Flight Center in Greenbelt, Md. Lingenfelter and Ramaty concluded that the gamma rays Levanthal detected probably came from a stellar black hole. The astronomers reached their conclusion on the basis of calculations showing how gamma rays are emitted and by studying gamma rays emitted from a probable stellar black hole known as *Cygnus X-1*. Their findings do not, however, contradict other evidence that indicates there may be a supermassive black hole at the galactic center.

New Views of Our Milky Way Galaxy

Our Milky Way Galaxy may not be a normal spiral galaxy, like the one above. After studying the motions of hydrogen gas in the outer regions of the Milky Way, astronomers reported in January 1990 that our Galaxy may resemble a barred spiral galaxy, *above right,* in which spiral arms begin at the end of a barlike section of stars. A false-color map of radio waves coming from the Milky Way's center, *right,* shows swirling gas clouds (blue, orange, and white) that surround what may be an invisible black hole.

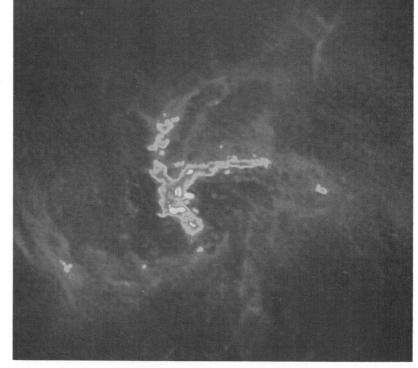

Explosions in the core. X rays are only slightly longer in wavelength than gamma rays, and they also require a source of high energy for their production, such as a *supernova*, the powerful explosion of a massive star. In June 1989, a team of scientists from Nagoya University in Japan reported a new form of X-ray emission from the galactic center detected by a Japanese satellite observatory called *Ginga*.

Although X rays from the galactic core had previously been detected, this discovery revealed a concentration of X rays of a particular wavelength. Atoms and *molecules* (combinations of atoms bonded together) each emit or absorb radiation at specific wavelengths. Because of this, astronomers can identify the chemical elements of which a distant object is made by analyzing the wavelengths of radiation the object gives off or absorbs.

The newly discovered X rays have wavelengths characteristic of iron. From this fact, the Japanese scientists determined that gas in the galactic core has been heated to extremely high temperatures and that the core contains a larger concentration of iron than is found in the outer regions of our Galaxy where our solar system is located. These two findings led to the conclusion that a massive explosion occurred in the galactic core, causing shock waves that heated the gas and also dispersed heavy elements such as iron into *interstellar space* (the space between the stars).

Most heavy elements are created as a result of nuclear reactions in the cores of stars or through explosive events such as supernovae. As the galaxy ages, the quantities of the heavy elements produced and dispersed in these ways increase. The central region of the galaxy must have undergone a greater amount of stellar "recycling" than the outer regions, because the iron content in the inner region is higher.

Chemicals in clouds. Between June and September 1989, astronomers identified three more chemical compounds in *interstellar clouds*. These clouds are concentrations of gas and dust that can become dense enough to collapse due to gravity, forming new stars. For this reason, astronomers want to gain a better understanding of the physical and chemical properties of interstellar gas clouds.

The gas in interstellar clouds can be in the form of atoms or, if it is dense enough and the temperature low enough, in the form of molecules. Molecules can be broken apart into atoms by high temperatures or intense radiation. Therefore, astronomers find molecules in deep space only inside interstellar clouds, where there is some protection from high-energy radiation and where the temperatures are very cold.

Silicon carbide molecules were detected in June by a group of astronomers from Spain and the United States, who analyzed data from telescopes that detected *infrared* (heat) radiation.

Molecules of acetylene were discovered in three interstellar clouds in July by astronomer John H. Lacy of the University of Texas in Austin, along with a group of coinvestigators. They also used an infrared telescope. Then, the discovery of carbon dioxide in solid form—commonly known as dry ice—was reported in August by French astronomers at the University of Paris and the Paris Observatory.

Carbon dioxide, a familiar gas in Earth's atmosphere, is produced by animals, decaying organic matter, and the burning of fossil fuels. But it is rarely found as a gas in space because it is unlikely to form at the low densities of interstellar clouds, where there are few collisions between atoms. The collisions that do occur between carbon and oxygen atoms are more likely to form other gas molecules, such as carbon monoxide (a molecule with one oxygen atom), rather than carbon dioxide (with two oxygen atoms). Under the conditions of interstellar space, it is easier for carbon dioxide to form as solid coatings on dust grains.

More complex molecules. How to detect more complex molecules—some containing as many as 30 or more atoms—in interstellar clouds was the subject of three separate studies reported in June 1989. These molecules belong to a class of chemicals called the *polycyclic aromatic hydrocarbons* (PAH's). They consist of interlocking six-sided rings of carbon atoms with an assortment of hydrogen or other kinds of atoms attached around the sides.

249

Because these molecules are very large and complex, astronomers have not known precisely what wavelengths of radiation they emit or absorb. The studies reported in June, however, indicated that by analyzing laboratory data, astronomers can determine what wavelengths correspond to these large molecules.

In one study, researchers at the University of Michigan in Ann Arbor found that infrared wavelengths from PAH's analyzed in the laboratory matched closely with infrared wavelengths detected in interstellar clouds. In a complementary study, astronomers at the NASA Ames Research Center at Moffett Field, California, measured interstellar infrared emissions and found that they corresponded to those predicted from laboratory measurements.

Finally, using theoretical calculations, astronomers at Pennsylvania State University in University Park described a process by which PAH molecules might form in the outermost regions of *red giant stars* (stars that have exhausted their nuclear fuel and have begun to expand and turn reddish in color). These outermost regions are where most interstellar dust grains form. Now, the Pennsylvania researchers have shown that PAH's can also form in these regions.

Brown dwarfs. Several faint objects found in the Pleiades star cluster may be *brown dwarfs*, according to a September 1989 report by a group headed by astronomer John R. Stauffer of the University of California at Santa Cruz. Brown dwarfs are objects that condense out of gas and dust in much the way stars do. But they lack sufficient mass to ignite nuclear reactions and actually become stars.

The faint objects detected by Stauffer have the properties expected of brown dwarfs. They are very cool, and their masses are less than 8 per cent the mass of the sun. According to theoretical calculations, nuclear reactions begin in the core of an object only if it has a mass greater than 8 per cent of the sun's.   [Theodore P. Snow]

In WORLD BOOK, see ASTRONOMY.

Astronomy,
Solar System

Astronomers obtained their best views ever of the distant planet Neptune and its moon Triton in August 1989 when the *Voyager 2* spacecraft flew by the planet, returning close-up images of its atmosphere. *Voyager 2* also flew extremely close to Triton and sent back detailed images of its surface. In the Special Reports section, see NEPTUNE: LAST STOP ON A GRAND TOUR.

Atmospheric escape. Pluto's atmosphere is escaping the planet, astronomers at the University of Arizona in Tucson, the University of Colorado in Boulder, and the Massachusetts Institute of Technology in Cambridge reported in November 1989. They calculated that all the gas presently in Pluto's atmosphere will escape into space in less than 100,000 years.

These findings were based on telescope observations of Pluto over several years as the planet approached the sun. On Sept. 12, 1989, Pluto's orbital path reached its nearest point to the sun. This close approach, called *perihelion*, was still very far away from the sun—about 29 astronomical units (AU's). (One AU equals about 150 million kilometers [90 million miles], or roughly the distance from Earth to the sun.) But it gave astronomers their best look at Pluto since the planet was discovered in 1930.

The observations were aided by a series of eclipses that occurred between Pluto and its moon, Charon. At times, Charon passed in front of Pluto, and at other times, behind Pluto, as seen from Earth. These eclipses, along with observations made as a star passed behind Pluto, enabled astronomers to obtain new information about the size and mass of Pluto and the composition of its atmosphere.

Gas and gravity. Planetary atmospheres escape when the gravity of the planet is not strong enough to keep gas molecules from breaking free of the planet after colliding with each other. There are many collisions of gas molecules in atmospheres every second. The speed at which molecules collide depends upon the temperature of the gas and the mass of the individual molecules. The higher the temperature and the less massive the molecule, the greater its speed or *velocity*. If the average speed of the molecules is greater than the *escape velocity* of the planet (the speed necessary to escape the planet's gravitational force), then molecules will move into space.

The more massive the planet is, the greater its gravitational force is. Earth's gravity is powerful enough to prevent its atmosphere from escaping. Pluto, however, is a tiny planet, less than one-fifth the size of Earth, so Pluto's gravitational force is not as strong and its escape velocity is much less than that of Earth.

The researchers found that the gases in Pluto's atmosphere leak slowly into space over time. The loss is more rapid when Pluto is close to the sun and its gases are heated by sunlight, which increases the speed of the colliding gas molecules. When Pluto is farthest from the sun—about 50 AU—the atmosphere hardly leaks away at all.

Microwaves from planets. After observing microwave radiation given off by Saturn and Uranus, space scientists at the California Institute of Technology in Pasadena, Calif., reported in September 1989 that they had mapped the deep inner atmospheres of those giant planets. Radio astronomers used the Very Large Array (VLA) radio telescopes near Socorro, N. Mex., to probe for the microwaves, a type of radio wave. They are part of the *electromagnetic spectrum* (the different wavelengths of radiation, ranging from high-energy gamma and X rays through visible light and radio waves).

Photographs of Saturn and Uranus returned by the *Voyager 1* and *2* spacecraft had shown only the upper parts of the atmospheres. The deeper regions are blocked by clouds of ammonia on Saturn and by a methane haze on Uranus. Microwave radiation generated by the heat of the atmospheres, however, penetrates these clouds and so can be detected with radio telescopes on Earth.

To map the atmospheres of these far worlds requires very high *spatial resolution* (the ability to discern small features at large distances). The VLA was the

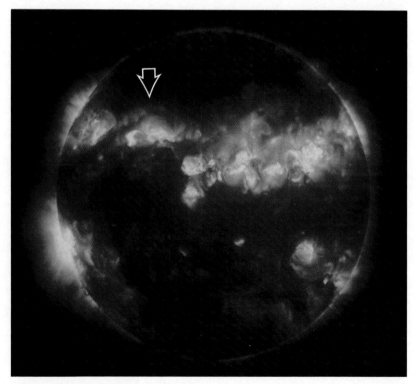

The sharpest X-ray image yet of the sun's *corona* (atmosphere) and of a *solar flare*—a magnetic disturbance that releases huge amounts of energy—was recorded by an X-ray telescope on board a sounding rocket in September 1989. The flare (arrow) reached a temperature of 10,000,000°C (18,000,000°F.). Other bright areas are also regions of magnetic activity but with temperatures of only 3,000,000°C (5,400,000°F.).

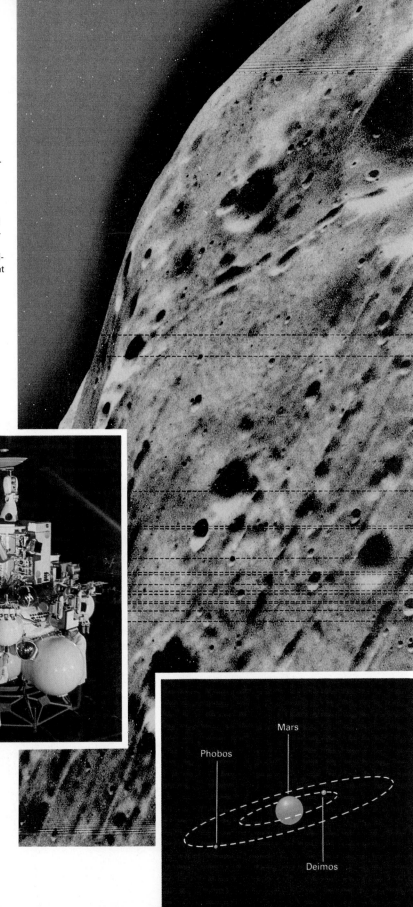

A Groovy Moon

Straight grooves and round meteorite craters mark the surface of Phobos, *right,* one of two moons that orbit Mars, *below right.* Pictures of the Martian moon, revealing 11 previously unknown grooves, were returned by the Soviet Union's *Phobos 2* spacecraft, *below,* and released by Soviet scientists in October 1989. Scientists think that Phobos and Deimos may be asteroids that were captured by Mars's gravity. What might have formed the grooves on Phobos is a mystery.

Mars

Phobos

Deimos

key to achieving this spatial resolution. Each of its 27 separate radio antennas, which are spaced along a Y-shaped set of railroad tracks, were "tuned" to receive microwave signals from the two planets. When the signals were combined by computers, the 27 separate antennas functioned as a single microwave receiver, or huge microwave "eye." Such a big receiver has very high spatial resolution.

Saturn's bands. The astronomers found that the bands or stripes that seem to encircle Saturn, so familiar from optical photographs, are also a feature of microwave radiation from the planet. The astronomers detected bands of higher microwave emissions from certain latitudes, indicating that ammonia and other obscuring gases that block microwaves were absent. The microwaves were therefore coming from hotter, deeper parts of the atmosphere. Other latitudes gave off less microwave emissions, indicating that these regions were cool and contained more of the microwave-blocking gases. Hence, gases in the deep atmosphere seem to be arranged in a banded structure that mimics the visible cloud bands higher up.

Scientists have long thought that the visible bands are caused by the atmospheric circulation of the planet: Heat deep within the planet causes warm air to rise, while cooler air sinks. The rising air columns produce clouds, and the sinking regions are clear. The rapid spin of the planet then smears the pattern out into the bands of clouds we see in optical photographs. The microwave data on Saturn imply that this spinning motion of the atmosphere extends deep below the visible tops of the clouds.

Bands in Uranus. The astronomers also reported similar observations of Uranus. Images from *Voyager 2* showed the planet was blanketed in a uniform blue haze with some hint of banding in this atmosphere. The microwave data showed more clearly that deep below the visible part of the atmosphere of Uranus, the amounts of the cloud-forming gas, ammonia, appear to vary in latitude, and this indicates a banded structure in the microwave part of the spectrum. The finding is significant, because even though Uranus has a weak source of heat coming from within its interior, it apparently is sufficient to cause warm gases to rise. It therefore appears that bands are common in the giant planets, regardless of how hot their interiors are.

Water on Io? The sulfurous, volcanic surface of Io, a moon of Jupiter, may contain some water, a group of astronomers reported in January 1990. The astronomers, based at the National Aeronautics and Space Administration's (NASA's) Ames Research Center at Moffett Field, California, observed Io from telescopes at Mount Lemmon, Ariz., and atop Mauna Kea in Hawaii.

By carefully measuring the spectrum of reflected sunlight from Io, the NASA astronomers were able to identify certain characteristics in the spectrum that indicated the presence of water. Careful comparison with spectra taken in the laboratory showed that the water was not in the form of ice but was probably chemically mixed with sulfur compounds. The scientists also found evidence for hydrogen sulfide.

The finding of water on Io's surface took astronomers by surprise because they had thought that Io was too hot for water to exist. Since the *Voyager* fly-bys of Io in 1979, astronomers have known that this moon is volcanically active, spewing sulfur and sulfur dioxide across the surface.

The source of energy for the volcanism is generally agreed to be the strong tidal pull of Jupiter's gravity. As Io moves in its orbit, the other satellites gently tug it and make Io's orbit noncircular. Consequently, Jupiter's pull becomes slightly unbalanced, causing twisting motions that heat up Io's rocky interior sufficiently to cause melting. Because of this long history of melting, astronomers thought that Io had been hot for so long that any water had long ago vaporized away.

The NASA astronomers speculated that a small amount of hydrogen may be left in Io's interior or, alternatively, that hydrogen atoms may come from other, icy moons, transported by Jupiter's magnetic field to Io, where the hydrogen combines with the sulfur dioxide to make water and hydrogen sulfide.   [Jonathan I. Lunine]

In WORLD BOOK, see ASTRONOMY; PLANETS.

Books
of Science

Here are 25 outstanding new science books suitable for the general reader. They have been selected from books published in 1989 and 1990.

Anthropology. *Native American Architecture* by Peter Nabokov and Robert Easton surveys Indian buildings and settlements in North America before and after the arrival of European settlers. (Oxford Univ. Press, 1989. 431 pp. illus. $50)

Astronomy. *Cosmic Catastrophes* by Clark R. Chapman and David Morrison studies natural catastrophes that have shaped our planet and could threaten it again. The authors cite evidence that catastrophic events, such as violent asteroid impacts, have changed the landscape of Earth and the other planets, contradicting the long-held belief that such planetary changes occur gradually. (Plenum, 1989. 302 pp. illus. $22.95)

Supernova!: The Exploding Star of 1987 by Donald Goldsmith records what scientists have learned from the appearance in 1987 of the brightest *supernova* (exploding star) in 400 years. Goldsmith also tells how stars form, how nuclear fusion fuels them, and how exploding stars create carbon, oxygen, and other chemical elements essential to life. (St. Martin's Press, 1989. 221 pp. illus. $15.95)

Biology. *The Darwinian Paradigm: Essays on Its History, Philosophy and Religious Implications* by Michael Ruse discusses how British naturalist Charles Darwin's ideas about evolution fit with the scientific thinking of his day. (Routledge, Chapman, & Hall, 1989. 299 pp. $25)

For the Love of Enzymes: The Odyssey of a Biochemist by Arthur Kornberg is a personal account of how steady advances in biochemistry have enabled us to understand heredity and the chemistry of life itself. Kornberg, an American biochemist, won the 1959 Nobel Prize in physiology or medicine for producing genetic material in a test tube. (Harvard Univ. Press, 1989. 336 pp. illus. $29.95)

Earth sciences. *Global Warming: Are We Entering the Greenhouse Century?* by Stephen H. Schneider reviews the evidence that Earth's climate is growing warmer and suggests ways that humankind may deal with rapid climatic change brought about by economic and population growth. (Sierra Club Bks., 1989. 317 pp. $18.95)

General science. *From Creation to Chaos: Classic Writings in Science*, edited by Bernard Dixon, gathers examples of scientific writing, some very short, chosen solely on the basis of literary quality. The book includes work by Sir Francis Bacon, an English philosopher of the 1600's; Charles Darwin, a British naturalist of the 1800's; and such modern writers as paleontologist Stephen Jay Gould, physician Oliver Sacks, and zoologist Sir Peter Medawar. (Blackwell, 1989. 280 pp. $29.95)

Seeing Voices: A Journey into the World of the Deaf by Oliver Sacks explores the extraordinary world of the deaf and the great subtlety and complexity of the sign language with which deaf people communicate. (University of Calif. Press, 1989. 180 pp. $14.95)

Mathematics. *Does God Play Dice?: The Mathematics of Chaos* by Ian Stewart explains the science of chaos, which is based on the idea that random variation directs many of the processes of everyday life, from changes in the weather to the metabolism of cells. (Blackwell, 1989. 320 pp. illus. $19.95)

Turbulent Mirror: An Illustrated Guide to Chaos Theory and the Science of Wholeness by John Briggs and F. David Peat looks at recent advances in biology, mathematics, and physics in light of chaos theory, which is leading to new ways of understanding the universe. (Harper & Row, 1989. 222 pp. illus. $22.50)

Natural history. *Africa's Mountains of the Moon: Journeys to the Snowy Sources of the Nile*, text and photographs by Guy Yeoman, is based on the author's journeys over 40 years in the magnificent Ruwenzori Range, mountains at the equator on the border between Uganda and Zaire. (Universe Bks., 1989. 176 pp. illus. $35)

Forest Primeval: The Natural History of an Ancient Forest by Chris Maser describes the diverse lives occupying a forest ecosystem. Maser traces the development of a wooded area in the Cascade Mountains of Oregon from A.D. 987 to the present. (Sierra Club Bks., 1989. 282 pp. illus. $25)

The Sagebrush Ocean: A Natural History of the Great Basin by Stephen Trimble is

Books
of Science
Continued

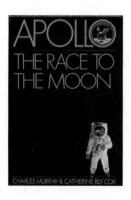

an introduction to the ecology and geography of the Great Plains of the United States. (University of Nev. Press, 1989. 260 pp. illus. $34.95)

Paleontology. *Dynamics of Dinosaurs and Other Extinct Giants* by R. McNeill Alexander uses the methods of physics and engineering to explain how dinosaurs lived and moved. Alexander uses available evidence to estimate dinosaurs' weight, their strength, how some swam or flew, and whether they were warm-blooded. (Columbia Univ. Press, 1989. 167 pp. illus. $30)

Wonderful Life: The Burgess Shale and the Nature of History by Stephen Jay Gould describes the unique fossil organisms discovered in the Burgess Shale, a deposit in British Columbia, Canada, and what the fossils tell us of the progress and predictability of evolutionary development. (Norton, 1989. 347 pp. illus. $19.95)

Physics. *Cosmogenesis: The Growth of Order in the Universe* by David Layzer explains the connection between *quantum physics*, a branch of physics that is based, in part, on the idea that matter and energy have characteristics of both particles and waves, and *cosmology*, the study of the general nature of the universe in space and time. Layzer argues that the universe did not begin as a fireball, but at temperatures close to absolute zero. (Oxford Univ. Press, 1990. 322 pp. illus. $24.95)

From Quarks to the Cosmos: Tools of Discovery by Leon M. Lederman and David N. Schramm shows how the small world of atoms and particles and the large world of stars and galaxies are being brought together by high-energy physics. The authors are using particle accelerators and astronomical observations to create a "theory of everything" that will explain how the universe began, how it got to be the way it is, and how it will end. (Scientific Am. Lib., 1989. 242 pp. illus. $32.95)

Memoirs by Andrei Sakharov, translated by Richard Lourie, is the personal account of the Soviet physicist who won the 1975 Nobel Peace Prize. The book tells of Sakharov's research on controlled nuclear fusion and his activities in defense of human rights. (Knopf, 1990. 740 pp. illus. $29.95)

Schrödinger: Life and Thought by Walter Moore offers fascinating insights into the life and work of the gifted Austrian physicist Erwin Schrödinger, winner of the 1933 Nobel Prize in physics for his mathematical equations describing the wavelike behavior of electrons. (Cambridge Univ. Press, 1989. 513 pp. illus. $39.50)

Space exploration. *Apollo: The Race to the Moon* by Charles Murray and Catherine Bly Cox is a history of the National Aeronautics and Space Administration project that culminated in astronaut Neil Armstrong's walk on the moon on July 20, 1969. (Simon & Schuster, 1989. 506 pp. illus. $24.95)

The Starflight Handbook: A Pioneer's Guide to Interstellar Travel by Eugene F. Mallove and Gregory L. Matloff discusses the challenges of interstellar travel, particularly the various forms of propulsion that might speed starships on their way and how people might cope with such lengthy voyages. (Wiley, 1989. 274 pp. $19.95)

Technology. *Robotics in Service* by Joseph F. Engelberger argues that the day of the service robot has arrived and describes advances in robot development, control systems, and artificial intelligence. (MIT Press, 1989. 250 pp. illus. $35)

Zoology. *Birds Asleep* by Alexander F. Skutch records the sleeping behavior of almost 500 species of birds. Birds spend almost half their time asleep, and Skutch tells us how, where, and how long they sleep. He also describes how they keep warm at night. (University of Tex. Press, 1989. 224 pp. illus. $24.95)

Birds of the Sea, Shore, and Tundra by Theodore Cross has more than 120 spectacular photographs of birds accumulated from more than 15 years of travel in the Arctic, the Central Pacific, and the Gulf Coast. Although there is no text, each picture is captioned, and the author provides a short guide to the art of photographing birds. (Weidenfeld & Nicolson, 1989. unpaged. illus. $65)

Crocodiles and Alligators, consulting editor Charles A. Ross, includes chapters on the reptiles' development over the past 200 million years, their behavior, their methods of reproduction, and their relationships with human beings. (Facts on File, 1989. 240 pp. illus. $35)   [William Goodrich Jones]

Botany

Plants detect and react to light reflected from neighboring plants, botanists at the University of Buenos Aires in Argentina reported in January 1990.

The Argentine scientists knew that a pigment called *phytochrome* enables plants to detect shade from other plants because it reacts to two kinds of red light—orange-red and far-red. When light strikes leaves, chlorophyll in the leaves absorbs most of the orange-red light, but the far-red light passes through. Therefore, far-red light is abundant in the shade from leaves. When phytochrome absorbs far-red light, it causes the plants' stems to grow. For this reason, plants in the center of a group of plants—where shade is deepest and comes from all sides—are tallest.

The researchers suspected that phytochrome also functions in much the same way when plants, though surrounded by other plants, are not in the shade. In such groupings, plants in the center are still tallest. In that case, the researchers theorized, phytochrome must be absorbing far-red light that is reflected from nearby plants. They tested that possibility with seedlings of mustard plants and of *Datura*, a plant related to the tomato.

The scientists placed transparent double cylinders around the plants' stems and filled the space between the inner and outer cylinders with either water—which allows both orange-red and far-red light to pass through—or a copper sulfate solution that absorbs far-red light. Thus, plants surrounded by cylinders containing copper sulfate solution could receive no far-red light coming from the side.

Among the seedlings at the center of a group, those that were surrounded by water-filled cylinders grew much more than those surrounded by cylinders containing copper sulfate solution. This result proved that the stem tissue of plants responds to far-red light reflected from nearby plants. When that source of light is cut off, the plants' growth is slowed.

Disturbed plants. If plants are shaken by water spray or wind, or if they are touched or damaged, they grow much less than protected plants. But why? In February 1990, researchers at Stanford University in California announced findings that may lead to an answer to that question.

Most outdoor plants are constantly subjected to mechanical stresses such as wind and being brushed by passing animals. Thus, stressed plants are the norm, while protected plants grow only in greenhouses. In an indoor environment, the difference can be striking between plants receiving experimental mechanical stresses and those left alone. Plants rubbed with the fingers just three times each day may be only one-fourth to one-third as tall as protected control plants, but their stems will be stronger.

Although scientists had studied this phenomenon for more than 20 years, they had been unable to explain it. The Stanford investigators discovered for the first time that at least four specific genes are involved in the plants' responses to disturbances.

The scientists studied a plant called *Arabidopsis*. They subjected potted *Arabidopsis* plants to stresses, including spraying them and cutting their leaves, and then did laboratory analyses of the substances produced by the plants. They found that within 10 to 30 minutes after the plants were stimulated, levels of four kinds of *messenger RNA* (mRNA) increased up to 100 times in the plants' cells. Messenger RNA is a molecule that carries out instructions in the genetic code—in this case, from four particular genes—for the production of proteins.

The researchers found that at least three of the four genes carry genetic instructions for making a protein called *calmodulin* or for related proteins. Calmodulin binds specific molecules so they can be used by the cell. When a plant is disturbed, calmodulin responds by binding calcium, which plays a key role in communication between cells. With calcium in short supply, communication is apparently disrupted, and that slows growth.

Auxin-binding proteins. A plant hormone called *auxin* regulates the growth of plant-stem cells in response to several influences, including gravity.

In July 1989, botanists at Oregon State University in Corvallis and the University of San Diego in California reported an important finding that may help us finally understand how

The Two Faces of Ozone

Ozone, a form of oxygen, can either help or harm plants. The yellowed leaf of a soybean plant, at right, *above,* shows the effect of ozone in smog. The green leaf (left) is from a plant inoculated with a microbe that increased its ozone tolerance. Ozone in the upper atmosphere blocks ultraviolet (UV) rays from the sun. A stunted cucumber plant, *right,* on the left of a normal plant, was exposed to UV levels equal to a 12 per cent depletion of the ozone layer.

Botany
Continued

auxin works on the molecular level.

When a horizontal stem bends upward, away from Earth's gravity, it is because auxin causes cells on the bottom side of the stem to grow more than cells on the top side. To determine the molecular basis for that response, the researchers began with the assumption that auxin must interact with one or more other molecules in plant cells.

To look for such molecules, the scientists conducted experiments with cell-membrane proteins taken from normal tomato plants and from a *mutant* (genetically altered) variety of tomato plant. The mutant plant does not respond to gravity, growing instead along the ground.

The investigators added radioactively labeled auxin to the proteins of both kinds of plants. The radioactivity enabled them to trace the auxin and determine which proteins it was binding with. They found that the hormone bound with at least two proteins from the normal plants but with none from the mutant. This result showed for the first time that the functioning of auxin can be directly related to its interactions with specific cell proteins.

Clue to plant evolution. A chemical "missing link" between land plants and the green algae that scientists believe were their ancestors about 400 million years ago was reported in August 1989 by researchers at the University of Wisconsin in Madison. The botanists found that a small green alga, *Coleochaete*, contains a compound very similar to the lignin that is common in most land plants. Lignin gives structural strength to plants, enabling them to stand upright.

Botanists had long considered *Coleochaete* to be the green alga most similar to land plants, but they did not think that any type of algae contained lignin because algae have no need of the rigidity required by a tree or a bush. The researchers speculated that lignin developed as an agent to protect *Coleochaete* from infectious microbes. Later, after the emergence of land plants, it evolved into a structural material.   [Frank B. Salisbury]

In WORLD BOOK, see BOTANY.

Chemistry

The development of fluids that can act as "chemical muscles," flexing and relaxing in a fraction of a second, was reported by researchers at the University of Michigan in Ann Arbor in March 1990. These substances, called *electro-rheological fluids* (ERF's), change from the consistency of water to the consistency of peanut butter in response to intense electric fields. The fluids could be used to make faster, simpler hydraulic controls for automobiles, airplanes, and submarines.

The technology of ERF's is the creation of materials engineer Frank E. Filiskoin. Two of his colleagues, Robert D. Ervin and Zheng Lou, have used ERF's to develop *actuators*—devices that move the ailerons, rudders, elevators, and other controls of aircraft—for the United States Air Force.

Their goal is to create actuators that will flex and relax up to 200 times per second, much faster than today's hydraulic systems operate. This quick response time would enable an ERF device to rapidly reduce dangerous vibrations of aircraft controls by absorbing energy from the vibrating control. Furthermore, because the consistency of an ERF depends upon the strength of an electric field, an ERF actuator could be managed directly— and instantaneously—by electric signals emitted by a computer.

Bioplastic factories. Bacteria in an experimental factory in Billingham, England, are producing 45 metric tons (50 short tons) a year of a biodegradable plastic, according to a September 1989 report from Imperial Chemical Industries Americas, Incorporated (ICI), in Wilmington, Del.

In their first experiments, researchers at the British ICI plant found that the bacteria produced a stiff, brittle plastic called PHB. This plastic plays the same role for the bacteria that fat does for animals and starch does for plants—it stores energy for later use.

More than 80 per cent of the solid materials in these bacteria can be PHB. Unfortunately, however, PHB's melt at a temperature of 170°C (338°F.). The high melting point is close to the temperature at which the substance begins

Chemical bonds form between copper and plastic in a copper-plating technique developed at the General Electric Research and Development Center in Schenectady, N.Y. The company says that these bonds are twice as strong as the mechanical bonds produced when copper fills microscopic gaps in a plastic surface during conventional plating.

Chemistry

Continued

to decompose, and this makes PHB difficult to work with.

The ICI researchers found they could solve this problem by feeding the bacteria a mix of *glucose* (a sugar) and certain organic acids. This new diet caused the bacteria to incorporate into the PHB molecules of a material that gave the PHB a lower melting temperature and also made it stronger and more flexible. They called the modified plastic PHB-V.

Biologically produced plastics, or *biopolymers*, may one day become less expensive than ordinary plastics, and they may be easier to custom-design at the molecular level for various uses. Scientists might vary the type of plastic being produced—as the ICI researchers did—by feeding different nutrients to the bacteria or by turning certain genes in these organisms on and off.

The main drawback of the ICI process is that the plastic is produced in small portions that must be extracted from the bacteria. The extraction process is time-consuming and expensive. First, the bacteria must be broken open

by, for example, subjecting them to *ultrasound* (sound too high for human beings to hear) or to a sudden change in pressure. Then, the plastic has to be separated from other solids by such processes as filtration.

To overcome this problem, scientists at Michigan State University in East Lansing are exploring the possibility of altering the genes of potato plants to make the plants produce plastics. This could be done by adding genes like those in the bacteria. The plants would then grow potatoes whose inside would be mostly plastic. To extract this material, one would peel the potato.

Lifelike molecules. The creation of a chemical system that could be considered a primitive form of life was reported in January 1990 by chemists at the Massachusetts Institute of Technology in Cambridge. By imitating natural processes, the scientists induced molecules to create copies of themselves in a laboratory solution.

The chemists used a stiff U-shaped molecule as a framework. To one end of the U, they chemically bound a

259

Chemistry

Continued

molecule that resembles an amino acid, a building block of proteins. To the other end, they attached a molecule that has characteristics of both proteins and deoxyribonucleic acid (DNA), the material of which genes are made.

What happened then was similar to the process that occurs in nature when a gene passes on the instructions for the creation of a protein. The chemicals in the laboratory reacted with each other, forming a bond that is characteristic of proteins and assuming a shape like an arched bridge. The DNA-like molecule then snapped loose from the U, forming a long, straight chain that became a model for making proteins and for replicating itself. Essentially, the chain stored, and then used, chemical information. The chain matched up free DNA-like and amino acid-like molecules around it and caused them to create a copy of the chain.

Clearing the air. A chemical process that cleans air pollutants such as sulfur dioxide and nitrogen oxides from the exhaust of coal-fired electric power plants—and helps pay for itself at the same time—seems almost too good to be true. But in September 1989, chemist Shih-Ger Chang of Lawrence Berkeley Laboratory (LBL) in Berkeley, Calif., announced the successful demonstration of such a process in the laboratory. Chang used a small-scale model of a *scrubber*, a device that mixes chemicals with the exhaust and purifies it before it goes up the smokestack.

The LBL process allows conventional sulfur dioxide scrubbers, already used on 190 coal-fired plants in the United States, to clean up nitrogen oxides as well. The cost of the operation is about half that of the conventional method of cleaning up nitrogen oxide alone. The conventional technique makes use of expensive *catalysts*, substances that facilitate chemical reactions while themselves remaining unchanged. The LBL process does not.

Instead, a series of chemical reactions convert the harmful compounds into valuable chemicals—gypsum, which is a construction material, and phosphate compounds, which are used to make fertilizers. These reactions

Sunlight concentrated by mirrors breaks down organic pollutants in wastewater pumped through a long glass tube in a test conducted in mid-1989 at Sandia National Laboratories in Albuquerque, N. Mex. The tube also contains water, hydrogen peroxide, and a *catalyst* (a substance that speeds up a chemical reaction while itself remaining practically unchanged).

Chemistry

Continued

remove 90 per cent of the sulfur dioxide and up to 100 per cent of the nitrogen oxides, compounds that lead to smog and acid rain.

A study by the Bechtel Power Corporation of San Francisco found that the LBL process is one of the most economical and efficient air-treatment systems yet devised for electric-power generating plants. LBL and Bechtel during 1990 were jointly testing a full-scale scrubber.

Cocaine stopper. With cocaine use a widespread problem, scientists are searching for safe chemicals that will act as drugs to help addicts kick the habit. In August 1989, psychologist Nancy K. Mello and her colleagues at Harvard Medical School-McLean Hospital in Belmont, Mass., reported that buprenorphine, a drug already used successfully to treat heroin addicts, may help to reduce the craving for cocaine as well.

The scientists worked with rhesus monkeys that had been taking cocaine daily for more than two months. The monkeys obtained the cocaine by pressing buttons at certain times of day. During the experiment, some of the monkeys received regular doses of buprenorphine but were still given the same opportunity to press the cocaine-releasing buttons. Those animals decreased their cocaine use by more than 90 per cent after 30 days.

Although the scientists do not understand how buprenorphine works, they noted that it does not reduce the animals' appetites. Buprenorphine is especially promising because it has already been proven safe and effective for heroin addicts, bringing it closer to approval by the United States Food and Drug Administration than are other experimental substances being evaluated for use against drug addiction. Additionally, buprenorphine could provide help for a growing population of "crank" addicts—individuals who smoke a mixture of heroin and cocaine. [Peter J. Andrews]

In the Special Reports section, see TWO SIDES TO THE OXYGEN STORY; LIFE AT THE DEEP-SEA "GEYSERS." In WORLD BOOK, see CHEMISTRY; HYDRAULICS.

Computer Hardware

An experimental processor that uses light, rather than electricity, to manipulate data was unveiled in January 1990 at AT&T Bell Laboratories in Holmdel, N.J. The processor, developed by researcher Alan Huang, uses mirrors, lenses, lasers, and special devices that can switch a laser beam on and off billions of times each second. One major advantage of optical processing is that more connections can be made between individual components, enabling the processor to run faster. See Close-Up.

Optical storage. The number of CD-ROM drives existing in the world reached 500,000 by February 1990, more than twice the number in February 1989. These drives for computer discs are similar to audio compact discs (CD's) and are read by laser beams. Computer CD's can store hundreds of *megabytes* (MB) of information, equivalent to tens of thousands of pages. (One MB is 1 million *bytes*. A byte is a letter, number, or other symbol.) Most such discs are *read-only memories* (ROM's), devices whose information cannot be changed once it is stored. The number of products available on CD-ROM also skyrocketed. See COMPUTER SOFTWARE.

Magnetic disks remained the dominant storage medium in 1989 and 1990, however, with typical hard disk drives in personal computers ranging in capacity from about 20 to 100 MB. This capacity could increase dramatically in the next few years, thanks to a development announced by International Business Machines Corporation (IBM) in January 1990.

Researchers at IBM's Almaden Research Center in Pasadena, Calif., reportedly squeezed 1 billion *bits* (the 0's and 1's that are the "letters" of computer "language") onto 6.5 square centimeters (1 square inch) of an experimental magnetic hard disk. This is 15 to 30 times the number of bits that can be stored in the same area on a conventional hard disk.

Portable Mac. Apple Computer, Incorporated, of Cupertino, Calif., in August 1989 introduced a long-awaited portable version of its Macintosh computer. The portable Mac

MicroTV, a circuit board for Macintosh II computers, allows a black-and-white TV picture to pop up on the monitor while the computer is also running page makeup, word processing, or other programs. Journalists could follow TV news stories, users could watch tapes to aid in learning new computer programs, or guards could match faces captured by a security TV camera with faces stored in the computer's memory. MicroTV, made by Aapps Corporation of Sunnyvale, Calif., accepts signals from cable, videocassette, or videodisc.

weighs about 7 kilograms (16 pounds), and the basic model sold for $5,799. The computer can run all Macintosh software. The new machine's battery operates for up to 8 hours, more than twice as long as batteries in most portable computers.

Faster than ever. The top computing speed possible in personal computers increased dramatically during the year with the introduction of the first personal computers based on the i486 processor chip produced by Intel Corporation of Santa Clara, Calif. (A personal computer's processor chip handles the machine's arithmetic and logic operations and controls the flow of information.)

The first computer employing the i486 chip was the PowerCache 33/4, introduced in January 1990 by Advanced Logic Research, Incorporated, of Irvine, Calif. Prices for this machine start at about $11,000.

A computer operates by sending pulses of electricity through electric circuits. The interval between the beginning of one pulse and the beginning of the next is one *cycle*. The version of the i486 chip available in early 1990 operates at a rate of 33 million cycles per second, or 33 megahertz (MHz). The fastest of the previous generation of microcomputers ran at 25 MHz.

Apple workstation. Apple in March 1990 introduced its first workstation, the Macintosh IIfx. Workstations are one step above personal computers. They are used by businesses and institutions that have need of rapid calculations and sharp graphics. Apple's new machine uses a 68030 processor that operates at a blazing 40 MHz. This processor is made by Motorola Corporation of Schaumburg, Ill. Prices for the IIfx start at around $9,000.

Super memory chip. Hitachi Limited of Japan announced on June 7, 1990, that it had developed the first working prototype of a chip that can store more than 64 *megabits* of data. (One megabit equals 1 million bits and is equivalent to about 125,000 bytes.) The prototype measures about 10 by 20 millimeters (0.4 to 0.8 inch). Hitachi did not say when it would begin commercial production of the chip.

Handwriting recognition. Sony Corporation of Japan in March 1990 announced a small computer that can recognize handwriting—even different handwriting styles. The Palmtop PTC-500 has no keyboard. Instead, users write on the computer's screen with an electronic pen.

This computer is intended for the Japanese market only and sells for about $1,300. With more than 3,000 characters, the Japanese alphabet is more suited for handwritten entry than for typewriter-style keys.

Laser printers continued to grow in power and decline in price during 1989 and 1990. Hewlett-Packard Company of Palo Alto, Calif., in February 1990 introduced the LaserJet III printer, which uses an integrated circuit to adjust its laser beam during printing. The adjustments result in crisper images and letters. The Laserjet III prints 8 pages per minute and sells for $2,395.

In September 1989, Hewlett-Packard introduced the LaserJet IIP. Although its printing speed is only 4 pages per minute, the IIP was priced at less than $1,500, making laser printing affordable for small businesses, schools, and many individual users.

IBM in October 1989 introduced its first laser printer—a $2,595 device called the IBM LaserPrinter. The machine can produce up to 10 pages per minute.

Game machines. Two video-game computers made their debut in late 1989. San Francisco-based Sega of America introduced Genesis, a *16-bit* machine—one that processes information 16 bits at a time. This is twice as fast as the previous generation of game machines. The fast speed of Genesis enables the machine to run more sophisticated games and produce sharper and more realistic pictures and a wider range of sounds.

NEC of Wood Dale, Ill., introduced Turbò-Grafx, a $149 machine that is extremely popular in Japan. The most notable features of Turbo-Grafx are a CD-ROM drive, which provides a tremendous amount of graphics, and sound that is comparable to recordings on audio CD's. [Keith Ferrell]

In the Special Reports section, see SCIENCE BY SUPERCOMPUTER. In the WORLD BOOK Supplement section, see COMPUTER.

Computing with Light

The demonstration of a complicated device made up of lasers, lenses, and superfast "light switches" on Jan. 29, 1990, focused public attention on a technology that may soon bring about a fundamental change in how computers operate. The device, called an *optical processor*, was designed and built at AT&T Bell Laboratories in Holmdel, N.J. It stood about 30 centimeters (1 foot) high and covered an area of about 0.4 square meter (4 square feet). Instead of using electric current to process information, this optical device used beams of light.

The AT&T optical processor was a great deal larger than an ordinary desktop computer. It was also much more primitive. The optical device had about the same capacity as an electronic chip used to control a dishwasher. But experts believe the parts, or components, of such optical computing devices can be miniaturized, and in other laboratories throughout the industrialized world, the technology of optical computing was already well underway. In fact, in 1984, scientists at GuilTech Research Company in Sunnyvale, Calif., had built a faster optical processor than the Bell Labs machine.

Today's computers are electronic digital machines in which numbers are usually encoded as a pattern of on and off signals, controlled by switches, representing either a 1 or a 0. The l's and 0's are called *binary digits*, or *bits*.

Since their development in the 1940's, electronic computers have undergone constant improvement. These computers, however, have fundamental limitations that designers must overcome if they are to continue to develop faster machines. The goal of AT&T and other laboratories is to overcome these limitations by computing with bits represented not by electricity but by light.

One major limitation of computing with electricity, for example, is that there is a restriction on the number of components that can be connected to each other within the machine. Even a relatively low-powered personal computer is made up of millions of components called *digital gates*. Several thousand gates can be built into a fingernail-size silicon chip. The connections between these components are lines of metal that *conduct* (carry) current. The more connections there are, the faster the computer can operate.

The number of connections that can be made, however, is limited by the size of these lines. All connections take up space. Roughly 80 per cent of the area of a typical computer chip is made up of the connections among the components.

In addition, there is a limit to the amount of current that can flow through any line without overheating the line. A conductor resists the flow of electricity, so as current flows through a line, it loses energy. The line absorbs this energy as heat. The greater the number of lines connected to a component, the greater must be the amount of current flowing through that component, and the greater the amount of heat produced.

Neither the wire size limitation nor the overheating problem would affect a digital computer that uses light beams instead of electric current for both calculations and connections. As in an electronic computer, data would be processed by on-off switches, but these switches would be operated by beams of laser light.

Electric current is a flow of subatomic particles called electrons, but a light beam may be thought of as either waves or particles—electromagnetic waves when it is traveling through space and *photons* when the light is detected. Light beams do not block other light beams. They pass through one another without interfering with one another. So an optical computer would have no wires that could overheat or take up precious space in a computer.

Another major advantage of an optical computer is that it would have superior ability in *parallel processing* (making more than one calculation at a time). Electronic computers also can operate in parallel, but not to the same degree. One electronic machine uses a whopping 65,000 processors, but each processor communicates in parallel with only a few others. An optical computer could have perhaps 1 million processors—each communicating in parallel with all the others. This would be equivalent to an electronic computer with about 1 trillion wires.

An electronic supercomputer can process millions of bits per second, but this requires a tremendous flow of electrons, which can cause the machine to heat up. To prevent an electronic supercomputer from overheating, a high-speed pump forces an extremely cold fluid, such as liquid nitrogen, through all the machine's parts.

An optical supercomputer, on the other hand, could process millions of bits without the overheating problem because of the dual wave-particle nature of light. Optical computers would have switches operated by light, not electricity. When a light beam passed through space from one switch to another, it would behave like a wave and lose essentially no energy due to resistance. When the light beam struck the second switch, it would behave like a hailstorm of photons, each depositing energy in the switch.

Electrical engineer Alan Huang of AT&T Bell Laboratories demonstrates an *optical processor*—a machine that uses beams of laser light, rather than electric current, to manipulate data.

Because no energy would be lost in conducting lines, the total amount of energy consumed by the optical supercomputer would be much less than that used by an electronic machine.

Despite the potential of digital optical processors, however, not all computer scientists are convinced that the future of optical processing lies in the development of digital computers. Many researchers foresee the emergence of hybrid computers that would be both electronic and optical. The electronic section would be digital, but the optical section would be an *analog* device in which quantities would be represented by light beams of different brightness. The optical section would attack a problem first and quickly come up with an estimate of the solution. It would then pass this estimate to the digital electronic section, which would produce the final, precise solution.

But for the present, the race is on to build a digital optical supercomputer. Before the year 2000, we could have a winner—or a decision to call off the race and develop a hybrid.

[Mir M. Mirsalehi and H. John Caulfield]

Computer Software

Indecision over the next generation of disk operating systems (DOS's) for IBM and IBM-compatible personal computers (PC's) dominated the software industry during 1989 and 1990. A disk operating system is a program that enables the computer to process information and run *applications software* such as programs for word processing, spreadsheets, and databases by controlling the flow of data among the various parts of the computer.

The most popular operating system, called MS-DOS, lacks the power to take advantage of the speed and memory capabilities of the newest generation of personal computers. These capabilities include *multitasking* (running more than one piece of software at a time).

The producer of MS-DOS, Microsoft Corporation of Redmond, Wash., also makes two systems that are the leading contenders to replace MS-DOS—programs called OS/2 and Windows. Both employ a graphical user interface (GUI), which enables the user to issue commands by pointing a cursor at *icons* (pictorial representations of programs and functions), rather than by typing instructions on a keyboard. This is the type of operating system used in the Macintosh computer, made by Apple Computer, Incorporated, of Cupertino, Calif.

OS/2 is more powerful than MS-DOS, but it requires the latest generation of computers. Windows is not a true operating system and can be used in less powerful computers along with MS-DOS. Windows makes complex operations simpler than they are with MS-DOS alone.

In May 1990, Microsoft introduced Windows 3.0, the most advanced version of this product. About 50 producers of software said that they would develop versions of their programs for Windows 3.0.

Many companies that had invested heavily in preparing applications software to run under OS/2 became concerned in 1989 when sales of the popular Windows program accelerated and OS/2 met with only lukewarm acceptance.

New OS/2 software. By early 1990, however, the picture brightened for these firms with the introduction of OS/2 desktop publishing packages such as Pagemaker from Aldus Corporation of Seattle and spreadsheets such as Excel for OS/2 from Microsoft. According to industry experts, OS/2 was likely to become the leading operating system for the next generation of IBM-compatible microcomputers. Windows was expected to retain much of its popularity as a transitional product between MS-DOS and OS/2.

More "user-friendly." Geovision, introduced in the spring of 1990, was designed to bring multitasking and other advanced capabilities to even the most basic MS-DOS computers. Produced by GeoWorks of Berkeley, Calif., this program runs on any PC that uses MS-DOS, and is expected to introduce many people to the use of icons.

HyperPad, a program for IBM compatibles that enables users to design their own GUI's, was introduced in the summer of 1989 by Brightbill-Roberts of Syracuse, N.Y. It is similar to the HyperCard program for the Macintosh. The user controls a mouse or another device to point a cursor at one of several "buttons" that are displayed on the screen. HyperPad can be used to create applications software, training programs, and even musical compositions.

New tools for desktop publishing. Adobe Systems, Incorporated, of Mountain View, Calif., continued to enhance its line of desktop publishing software. Adobe's Type Manager, shipped in August 1989, helped to eliminate jagged edges on the curved parts of letters as they appear on the computer screen. It also creates smoother letters on pin-type printers.

Corel Draw!, introduced in May 1990 by Corel Systems Corporation of Ottawa, Canada, is a Windows-based drawing and desktop publishing package for IBM computers. Corel designed this program especially for documents that contain many pictures.

Encyclopedias on CD-ROM. Two major publishers of encyclopedias in 1989 and 1990 took advantage of the immense capacity of CD-ROM (*compact disc, read-only memory*) storage, in which information is held on CD's similar to those used to record music. (*Read-only memory* means that a computer can "read" the data but cannot change it.) A single disc can store tens

Computer Software

Continued

of thousands of pages of information, so CD-ROM is an excellent medium for distributing large amounts of material such as databases, collections of images, or encyclopedias.

World Book, Incorporated, of Chicago in December 1989 released Information Finder, a CD-ROM version of *The World Book Encyclopedia*. Information Finder contains the text of more than 17,000 encyclopedia articles as well as 139,000 entries from *The World Book Dictionary*. This software is for PC's and PC-compatible machines.

Compton's MultiMedia Encyclopedia was introduced in February 1990 by Britannica Software of San Francisco. This product incorporates both graphics and sound, enabling users to hear samples of music or spoken words, and to view photos and illustrations. The MultiMedia Encyclopedia is for PC's and PC-compatibles.

Educational software. The Playroom, a program for preschool children, produces images with which a child can interact by striking keys or controlling a mouse. The program, introduced in September 1989 by Broderbund Software, Incorporated, of San Rafael, Calif., helps teach such subjects as reading, simple mathematics, and telling time. Playroom is available for PC's, PC-compatibles, and Macintosh computers.

SimCity: The City Simulator, designed for adults, presents an image of an area of land and provides the tools for developing the land. The user can create roads, buildings, factories, homes, and other urban structures. SimCity monitors traffic, crime, pollution, and other problems and generates graphs, reports, and even evaluations of the user's performance. Maxis of Moraga, Calif., introduced SimCity in September 1989 for PC's, PC-compatibles, Macintoshes, and two machines made by Commodore Business Machines, Incorporated, of West Chester, Pa.—the Commodore 64 and the Amiga.   [Keith Ferrell]

See also COMPUTER HARDWARE. In the Special Reports section, see SCIENCE BY SUPERCOMPUTER. In the World Book Supplement section, see COMPUTER.

The BlockAIDS computer game, *right,* developed at the University of Texas in Austin, teaches players about AIDS. A correct answer to a question about the disease fills one space with a character named "Blocky," *below.* Incorrect answers produce the AIDS Virus character, *bottom.* The game is similar to tick-tack-toe. By filling a line of squares with Blocky —across, down, or diagonally—the player wins.

Deaths of Scientists

Notable scientists and engineers who died between June 1, 1989, and June 1, 1990, are listed below. Those listed were Americans unless otherwise indicated in the biographical sketch.

Bailey, William John (1921-Dec. 17, 1989), chemist who specialized in large, chainlike molecules called *polymers*. He developed a biodegradable plastic that could be broken down by microorganisms in water.

Bargmann, Valentine (1908-July 21, 1989), German-born theoretical physicist who worked with Albert Einstein and made important contributions to Einstein's theory of relativity, which revised ideas of space and time.

Beadle, George W. (1903-June 9, 1989), geneticist who shared the 1958 Nobel Prize in physiology or medicine with biologists Edward L. Tatum and Joshua Lederberg. The three scientists discovered that genes direct the formation of *enzymes*, proteins that control chemical reactions in living cells.

Bettelheim, Bruno (1903-March 13, 1990), Austrian-born psychiatrist and psychoanalyst who gained world fame for his work with emotionally disturbed children.

De Hoffmann, Frederic (1924-Oct. 4, 1989), Austrian-born nuclear physicist who worked on the Manhattan Project, the secret U.S. government project that produced the first atomic bomb in 1945. He later helped develop the hydrogen bomb, and he directed the Salk Institute for Biological Studies, in San Diego, from 1972 to 1988.

De Mestral, Georges (1908?-Feb. 8, 1990), Swiss engineer who in 1948 invented Velcro, a fastener based on a strip of tiny nylon hooks that grasp a strip of dense nylon loops. He reportedly was inspired to create Velcro by wondering why burrs stuck to the legs of his trousers.

Edgerton, Harold E. (1903-Jan. 4, 1990), electrical engineer who pioneered in high-speed photography, a technique that uses blinking strobo-scopic lights to freeze action. He also developed improved underwater cameras and sonar equipment that helped locate underwater wrecks. Edgerton joined the faculty of the Massachusetts Institute of Technology in Cambridge in 1931 and spent his entire academic career there.

Fairbank, William M. (1917-Sept. 30, 1989), physicist known for his work in *superconductivity*, the ability of certain materials to conduct electricity with little or no resistance. He served as professor of physics at Stanford University in California from 1959 to 1987.

Hirschfelder, Joseph O. (1911-March 30, 1990), a founder of modern theoretical chemistry and a key participant in the Manhattan Project. He received the National Medal of Science in 1976.

Hubbert, Marion King (1903-Oct. 11, 1989), geologist and geophysicist whose research showed that oil and gas flow through cracks and pores in underground rocks, rather than standing in pools as previously thought. His work helped change methods of oil and gas exploration.

Korff, Serge A. (1906-Dec. 1, 1989), United States physicist, born in Finland of Russian parents, who discovered and mapped the shower of *neutrons* (electrically neutral subatomic particles) produced by high-energy radiation from outer space striking gases in Earth's atmosphere.

Laing, R. D. (Ronald David Laing) (1927-Aug. 23, 1989), British psychiatrist who pioneered new treatment for schizophrenics, believing them victims of family stress.

Mangelsdorf, Paul C. (1899-July 22, 1989), geneticist and botanist known as an expert in the origins and breeding of *maize* (corn). He also developed the first variety of winter wheat with stems resistant to the fungus disease called rust.

Mauro, Alexander (1921-Oct. 6, 1989), biophysicist who, with heart surgeon William W. L. Glenn, developed the radio frequency cardiac pacemaker, a device implanted in the heart to maintain a normal heartbeat.

McConnell, James V. (1925-April 9, 1990), author of *Understanding Human Behavior*, a leading college textbook on introductory psychology; psychology professor at the University of Michigan in Ann Arbor from 1956 to 1988; and former member of the editorial advisory boards of SCIENCE YEAR and THE WORLD BOOK HEALTH & MEDICAL ANNUAL.

Moloney, Peter Joseph (1891-Aug. 12, 1989), Canadian chemist who helped produce a combined vaccine for

Bruno Bettelheim

Harold E. Edgerton

James V. McConnell

Deaths
of Scientists
Continued

Andrei D. Sakharov

William Shockley

An Wang

diphtheria and *pertussis* (whooping cough) and a chemically altered form of insulin effective for certain insulin-resistant diabetics.

Pedersen, Charles J. (1904-Oct. 26, 1989), U.S. industrial chemist, born in Korea of Norwegian and Japanese parents, who shared the 1987 Nobel Prize in chemistry with Donald J. Cram of the United States and Jean-Marie Lehn of France. Pedersen was honored for his discovery of compounds called *crown ethers* that couple with electrically charged atoms called *ions*. His discovery enabled scientists to create complex organic compounds that mimic the function of natural molecules. From 1927 until his retirement in 1969, Pedersen worked for the Du Pont Company, where his research yielded 65 patents.

Pimentel, George C. (1922-June 18, 1989), chemist who invented the chemical laser and a special *spectrometer* (an instrument that analyzes light by spreading it into a spectrum) for use on interplanetary spacecraft. Pimentel taught at the University of California at Berkeley from 1949 until his death and received the National Medal of Science in 1985.

Roberts, Walter Orr (1915-March 12, 1990), solar astronomer who studied the sun's *corona*, the outer edge of its atmosphere. His interest in solar activity led to studies of Earth's changing climate, and he founded the National Center for Atmospheric Research in Boulder, Colo., in 1960.

Rusk, Howard A. (1901-Nov. 4, 1989), physician who pioneered in the rehabilitation of the physically disabled in the United States. He founded the Institute of Physical Medicine and Rehabilitation (now the Howard A. Rusk Institute of Rehabilitation Medicine) at New York University.

Sachs, Allan M. (1921-Sept. 20, 1989), physicist who took part in early experiments that established the properties of subatomic particles.

Sakharov, Andrei D. (1921-Dec. 14, 1989), Soviet physicist who helped develop the Soviet Union's hydrogen bomb in the early 1950's but then turned to working for disarmament. He won the 1975 Nobel Peace Prize for promoting human rights and world peace.

Shapiro, Harry L. (1902-Jan. 7, 1990), anthropologist widely considered the dean of forensic anthropology, which uses anthropological techniques to investigate crimes. He served as curator of physical anthropology at the American Museum of Natural History in New York City from 1926 to 1970.

Shock, Nathan W. (1906-Nov. 12, 1989), psychologist and gerontologist often called the father of modern research on aging.

Shockley, William (1910-Aug. 12, 1989), electrical engineer who shared the 1956 Nobel Prize in physics with physicists John Bardeen and Walter Brattain for discovering the principles that make possible the transistor, a tiny device used to control the flow of electric current.

Sitterly, Charlotte M. (1898-March 3, 1990), physicist who devoted much of her career to the study of the sun's spectrum. Her analysis of sunlight first showed that the element technitium exists in nature.

Street, J. C. (Jabez Curry Street) (1906-Nov. 7, 1989), physicist who, along with Edward C. Stevenson, discovered an elementary particle known as the *muon* in 1937.

Titterton, Sir Ernest (1916-Feb. 8, 1990), British nuclear physicist who helped build Great Britain's first atomic bomb in the late 1940's. He then became an adviser to the Australian government and was responsible for monitoring radioactive fallout on the Australian continent.

Wang, An (1920-March 24, 1990), Chinese-born electrical engineer, physicist, and inventor. Wang developed the magnetic core, the basic unit of computer memory until the introduction of the microchip. He also founded Wang Laboratories, Incorporated, a leading manufacturer of office computers and word processors.

Weiss, Paul A. (1898-Sept. 8, 1989), Austrian-born biologist who won the National Medal of Science in 1979 for his pioneering work in the theory of cellular development. Among other breakthroughs, he established the principle of cellular self-organization, the ability of a mixture of cells from different organs to reassemble themselves according to the organ from which they came. [Sara Dreyfuss]

Dentistry

Human saliva may provide natural protection against AIDS, according to new evidence reported in June 1989 by dental researchers. Scientists at the National Institute of Dental Research in Bethesda, Md., collected saliva samples from nine healthy men, nine healthy women, and seven healthy children. They also obtained samples from nine men infected with human immunodeficiency virus (HIV), the virus that causes AIDS.

The researchers incubated the saliva samples with a concentration of HIV, then measured how much the virus had reproduced. The salivas of all the women and children in the study prevented the virus from multiplying. Six of the nine saliva samples from healthy men and seven of the nine samples from HIV-infected males also completely blocked viral reproduction, and the remaining samples reduced the rate at which the virus multiplied.

Lead in teeth. Scientists have long known that exposure to lead results in the metal accumulating in bones and teeth. In January 1990, a group of French scientists reported a study that explored whether the lead content of people's teeth correlated with the concentration of lead in gasoline and the intensity of motor vehicle traffic where the people lived.

The researchers analyzed decay-free molars from patients aged 10 to 80 who had lived all their lives in one of three areas: Strasbourg, a city of about 250,000 people in France; the rural area surrounding Strasbourg; or Mexico City, which, with more than 10 million people, is the largest city in the world and one of the most polluted.

There was no difference in the lead in teeth from Strasbourg compared with those from rural areas. The lead concentration in the Mexico City teeth, however, ranged from 5.7 to 8.9 times higher than that in the French teeth. The researchers attributed the difference to higher lead content in Mexican gasoline and to Mexico City's greater traffic congestion.

Social effects of missing teeth. Dental researchers from the State University at Groningen in the Netherlands

Ariadne was shunned by her fellow witches because she had good teeth.

reported in June 1989 on a study assessing the psychological and social impact of missing teeth. The scientists compared three groups of patients: those with a missing front tooth, those with missing back teeth, and a control group who had kept all their teeth.

Compared with people who had a full set of teeth, those with missing front teeth tended to avoid contact with people, laughed less, and covered their mouths more often when they did laugh. Such behavioral changes also occurred occasionally in the group with missing back teeth.

TMJ sounds in teen-agers. Many teen-agers and young adults experience clicking or cracking sounds when they open and close their mouths to chew or speak. The noises originate in the *temporomandibular joints* (TMJ's), two joints at the temples where the *mandible* (lower jaw) is attached to the skull. Scientists know little about the cause or significance of such sounds.

To learn more about TMJ clicking, dental researchers from Umeå University in Sweden conducted a two-year study of 285 17-year-olds. They monitored clicking sounds reported by the volunteers as well as those recorded by dental examiners and also assessed the volunteers' jaw function.

Among all 285 volunteers, 36 per cent experienced TMJ clicking at some time during the study. Only 9.3 per cent of the volunteers heard clicking sounds throughout the period.

Reports of TMJ clicking decreased over time. Almost one-third of the volunteers with clicking during the first year reported themselves free of the sounds during the second year. Dental examiners found almost half of those with sounds to be free of them the following year.

Annual examinations revealed no significant connection between TMJ clicking and jaw problems such as impaired range of jaw movement or joint pain. These findings suggest that dentists should treat TMJ clicking conservatively because it will likely disappear over time without medical intervention. [Paul Goldhaber]

In WORLD BOOK, see DENTISTRY.

Drugs

Two separate studies in 1989 revealed that a drug called deprenyl significantly slows the development of Parkinson's disease, a disorder of the nervous system that progressively reduces the brain's ability to control the muscles. This finding may enable patients with the disorder to delay the use of levodopa (L-dopa), a drug that quickly relieves the symptoms of Parkinson's disease but whose benefits often wear off with time. L-dopa also can cause severe side effects.

The idea of using deprenyl to treat Parkinson's disease grew from research into the cause of a type of Parkinson's disease affecting some drug abusers in California. These drug abusers had used a substance intended to be a synthetic version of heroin but which was actually a toxic chemical. In 1983, neurologist J. William Langston and colleagues at the California Parkinson's Foundation in San Jose found that a particular chemical in the heroinlike drug called MPTP was responsible for the addicts' condition.

Also that year, researchers at the National Institutes of Mental Health in Bethesda, Md., discovered that monkeys injected with MPTP developed the same symptoms and brain damage suffered by the California addicts. They also found that animals that were given MPTP did not develop drug-induced Parkinson's disease if they were also given deprenyl.

Delaying Parkinson's. In 1989, two groups of researchers discovered that although deprenyl does not prevent the development of Parkinson's disease in people, it can slow the progress of mild cases of the disorder.

In August 1989, Langston and neurologist James Tetrud reported on their study of 54 Parkinson's patients, half of whom received deprenyl. The other half received a *placebo* (inactive substance). The researchers found that patients who received deprenyl took twice as long to develop symptoms severe enough to require treatment with L-dopa than did the patients who received the placebo.

Similar results were reported in November by the Parkinson Study Group,

Parallel Track Drug-Testing Program

More than 10,000 patients with AIDS in 1990 were taking an experimental anti-AIDS drug called dideoxyinosine (ddI) every day. Yet ddI had not yet been approved for general use by the Food and Drug Administration (FDA), the agency charged with ensuring the safety and effectiveness of drugs used in the United States. There was nothing illegal about these patients' use of ddI, however. They were participants in a new streamlined drug-approval program called the *parallel track*. Under this program, people with life-threatening illnesses, such as AIDS, who have not responded to conventional treatments can obtain experimental drugs while researchers are still conducting tests of the drugs' safety and effectiveness. DdI is the best known of nearly a dozen experimental drugs on the parallel track.

Ordinarily, the only people who receive experimental drugs are patients participating in clinical trials being conducted under strict guidelines approved in advance by the FDA. Clinical trials are an important part of the drug-approval process. In most clinical trials, patients are assigned at random to take the experimental drug, a *placebo* (inactive substance), or an already approved drug being compared with the experimental drug. Patients in the test do not know which drug they are taking.

Clinical trials are used to determine whether an experimental drug is generally safe to use, which doses of the drug are the most effective, and whether the drug has any advantages over other drugs used to treat the same condition. The physicians and medical researchers who conduct clinical trials are required to keep detailed records on the patients' responses to the drugs. The FDA uses these data in deciding whether to approve the drugs for general use.

This testing and approval process can take up to 10 years, and many physicians and patients have criticized the FDA for taking what they consider an unnecessarily long time to make promising new drugs available. Patients with AIDS and their physicians have been particularly critical of the FDA's approval process. They have demanded that the agency speed up the process for drugs that appear to show any promise at all in reducing the ravages of that deadly disease.

In winter 1986, in response to these criticisms, the FDA began to release the then-experimental drug AZT to physicians of patients in the last stages of AIDS. The drug was so effective in prolonging the life of some AIDS patients that in May 1987 the agency formally established the parallel track. This program was created by expanding the use of an FDA regulation that allowed the agency to occasionally authorize release of experimental drugs to private physicians treating seriously ill people who failed to respond to any other treatment.

The parallel track, though hailed by AIDS activists, was not without its critics when it was instituted. Many physicians and medical researchers feared that the speeded-up approval process would interfere with the traditional drug-approval process. They predicted that drug companies would not complete clinical trials once their product was being widely distributed. They worried that already ill people would suffer serious side effects from inadequately tested drugs.

Some people also feared that patients would be financially exploited because drug companies are allowed to charge patients for drugs administered through the parallel track but not for drugs used in clinical trials. Finally, opponents of the parallel track warned that people would be unwilling to enroll in clinical trials—where they

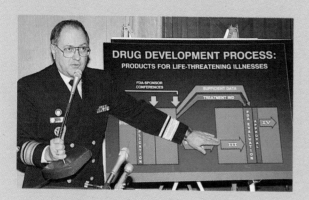

Frank E. Young, commissioner of the U.S. Food and Drug Administration, testifies before a congressional committee about the parallel track, a new streamlined drug approval process that allows people with life-threatening illnesses to obtain experimental drugs while researchers are still testing the drugs' safety and effectiveness.

might not be in the group getting the potentially helpful drug—because they would be able to get the drug from their physician.

None of these problems has developed, however, chiefly because of the requirements built into the FDA regulation governing the parallel track. Manufacturers of experimental drugs released on the parallel track are required to continue testing the drug in clinical trials. Also, the drug manufacturers must first conduct small clinical trials to ensure that the drugs are relatively safe. In addition, most of the drugs on the parallel track have been provided by the manufacturer free of charge.

Finally, medical researchers have had little difficulty in recruiting participants for clinical trials. That is because in order to receive experimental drugs on the parallel track, patients must meet certain conditions. For example, they must already have failed to respond to, or suffered serious side effects from, other drugs used to treat their condition. Or they must live too far away from a medical center where a clinical trial of the experimental drug is being conducted to participate.

While almost half the drugs released on the parallel track are for the treatment of AIDS or AIDS-related infections, a sizable number are cancer-fighting drugs. Other drugs on the parallel track include medication to improve the breathing ability of premature infants, drugs to help organ transplant patients ward off infections, and drugs for treating psychiatric and neurological conditions and some hereditary diseases.

Many medical experts believe that if the parallel track is successful, it will fundamentally change the way in which drugs for life-threatening diseases are approved in the United States. For example, they believe it will lead the FDA to reevaluate the need for clinical trials. They also speculate that future information on drugs' safety and effectiveness may be gathered in other ways. For example, less detailed data from large numbers of people taking a drug may be as scientifically valid as highly detailed information from a limited number of volunteers in clinical trials. Currently, most trials of a new drug involve no more than 2,000 volunteers, less than one-fifth the number of people currently taking ddI on the parallel track.

Meanwhile, the standard approval process goes on. Several drugs, such as AZT, have been removed from the parallel track because they have received the FDA's approval for general use. New drugs are added to the list, however, at the rate of about one a month. As of now, FDA officials see no end to the stream of drugs entering the parallel track.   [Beverly Merz]

a team of scientists from 28 medical centers in the United States. These researchers studied 800 patients with Parkinson's disease who received either deprenyl, another drug that researchers thought might relieve the symptoms of the disease, or a placebo.

The scientists found that deprenyl appeared to slow the progress of Parkinson's disease and delay the need for treatment with L-dopa. The researchers also noted that the patients who received deprenyl were better able to care for themselves and were much more likely to continue working full time than patients who did not receive the drug. See NEUROSCIENCE.

Alcohol and women. Alcohol is a drug, and its abuse can lead to serious medical problems. Women tend to react more strongly to alcohol than do men, and an enzyme produced by the stomach may be the reason. That finding was reported in December 1989 by a group of researchers headed by internist Charles S. Lieber of The Mount Sinai School of Medicine in New York City. The research also may explain why female alcoholics are more likely than male alcoholics to develop severe liver damage.

In a study of 20 men and 23 women, Lieber and his colleagues found that, compared with men of the same weight, women had about 30 per cent less of an enzyme called *alcohol dehydrogenase.* This enzyme, produced by the lining of the stomach, breaks down some of the alcohol a person drinks before it passes through the stomach wall into the bloodstream. Once in the bloodstream, alcohol travels to the brain and, eventually, to the liver, where it is broken down completely. Because women produce less of the enzyme than do men, more of the alcohol women consume is absorbed into the bloodstream.

Lieber and his colleagues also found that long-term heavy drinking significantly reduced the ability of the male alcoholics in the study to produce alcohol dehydrogenase. The alcoholic women seemed to lose the ability completely. Almost all the alcohol these women drank passed directly into the bloodstream and on to their liver. Heavy drinking over many years can cause serious damage to the liver. Ac-

Drugs
Continued

cording to the researchers, their findings may explain why women alcoholics tend to develop liver disease earlier than do men and why their liver disease is often more severe.

Treating colon cancer. Treatment with a combination of two well-known drugs significantly improved the survival rate of patients with advanced colon cancer. That finding was reported in February 1990 by a team of researchers headed by internist Charles G. Moertel of the Mayo Clinic in Rochester, Minn. The success of the drug therapy represents the first significant progress in the treatment of this deadly cancer.

Colon cancer is the second leading cause of cancer deaths in the United States, behind lung cancer. If colon cancer is detected at an early stage—before it has spread outside the wall of the colon—the cure rate is 70 to 90 per cent. Many cases of colon cancer, however, are not detected until after the disease has spread to the lymph glands surrounding the colon wall. Only 35 to 60 per cent of patients with this stage of colon cancer survive after undergoing surgery to remove their cancer. An estimated 21,000 Americans develop advanced colon cancer each year.

Moertel and his colleagues studied 1,296 patients with advanced colon cancer who had undergone surgery. Half of these patients received no further treatment. The other half received two drugs: fluorouracil, a drug previously used, with only modest results, to treat colon cancer; and levamisole, a drug used to rid farm animals of worms.

The researchers found that the patients who received both drugs were 41 per cent less likely to have a recurrence of their cancer after five years. In addition, the death rate among these patients was 33 per cent less than among the patients who took no drugs.

The researchers are unsure why the combination of the two drugs was effective. Some studies have shown that levamisole strengthens the ability of weakened immune systems to fight disease. [B. Robert Meyer]

In WORLD BOOK, see DRUG.

Ecology

The study of global changes in climate brought about by human activity and their potential effect on Earth's plant and animal life was a major area of concern among ecologists in 1989 and 1990. A number of human activities, such as the destruction of tropical rain forests, may be altering the world's climate—probably making it significantly warmer in coming centuries. How would Earth's species respond to such a change? At the 1989 annual meeting of the Ecological Society of America—held in August in Toronto, Canada—the society's retiring president, Margaret B. Davis, said studies of the past can give clues to the present and future.

Learning from the past. Davis said the fossil record indicates that some species will do well and others will suffer. She pointed out that species respond to climatic changes in an individual fashion. Over the past 20,000 years or so—a period that includes the most recent ice age—some kinds of trees, for example, have flourished while others have become rare or extinct. Scientists have determined that fact by analyzing ancient pollen grains found in lake sediments. The types and amounts of pollen show which trees were present, and in what numbers, at various times in the past.

Spruce was a variety that went from being abundant to being rare, and today is abundant again. The same climatic conditions that caused those fluctuations in spruce trees had different effects on other tree species.

Another lesson learned from studying the past, Davis said, is that there is often a time lag in the response of species to climatic changes. And, again, different species respond differently. For example, small animals such as beetles can adapt rapidly, whereas trees might take decades or hundreds of years to respond.

The ozone hole and ecology. The "hole" in the ozone layer over Antarctica may eventually have harmful effects on the antarctic ecology, oceanographer Sayed El-Sayed of Texas A&M University in College Station reported in February 1990.

Alaska's Walrus Population Explosion
A beach on the Bering Strait in Alaska is jammed with once-endangered Pacific walruses, *right.* Ecologists fear that the huge animals, estimated to number at least 250,000, have overbred and are due for another population plunge as food becomes harder for them to find. The walruses ordinarily feed on clams, *inset,* and mussels, but the walruses are depleting this food source. Some ecologists have called for the development of a management plan to stabilize the walrus population.

A multicolored blimp lowers a "raft" constructed of air-filled pontoons and netting into the upper treetops, or *canopy,* of the Amazon rain forest of French Guiana in South America. The raft, developed by scientists at the University of Montpellier in France, provides a working platform for researchers studying how insects and other animals live in the rain forest canopy.

Ecology
Continued

A layer of ozone—a form of oxygen—in the upper atmosphere protects Earth from ultraviolet radiation from the sun. Since the 1970's, scientists have detected a thinning of the ozone layer over Antarctica, most likely caused by air pollutants—notably ones called *chlorofluorocarbons.* These gases rise into the upper atmosphere and react with the ozone, destroying much of it. Such reactions may lead to ozone holes over other parts of Earth as well.

Ultraviolet radiation can damage the genetic material in cells. In laboratory experiments, Sayed found that ultraviolet rays can also kill *phytoplankton,* microscopic marine organisms that form the base of the food chain in the world's oceans. Many scientists believe that a reduction of as little as 10 per cent in the numbers of these organisms would have far-reaching effects on Earth's ecology.

Sayed said that ultraviolet radiation coming through the antarctic ozone hole could destroy enough phytoplankton in southern waters to affect the local food supply. That would lead to a diminished population of birds and mammals in Antarctica.

But some scientists disagree with Sayed's conclusions. They point out that phytoplankton are often well below the ocean surface, where ultraviolet light is filtered out by seawater. Also, they say, the cells of many organisms in polar regions not only have the ability to repair genetic damage but also contain compounds that absorb ultraviolet light, making it less harmful.

The mysterious grouse. Why do populations of the red grouse, a bird that is economically important in parts of Great Britain, periodically plummet? In December 1989, a group of biologists met at a rural facility of Imperial College near Ascot, England, to debate that question.

A solution to the mystery is important because it would have implications extending far beyond Great Britain. Similar rises and drops in population—affecting birds, rodents, hares, and their predators—are quite common throughout the northern temperate and arctic regions. Biologists have stud-

Ecology

ied such cycles in population density since the mid-1900's but have not yet learned why they occur.

The population density of the grouse in different regions of Great Britain rises and falls in cycles of three to four years. The number of grouse in an area has been known to decline by as much as 97 per cent. These drastic variations in the birds' population are of major economic importance in northern England and Scotland, where grouse hunting is an important source of income for many estates; recreational hunters pay landowners $95 to $115 for the right to shoot a pair of the birds.

There are two major schools of thought on the question of grouse population cycles. Some of the participants at the Ascot meeting argued that the cycles result from a natural mechanism, possibly involving the competitive behavior of the birds, and cannot be prevented. Others contended that a parasitic *nematode* (a tiny worm) that infects grouse causes the cycles, sickening the birds and reducing their ability to reproduce.

The rift in thinking extended to recommendations on what steps to take to stabilize grouse populations. The scientists holding the view that the cycles cannot be prevented said improved maintenance of the *heather* (an evergreen bush) that the birds eat and make their nests in would result in higher numbers of grouse.

But the biologists who think that nematodes are the problem said the grouse should be treated with a medicine that kills the parasites. That could be done, they said, either by putting the drug in the fine sand or gravel that the grouse eat to aid their digestion or by sneaking up on the birds at night and giving them the antiparasite medication directly.

By the end of the conference, some of the scientists had concluded that perhaps both views are correct. In some areas, they speculated, deteriorating heather may be the cause of a declining grouse population, while nematodes are the primary culprit elsewhere. [Robert H. Tamarin]

In WORLD BOOK, see ECOLOGY.

Electronics

The family of consumer electronic products that use information stored on compact discs (CD's) and laser discs continued to grow in 1989 and 1990. Digital audio tape (DAT) players finally reached the United States market in 1990. And the U.S. Federal Communications Commission (FCC) approved a method of broadcasting high definition television (HDTV) signals, which would enable special TV sets to produce extremely sharp pictures.

Combination CD players. Pioneer Electronics of Long Beach, Calif., in June 1989 introduced a player that can play both standard audio CD's and 29.4-centimeter (12-inch) LaserVision videodiscs. LaserVision uses a technology similar to that of CD's. The player sells for less than $500.

Since their introduction in the early 1980's, CD's have become the recording industry's most successful product. LaserVision, however, has lagged far behind the videocassette recorder (VCR). But the low price of the new combination player sparked renewed interest in LaserVision. Several other firms announced that they would release combination players in 1990.

Interactive discs. The first disc players belonging to a new technology called CD Interactive (CD-I) were shipped in autumn 1989 by Philips of the Netherlands. The new deck, developed jointly by Philips and Sony Corporation of Japan, is based on a microprocessor chip produced by Motorola Corporation of Schaumburg, Ill. This chip belongs to the same family as microprocessors used in Apple Macintosh computers.

The deck connects to an ordinary television set and enables the user to interact with both sound and moving pictures. In a program called Cartoon Jukebox, for example, the user can change the colors of characters on the screen by manipulating a joystick or a mouse.

DAT reaches U.S. market. Sony Corporation of Japan introduced DAT's to the United States market in June 1990. DAT players had already been available in Japan.

The introduction stemmed from the

Forgotten World and other games played on the Genesis system introduced in late 1989 offer highly detailed pictures, with more realistic motion than provided by earlier home video games. Genesis, a product of Sega of America in San Francisco, processes data 16 *bits* at a time, compared with 8 bits for conventional systems. (Bits are 0's and 1's, the "alphabet" of computer languages.)

Electronics

Continued

Japanese government's adoption in May 1990 of a DAT standard incorporating an agreement between manufacturers of DAT equipment and the Recording Industry Association of America (RIAA). DAT decks must contain circuitry enabling the user to make a DAT copy from a copyrighted digital source such as a CD or a DAT recording, but preventing this copy from being used to make more copies. The Sony players contained such circuitry. Industry experts expected the U.S. Congress to adopt essentially the same standard.

DAT technology gives consumers the ability to digitally record music for the first time. Digital technology records sounds as a series of 0's and 1's. When the digits are converted back to sound, this reproduces faithfully the original music. The RIAA, worried that the excellent recording capabilities of DAT's would lead to illegal taping of prerecorded music, had opposed the introduction of the devices in the United States. In the Science You Can Use section, see ALL ABOUT DAT.

HDTV proposal approved. To enable special HDTV sets to produce supersharp pictures, an HDTV broadcast signal must have a *bandwidth* (range of frequencies) much broader than the bandwidth used for conventional TV signals. Unfortunately, however, existing conventional TV's could not use an HDTV signal to produce an ordinary picture. But the FCC ruled in September 1988 that whatever HDTV system it eventually approves for use in the United States must not make these sets obsolete overnight.

As a result, TV manufacturers and U.S. broadcasters have been experimenting with various methods of broadcasting HDTV and conventional TV signals at the same time. In April 1990, the FCC ruled that the United States would use a *simulcast* system. Stations would broadcast two complete signals simultaneously over different channels—one signal for conventional TV sets only and the other for HDTV sets only. [Elliot King]

In WORLD BOOK, see COMPACT DISC; ELECTRONICS; VIDEODISC.

Earth Day 20 Years Later

The 20th anniversary of "Earth Day" was observed on April 22, 1990. The event involved hundreds of millions of people in more than 140 countries.

The first Earth Day—the first political demonstration on behalf of an entire planet, on April 22, 1970—had been largely confined to the United States. It addressed environmental issues ranging from air and water pollution to the near extinction of dozens of species, including the national bird of the United States, the bald eagle.

Environmental issues in 1970 were viewed, for the most part, as local and regional problems. But 20 years later, they were recognized as being global, and the slogan for Earth Day 1990 was "Save the Planet."

The first Earth Day—on which millions of people demonstrated—helped provide the political momentum needed to pass a new generation of environmental legislation. The U.S. Congress extended and strengthened the Clean Air Act and created the Environmental Protection Agency. Also in 1970, the U.S. Department of the Interior banned the use on federal lands of many pesticides, including DDT, which had been blamed for the dwindling bald eagle population. Two years later, the EPA banned all use of DDT.

The reform laws had a measurable impact. The strengthened Clean Air Act helped reduce the three main types of pollutants emitted by automobile exhausts. As a result, the exhausts of automobiles manufactured in 1990 give off 96 per cent less carbon monoxide and hydrocarbons and 76 per cent less nitrogen oxides than

An Earth Day 1990 celebration in New York City.

older models. Local water pollution laws helped with the cleanup of many lakes and streams. And the banning of DDT helped restore the bald eagle population, so that 20 years later, government biologists considered removing it from the endangered species list.

But just as some environmental problems seemed on the brink of resolution, scientists were gathering evidence indicating that larger problems were looming on the horizon. The concerns of Earth Day 1990 were worldwide—global climate warming, depletion of the atmosphere's protective ozone layer, destruction of the tropical rain forests, and mounting piles of the world's garbage.

As recently as the first Earth Day in 1970, carbon dioxide had been thought of as a harmless gas, essential to plant *photosynthesis* (the process by which plants convert carbon dioxide to food energy). But in 1990, scientists were warning that the continued release of carbon dioxide from burning large amounts of fossil fuels could cause a global warming. Carbon dioxide is a so-called greenhouse gas that, like glass in a greenhouse, traps heat from the sun. Too much carbon dioxide and other greenhouse gases could raise Earth's temperature, altering the world's climate and raising sea levels.

Damage to Earth's atmosphere was also apparent when a hole in the ozone layer over Antarctica was discovered by scientists in 1985. Ozone is a gas that in the upper atmosphere blocks the sun's ultraviolet radiation, known to cause skin cancer. Subsequent research showed that ozone was being depleted on a global basis, and that chlorofluorocarbons (CFC's), chemicals used mainly as cooling agents in refrigerators and air conditioners and as a propellant in some spray cans, seemed the likely cause.

Meanwhile, destruction of the rain forests threatened a million species of plants and animals with extinction. Burning and cutting of the rain forests also contributed to the greenhouse effect. Not only did the burning of rain forest trees send more carbon dioxide into the atmosphere, but, more significantly, the loss of those trees meant that much less carbon dioxide was being removed from the atmosphere through the process of plant photosynthesis.

But along with the realization that human activity was damaging the global environment, there was also encouragement that the environment was becoming an international concern. In 1987, 24 nations signed a treaty, agreeing to limit the use and production of CFC's. This kind of international agreement seemed to hold out the promise on Earth Day 1990 that although we pollute the planet together, we can also act together to help save it.   [Rod Such]

Environment

Continued

Fireboats spray water on flaming oil that leaked from a Norwegian oil tanker, the *Mega Borg,* following an explosion in the ship's pump room that killed two crew members in June 1990. The explosion occurred in the Gulf of Mexico off Galveston, Tex., and spilled about 14 million liters (3.7 million gallons) of light crude oil into the gulf. Most of it reportedly burned or evaporated in the blaze.

ests. By contrast, the report said that ozone-smog may have accounted for $5 billion in losses in U.S. crop yields and may have significantly damaged many U.S. forests.

Acid rain effects can be severe on a regional basis, however. At a February 1990 NAPAP meeting in Hilton Head Island, S.C., researchers reported cause for concern in many regional areas, including the southwestern Adirondack Mountains, New England, the Atlantic coastal plain, and the Appalachian Mountains as far south as North Carolina.

At the meeting, aquatic ecologist Joan P. Baker and her colleagues reported results of a new survey sponsored by New York state and several electric utilities that burn fossil fuels. The survey found that 24 per cent of the lakes in New York's Adirondacks have no fish. Baker estimated that acid rain was responsible for the absence of fish in roughly one-third of those lakes.

Arctic ozone. Preliminary evidence that a small, seasonal "hole" may be developing in the ozone layer in the

upper atmosphere over the Arctic was reported in July 1989. Data collected by a team of atmospheric scientists headed by David J. Hofmann of the University of Wyoming in Laramie showed that significant thinning in the ozone layer occurred in a region 22 to 26 kilometers (14 to 16 miles) above the Arctic. See METEOROLOGY.

X-ray dangers. Low doses of X rays pose a 2½ times greater risk of causing human cancers other than leukemia and a 4 times greater leukemia risk than previously estimated, according to a major study published by the National Academy of Sciences in January 1990. The report, which was based on a review of studies performed over the previous 10 years, also indicates that age affects radiation risk. Exposures during childhood pose roughly twice the lifetime cancer risk of those received by adults.

Curbing benzene. Rules to limit nonoccupational exposure to industrial emissions of benzene, the 16th most widely used chemical by U.S. manufacturers, were proposed on Aug. 31,

1989, by the U.S. Environmental Protection Agency. The new pollution controls, expected to cost industries more than $1 billion, were targeted at industrial-plant emissions of this cancer-causing chemical. Such emissions may account for 4 of the 960 benzene-related leukemias estimated to occur each year in the United States, according to the EPA.

The new regulations do not apply to other emissions of this chemical. But data from an EPA indoor air pollution study published in October indicated that exposure to benzene in and around the home, from such things as cigarette smoke, paint, and auto exhaust, probably cause 99 per cent of the benzene-related leukemias. If these findings are upheld, benzene would rank among the leading nonoccupational sources of chemically caused cancers in the United States.

Lead poisoning. Childhood exposures to levels of lead that were once considered moderate or low can seriously influence adult intellectual performance, according to a January 1990 report by a team of researchers headed by Herbert L. Needleman at the University of Pittsburgh in Pennsylvania. The researchers tested the baby teeth of 122 individuals. The level of lead in baby teeth is an indicator of lead exposures in childhood.

The researchers then divided the adults into three groups: those whose baby teeth had shown lead levels under 10 parts per million (ppm), those whose teeth had contained 10 to 20 ppm lead, and those whose baby teeth had contained 20 to 24 ppm lead. All these childhood lead levels were well below those considered toxic.

Adults from the highest lead group performed less well than those in the lower groups on reading, vocabulary, and grammar-reasoning tests. In 1979, Needleman was the first to observe that the more lead a child had been exposed to, the more poorly that child performed at school. He now concludes that lead's harmful effects on the brain are permanent.   [Janet Raloff]

In WORLD BOOK, see ENVIRONMENTAL POLLUTION.

Genetics

The discovery of a gene that may control the process by which different pieces of *deoxyribonucleic acid* (DNA) are joined together to produce *antibodies* was announced in December 1989 by scientists at the Whitehead Institute for Biomedical Research and the Massachusetts Institute of Technology (MIT), both in Cambridge. Antibodies are protein molecules produced by the immune system to defend the body against infections. DNA is the molecule of which genes are made.

The interest in the newly discovered gene stems from the fact that the immune system is capable of responding to a huge number of *antigens* (infectious agents), including hundreds of thousands that it encounters for the first time. To cope with these legions of foreign invaders, certain white blood cells, called *lymphocytes*, must produce antibodies that are specific enough to react to each individual type of antigen and to "recognize" any particular antigen the next time they encounter it.

Reshuffling antibody genes. Although antibodies are produced under the direction of genes, we do not have a gene for every potential antigen—there are simply too many antigens around. Instead, various segments of DNA are joined together in a lymphocyte to "build" a gene to produce an antibody specific to an invading antigen. The Cambridge scientists isolated a gene they called the RAG-1 gene, which may control the process by which the pieces of DNA are joined together.

To isolate the RAG-1 gene, the scientists conducted experiments with two kinds of cells—skin cells called *fibroblasts* that normally lack the ability to shuffle DNA segments around to build antibody-producing genes and a type of lymphocyte that seems to have an overactive immune response caused by a very active RAG-1 gene. The researchers also designed a system of "markers"—a sort of easily seen genetic identification tag—that enabled them to track DNA segments.

Using these tools, the scientists painstakingly introduced tiny pieces of genetic material from the lymphocytes into the fibroblasts. Each time they did so, they checked to see if the marker indicated a shuffling of DNA segments. Finally, a piece of genetic material they added caused a rearrangement of DNA segments in the fibroblasts. The fibroblasts had in a sense gained the ability to produce antibody genes.

The bit of genetic material that caused that transformation in the fibroblasts, the researchers concluded, contained the RAG-1 gene. The scientists also found what appeared to be a similar gene in DNA from rabbits, dogs, goats, horses, and mice.

Although scientists have long known about the process of building antibody-producing genes, this was the first time that a gene specific to the DNA shuffling process had been identified and isolated. The researchers hope that continued studies of this gene will help to further our understanding of how the immune system works and how problems with it might be corrected.

Genetically altered mice. In other research at MIT and the Whitehead Institute, scientists reported in April 1990 that they had developed an unusual strain of mice with a deficiency in their immune system. The researchers created the deficiency by substituting a defective form of a gene for the normal one in the animals' cells.

Using a recently developed technique called *targeting*, the researchers disrupted the functioning of a gene that plays an important role in the mice's immune system. Targeting, originally developed in research with simple organisms such as bacteria and yeast, enables scientists to zero in on just one gene and change or replace it.

Targeting is much more complex with mammal cells, which contain as many as 100,000 genes, as opposed to only a few thousand in yeast and bacterial cells. The procedure had been used previously with mammal cells growing in laboratory cultures. In developing a strain of living mice with a targeted mutation, the Whitehead and MIT scientists pushed the technique to a more advanced level.

The researchers first replaced the normal immune-system gene with a defective gene in cultured cells from mouse embryos. The cells from each embryo were at a stage when they could be manipulated and still develop into a fetus when put back with the other cells from the embryo. The mice that developed from the combination of these cells had some body cells with a normal copy of the targeted gene and some cells with a mutated copy of the gene. By selectively breeding the mice for several generations, the researchers developed a line of mice with the defective gene in all of their cells.

The investigators predicted that the new technique would have wide application in medical research. They said it should be possible to develop mice and other animals with various mutations that cause human diseases, including some forms of cancer. The animals would then serve as experimental "models" for the study of those genetic defects and diseases.

Second genetic code. New findings on the so-called second genetic code were announced in December 1989 by researchers at Yale University in New Haven, Conn. The second genetic code governs the way in which protein molecules are assembled in cells.

What scientists call the first, or primary, genetic code is contained in DNA, which is shaped like a twisted ladder. The steps of the ladder are made of molecules called *bases*, and the genetic code is contained in the order in which these bases are arranged.

A gene is a sequence of bases encoding the instructions for constructing a protein, which is made from units called *amino acids*. In the DNA code, bases are organized into three-base segments called *codons*; each codon specifies 1 of 20 amino acids.

In order for a given protein to be manufactured, the coded information in DNA is first copied into a similar molecule called *messenger ribonucleic acid* (mRNA). The mRNA then travels out of the cell nucleus to the main body of the cell. There, at a molecule called a *ribosome*, the information carried by the mRNA is "read" one codon at a time by molecules of another kind of RNA, known as *transfer RNA* (tRNA). Each tRNA molecule has a single amino acid attached to it, and the amino acids are linked together, one by one, as the codons are read.

Although this process may seem relatively straightforward, it is actually quite complex. In addition to the 20

Genetics

Continued

different amino acids, there are 45 to 50 different types of tRNA molecules. Geneticists did not know how a particular amino acid connects with the right tRNA molecule in order to be carried into place at the ribosome.

Researchers did know that a protein called a *synthetase* was necessary to physically connect an amino acid with a tRNA molecule. The Yale scientists used a technique called *X-ray crystallography* to analyze the various stages of this process. By exposing crystallized forms of the various substances involved to X-ray bombardment, the investigators learned about the detailed structures of the molecules and how they worked together. They discovered that the synthetase "recognizes" the part of the tRNA molecule that reads the mRNA code. In addition, the scientists learned when and how the actual joining of the tRNA and amino acid is accomplished.

Although this finding was hailed by many molecular biologists as a landmark step in understanding the process of protein assembly, the Yale re-

searchers studied only two amino acids and their tRNA "mates." Given the number of possible combinations of tRNA and amino acid molecules, there is still a great deal more to be learned.

New leukemia findings. Discoveries relating to the genetic basis of two different types of leukemia were announced in late 1989 and early 1990 by research groups at the Whitehead Institute and the Stanford University School of Medicine in California. Both of the leukemias—cancers of the white blood cells—appear to involve breaks in chromosomes, the threadlike structures in the cell nucleus that carry the genes.

Each normal human cell contains 46 chromosomes, which come in pairs numbered 1 to 23. One of the leukemias studied by the scientists, chronic myelogenous leukemia, has been linked with breaks at particular points in chromosomes 9 and 22. The other type of leukemia, acute lymphoblastic leukemia, involves breaks in chromosomes 1 and 19.

In the case of acute lymphoblastic

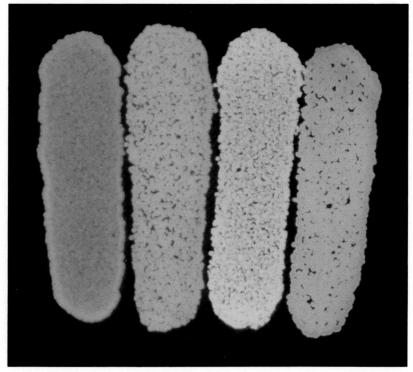

Spliced-in genes from a Jamaican beetle called the kittyboo make colonies of bacteria glow. Each colony has one of four genes from the kittyboo, a *bioluminescent* animal (an animal that produces light). Researchers plan to use the newly discovered genes to study the functioning of other genes. For example, a kittyboo gene could be inserted into a human cell next to any particular gene in such a way that the two genes are always "turned on" together. When the kittyboo gene was activated, it would light up the cell, showing scientists that the other gene was also active.

Striking New Images of DNA

Detailed images of deoxyribonucleic acid (DNA), the molecule of which genes are made, were produced in 1989 and 1990 by the scanning tunneling microscope (STM), an instrument that uses an ultrafine needle to sense areas as small as an atom. The first undistorted image of DNA, *right,* was produced by researchers at Arizona State University in Tempe, by placing the STM and the molecule underwater. With other microscope techniques, scientists had to remove all the water from DNA to create an image. A computer-enhanced STM image of DNA, revealing its many twists, peaks, and valleys, *bottom,* was produced at the Lawrence Berkeley Laboratory in California.

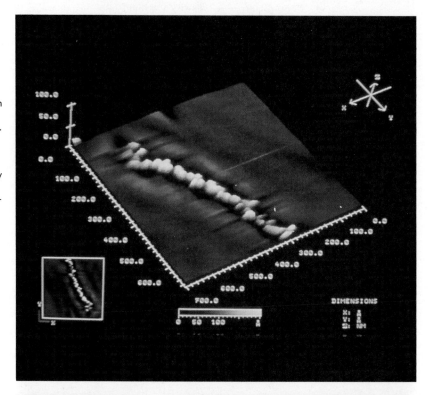

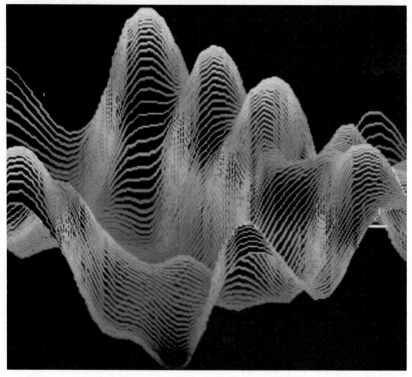

leukemia, the Stanford researchers were able to identify the genes at the break points in the two chromosomes. One of the genes makes a protein called an *enhancer* that is important for the proper functioning of the immune system. Because the white blood cells affected by leukemia are a critical component of the immune system, this was a significant finding. The scientists speculated that acute lymphoblastic leukemia may result from changes that the chromosome breaks cause in the enhancer gene and other genes.

In studies of chronic myelogenous leukemia, researchers had already shown that an unusual chromosome known as the Philadelphia chromosome (named after the city where it was discovered) was almost always present in patients with the disease. The Philadelphia chromosome is formed by the joining of broken pieces of chromosomes 9 and 22.

The investigators at the Whitehead Institute found that a new gene is created at the point where these two chromosome pieces join. The scientists isolated the protein produced by this gene and found it to be very similar to an abnormal protein thought to cause a type of cancer that affects mice.

To see whether the protein coded for by the newly discovered gene would also cause cancer, the researchers injected copies of the gene into healthy mice. The mice soon developed a disease resembling chronic myelogenous leukemia.

The scientists at the two institutions expressed optimism that their findings will lead to a better understanding of leukemia. They said more effective treatments of this form of cancer may also result.

Tumor-suppressing genes. An important finding supporting the idea that there is a whole class of human genes that help prevent the development of cancer was reported in December 1989 by researchers at MIT and the University of Colorado in Denver. These genes, called *tumor suppressor genes*, appear to play a crucial protective role in the multistep process that can ultimately lead to cancer.

The research groups found a gene on chromosome 11 that apparently prevents a form of kidney cancer known as Wilms' tumor. Because chromosomes come in pairs, there are two copies of this gene, and both copies seem to be missing or defective in patients with Wilms' tumor.

This finding indicated that just one copy of the normal gene in a cell will prevent a tumor from forming, which supports the theory that the development of cancer is a multistep process. Scientists believe that at least three other genes, of a type that promotes rather than suppresses the cancer process, are involved in Wilms' tumor.

The new evidence places Wilms' tumor in a growing class of cancers—including cancers of the colon, lung, and breast—that researchers now think are caused by a series of genetic changes. Scientists hope that unraveling the genetic basis of these common cancers will lead to better ways of treating them, and perhaps also of preventing them.

In a related development, investigators at the School of Medicine of the University of California at San Diego announced in February 1990 that they had found evidence for a gene capable of suppressing the development of prostate cancer. The scientists introduced a normal copy of a gene called the RB gene into cells that are known to form prostate tumors in experimental animals. When these modified cells were injected into mice, tumors did not develop. Cancer of the prostate gland is one of the most common types of cancer found in men, and this research finding holds out hope for a more effective treatment of this disease.

Cystic fibrosis gene found. Research groups at the University of Toronto in Canada and other institutions announced in September 1989 that they had identified the gene that causes cystic fibrosis, a fatal hereditary disease that involves thick mucus in the lungs and digestive tract. The discovery of the gene may lead to new treatments for cystic fibrosis. In the meantime, patients may be helped by a new drug, being readied for human tests in mid-1990, that in laboratory tests thinned the sticky mucus. In the Special Reports section, see TRACKING DOWN A DEADLY GENE. [David S. Haymer]

In WORLD BOOK, see CANCER; CELL; GENETICS; IMMUNITY.

Geology

Two major earthquakes struck opposite sides of the world in late 1989 and mid-1990. A quake measuring 7.1 on the Richter scale struck the San Francisco area on Oct. 17, 1989. The quake, known as the Loma Prieta earthquake, killed at least 62 people and caused $6.2 billion in damage. On June 21, 1990, a quake measuring 7.7 on the Richter scale struck Iran, reportedly killing about 40,000 people.

Radio warning of quake? Surges in ultralow-frequency (ULF) radio waves were detected about three weeks and again three hours before the Loma Prieta earthquake struck. But researchers at Stanford University in Palo Alto, Calif., are unsure whether the waves were related to the earthquake.

ULF waves can travel very long distances through ground or water and often are caused by solar magnetic storms and other conditions in Earth's upper atmosphere. By chance, a team of Stanford scientists headed by electrical engineer Anthony Fraser-Smith had set up equipment that records ULF radio waves only 7 kilometers (4⅓ miles) from Loma Prieta, a mountain near where the earthquake began.

On October 5, the scientists noticed an increase in the strength of the ULF waves. Three hours before the quake began, the intensity of the waves increased to 30 times its normal level.

If scientists can demonstrate that the signals were in fact related to the earthquake, the signals may provide a short-term warning that a quake is about to occur. It will be necessary, however, to set up monitoring instruments near known earthquake zones to determine if there is an increase in the strength of ULF radio waves before other earthquakes.

Oldest rocks. The discovery of the oldest rocks ever found on Earth was reported in November 1989 by geologists Samuel A. Bowring of Washington University in St. Louis, Mo., and Ian S. Williams and William Compston of Australian National University in Canberra. The rocks, which were found near Great Slave Lake in the Northwest Territories of Canada, are 3.96 billion years old. They are only about 600 million years younger than Earth itself, which formed about 4.6 billion years ago.

The rocks are a type of *metamorphic* rock called *gneiss*. Metamorphic rock is rock that has been altered by heat and pressure deep within Earth. Gneiss is a coarse-grained rock made of alternating bands of light and dark minerals.

Embedded in gneiss are tiny grains of zircon less than 1 millimeter (1/25 inch) in diameter. They contain small amounts of the radioactive elements uranium and thorium. These elements undergo radioactive decay at a known rate to form *isotopes* (forms) of lead. This process goes on over millions or billions of years. By determining the proportion of uranium and thorium to lead in the zircon crystals, scientists can calculate the age of the crystals and, thus, that of the rock containing them.

Determining these proportions in the gneisses was difficult, however, because the rocks contain only minute amounts of the radioactive elements. For their study, Williams and Compston relied on a one-of-a-kind instrument that can analyze extremely small sections of zircon crystals.

The device shoots a stream of *ions* (charged atoms) at the crystals, breaking off individual atoms. The atoms can then be analyzed to determine their mass. Different elements and isotopes have different masses. These measurements provided the scientists with a way of identifying the uranium and thorium atoms and lead isotopes, and, thus, determining the proportion of each in the sample. The scientists calculated the age of the rocks at 3.964 billion years. Previously, the oldest known rocks were gneisses from Antarctica calculated to be 3.87 billion years old.

First oceans. How did water condense onto the surface of Earth to form oceans? A catastrophic collision of a huge planetary body with Earth more than 4 billion years ago may have been the cause. That theory was reported in March 1990 by geophysicist William Kaula of the University of California, Los Angeles.

Geologists believe that early in Earth's history its crust was very hot and that it probably had an atmosphere much like that of Venus, composed mostly of carbon dioxide. This dense atmosphere traps heat from the sun, raising temperatures on the surface of

Icy Speedometer
A geologist buries a device that measures movement in an *ice stream,* a fast-moving river of ice, in the West Antarctic Ice Sheet. The device will help geologists determine whether the speed of the ice stream is increasing, which may indicate that the entire ice sheet is sliding into the sea. The melting of the ice sheet would raise global sea levels, flooding coastal areas.

Venus to about 450°C (840°F.). The early Earth may have had similar surface temperatures, far too hot for water vapor in the atmosphere to condense as rain.

Kaula theorized that the differences between Venus and Earth today can be explained by catastrophic events that happened early in Earth's history. Some scientists believe that a planet about the size of Mars collided with Earth, forming the moon. Kaula suggested that this collision also blew away Earth's original carbon-dioxide-rich atmosphere, allowing the surface to cool dramatically.

Soon, a second atmosphere formed from the gases given off by the many volcanoes active on Earth at that time. Volcanic gases are made up largely of steam. Because Earth's surface was cooler, this steam condensed as rain, which filled the oceans.

Did meteorites destroy early life? The bombardment of Earth by huge asteroids and meteorites may have affected when and where life evolved. This theory was proposed in February 1990 by a team of researchers headed by geologist James F. Kasting of the Pennsylvania State University in University Park.

Kasting and his colleagues suggest that the periodic evaporation and reformation of the oceans may have prevented life from gaining a permanent foothold on Earth until 3.5 billion years ago. Fossil evidence indicates that life has existed continuously on Earth since at least that time.

Most geologists agree that Earth was frequently struck by asteroids and meteorites from the time of its formation about 4.6 billion years ago until about 3.8 billion years ago. According to Kasting and his colleagues, when the asteroids and meteorites hit Earth, they and the land or water they struck were *vaporized* (transformed to gas). This gas, whose temperature reached 2000°C (3600°F.), rose and heated the atmosphere. The hot atmosphere, in turn, radiated heat into the oceans, causing them to boil and evaporate. The scientists calculated that if an asteroid 435 kilometers (270 miles) in

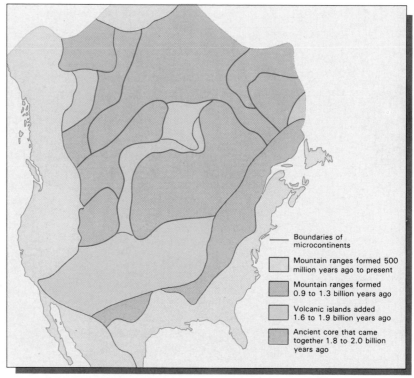

The ancient core of North America is made up of seven microcontinents (shown in blue) that came together in a series of collisions between 2 billion and 1.8 billion years ago, according to research reported in summer 1989. The collisions were caused by the movement of the huge tectonic plates that make up Earth's outer layers, including the crust. Part of the southern part of North America (shown in green) consists of volcanic islands that became attached to the core between 1.9 billion and 1.6 billion years ago. Other parts of the continent (shown in orange and yellow) were formed later.

Boundaries of microcontinents

Mountain ranges formed 500 million years ago to present

Mountain ranges formed 0.9 to 1.3 billion years ago

Volcanic islands added 1.6 to 1.9 billion years ago

Ancient core that came together 1.8 to 2.0 billion years ago

Source: Paul F. Hoffman, Geological Survey of Canada.

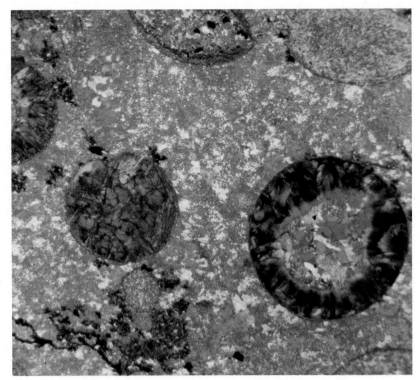

Spherical particles of rock about the size of grains of sand are the first solid evidence that huge meteors bombarded Earth early in its history, according to research reported in April 1990. The particles, embedded in sedimentary rock and discovered in South Africa, are at least 3.2 billion years old. Geologists believe they were created from vaporized rock sent into the atmosphere when the meteors crashed into Earth. The vaporized rock later condensed to liquid droplets that rained down on Earth, eventually solidifying as glassy particles.

Geology

Continued

diameter had collided with Earth, this could have caused the evaporation of all the world's oceans. As a result, any life forms in the oceans would have been wiped out. The scientists estimated that it would have taken at least 1,000 years for the steam in the atmosphere to cool enough to turn to liquid rain and refill the oceans.

But, they note, all ocean life may not have been destroyed. Most of the asteroids striking the Earth were probably no more than 190 kilometers (120 miles) in diameter. An asteroid this size, they estimate, would have evaporated only the top 200 meters (650 feet) of the oceans.

Life may have survived in the deep sea around vents, or openings, in the sea floor from which spew plumes of hot water rich in sulfur and other minerals. Kasting noted that some of the oldest known bacteria favored a hot environment and obtained their nourishment from hydrogen sulfide gas and minerals dissolved in seawater. Bacteria that live near deep-sea vents today also obtain energy in this way. Thus,

Kasting speculated, life may have evolved first in the deep oceans, where it was protected from the catastrophic events taking place on the surface. In the Special Reports section, see LIFE AT THE DEEP-SEA "GEYSERS."

North American core. North America is one of the most ancient of all the continents, with more than half of its core dated to at least 2.5 billion years ago. That ancient core is composed of seven microcontinents that came together in a series of collisions that lasted about 150 million years. The collisions were caused by movements of *tectonic plates*, the gigantic plates that make up Earth's outer layers.

Those conclusions were contained in the first comprehensive summary of the ancient geologic history of North America, published in summer 1989 by geologist Paul F. Hoffman of the Geological Survey of Canada. Hoffman, citing the research of many geologists, surveyed the geologic history of North America during the Precambrian Time. This period extended from about 4 billion years ago, when the first rocks were formed, to 570 million years ago, when the first marine *invertebrates* (animals without backbones) appeared.

Hoffman reported that rocks more than 2.5 billion years old formed seven microcontinents that collided about 1.9 billion years ago to form the core of North America. Chains of volcanic islands were added until about 1.1 billion years ago.

Sliding or colliding? The tectonic plate on which Australia and India sit seems to have changed directions and now appears to be sliding beneath the Pacific Plate. That conclusion was reported in December 1989 by a team of scientists headed by seismologist Susan L. Beck of the University of Michigan in Ann Arbor.

For at least 50 million years, the Australian Plate has been sliding past the Pacific Plate. If the two plates continue to collide, scientists will have a rare opportunity to study the formation of a *subduction zone*, a region where one tectonic plate is descending beneath another. Although geologists have identified many subduction zones,

they are uncertain about how such a region is formed.

The Michigan scientists analyzed the movement of crust that caused a huge earthquake on May 23, 1989. The earthquake, which measured 8.2 on the Richter scale, struck the Macquarie Ridge, a chain of underwater mountains extending south from New Zealand toward Antarctica. The Macquarie Ridge marks part of the boundary between the Pacific and Australian plates. They reported that, as in past earthquakes at this site, the two plates slid sideways past each other. But they also found that at some places the two plates collided.

According to the scientists, the existence of two trenches on the sea floor just west of the Macquarie Ridge is additional evidence that a subduction zone is forming. These deep, narrow depressions in the ocean floor commonly form near subduction zones. [William W. Hay]

In the Special Reports section, see EARTH'S DEADLY MOVEMENTS. In WORLD BOOK, see EARTH; GEOLOGY.

Immunology

Vaccine tests with monkeys indicate that it may be possible to immunize people against the AIDS virus, researchers at Tulane University in New Orleans reported in December 1989. Although monkeys do not get AIDS, they can be infected by a related virus called the *simian immunodeficiency virus* (SIV). SIV causes an immunity-destroying condition similar to AIDS.

The Tulane scientists immunized nine rhesus monkeys with an experimental SIV vaccine and later injected them with the virus. The investigators used a virus dose level that previous research had shown will kill 75 per cent of injected monkeys within seven months. One year after being infected, all the monkeys in the Tulane study were well, and only one had detectable amounts of the virus in its body.

Eliminating the AIDS virus. Doctors at Johns Hopkins University in Baltimore reported in December 1989 that they had succeeded in eliminating the AIDS virus in a patient. The patient, a 41-year-old man, was suffering from both AIDS and lymphoma, a cancer of

the lymph glands that often occurs in people with AIDS.

The physicians' goal was to eliminate both the cancer cells and the AIDS-infected cells from the patient's body. To do that, they destroyed the man's bone marrow—the source of both kinds of cells—with powerful drugs and radiation. They then replaced it with normal marrow from a donor. They also administered the anti-AIDS drug *azidothymidine* (AZT), which prevented any lingering traces of the AIDS virus from attacking cells in the transplanted marrow.

Although the new bone marrow was accepted by the patient's body, he ultimately died from a recurrence of the cancer. But no AIDS virus could be detected in tissues from the patient's body in autopsy studies.

Bone marrow transplants are a standard treatment for lymphoma and leukemia, a cancer of the white blood cells. But in combination with AZT, marrow transplants might offer hope to AIDS patients who are not also suffering from one of those cancers.

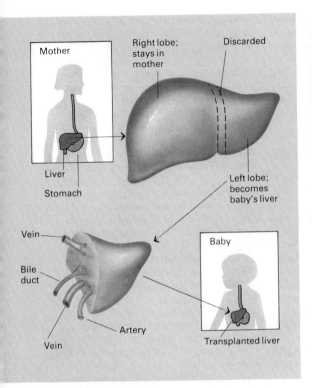

Mother

Right lobe; stays in mother

Discarded

Liver

Stomach

Left lobe; becomes baby's liver

Vein

Bile duct

Vein

Artery

Baby

Transplanted liver

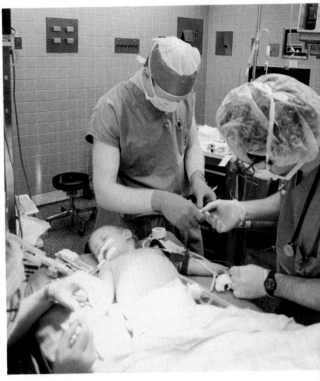

Medical Research

Continued

Live-Donor Liver Transplant

Surgeons at the University of Chicago Medical Center, *above right,* prepare to perform the first liver transplant in the United States using liver tissue from a living donor in November 1989. The surgeons successfully replaced the diseased liver of 21-month-old Alyssa Smith with a section of her mother's liver, *above.*

removed the left lobe of the mother's liver, the second largest of the liver's four lobes. They left the bile ducts and the three major blood vessels that supply the liver attached to her right lobe, the liver's largest section.

When the surgeons removed Alyssa's diseased liver, they did not take out the three blood vessels. These were attached to the transplanted lobe. Alyssa's new liver began to work almost immediately.

Because the liver is the only organ capable of regenerating, the mother's liver grew back to its original size within a few weeks. Alyssa's transplanted section of liver, which is the size of a healthy liver in a child her age, will grow to normal adult size as she grows.

The Chicago surgeons successfully performed a second live-donor liver transplant in December 1989. Fifteen-month-old Sarina Jones, who was also suffering from biliary atresia, received the transplant from her father.

The use of partial livers from live donors is expected to increase the supply of organs for transplantation in

children. Because the waiting time for livers will be reduced, fewer children will die while awaiting a transplant. In addition, the children will receive their transplants while they are still relatively healthy. This should improve their ability to survive the surgery.

Reducing paralysis. For the first time, researchers have discovered a drug treatment that reduces the level of paralysis caused by injury to the spinal cord. This finding was announced in March 1990 at a press conference at the National Institute of Neurological Disorders and Stroke in Bethesda, Md. To be effective, however, the drug must be administered within hours after the injury occurs.

These findings were so significant that they were announced before the details of the study were published so that doctors would learn about the treatment as quickly as possible. More than 10,000 Americans suffer spinal cord injuries each year.

The study of the drug treatment involved 487 patients with injured spinal cords at 10 U.S. medical centers.

Medical Research

Continued

An experimental ultrasound imaging technique developed at the University of Rochester in New York may enable physicians to find some hard-to-detect cancerous tumors at an early stage. A cancerous prostate tumor that appears only as an indistinct impression in a conventional ultrasound image, *below,* is clearly visible as a dark mass in an image made using the new technique, *below right.* The technique, which also can detect tumors that cannot be seen with conventional ultrasound, maps differences in the rate at which tissue vibrates when stimulated by low-frequency sound waves. Cancerous tissue vibrates less rapidly than does healthy tissue.

One group of patients received intravenous injections of *methylprednisolone,* an anti-inflammatory drug that slows cell damage in injured tissue. Another group received *naloxone,* a drug that improves blood flow to the spinal cord. The remaining patients received a *placebo* (inactive substance).

Both methylprednisolone and naloxone had previously been tested in patients with spinal injuries with varying results. In this study, however, the methylprednisolone was administered in doses up to 15 times higher than that given in previous studies.

The researchers tested the nerve and muscle function and the sense of touch of all the patients when they were admitted to the hospital after being injured and then at six weeks and six months. Only a few of the patients who received naloxone or the placebo showed even slight improvement.

But most of the patients who received methylprednisolone were significantly improved, both at six weeks and six months after they were injured. Methylprednisolone had no effect, however, in the patients who received it more than eight hours after being injured.

According to the researchers, the findings provide the first direct evidence that the paralysis that often follows spinal injuries does not result from the injury itself. Few spinal injuries sever the spinal cord. Instead, the injury causes swelling of the spinal tissue and triggers a series of chemical reactions that kill nerve cells.

The researchers are not sure why methylprednisolone is effective in limiting damage to the spinal cord. They speculate that the drug may help maintain the flow of blood—and thus, oxygen—to the swollen spinal tissue. The drug may also interrupt the chemical reactions that destroy the nerve cells.

Treating muscular dystrophy. Injections of healthy muscle cells may offer a promising therapy for children with muscular dystrophy. Researchers at four medical centers in the United States began trials of this experimental therapy with 40 boys in early 1990.

Muscular dystrophy is a hereditary

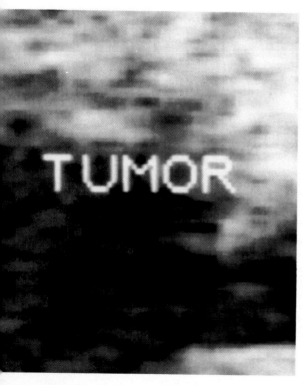

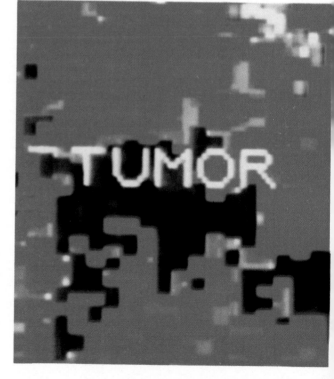

disease, usually affecting boys, in which the muscles become progressively weaker. The disease is caused by reduced levels of a protein called *dystrophin*, which is essential for proper muscle function. Patients with the most severe form of muscular dystrophy rarely live beyond their teens. There is no known treatment that will slow or reverse the progress of the disorder.

The researchers obtained small pieces of muscle from volunteer donors. They then separated out the *myoblasts*, immature muscle cells. These cells contain the gene that *codes for* (directs the production of) dystrophin. Finally, the researchers grew the myoblasts in laboratory cultures to increase their number.

The researchers at the different centers injected the cells into a particular muscle in the boys with muscular dystrophy. At the University of Tennessee in Memphis, the cells were injected into the muscle that controls the movement of the big toe on the left foot. Researchers at the Montreal Neurological Institute and Hospital in Canada injected the myoblasts into the biceps muscle in one arm of the boys studied there. At the University of California, San Francisco, the cells were injected into a shin muscle. Researchers at Tufts New England Medical Center in Boston were scheduled to begin injections into the small muscle between the thumb and the index finger in October 1990.

In earlier animal studies of the experimental therapy, the researchers found that the healthy myoblasts fused to the surface of the muscles weakened by muscular dystrophy, forming hybrid cells. These hybrid cells then produced dystrophin. The researchers hope that an increase in dystrophin in the boys' muscles will reverse some of the damage caused by the disease.

Obesity and heart attack. Obese women have a much higher risk of heart attack than do women of normal weight, according to results reported in March 1990 from an ongoing study. The data presented the first clear evidence of a link between obesity and heart disease in women.

Researchers from Harvard University Medical School in Boston have been studying the health of 115,886 women since 1977. At the beginning of the study, all the women were between the ages of 35 and 55. None had been diagnosed as having heart disease or had suffered a stroke.

For comparison purposes, the researchers computed a body/mass index for each woman by dividing her weight in kilograms by the square of her height in meters. They then arranged the women by index number from lowest to highest and noted what percentage of the women at each level had developed heart disease. The researchers also adjusted statistically for other heart disease risk factors, including age and smoking.

They found that women of below-average to average weight had a low risk of heart disease. Women who were moderately heavy were nearly twice as likely as the first group to develop heart disease. The heaviest women were three times more likely.

The research results indicated that excess weight was responsible for 40 per cent of all heart disease in the women in the study. According to the researchers, 70 per cent of the heart disease in obese women was due to the extra weight they carry. The scientists also found that women who gained weight after age 35 were more likely to develop heart disease than women who had maintained the same weight since age 18.

Diet and atherosclerosis. Even relatively small increases in the amount of dietary fat a person consumes can influence the development of atherosclerosis, a build-up of fatty substances on the walls of the arteries. That finding was reported in March 1990 by researchers at the University of Southern California School of Medicine in Los Angeles. Atherosclerosis often results in heart disease, heart attack, or stroke.

The California team studied 82 men ages 40 to 59 who had undergone coronary artery bypass surgery to replace one or more clogged arteries in their heart. The men were asked to follow a diet in which fats made up only 25 per cent of the calories they ate.

All the men were given *angiograms*—X rays of the arteries in the heart—when they entered the study. The researchers noted all the areas in the arteries where fatty materials blocked

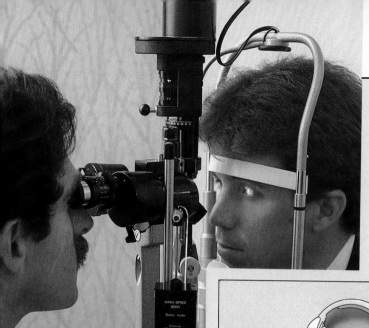

Using Lasers to Correct Vision

Lasers have long been used in eye surgery. Researchers are currently conducting studies to determine whether lasers can be used safely and effectively to correct myopia, or near-sightedness.

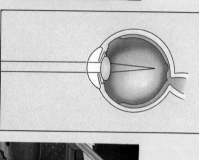

Near-sightedness occurs when the cornea, the transparent dome over the front of the eye, is too long or too curved. As a result, light rays are focused in front of instead of on the retina, forming a blurred image.

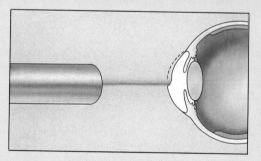 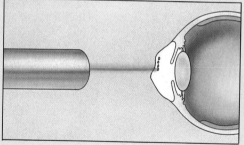

Two experimental laser techniques change the focus of the eye by reshaping the cornea. An excimer laser, *above left,* vaporizes several layers of cells on the surface of the cornea. A solid-state laser, *above right,* produces a much narrower light beam that penetrates the cornea and vaporizes tiny pockets of cells within it, causing the outer layer of the cornea to collapse.

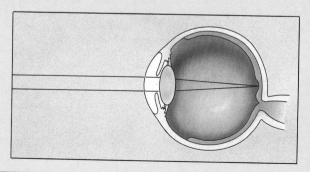

Both techniques cause the cornea to become shorter and flatter. After the cornea is reshaped, light rays are focused on the retina, creating a sharp image.

more than 20 per cent of the diameter of the artery. When the researchers took new angiograms two years later, they found that 18 of the men had developed new clogged areas.

The researchers then compared the diets of these 18 men with those of the rest of the men. They found that fat made up 34 per cent of the calories, on average, consumed by the 18 men. The men who did not develop new deposits obtained only 27 per cent of their calories from fat. The researchers concluded that cutting back even slightly on the amount of fat consumed may significantly benefit the heart.

Fetal surgery. In the first successful major surgery performed on a fetus, a team of surgeons headed by Michael R. Harrison of the University of California, San Francisco, reported in May 1990 that they had repaired an abdominal defect that is usually fatal. Surgeons had previously performed only minor surgery on fetuses while the fetuses were in or partially outside the womb.

An ultrasound test had revealed a hole in the baby boy's *diaphragm*, the layer of muscle separating the abdominal cavity from the chest. The baby's stomach, intestines, liver, and spleen had pushed through the hole into the chest cavity and were pressing against the lungs. If uncorrected, the condition would have prevented the baby's lungs from developing properly, and he almost certainly would have died at birth.

In the procedure, the surgeons cut open the mother's abdomen and uterus and pulled out the baby's left arm, exposing his left side. They then made an incision in the upper left side of the baby's abdomen and lifted out his stomach, spleen, and intestines and part of his liver.

The surgeons repaired the hole in the baby's diaphragm with a patch made from a fabric used in outdoor clothing and then replaced his organs in his abdomen below the repaired diaphragm. Next they sewed another fabric patch over the baby's abdominal incision. This step enlarged his abdominal cavity, making room for the organs. Finally, the surgeons put the baby's arm back into the uterus and closed the incisions in the mother's uterus and abdomen.

The baby was born prematurely seven weeks later. When he was three months old, the surgeons removed the fabric patch on his abdomen and closed the abdominal wall. The surgeons later successfully performed the same procedure on another fetus, a girl, who was born two months later.

Artificial lung. A temporary artificial lung that adds oxygen to and removes carbon dioxide from the bloodstream was tested in a human being for the first time in February 1990. The device, called an intravenous oxygenator (IVOX), was implanted in a teen-age girl whose lungs had failed. The operation was performed by surgeons at LDS Hospital in Salt Lake City, Utah. The team was headed by surgeon J. D. Mortensen, who developed the device.

The device was tested in a second patient in March. The researchers did not expect that the device would save the lives of these terminally ill patients.

IVOX consists of about 1,000 hollow fibers, each about as thick as a human hair, bundled together and bound at either end to a thin tube. The device is inserted through a small incision in the neck into the vena cava, the major vein in the chest.

One end of the tube, which protrudes from the body, is attached to an oxygen tank. Oxygen pumped through the tube passes into the bloodstream through pores in the fibers. At the same time, carbon dioxide is filtered out of the blood through the fibers.

According to Mortensen, IVOX causes less damage to the lungs than mechanical respirators—machines that pump oxygen into a patient's lungs by means of a tube inserted into the windpipe. As a patient's lungs lose the ability to exchange oxygen for carbon dioxide, the respirator pumps increasingly larger amounts of oxygen at increasingly higher pressures into the lungs. The force of the pressure often causes additional damage to the lung tissue. IVOX exchanges gases in the blood much as air sacs in the lungs do, and so pumps less oxygen at lower pressures.   [Beverly Merz]

In the Special Reports section, see TRACKING DOWN A DEADLY GENE; TWO SIDES TO THE OXYGEN STORY. In WORLD BOOK, see HEART; LIVER; LUNG; MUSCULAR DYSTROPHY.

Meteorology

The upper atmosphere above Antarctica during early October 1989 again contained a prominent "hole" in the ozone layer, according to a report by atmospheric physicist Arlin Krueger of the National Aeronautics and Space Administration's (NASA's) Goddard Space Flight Center in Greenbelt, Md. Ozone is a gas molecule consisting of three oxygen atoms. In the upper atmosphere, this gas absorbs biologically harmful ultraviolet radiation from the sun and prevents it from reaching Earth.

Krueger found that the concentration of ozone in the central region of the hole was about 50 per cent lower than normal. It was only slightly above the record-setting low level reported for October 1987. The hole in October 1989—spring in Antarctica—covered an area of some 16 million square kilometers (10 million square miles) and was roughly centered over the South Pole.

Krueger and other NASA scientists have monitored the amount of ozone over the Southern Hemisphere since 1978. Their primary research tool is the Total Ozone Mapping Spectrometer (TOMS), an instrument on board NASA's *Nimbus-7* satellite. The TOMS measures the amount of ultraviolet light absorbed in the atmosphere. Based on this measurement, scientists deduce the amount of ozone present in the atmosphere.

Hurricane Hugo. Over a period of 12 days in mid-September 1989, Hurricane Hugo became the most costly hurricane in history, killing at least 71 people in the United States and on islands of the Caribbean Sea and causing an estimated $8 billion in property damage. Hugo was also perhaps the best-observed hurricane in history.

Hurricane specialists with the National Oceanic and Atmospheric Administration (NOAA) flew through the storm on Sept. 15, 1989. As their NOAA weather reconnaissance aircraft penetrated into the storm's central eye, they encountered a *suction vortex* (a small, intense swirl in which the highest wind speeds occurred). The 1-kilometer- (0.6-mile-) diameter vortex was like those commonly found swirling around the centers of intense tornadoes. This was the first time detailed measurements were made inside such a feature in a hurricane.

Inside the suction vortex, the researchers observed a low air pressure of 918 millibars (27.10 inches of mercury). The average air pressure at sea level is 1,013 millibars (29.92 inches of mercury). The air pressure indicated the hurricane's intensity because the lower the pressure, the more intense the storm.

The researchers also measured wind speeds of 85 meters per second (equivalent to 190 miles per hour) at an altitude of 500 meters (1,600 feet). Estimated surface wind speed at an altitude of 10 meters (33 feet) was 72 meters per second (160 miles per hour). This identified Hugo as a Category 5 hurricane, the most severe type, according to a scale used by the United States National Weather Service.

Hugo crossed the islands of Guadaloupe and St. Croix on September 17 and 18 with 63 meter-per-second (140 mile-per-hour) surface winds and a central pressure of 941 millibars (27.78 inches of mercury). The center of the storm then passed over Puerto Rico with slower wind speeds of 56 meters per second (125 miles per hour).

Hugo reached the South Carolina coast at Sullivans Island, just outside Charleston, on September 22. As it moved onshore, aircraft measured a central pressure of 934 millibars (27.58 inches of mercury). The surface wind speed had risen to an estimated 63 meters per second.

The 1989 hurricane season in the Atlantic Ocean, the Caribbean, and the Gulf of Mexico produced seven major hurricanes. This was the second consecutive year of intense hurricane activity.

Link to global warming? The appearance of Hugo may also have been a signal that high-intensity hurricanes can be expected more often in the future as a result of global climate warming, according to research meteorologist Richard Anthes of the University Corporation for Atmospheric Research in Boulder, Colo.

Many scientists believe that the world's climate is warming due to increasing levels of atmospheric *greenhouse gases* (gases that absorb heat radiated from Earth's surface). Anthes

A satellite photograph of Hurricane Hugo, superimposed on a map, shows the storm's swirling clouds (white area at center) as Hugo approached the southeastern coast of the United States, on Sept. 21, 1989, with wind speeds of 217 kilometers (135 miles) per hour.

Meteorology

Continued

reported in September 1989 that global warming may increase the frequency of Category 4 and Category 5 hurricanes. Although Anthes noted that it is impossible to link a single storm, such as Hugo, to climate change, computer models show that warming of the tropical oceans and of the atmosphere in tropical regions will tend to provide more energy for such superstorms.

Clouds and climate. Greenhouse gases, such as carbon dioxide, trap heat energy from the sun and may be causing global temperatures to rise. To understand how the release of greenhouse gases into the atmosphere may affect climate, scientists use computers to create complex models of the atmosphere. In August 1989, atmospheric scientist Robert D. Cess of the State University of New York at Stony Brook reported preliminary results from a comparison of 14 different climate models developed by scientists from around the world. When the effects of clouds were removed from the models, Cess found that all 14 predicted similar results. But when the effects of clouds

were included, the predictions of the models differed greatly.

Cess's study underscored the lack of agreement among scientists on the role that clouds play in global warming, due to the many properties clouds have. For example, clouds reflect sunlight, so less heat reaches the ground. But clouds also trap heat radiated from Earth's surface, warming the lower atmosphere. Clouds also transport heat into the upper atmosphere. Clouds appear to have properties that promote both heating and cooling, and scientists do not yet know which properties have the greatest effect.

Not so hot? In September 1989, uncertainties about the properties of clouds led meteorologist John Mitchell and colleagues at the United Kingdom Meteorological Office in Bracknell, England, to revise their earlier estimate of how much warmer the planet might become. Earlier, they had predicted a 5°C (9°F.) warming by the middle of the next century if the amount of carbon dioxide in the atmosphere doubles. Mitchell now estimates that there will

Sunspots and Weather

The number of sunspots was rising toward a record level in the summer of 1990, renewing interest in an age-old question: Do sunspots affect the weather?

The fact that the sun is blemished with dark "spots" was first observed around 1611. Then Heinrich Schwabe, a German amateur astronomer, discovered in 1843 that the number of these sunspots rises and falls in cycles. Since then, researchers have learned what causes sunspots and have measured their cycles precisely.

Astronomers believe sunspots are areas where huge, stringlike magnetic fields generated within the sun break through the solar surface. Sunspots appear dark because they are cooler than the sun as a whole and therefore emit less light. In addition, sunspots are often surrounded by extremely bright patches called *faculae*.

The current sunspot cycle, which began in 1987, is the 22nd known cycle. The duration of sunspot cycles varies from 8 to 15 years, with the average being 11 years. The number of sunspots also varies from cycle to cycle. The largest number seen on any single day was 355 spots, viewed on Dec. 24 and 25, 1957. Those days were in cycle 19, which lasted from 1955 to 1966.

Over the years, meteorologists have looked for links between the rise and fall of the sunspot cycle and a wide variety of changes on Earth, such as shifts in amounts of rainfall, the population of rabbits in Australia, the length of the winegrowing season in France, and even prices

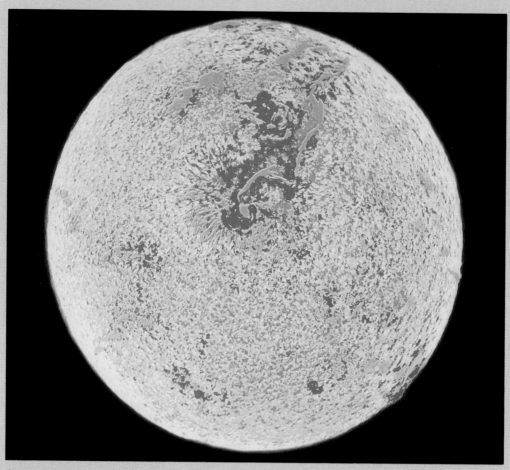

Sunspots appear as green splotches on the solar surface in this artificially colored image. Long, thin patches of green represent huge arches of gas, and red areas indicate bursts of extremely bright light.

on the stock market. All these factors are affected directly and indirectly by weather events such as droughts, floods, the onset of frost, and heat waves.

If sunspots affect the weather, matching cycles should show up in records of these phenomena. Scientists have found some match-ups that have lasted for a few sunspot cycles, but these correlations eventually have broken down.

Meteorologists have long believed that, if there is a physical mechanism linking the sunspot cycle to Earth's weather, this mechanism is driven by variations in the amount of energy the sun gives off as visible light during sunspot cycles. In addition to visible light, the sun emits other forms of radiation, such as X rays and ultraviolet rays. Very little of this radiation, however, penetrates into the *troposphere*, the part of the atmosphere where what we know as "the weather" occurs. The troposphere extends from Earth's surface to 10 kilometers (6 miles) above the surface.

Because the faculae are so much brighter than the sunspots, solar physicists have reasoned that the total amount of light energy emitted by the sun might well increase as the number of sunspots increases and decrease when sunspots decrease. As a result, the amount of light energy reaching Earth's surface might rise and fall during the sunspot cycle, changing the air temperature—and thereby affecting droughts, floods, and other weather phenomena generated in part by air temperature.

It is not possible for instruments on Earth to reliably measure changes in the light energy emitted by the sun because air turbulence can make the amount of energy appear to fluctuate more than it actually does. Accurate measurements had to await the launching of satellites that could measure solar radiation outside Earth's atmosphere.

The satellite record so far covers only the period from 1978 to 1989—about one sunspot cycle. This record shows a decrease in energy from about 1980 to mid-1985, matching a decrease in sunspots. The amount of light energy emitted by the sun remained constant from mid-1985 until mid-1987, and began to rise with a new increase in sunspot activity.

There was a variation of only 0.09 per cent from least to greatest energy given off by the sun during this time. This may not seem like much of a variation. In fact, it appears to be only about 1/1,000th as large as it would have to be to compete with the enormous energy contained in weather systems generated by the heating or cooling of air masses. The measurement has excited researchers, however, because it was large enough to indicate that there could be some unknown—and complicated—mechanism linking sunspot cycles to weather changes.

What might be a key part of this mechanism was discovered in 1987 by German meteorologist Karin Labitzke of the Free University in West Berlin. Labitzke specializes in the meteorology of the *stratosphere*, a region of Earth's atmosphere extending from about 10 to 48 kilometers (6 to 30 miles) above the surface.

At the time of her discovery, Labitzke had been spending a weekend in Washington, D.C., before traveling to Boulder, Colo., where she was going to meet her United States collaborator, meteorologist Harry Van Loon of the National Center for Atmospheric Research. She had with her some data on air temperature and circulation in the stratosphere above the North Pole.

In a hotel room, Labitzke started plotting the data on graph paper to determine whether she could find some link with the sunspot cycle. A graph of stratospheric, polar air temperature at various intervals showed no link between temperature and sunspot number.

But then Labitzke tried a different approach—sorting the data according to whether the stratospheric wind at the equator was blowing eastward or westward. This wind has a cycle of its own, a variation of about 28 months known as the quasi-biennial oscillation.

Labitzke then plotted a graph of polar air temperature for only the years when the equatorial wind in the stratosphere blew eastward. She could hardly believe her eyes. The graph showed a very strong relationship between air temperature and the sunspot cycle: The rise and fall of polar air temperature matched the increases and decreases in the sunspot number.

For years in which winds in the stratosphere above the equator blew westward, the opposite was true: As the sunspot number increased, the stratospheric air temperature above the North Pole fell. And as the sunspot number decreased, this temperature rose. Since Labitzke made her discovery, she and Van Loon have found similar relationships in the mesosphere, which ranges from 48 to 80 kilometers (30 to 50 miles) above the surface, and even in the troposphere.

Data on the direction of the stratospheric winds above the equator are available for 1953 to 1990, during which time three sunspot cycles occurred. Labitzke and Van Loon's findings hold for all those years.

Thus far, however, the linkage between sunspots and the weather is only statistical. Meteorologists now have another question: How could a tiny variation in the light energy emitted by the sun possibly affect Earth's weather? The answer—if there is an answer—may be blowing in the wind.   [Raymond G. Roble]

be less than a 2.8°C (5°F.) temperature rise, about half the old estimate.

There is no evidence of global warming from an enhanced greenhouse effect, according to an analysis of 10 years of temperature data from a satellite. This finding was reported in March 1990 by atmospheric scientists Roy W. Spencer of NASA's Marshall Space Flight Center in Huntsville, Ala., and John R. Christy of the University of Alabama in Huntsville. Although they found that Earth's atmosphere goes through large year-to-year temperature changes, they also found that over the 10-year period from 1979 through 1988, there was no detectable upward trend in overall global temperature. A small warming trend in the Northern Hemisphere was offset by a similar cooling trend in the Southern Hemisphere.

This study was the first involving temperature measurements from satellites to monitor global temperatures. Most other studies of temperature trends have been based on readings made at ground-based stations. These studies often have had to adjust reported temperatures to obtain values representative of a region. This is because over a period of years, urban areas have been built around many of the ground stations. For example, many stations are based at airports that previously recorded temperatures when the airports were surrounded by rural farmland. But as cities grew up around the airports, they absorbed more heat. Therefore, recorded temperatures became higher and were no longer representative of the region.

Furthermore, few surface-based data have been available from over the oceans. Satellite observations, on the other hand, provide regional temperature data from over the entire globe.

Satellite measurements of the sun's luminosity during sunspot cycles have also become important to researchers monitoring temperatures in Earth's upper atmosphere. This research may one day tell us whether the sunspot cycle affects weather. See the Meteorology Close-Up. [John T. Snow]

In WORLD BOOK, see METEOROLOGY.

Neuroscience

Genetic factors alone cannot account for the development of schizophrenia, researchers at the National Institute of Mental Health (NIMH) in Rockville, Md., reported in March 1990. Schizophrenia is a severe form of mental illness marked by bizarre behavior and thinking.

Although the cause of schizophrenia is unknown, findings from studies of families in which there are schizophrenics have indicated that schizophrenia victims inherited a tendency to develop the disease. But the NIMH investigators reported that brain abnormalities, apparently caused by environmental factors, also seem to play a significant role.

The NIMH researchers used a technique called *magnetic resonance imaging* to study the brains of 15 sets of identical twins. Identical twins have the same genetic makeup. But one of the twins in each set suffered from schizophrenia, though the other was normal.

The scientists asked a colleague, who did not know which of the twins were schizophrenic, to examine all the images. On the basis of abnormalities revealed by the scans, that researcher was able to tell which twin had the disease in 12 of the 15 cases. Some of the abnormalities involved an area believed to be involved in emotion and learning.

The researchers concluded from these brain abnormalities that schizophrenia must be caused, at least in part, by environmental factors. If the cause of schizophrenia were strictly genetic, they reasoned, the brains of the twins would be the same—as they most likely were when the twins were born.

Dangers—and uses—of PCP. New findings about the street drug phencyclidine (PCP) were announced in June and November 1989 by neuroscientists at the Washington University School of Medicine in St. Louis, Mo. Their studies showed that the use of PCP involves a risk of possible permanent brain damage as well as mental and emotional upset. But, surprisingly, the investigators also found that the drug—or at least one very similar to it—may prove useful in treating some kinds of

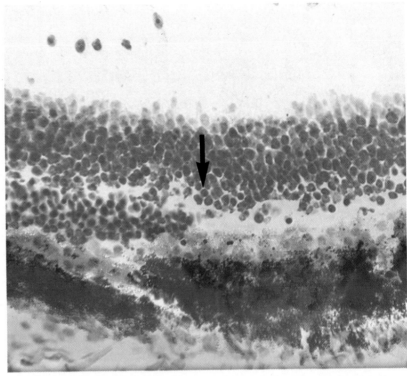

A layer of light-sensitive cells (left of arrow) was transplanted into an area of a mouse's eye that was missing a row of these cells (right of arrow). Four weeks later, the cells were still alive and producing a protein essential to vision. This work, reported in August 1989 by researchers at Washington University in St. Louis, Mo., indicates that some diseases of the retina, the light-sensitive tissue at the back of the eye, may someday be treated with retinal cell transplants.

Neuroscience

Continued

brain disorders. PCP, also called "angel dust," causes symptoms that mimic *psychosis,* a severe form of mental illness. Over the past 20 years, PCP has become a major drug of abuse.

Most neuroscientists had thought the effects of PCP were temporary and primarily psychological, with little, if any, physical harm done to the brain. The Washington University researchers found, however, that PCP causes structural damage to certain groups of brain cells.

The scientists gave relatively low doses of PCP to rats and then examined the animals' brain tissues under a microscope. They found damage in all of the rats' brains. In some of the brains, the changes appeared to be temporary, but in others there appeared to be permanent damage.

The researchers also reported on a compound called MK-801, which is chemically similar to PCP. They said MK-801 may relieve the effects of degenerative brain diseases, though it, too, may cause harmful changes to brain cells. Neuroscientists at a number

of institutions in the United States are now working to develop the potential of MK-801 for the treatment of brain diseases, while at the same time eliminating its damaging effects.

Brain cells grown in laboratory. Researchers at Johns Hopkins University in Baltimore announced in May 1990 that they had succeeded in maintaining human brain *neurons* (nerve cells) in the laboratory. Unlike other kinds of cells, neurons do not grow and divide after reaching maturity, and they usually do not survive for long outside the brain or nervous system. Until now, scientists were unable to grow neurons in laboratory cultures.

Neuroscientists Gabriele Ronnett and Solomon Snyder and their co-workers at the Johns Hopkins School of Medicine studied neurons that had been surgically removed from the brain of a baby girl during an operation to relieve uncontrollable seizures. The seizures were caused by *megalencephaly,* a rare disorder in which cells in one half of the brain of a developing fetus undergo too many divisions, re-

Neuroscience

Continued

A developing nerve in a grasshopper's leg fails to make a connection (arrow) with other nerves in the absence of cells called *pioneer neurons*. These help nerve fibers make connections with the central nervous system by "blazing a trail" for them. Researchers at the University of California at Berkeley used heat to destroy pioneer neurons in the grasshopper's leg. The resulting inability of the nerves to connect with other nerves showed that pioneer neurons are essential in forming the grasshopper nervous system. Pioneer neurons have been found in other animals, including fish and amphibians, and they may also occur in mammals.

sulting in that half of the brain becoming overly large.

The investigators placed the neurons in an enriched culture solution. After 21 days, nearly all the cells had died, but a few survived. Those surviving cells grew and divided, just as normal neurons do in the developing brain. The cells also showed other characteristics typical of normal neurons. They developed into different types of neurons when stimulated with brain substances called *nerve growth factors*, and they secreted many of the same *neurotransmitters* (chemicals that transmit nerve impulses) as do cells of the cerebral cortex, the outermost layer of the brain.

Cells from the Johns Hopkins study will undoubtedly be analyzed by neuroscientists at a number of institutions. Researchers hope the neurons will help them learn more about brain cells, including how they grow and how they are affected by such factors as drugs and disease. Scientists may also gain a better understanding of why the brain and spinal cord do not recover well

after being damaged. Such knowledge might lead to effective new treatments for brain and spinal cord injuries.

Drug for Parkinson's disease. The drug deprenyl is very effective in slowing the progression of Parkinson's disease, neurologist Ira Shoulson of the University of Rochester in New York reported in November 1989. Parkinson's disease is a so-far incurable neurological disorder that afflicts about half a million people in the United States alone, mostly people in their 50's and 60's. It causes muscle rigidity, tremors, and a shuffling gait.

Shoulson headed a study of deprenyl involving 800 Parkinson's patients at 28 U.S. medical centers. Half the patients received deprenyl and the other half were given either a *placebo* (an inactive substance that looked the same as the drug) or a different medication. This phase of the study had been planned to last five years, but Shoulson announced in November that because the results after just two years were so impressive, all the patients would begin receiving deprenyl.

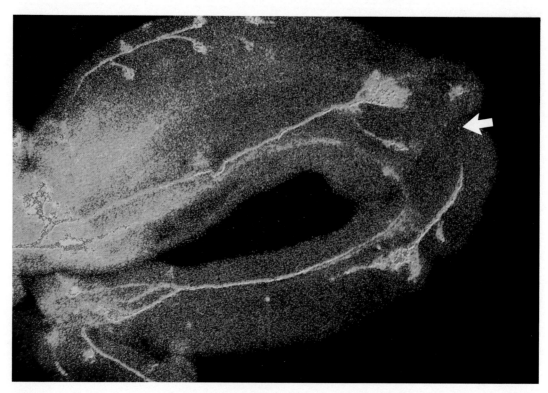

Neuroscience

Shoulson said deprenyl had reduced the development of severe Parkinson's symptoms by 57 per cent. That result confirmed similiar findings in another study, reported in August 1989, with a group of 54 patients at the California Parkinson's Foundation in San Jose.

Earlier studies with laboratory animals, in which symptoms of Parkinson's disease were induced with a form of synthetic heroin, had shown that deprenyl slows the deterioration of brain cells that produce *dopamine,* an important neurotransmitter. A deficiency of dopamine in the brain causes the symptoms of Parkinson's disease.

Although deprenyl is not a cure for Parkinson's disease, it should be a valuable addition to the medical arsenal. Neuroscientists hope that deprenyl will also prove useful as a research tool that will help investigators develop drugs to treat other brain diseases.

Brain communication. Brain cells called *astrocytes* may provide a pathway for rapid communication between the various parts of the brain, neuroscientists at the Yale University School of Medicine in New Haven, Conn., reported in January 1990. If that theory is correct, it would help explain how so much information can be transmitted so quickly from one brain area to another and how the brain is capable of directing such an enormous range of physical and mental activities.

Astrocytes are the most common of the five kinds of *glial cells,* brain cells that form a supporting network for the neurons and outnumber them by at least 10 to 1. Astrocytes are star-shaped cells that guide the development of neurons. They are also involved in the formation of scar tissue after a brain injury and help regulate blood flow through the brain. But the Yale researchers suspected that astrocytes might also function much like neurons, relaying nerve impulses.

The investigators placed astrocytes from rat brains in test tubes. They then added a chemical that, in the presence of calcium, glowed when exposed to ultraviolet light. This allowed the scientists to monitor the movement of calcium, which they thought astrocytes might use in communicating.

The researchers noted an *oscillating* (back and forth) movement of calcium in the astrocytes when the cells were exposed to a neurotransmitter called glutamate. In some cases, the waves of calcium traveled to nearby astrocytes, triggering similar oscillations in those cells. Thus, there seems to be a system of communication among astrocytes that is activated by glutamate released from neurons.

Spinal cord repair? Injury to the central nervous system—the brain and spinal column—of human beings and other animals can result in permanent paralysis. But neuroscientists at the University of Zurich, Switzerland, presented experimental evidence in January 1990 that it may be possible to restore the functioning of a damaged central nervous system.

Lower *vertebrates* (animals with backbones) such as fish and frogs can regenerate injured central nerves. But in mammals, only *peripheral nerves*—those outside the central nervous system, such as in the limbs—regenerate on their own.

The Zurich researchers studied the *myelin* (a fatty sheath surrounding nerve fibers) of rat spinal nerves and found it contains two proteins that slow or stop nerve growth. Stopping nerve growth is essential during the normal development of an organism when the organism has reached maturity.

The scientists treated the severed nerve fibers of rat spinal cords with *antibodies*—molecules produced by the immune system—that inactivated the growth-stopping proteins. Microscopic examination of the fibers following the antibody treatment revealed a massive regrowth of cells in the cut nerve endings. Severed nerves that were treated with an inactive chemical showed little sign of this regeneration. This showed that the antibody was responsible for allowing the regrowth to occur. These results raise the possibility of developing similar antibodies against human proteins that stop or slow nerve growth—and of ending the paralysis that is caused by spinal cord injuries.   [George Adelman]

See also DRUGS; MEDICAL RESEARCH. In the World Book Supplement section, see MAGNETIC RESONANCE IMAGING. In WORLD BOOK, see BRAIN; NERVOUS SYSTEM.

Nobel Prizes

In October 1989, the Royal Academy of Sciences in Stockholm, Sweden, awarded the Nobel Prize in chemistry to a United States chemist and a Canadian-born molecular biologist and the Nobel Prize in physics to one West German and two American physicists. The Karolinska Institute in Stockholm awarded the Nobel Prize for physiology or medicine to two U.S. physicians. The recipients of each prize shared a cash award of about $470,000.

The chemistry prize was shared by Thomas R. Cech, 41, of the University of Colorado in Boulder and Sidney Altman, 50, of Yale University in New Haven, Conn., who holds both U.S. and Canadian citizenship. The two scientists discovered a previously unknown role for RNA (ribonucleic acid), the chemical that reads the genetic blueprint in DNA (deoxyribonucleic acid), the molecule of which most genes are made. RNA's chief role is to copy instructions for making proteins coded for by DNA in the cell nucleus and help assemble the proteins from materials in other areas of the cell.

In a series of experiments in the late 1970's and early 1980's, Cech and Altman independently discovered that RNA can act as an enzyme, triggering chemical reactions inside a cell without being changed or consumed. Previously, scientists thought that only proteins acted as enzymes. Their findings also led scientists to wonder whether RNA was the first biochemical to appear billions of years ago and whether DNA evolved from it.

The physics prize was divided between Norman F. Ramsey, Jr., 74, of Harvard University in Cambridge, Mass., who won half of the $470,000 prize, and Hans G. Dehmelt, 67, of the University of Washington in Seattle and Wolfgang Paul, 76, of the University of Bonn in West Germany, who shared the other half. The three physicists, working independently, advanced scientists' ability to study the properties of individual atoms.

In the late 1940's, Ramsey invented a technique for measuring the differences between energy levels of atoms by firing a stream of atoms through two

Winners of the 1989 Nobel Prize in physiology or medicine were cancer researchers Harold E. Varmus, left, and J. Michael Bishop of the University of California at San Francisco. They were honored for discovering that growth-regulating genes present in nearly all animal cells could undergo changes that lead to uncontrolled cancerous growth.

separate electromagnetic fields. Ramsey's technique, called the *separated oscillating fields method*, has many applications. Perhaps the best-known device based on his technique is an extremely accurate timepiece called the *cesium atomic clock*, which measures time based on the frequency with which a cesium atom alternates between energy levels.

In the 1950's, Paul devised a greatly improved version of a device known as an *ion trap*, which uses electromagnetic fields to capture and hold electrically charged atoms called *ions*. By suspending ions in electrical fields and illuminating them with laser beams, scientists can study the ions in great detail.

Dehmelt used ion-trap technology to study electrons and other charged particles. In 1973, he became the first researcher to isolate a single electron in a trap, opening the way for precise measurement of many properties of electrons.

The physiology or medicine prize was shared by cancer researchers J. Michael Bishop, 53, and Harold E. Varmus, 49, of the University of California at San Francisco. They revolutionized scientists' understanding of how cancer develops by discovering in the mid-1970's that normal genes can go awry and cause cancer.

Previously, scientists had speculated that cancer-causing viruses inserted their own genes into normal cells, turning the cells cancerous. But in studying a virus called the *Rous sarcoma virus*, which causes cancer in chickens, Bishop and Varmus discovered that the virus' cancer-causing gene is a modified copy of a normal gene.

Scientists have since discovered normal but potentially cancer-causing genes in almost all animal cells, including those of human beings. These genes seem to play a vital role in cell growth and development. Later in life, however, genetic damage may transform these genes into *oncogenes*, genes that cause malignant tumors by allowing cells to grow wildly. A number of environmental factors, including toxic chemicals, viruses, and radiation, may trigger the change.   [Sara Dreyfuss]

In WORLD BOOK, see NOBEL PRIZES.

Nutrition

Nutrition news in 1989 and 1990 included reports that oat bran might not provide the health benefits once hoped (see Close-Up). In other news, revisions of the Recommended Dietary Allowances (RDA's) were released by the National Research Council in Washington, D.C., in October 1989. First published in 1943 and last updated in 1980, the RDA's are the amounts of essential nutrients recommended daily for the majority of healthy adults and children. Because nutrient needs vary by such factors as age, sex, and whether a woman is pregnant, the RDA's also vary accordingly.

The new RDA's. The RDA's for many nutrients did not change, and others were revised only slightly, but the National Research Council altered some of its recommendations substantially. The RDA for vitamin C remained at 60 milligrams for most individuals, about the amount found in one orange. (A milligram is one-thousandth of a gram.) But the RDA of vitamin C for cigarette smokers was boosted to 100 milligrams per day because smokers process and eliminate the vitamin faster than nonsmokers do.

The calcium RDA was increased to 1,200 milligrams per day for teen-agers and young adults through age 24—a critical period for bone growth. Nutritionists believe that a diet high in calcium during this period may help prevent *osteoporosis*, a condition that makes bones susceptible to fractures later in life.

For the first time, the board established RDA's for vitamin K, which helps in blood clotting. The panel advised that men get 80 micrograms of the vitamin per day; and women, 65 micrograms. (A microgram is one-millionth of a gram, and both RDA amounts are less than a grain of salt.) Green leafy vegetables are the best source of vitamin K.

The RDA's issued in 1980 suggested a range of 50 to 200 micrograms per day for the mineral selenium, which protects cells from damaging chemical reactions. Subsequent studies established a more precise requirement. The 1989 recommendations set the

Is Oat Bran Really Good for Us?

Two studies published in January 1990 indicated that oat bran might not have the cholesterol-lowering benefits for which it was widely acclaimed. Until then, it had been hard to avoid hearing about the health benefits to be gained from eating oat bran. Following reports in the early 1980's that oat bran helped lower blood cholesterol levels, food manufacturers began putting oat bran into all types of food products—more than 300 food items, in fact, ranging from cereal and muffins to potato chips, doughnuts, and even beer.

Cholesterol is a fatty substance, and high levels of cholesterol in the blood have been linked to heart disease. Based on the earlier reports of oat bran's cholesterol-lowering benefits, many health professionals recommended oat bran as a regular part of people's diets.

The first study casting doubt on—but not disproving—oat bran's benefits was done by researchers at Brigham and Women's Hospital in Boston and published in *The New England Journal of Medicine*. The purpose of the study was to determine whether oat bran directly lowered blood cholesterol levels due to its fiber content or whether oat-bran diets lowered cholesterol levels indirectly simply by replacing fatty foods in the diet. Fiber comes in two forms: soluble and insoluble. Soluble fiber dissolves in water; insoluble fiber does not. Oat bran contains both types of fiber, but it consists mostly of soluble fiber. Insoluble fiber, found mainly in wheat bran and corn bran, helps speed waste matter through the intestines and is recommended for people with constipation and *diverticulitis* (inflammation of the colon).

The Boston study involved 20 healthy people under 50 years of age who already had desirable levels of cholesterol. Cholesterol is measured in milligrams (mg) per deciliter (dl), and a desirable level is 200 mg/dl and below. The people taking part in the study were placed on a regular diet plus 90 grams (3 ounces) of oat bran—the equivalent of three bowls of hot oat bran cereal—every day for six weeks. The same participants then ate a regular diet plus refined wheat products containing low amounts of fiber for another six weeks. The participants were not told that they were eating oat bran or low-fiber wheat products. The oat bran was added to muffins and entrees that were produced in a dietetic kitchen to resemble similar foods made from refined wheat. After both diets, the cholesterol levels of the participants dropped by a

"Overdosed on oat bran. And you?"

similar amount, 7.5 per cent—in other words, neither diet significantly lowered cholesterol.

The researchers concluded that oat bran had no significant effect on these volunteers' blood cholesterol levels. They reasoned that both the oat-bran diet and the low-fiber wheat diet reduced blood cholesterol levels about equally because the participants simply substituted oat or wheat products for such fatty foods as bacon and eggs at breakfast time.

The second study, conducted at Syracuse University in New York, was published in the *Journal of the American Dietetic Association.* Researchers at Syracuse University assigned 68 individuals with high cholesterol levels to one of four diets. One was a low-fat, low-cholesterol diet that did not include oat bran; the second was a low-fat, low-cholesterol diet that included 57 grams (2 ounces) of oat bran daily; the third was a regular diet plus 57 grams of oat bran; and the fourth was a regular diet plus about 43 grams (1½ ounces) daily of ready-to-eat oat bran cereal. After 12 weeks, cholesterol levels of all participants dropped an average of 10 to 17 per cent; there was no significant difference among the diet groups. The diets containing oat bran were no more effective at lowering cholesterol than the low-fat, low-cholesterol diet that did not include oat bran.

The new studies raised questions in some consumers' minds about the validity of scientific research. Why was it, many wondered, that more than a dozen studies since the early 1980's seemed to confirm the cholesterol-lowering value of oat bran? Were those previous studies unreliable? Should they now be ignored? In order to answer those questions, it is necessary to compare previous studies to the two new ones that seemingly dethroned oat bran.

In the Boston study, all of the participants already had low cholesterol levels. But earlier studies seemed to show that oat bran has its greatest effect on individuals with high cholesterol levels. For example, in a study performed by researchers at the University of Kentucky in Lexington, in 1981, individuals with high cholesterol levels had a 13 per cent reduction in cholesterol when they ate about 100 grams (3½ ounces) of oat bran daily. Researchers at the Northwestern University School of Medicine in Chicago reported in 1986, however, that individuals with low cholesterol levels had only a 3 per cent drop when they consumed almost 43 grams of oat bran daily.

The amount of fiber already in the diet might also play a role in oat bran's ability to lower cholesterol. Although the Syracuse study used individuals with high cholesterol levels, the total amount of fiber in their diet at the end of the study was extremely low. It is possible that the fiber intake of the Syracuse participants was so low that a large cholesterol-lowering effect due to fiber was not possible.

The Boston study had the opposite problem. The normal diets of the participants contained twice as much fiber as the average American diet. Perhaps adding extra fiber in the form of oat bran to a diet already high in fiber would have little additional effect on cholesterol.

In a well-designed scientific study, scientists manipulate only one variable while the others remain constant. To investigate the value of oat bran in the diet, the rest of the diet (for example, the intake of fat, saturated fat, and cholesterol) should remain unchanged. Although participants in the Boston study were told to continue eating their normal diets, their actual fat, saturated fat, and cholesterol intakes dropped slightly. The Boston investigators hypothesized that the small drop in saturated fat and cholesterol intake explains the 7.5 per cent cholesterol reduction among participants in their study. In the Syracuse University study, saturated fat intake dropped by almost 50 per cent among those on the low-fat diets and 22 per cent among those on the oat-bran diet.

Some previous studies, however, that showed the cholesterol-lowering effects of oat bran had involved tight control of fat and cholesterol intake among study participants. In the Kentucky study, for example, the participants ate all their meals in a hospital so that researchers could precisely monitor and control their diet.

Earlier investigations also showed that adding oat bran to a diet already low in fat and cholesterol probably provides little additional benefit. The participants in the Boston study were not eating the typical American high-fat diet. The fat intake of the study participants was only 31 per cent of all the calories they consumed, compared with the typical diet in which fat intake is 37 per cent of all calories.

As a result, the Boston and the Syracuse studies raise questions about, but do not disprove, oat bran's cholesterol-lowering ability. Further studies are needed to determine how much of an effect oat bran may have when it is not part of a low-fat diet.

Meanwhile, most health professionals agree that the best diet is one that is low in fat, saturated fat, and cholesterol and high in fiber, particularly soluble fiber. Soluble fiber can be found plentifully not only in oat bran but also in fruits, vegetables, and legumes, such as beans and lentils. So there is no reason to throw out your boxes of oat bran. Until more is learned about oat bran, simply make it part of an overall low-fat, high-fiber diet.   [Jeanine Barone]

Nutrition

Continued

RDA at 70 micrograms for men and 55 for women. Seafood is a good source of the mineral.

Largest diet study. Early findings from the largest study ever of the relationship between diet and disease were reported in May 1990. Chinese and U.S. nutritionists gathered data about eating habits, health, and life style from 6,500 people throughout China. Nutritional biochemist T. Colin Campbell of Cornell University in Ithaca, N.Y., directed the research along with scientists at the Chinese Institute of Nutrition and Food Hygiene. They began the study in 1983 to explore dietary causes of cancer but then expanded the research to include heart, metabolic, and infectious diseases. Among the early findings was evidence that obesity is caused more by the amount of fat in the diet than by the total calories consumed.

Recall of a supplement. In December 1989, the U.S. Food and Drug Administration (FDA) halted sales of the dietary supplement L-tryptophan, which had been linked with a rare blood disorder known as *eosinophilia-myalgia syndrome*. L-tryptophan is an amino acid, one of the building blocks of proteins. Many people take it in an effort to relieve insomnia, depression, and stress—though there is no conclusive scientific evidence that L-tryptophan supplements provide any health benefit.

Health professionals first recognized the syndrome associated with L-tryptophan in October 1989. By May 1990, more than 1,400 cases had been reported throughout the United States, with at least 21 deaths. The disorder is characterized by an abnormal increase in the white blood cells known as *eosinophils*. The symptoms include severe muscle and joint pain, skin rash, and swelling of the arms and legs.

Researchers still have not determined how L-tryptophan is linked to this syndrome. A report in the March 1990 issue of *The Journal of the American Medical Association* speculated that some individuals may have a biochemical defect causing them to abnormally metabolize the amino acid.

Volunteers in a nutrition study at the U.S. Department of Agriculture's Western Human Nutrition Research Center in San Francisco lick their plates to ensure that they have consumed every bit of a carefully measured diet. This type of highly controlled food consumption is necessary to gather accurate data for making decisions about such dietary matters as Recommended Dietary Allowances of vitamins and minerals.

Nutrition

Continued

In April, however, scientists at the federal Centers for Disease Control in Atlanta, Ga., reported that three independent studies seemed to focus suspicion on the L-trypotophan made by a single manufacturer. In studies of the blood disorder in Minnesota, New York, and Oregon, researchers found that the supplement taken by people who became ill was manufactured by the same chemical company. Scientists speculated that the L-tryptophan may have become contaminated during manufacture.

A fat substitute. In February 1990, the FDA approved the first low-calorie substitute for fat. The artificial fat, called Simplesse, consists of small, round protein particles that create a creamy texture similar to fat.

The proteins in Simplesse come from egg whites and milk. As a result, the fat substitute cannot be used in foods that require cooking because heat will make the product stiffen. Another drawback is that people with allergies to milk or eggs may be allergic to Simplesse.

The manufacturer, the NutraSweet Company of Deerfield, Ill., introduced Simplesse in a frozen dessert called Simple Pleasures. A 4-ounce (120-milliliter) scoop of Simple Pleasures contains 120 calories and no fat, while the same amount of super-premium ice cream contains 250 calories and 15 grams (0.53 ounce) of fat.

New food labeling regulations. In March 1990, the FDA proposed substantial changes in food labeling requirements. The proposed changes include mandatory nutrition labeling for most foods. Existing FDA regulations required such labeling only on products that made a special nutritional claim or that contained added vitamins, minerals, or protein.

The FDA proposals were only the first step in a process that may take years to affect food products in the marketplace. The United States Congress was also considering several food-labeling bills that would be tougher than the FDA proposals and might be enacted sooner.   [Jeanine Barone]

In WORLD BOOK, see NUTRITION.

Oceanography

Scientists during 1989 and 1990 continued their efforts to determine the cause of *El Niño*, a warm ocean current that occurs periodically in the Pacific Ocean and appears to affect weather conditions worldwide. Most researchers suspect that the cause is linked to changes in air and sea conditions stretching across the Pacific. In July 1989, seismologist Daniel Walker of the University of Hawaii in Manoa suggested the possibility that heat energy from undersea volcanic activity may trigger those changes.

Walker based his ideas on two sets of data. The first included changes in atmospheric pressure across the Pacific, which were linked closely with El Niño events that occurred between 1964 and 1987. The second set of data was a record of earthquakes on the *East Pacific Rise*, a mountain chain on the ocean floor that marks the boundary between two of the gigantic plates that make up Earth's crust. According to the theory of *plate tectonics*, these plates move slowly, coming together in some places and moving apart in others. The

plates at the boundary on the East Pacific Rise are moving apart at a rate of up to 15 to 18 centimeters (6 to 7 inches) per year, as molten rock pushes up between them to form new crust on the sea floor. This volcanic activity causes strains on the old crust that can trigger earthquakes.

Walker found that prior to the five El Niño events that occurred between 1964 and 1987, clusters of earthquakes occurred along the East Pacific Rise during or just before there were five big changes in atmospheric pressure conditions across the Pacific. Walker speculated that the earthquakes were due to increased underwater volcanic activity that warmed the ocean, which in turn warmed the air. This caused major changes in atmospheric pressure, triggering the changes in air and sea conditions linked to El Niño.

Old sea floor rocks. Geologists have recovered what they believe to be samples from one of Earth's oldest ocean floor regions, according to a February 1990 report by Roger Larson of the University of Rhode Island in Kingston

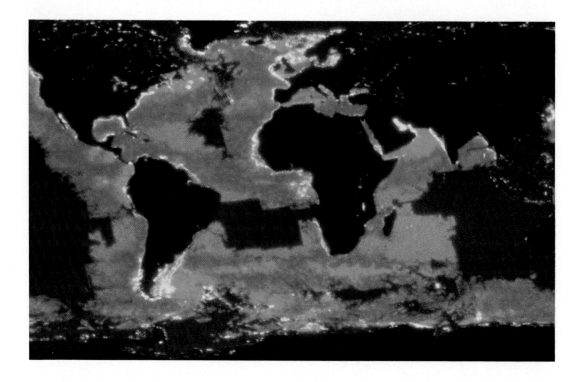

Oceanography

Continued

When Plankton in the Oceans Blooms
Satellite images of the world's oceans reveal seasonal differences in blooms of *phytoplankton* (one-celled water plants). There is very little phytoplankton in the ocean during the winter months, *above,* in the Northern Hemisphere. Purple areas have the least phytoplankton and orange areas the most.

and Yves Lancelot of the Université Pierre et Marie Curie in Paris. The two geologists were co-chief scientists aboard the drillship *JOIDES Resolution*, which obtained the samples.

The 175-million-year-old fragments were recovered from an area in the far western Pacific Ocean 2,400 kilometers (1,500 miles) south of Japan in the Pigafetta Basin. They were retrieved by lowering a drill bit and pipe through 5.8 kilometers (3.6 miles) of seawater and then penetrating almost 0.8 kilometer (0.5 mile) into the underlying sediments. Marine fossils enabled geologists to date their find to the Jurassic Period, a time when a giant ocean covered two-thirds of Earth's surface and the land was clustered in a supercontinent called *Pangaea*.

Scientists also used the fossil record to infer the climate that probably existed during the Jurassic. The only fossils found in these Jurassic sediments were *radiolaria*—organisms that construct their shells with silica (sand). Single-celled organisms build their shells from either silica or calcium

carbonate. Organisms with silica shells are better able to survive with few nutrients than are those with carbonate shells. So, the radiolaria fossils with their silica shells provide evidence that there was weak ocean circulation, probably because winds were very calm worldwide. Under these conditions, few nutrients would be stirred up from the ocean depths, and only radiolaria would be likely to survive. Another probable result of weak ocean and atmospheric circulation would be warmer climates and smaller temperature differences between the poles and the equator.

Young oil. Oil can be formed on the sea floor in much less time than was previously thought, according to findings reported by two geologists in November 1989. Oil usually results from processes that take millions of years. As plants and animals decay and form sediments, heat and chemical reactions convert them to *hydrocarbons* (molecules made up of the elements hydrogen and carbon). Crude oil, or petroleum, is a mixture of different hydrocarbons.

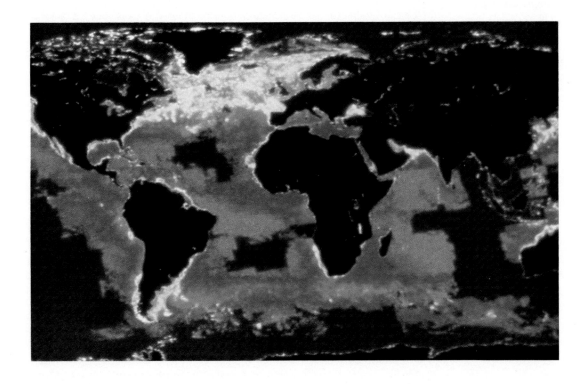

Oceanography

Continued

In spring, phytoplankton blooms around North America on a larger scale than scientists previously thought, *above.* This indicates that the ocean is absorbing huge amounts of the gas carbon dioxide (CO_2). Excess CO_2 in the atmosphere could lead to global warming. Since the tiny ocean plants absorb CO_2 from the atmosphere, knowing more about when and how much phytoplankton blooms could help scientists make better predictions about possible world climate changes.

The lengthy process of formation usually occurs on the floor of inland seas or river deltas where sediments thicken to tens of thousands of meters over millions of years. As the hydrocarbon-laden sediments become buried deeper and deeper, they are subjected to increasingly higher temperatures. Eventually, temperatures reach the point where oil forms readily.

Geologists Borys M. Didyk of Refineria de Petroleo Concón in Chile, and Bernd R. T. Simoneit of Oregon State University in Corvallis discovered petroleumlike hydrocarbons in the sediments of the Guaymas Basin, a trench 2,000 meters (6,500 feet) deep in the Gulf of California. Through observations and samples taken from the research submersible *Alvin,* they located a layer of olive-green ooze 460 meters (1,500 feet) thick. Although these sediments were not buried deep enough to produce the temperatures that create hydrocarbons in the usual way, the geologists found that, nevertheless, oil rose from these sediments into the water above.

The geologists speculated that the temperatures needed to form hydrocarbons were provided by nearby *hydrothermal vents* (hot springs) on the sea floor. Two segments of sea floor are pulling apart along a continuation of the San Andreas Fault in the Guaymas Basin. Molten rock pushes into this rift and in the process creates water temperatures up to 315°C (599°F.) In the Special Reports section, see LIFE AT THE DEEP SEA "GEYSERS."

This intense heat appears to produce oil that is similar to crude oil. Analysis of the oil indicated that a large part of its carbon content was converted from decaying organic material to oil in less than 5,000 years, a very short period by geological time scales.

So far there is no evidence to show how much this short-cut process has contributed to known oil reservoirs. Detection and confirmation of this hydrothermal process promises to advance our understanding of how oil forms and eventually aid in locating new oil resources. [Lauriston R. King]

In WORLD BOOK, see OCEAN.

Paleontology

The discovery in Colorado of fossils of a ferocious dinosaur so large that it could have gobbled down a 635-kilogram (1,400-pound) cow in one gulp was reported in January 1990 by a team of scientists headed by paleontologist Robert T. Bakker of the University of Colorado, Boulder. The dinosaur, called *Epanterias amplexus*, was 15 meters (50 feet) long, as large as the largest *Tyrannosaurus rex*. It lived about 130 million years ago, during the mid-Jurassic Period.

Impact crater. The largest meteor crater in the United States may be the site of a meteorite collision with Earth that led to the extinction of the dinosaurs and many other animal and plant species about 66 million years ago. That was the conclusion of a new study of the crater's age reported in June 1989 by geologists from the United States Geological Survey (USGS). They reported that the crater, part of which lies beneath the town of Manson in central Iowa, is about 65.7 million years old. The crater is 35 kilometers (22 miles) in diameter and is covered by about 30 meters (100 feet) of sediment.

Since the early 1980's, scientists have discovered mounting evidence supporting the theory that a mass extinction of species about 66 million years ago, at the end of what is known as the Cretaceous Period, was linked to the impact of a giant meteorite. One of the main arguments against the theory, however, has been that there is no known impact crater of the right size and age.

Dating the crater. Although other geologists have attempted to date the Manson crater, the USGS scientists were the first to use *radiometric dating* to establish its age. This system of dating measures the levels of *isotopes* (forms) of chemical elements created by the *decay* (breakdown) of other radioactive isotopes over time at a known rate.

Some scientists, however, argued that although the Manson crater is the right age, it is too small to account for all the impact-related debris discovered around the world in rock from the K-T boundary, the boundary between the Cretaceous Period and the Tertiary Period that followed. It may be, however, that the meteorite broke into a number of pieces when it entered Earth's atmosphere and that the Manson crater was only one of several craters created by their impact.

Extinction and climate change. A study of fossilized leaves and pollen from the Western United States suggests that a meteorite impact at the end of the Cretaceous Period may have delivered only a final blow to some plant species already dying out because of climate change. The research was reported in August 1989 by a team of scientists headed by geologist Kirk Johnson of Yale University in New Haven, Conn.

Johnson and his colleagues studied about 11,500 leaf samples collected from layers of sediment above, at, and below the K-T boundary in North Dakota. The researchers found three distinct stages in the history of the fossils.

The first two stages occur about 17 meters (55 feet) and 25 meters (82 feet) below the boundary. At each of these levels, the number of plant species fell. Only about a quarter of the species lasted into the Cretaceous Period. According to Johnson and his colleagues, this suggests that the climate was changing.

They discovered that the vegetation changed from temperate-climate plants to warm-climate plants, which led them to conclude that the climate was growing warmer. Evidence of climate warming in the late Cretaceous Period has been discovered elsewhere in the world, suggesting that the effect was global. Scientists are unsure why this warming occurred.

At the K-T boundary itself, the number of plants suddenly decreased. The scientists view this as evidence of a mass extinction, perhaps related to the impact of a meteorite. Above the K-T boundary, the scientists found new forms of vegetation. Johnson and his colleagues concluded that a large-scale extinction related to climate change already may have been in progress when a meteorite struck, finishing off many plant species.

Extinction and leaf shape. Changes in the sizes and shapes of fossilized leaves found in rocks above and below the K-T boundary also supports the theory of climate change at the end of the Cretaceous Period. That conclusion

Ferocious Dinosaur

The discovery in Colorado of many fossils of a little-known dinosaur called *Epanterias amplexus* was reported in January 1990. *Epanterias* lived about 130 million years ago and had expandable jaws that would have enabled it to swallow a 635-kilogram (1,400-pound) cow in a single gulp. It was a ferocious hunter with a row of small teeth that could inflict buzz-sawlike wounds. The fossils were found by a team of University of Colorado paleontologists, *right,* headed by Robert T. Bakker (at left), who used the fossils to draw a reconstruction of *Epanterias* attacking another dinosaur, *above.*

Paleontology

was reported in January 1990 by paleobotanist Jack A. Wolfe of the USGS in Denver.

In studying the leaves of plants alive today, Wolfe found a strong relationship between their shape and temperature and humidity. For example, the leaves of tropical plants nearly always have smooth edges. Those from temperate plants often have jagged edges.

Applying this information to fossilized leaves from the Cretaceous Period, Wolfe concluded that at the very end of this period, average temperatures rose by about 10 Celsius degrees (18 Fahrenheit degrees) and the amount of rainfall increased significantly. These warm, humid conditions lasted for about the first 1 million years of the Tertiary Period. After this, however, both the temperature and rainfall dropped.

Ancient silk? Spiders may have spun silk as long as 385 million years ago, according to a study reported in October 1989 by a team of scientists led by paleontologist William A. Shear of Hampden-Sydney College in Virginia.

In a fossilized spider discovered in upstate New York and dating from the Middle Devonian Period about 385 million years ago, the scientists found a well-preserved *spinneret*, an organ in the abdomen of modern spiders that is used to spin silk.

Shear and his colleagues are unsure how the ancient spider used its silk. Flying insects, like those caught in webs by modern spiders, did not appear in the fossil record until 320 million years ago. The scientists speculated that the ancient spider may have used its silk to wrap its egg sacs or to line the burrows in which it lived. The Devonian spiders probably did not produce webs. In August 1989, however, the discovery of the oldest known true web-spinning spiders was reported by paleontologist Andrew Jeram of the University of Manchester in England. The fossils, which were found in rocks about 120 million years old, show hairlike structures on the legs that were used for weaving webs.   [Carlton E. Brett]

In WORLD BOOK, see DINOSAUR; FOSSIL; PALEONTOLOGY.

Physics, Fluids and Solids

Researchers continued in 1989 and 1990 to overcome barriers blocking the application of so-called *high-temperature superconductors*. A superconductor is a material that conducts electricity with no resistance when chilled to an extremely low temperature. The highest known *critical temperature* (temperature at which superconductivity begins) was −250°C (−418°F.) until 1986. Then scientists discovered a *ceramic* superconductor with a critical temperature of −243°C (−405°F.).

Ceramics are solids that are neither metals nor plastics. Most dinnerware, for example, is made of ceramics. By contrast, most superconductors known before 1986 were metals or *alloys* (metal mixtures).

Engineers who design powerful magnets and electric generators are excited by the prospect that the new ceramics would be less expensive to use than are conventional superconductors. Many superconducting substances discovered since 1986 can be chilled below their critical temperatures by liquid nitrogen, whose boiling point is

−196°C (−321°F.). Liquid nitrogen is much less expensive to buy and use than liquid helium, which has a much lower boiling point and is the only practical coolant for conventional superconductors.

But before the new ceramic materials can be used extensively, researchers must solve some problems that stem from their crystal structure. One problem is that the new ceramics are brittle and are therefore difficult to form into wires that can be wound to build electromagnets.

Current limits. A more important problem, however, is the inability of the ceramic materials to carry currents as large as those that can flow through conventional metal superconductors. One reason for this low current capacity is the microscopic structure of ordinary ceramic superconductors, with grains, or clumps, of superconducting crystals surrounded by crystals of substances that do not superconduct. Researchers in several laboratories have worked their way around this barrier by producing superconducting ceramic

Physics,
Fluids
and Solids

Continued

films, which do not have a granular structure.

A more serious limitation was under study, however, in 1989 and 1990. It involved the discovery made in late 1988 that the amount of current that can pass through a high-temperature superconductor is limited by the behavior of a three-dimensional magnetic structure called a *flux lattice*. When a ceramic superconductor is placed in a magnetic field, the field forms intermeshing, stringlike concentrations of magnetism called *fluxoids*.

An electric current can move fluxoids about and thus transfer some of the current's energy to the superconductor. This causes the superconductor to lose its zero electrical resistance. The higher the temperature at which the superconductor operates, the looser the lattice becomes, and so the easier it becomes for a current to move fluxoids about—increasing the material's resistance.

To prevent lattices from loosening, researchers at American Telephone and Telegraph Company (AT&T) Bell Laboratories in Murray Hill, N.J., took advantage of a characteristic of certain conventional superconductors. In those materials, fluxoids can be immobilized, or "pinned down," by defects in the crystal of the material.

Pinning flux with defects. Physicist Sungho Jin and his colleagues announced at the November-December 1989 meeting of the Materials Research Society in Boston that they had pinned down lattices in a high-temperature superconductor by introducing defects in an unusual way. The researchers began with a crystalline material made up of certain portions of atoms of four chemical elements. For each atom of yttrium, there were two barium atoms, four copper atoms, and eight oxygen atoms. The AT&T scientists rapidly heated this material to a temperature of 920°C (1688°F.). This changed the basic atomic structure of the crystal so that for each atom of yttrium there were still two barium atoms but only three copper atoms and only seven oxygen atoms. The extra copper and oxygen atoms settled into

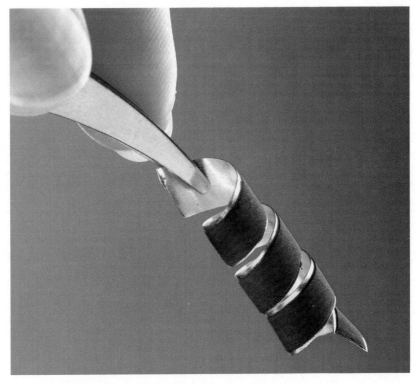

A coil made of superconducting ceramic material was developed by researchers at Argonne National Laboratory in the summer of 1989. Superconductors carry electricity without resistance, but the so-called high-temperature ceramic superconductors are brittle and difficult to shape into coils and wires. The Argonne researchers made a paste of the ceramic material and silver powder and spread it onto silver foil. They then formed it into a coil and heated it, solidifying the paste.

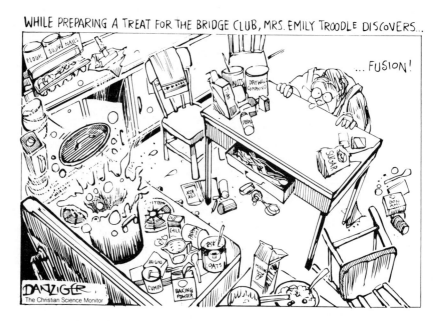

WHILE PREPARING A TREAT FOR THE BRIDGE CLUB, MRS. EMILY TROODLE DISCOVERS...

...FUSION!

DANZIGER
The Christian Science Monitor

Physics,
Fluids
and Solids

Continued

the material at random, causing tiny crystal defects.

Jin and his colleagues reported that the *current density* of their altered crystalline material was about 10 times that of the material without the defects. (Current density is the amount of current flowing through a given cross-sectional area of a material.)

Another technique for altering the crystal structure of a high-temperature superconductor by introducing crystal defects was announced by physicists Bruce van Dover, Michael Gyorgy, Lynn Schneemeyer, and their colleagues at AT&T Bell Laboratories in November 1989. Their technique produced a 100-fold increase in the current passing through the crystal.

The researchers measured the density of a current flowing through a crystal made up of yttrium, barium, copper, and oxygen. Then they bombarded the crystal with neutrons, creating defects very much like cracks in a brick wall. When they again passed a current through the crystal, the fluxoids stuck to the defects and did not

interfere with the current. As a result, the current density increased sharply to an amount that would make these materials useful for magnets.

Metallic hydrogen created. The first metallic hydrogen ever created in a laboratory was reported in June 1989 by physicists H. K. Mao and R. J. Hemley at the Carnegie Institution in Washington, D.C. They accomplished this by cooling hydrogen to a solid a few thousandths of a millimeter thick at a temperature of $-196°C$ ($-321°F$.). They then compressed it to a pressure of more than 2½ million *atmospheres*. (One atmosphere equals 1,033.2 grams per square centimeter or 14.7 pounds per square inch—approximately the pressure exerted by the air on Earth's surface at sea level.)

The scientists compressed the hydrogen with a diamond anvil cell, a recently developed instrument made up of two slightly cone-shaped diamonds that are mechanically pressed together. The scientists observed the hydrogen as it was compressed by looking through the diamonds.

Physics,
Fluids
and Solids

Continued

At pressures up to 2 million atmospheres, the hydrogen was transparent. As the anvil increased the pressure, the hydrogen gradually lost its transparency, becoming completely opaque at about 3 million atmospheres. At that pressure the material also reflected light like a mirror. No piece of any known metal the thickness of the hydrogen could be transparent, and all known metals reflect light. So the researchers concluded that their sample of solid hydrogen had become a metal at high pressure.

Quasicrystal's atoms scanned. The first pictures ever obtained of the atomic structure of an unusual kind of solid known as a *quasicrystal* were published by Bell Labs researchers led by physicist A. Refik Kortan in January 1990. The fundamental structure of a quasicrystal differs from that of a crystal. In a crystal, atoms are arranged in a repeating pattern called the *unit cell*. The distance between unit cells is the same throughout the crystal. Physicists call this arrangment *periodic*. A quasicrystal also has unit cells, but these cells do not form a periodic pattern.

Quasicrystals were discovered in 1984. Physicists theorized that their unit cells fit together in a peculiar pattern known as *Penrose tiling*. This pattern, named for English mathematician Roger Penrose, who developed it at Oxford University in the 1970's, is a way of fitting together flat, regularly shaped objects as one would fit tiles together to cover a surface—with no gaps between tiles.

Kortan and his colleagues obtained pictures of quasicrystals on the surface of a solid made up of aluminum, cobalt, and copper. To obtain the pictures, the scientists used a device called a scanning tunneling microscope (in the Special Reports section, see THE NEW MICROSCOPES).

The pictures obtained by Kortan and his colleagues confirmed that the arrangement of unit cells in quasicrystals fits the tiling pattern described by Penrose. [Alexander Hellemans]

In WORLD BOOK, see CRYSTAL; HYDROGEN; PHYSICS; SUPERCONDUCTIVITY.

Physics,
Subatomic

Hopes for so-called "cold" nuclear fusion received a severe blow in March 1990, a year after they first arose—and at the same institution, the University of Utah in Salt Lake City. In March 1989, chemists Martin Fleischmann and B. Stanley Pons had announced at a press conference in Salt Lake City that they had produced *nuclear fusion* (a fusing, or joining, of atomic nuclei) in a simple, tabletop device that has been common in chemical laboratories for more than 100 years. The blow came from a team of physicists headed by Michael H. Salamon, working with the very same device that had started the uproar.

A fusion reaction gives off a tremendous amount of energy. In fact, fusion powers the sun and other stars. In an effort to tap fusion's potential as a commercial source of energy, governments throughout the world have spent tens of billions of dollars to build and test fusion devices.

Atomic nuclei on Earth normally stay too far apart to fuse. Their protons have positive electric charges, and the mutual repulsion of like charges keeps the nuclei separated. To overcome this repulsion, fusion research since the 1950's has centered on heating heavy *isotopes* (forms) of hydrogen to temperatures of tens of millions of degrees. At such temperatures, atoms are moving so swiftly that they can get close enough to fuse.

At high temperatures, however, the nuclear fuel expands with explosive force, cutting off the fusion reaction long before usable amounts of energy can be produced. To counteract this expansion, some researchers have built machines that use powerful magnetic fields to contain the nuclear fuel. Other scientists have constructed devices that use intense beams of light or subatomic particles to heat the fuel so rapidly that a significant amount of fusion occurs before the fuel can expand. Over the years, fusion devices have increased in size, complexity, and cost but are not yet capable of producing more energy than they consume.

The cold-fusion claim. Fleischmann and Pons claimed that they produced fusion in a simple electrolytic cell—a jar containing two electric terminals and filled with *heavy water*, which is formed of oxygen and a heavy isotope of hydrogen. The chemists claimed that when they passed a current from one terminal to the other, a large amount of heat was generated in the water and the cell emitted neutrons and gamma rays—all telltale signs of a fusion reaction. The researchers theorized that atoms of the heavy isotope trapped in the terminals had been crowded close enough together to fuse.

Cold fusion doubts. From the beginning, other scientists said there were inconsistencies in the Fleischmann-Pons data. The rates of neutron and gamma ray emission, for example, were at least 1 million times too small to account for the observed rise in temperature.

In the following months, many researchers tried to duplicate Pons and Fleischmann's results. Most failed completely, though a few reported some excess heat or a bit of radiation—but always too feeble to be of practical significance.

Salamon's team repeated the work of Pons and Fleischmann, using the same electrolytic cell. The team improved the measurement by using much more sensitive instruments, but they detected no sign of fusion. Many scientists are now convinced that the "cold fusion" approach is a blind alley unworthy of further investigation.

Particle quest near an end. Two particle accelerators that began operation in 1989 quickly provided a clear sign that a century-old quest for the *fundamental particles* (the "building blocks" of matter) may finally be coming to an end. The accelerators are the Stanford Linear Collider (SLC), near Palo Alto, Calif., and the Large Electron-Positron collider (LEP), which straddles the French-Swiss border near Geneva, Switzerland. Data generated by these machines indicate that one long-sought particle may be the last of the fundamental-particle types.

The quest began in 1897 with the discovery of the *electron*, a negatively charged particle that orbits atomic nuclei. A close relative, the *electron neutrino*, was first observed in 1954. This particle, which is electrically neutral, is not a part of ordinary matter but is produced in some nuclear reactions, including those that produce the sun's energy.

The protons and neutrons that make up the atomic nucleus were once thought to be as simple as the electron. But by the 1960's it had become clear that they were made of objects called *u-quarks* and *d-quarks*. The u-quark carries a fractional electric charge of $+\frac{2}{3}$, while the charge of the d-quark is $-\frac{1}{3}$.

Although this quartet of particles—electron, electron neutrino, u-quark, and d-quark—could be enough to build all the familiar forms of matter, two additional quartets have been discovered. Physicists call each quartet a *generation* of particles. The new data from the SLC and LEP seem to rule out any additional generations.

The electrically charged particles in the second and third generations are much heavier than their first-generation counterparts. This extra mass makes these particles unstable; in less than 1 millionth of 1 second, they break up into first-generation particles.

None of the three types of neutrinos, on the other hand, shows any sign of having any mass at all. Each is at least thousands of times lighter than the charged members of its generation.

Matter and antimatter. Physicists call all of these building-block particles *fermions*. Fermions can be created only along with *antiparticles*, which have the same mass as corresponding particles but respond oppositely to some forces such as a push or pull exerted by an electric charge.

Although one kind of fermion can be transformed into another, it can be destroyed only if it encounters an antiparticle. When an antifermion encounters the corresponding fermion, both particles vanish.

Although fermions and antifermions are normally created and destroyed in equal amounts, in the early history of the universe that was not the case. Today, there are many fermions but few antifermions in the universe. Objects made of first-generation fermions are the most enduring forms of physical substance.

In addition to these particle "bricks," nature needs "mortar" in the form of other particles to transmit the forces

Matter-Antimatter Atom Smasher

A new particle accelerator, or atom smasher, went into operation in August 1989 at the CERN Laboratory near Geneva, Switzerland. This Large Electron-Positron Collider sends beams of sub-atomic particles called *electrons* and their anti-matter counterparts, called *positrons,* in opposite directions around a ring-shaped tunnel, *right,* 27 kilometers (17 miles) in circumference. The beams, traveling at nearly the speed of light, collide and produce a shower of particles that are measured in four huge particle detectors. One of the detectors, the Delphi, *below,* is especially effective in identifying individual particles. The Opal detector, *below right,* is best at reconstructing the paths of the particles created by the collisions. Physicists then analyze this information to learn more about the fundamental particles of our universe and the forces that govern them.

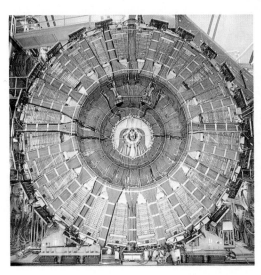

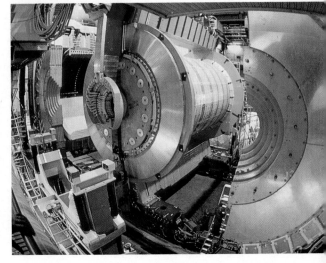

that bind the "bricks" together. These particles are called *bosons*, and four kinds have been discovered. They are the *photon*, which carries electromagnetic forces; the *gluon*, which carries the strong force that holds quarks together inside protons and neutrons; and the W and Z^0 particles, which are responsible for certain radioactive processes. Bosons are easy to create and destroy, so these "mortar" particles have no permanence.

Accelerators can produce unstable particles by colliding beams of swiftly moving particles. When particles collide, their energy of motion can be converted to mass, creating unstable combinations of second- and third-generation particles in addition to bosons. Electronic detectors surround the collision points.

Making Z's. The SLC and LEP were specifically designed to be "Z factories." Both machines produce Z^0 bosons in head-on collisions of beams of electrons and their antimatter opposite, positrons. SLC produced its first Z^0 particle in April 1989 and LEP followed in August 1989.

The Z^0 boson is the heaviest known subatomic particle. Physicists usually state particle masses in terms of the equivalent energy, which for the Z^0 is 91.16 billion electron volts (GeV).

Because of its large mass, the Z^0 breaks up quickly—first into a fermion and its antifermion. Further breakups and transformations may result in a large number of particles. In fact, a breakup of many Z^0's will eventually produce at least some examples of all the lighter particles. This makes the Z^0 an ideal tool to use in the search for particles not yet discovered.

When the initial fermion-anitfermion pair is one of the three kinds of neutrinos, it escapes detection because neutrinos interact only feebly with matter and therefore leave no trace in particle detectors. Because the rate at which Z^0's are produced can be predicted with some accuracy, it is possible to estimate from the number "missing" how many kinds of neutrinos there are.

The last generation. Physicists are virtually certain that, if there were a fourth generation of fermions, the neutrino in this generation would be light enough to emerge from the breakup of a Z^0. If a fourth-generation neutrino existed, 4 per cent of all Z^0 decays would break up in this particular fashion. And researchers therefore would observe 4 per cent fewer Z^0 decays in all their particle accelerator experiments than the number expected for only three generations of neutrinos.

The types of decays physicists had observed by October 1989 were consistent with the percentage expected for three neutrinos. This ruled out a fourth neutrino.

Further evidence against the existence of a fourth neutrino came from measurements of the Z^0's *half-life* (the time it takes for half the Z^0's created to decay into other particles). If there were a fourth neutrino, this would provide the Z^0 with an additional way to break up, shortening its half-life by about 6 per cent. By the end of 1989, physicists had observed enough Z^0's to estimate that particle's half-life at 1.8 ten-trillionths of 1 trillionth of 1 second—6 per cent too long for there to be a fourth neutrino.

T-quark still not found. Physicists have found all but one of the particles in the first three generations. Missing is the *t-quark*, the third-generation equivalent of the u-quark.

If the t-quark were lighter than 45 GeV, which is about half the mass of the Z^0 (91.16 GeV), t-quarks would be produced just as often as u-quarks. The detectors at LEP and SLC saw no sign of the t-quark. This did not surprise the experimenters, however, because they have indirect evidence that the t-quark mass must be somewhere between 100 and 200 GeV.

SSC land purchases approved. The United States government in March 1990 approved the start of land acquisition for what would be the world's largest particle accelerator, the Superconducting Super Collider (SSC). This machine is to be built in an underground oval "racetrack" 85 kilometers (53 miles) in circumference, surrounding the city of Waxahachie, Tex. It seems unlikely that experiments run on the SSC will produce useful data before the year 2000.   [Robert H. March]

In WORLD BOOK, see BOSON; LEPTON; PARTICLE PHYSICS; QUARK.

Psychology

Research in psychology covered a broad range of subjects in 1989 and 1990, from the use of computers in psychotherapy to effective child-rearing styles. Other studies dealt with nightmares and painful memories and how they affect emotional health.

Computers in psychotherapy. Computers may someday give human psychotherapists a run for their money. Researchers reported in January 1990 that a computer programmed to use specific psychological techniques relieved depression as effectively as a human therapist.

Paulette M. Selmi, a psychologist in private practice in Mesa, Ariz., developed the computer program. It used the techniques of a type of psychotherapy called *cognitive-behavioral therapy*, which emphasizes practical exercises to overcome negative attitudes and modify self-defeating behavior.

Rather than carrying on a dialogue with the depressed person, the computer asked open-ended and multiple-choice questions. The machine was programmed to pick up key words and phrases in the patient's answers. It then incorporated those words and phrases into suggestions that might change the beliefs and behavior contributing to the individual's depression.

Selmi along with colleagues at the University of Wisconsin-Madison randomly assigned 36 mildly or moderately depressed volunteers to either six appointments with the computer, six sessions with a human psychotherapist, or a waiting list, which served as a control group. Two months after the psychotherapy sessions ended, about three-fourths of the people treated either by the computer or by the human therapist reported that their mood had significantly improved. Only 1 out of 12 people on the waiting list felt significantly better.

Selmi noted that some computer-treated patients related to the machine and spoke about it as if it were a person. For example, several of them reported that they had felt "therapist understanding." Selmi was unsure why the computer therapy worked so well. She speculated that the novelty of the

Gary Larson, *The Far Side;* reproduced by permission of Chronicle Features

Primitive peer pressure

Psychology

method may have helped. In addition, working with the computer forced patients to put their feelings into words and review what they had written—a process that may have been beneficial.

Frequent nightmares. A study reported in February 1990 challenged the view that people who have frequent nightmares suffer from intense anxiety and may even have emotional disorders. Emotionally stable people have the same number of nightmares as those who are highly anxious, according to psychologists James M. Wood and Richard R. Bootzin of the University of Arizona in Tucson.

Wood and Bootzin asked 220 college students to estimate the number of nightmares they had during the previous year. The researchers also had the students keep a dream log. For two weeks, each student recorded his or her nightmares after waking.

Based on the dream logs, each student had an average of 24 nightmares per year, more than twice as many as they had earlier estimated. The students who described themselves as having more symptoms of anxiety than average did not have an excess number of nightmares.

Effects of parental styles. The best way to bring up a psychologically healthy child is with supportive control, not permissiveness. This is the latest finding, announced in August 1989, of an ongoing study begun in 1965 at the University of California at Berkeley. Parents who set clear standards for conduct and offer children freedom within specific limits are most likely to raise teen-agers who do well academically, emotionally, and socially, said psychologist Diana Baumrind, director of the project.

The 124 teen-agers in the study were examined when they were 3 years old and again when they were 10 and 15 years old. The investigators conducted extensive interviews with the children and their parents. They also made videotapes of each set of parents interacting with their child.

Children raised by firm but supportive mothers and fathers—called "authoritative" parents in the study—use alcohol and illegal drugs markedly less than youngsters from other types of families, Baumrind noted. Single parents who used the authoritative parenting style had teen-agers who did just as well as youngsters from two-parent authoritative families, she added.

Teen-agers from "democratic" families—where parents stressed permissiveness instead of laying down limits—also did well academically, emotionally, and socially but were more likely to use drugs. "Authoritarian," as opposed to authoritative, parents—defined as restrictive parents who provided little emotional support—had the unhappiest teen-agers with the most academic and emotional problems.

Recovering from painful experiences. *Repressing* painful memories (keeping them out of conscious awareness) may improve psychological functioning, according to a surprising study released in June 1989. Psychologists Peretz Lavie and Hanna Kaminer of the Technion-Israel Institute of Technology in Haifa, Israel, studied survivors of the Holocaust, the mass murder of European Jews by the Nazis during World War II (1939-1945). The study involved 23 people who had been in a concentration camp or who had hidden from the Nazis for months or years.

Lavie and Kaminer reported that well-adjusted survivors were largely unable to remember events and feelings associated with the Holocaust. Poorly adjusted survivors, suffering from emotional problems and difficulties at work and at home, were more likely to remember Holocaust events.

Another Holocaust-survivor study, reported in September 1989, yielded a different conclusion. Talking candidly with others about horrifying experiences improves physical and mental health, according to psychologist James W. Pennebaker of Southern Methodist University in Dallas. Pennebaker and his co-workers found that survivors who readily showed emotion while describing their ordeals and who talked about the Holocaust with friends and relatives reported far fewer physical and emotional problems than survivors who had difficulty discussing their Holocaust experiences. Until more is learned, most mental health workers continue to recommend carefully confronting, rather than repressing, painful memories.   [Bruce Bower]

In WORLD BOOK, see PSYCHOLOGY.

Public Health

The epidemic of AIDS remained a major public-health problem in 1989 and 1990. As of April 30, 1990, 130,252 people in the United States had contracted AIDS and 79,587 of them had died of the disease, according to the federal Centers for Disease Control (CDC) in Atlanta, Ga. Although most AIDS cases continued to occur in large urban areas, the CDC reported that there was an increase in cases in smaller communities.

The rate of increase among homosexual and bisexual men declined. This decline may reflect an actual drop in new cases or may result from medical treatment delaying the onset of AIDS symptoms.

Early death in Harlem. Black men in the Harlem section of New York City are less likely to live to age 65 than are men in Bangladesh, one of the poorest countries in the world. Researchers from Columbia University and Harlem Hospital reported this finding in January 1990 based on a study of census data and death certificates for the period from 1979 to 1981.

Compared with white men and women in the United States, blacks in Harlem have more than double the expected rate of death at young ages. Even when compared with other U.S. blacks, Harlem residents have a 50 per cent higher rate of early death.

The researchers also reported that the chief causes of the excess death rate in Harlem residents under age 65 are heart disease, cirrhosis of the liver, homicide, cancer, and deaths related to drug dependency. From 1960 to 1980, the death rate from homicide rose from 25 to 91 per 100,000 people. Since 1980, the number of deaths in black males between age 25 and 44 has increased by 31 per cent, largely due to AIDS.

The researchers noted that mortality rates for Americans in general have fallen steadily since 1930 because of improved standards of living, better education, and better access to health care. In Harlem, however, the standard of living has not kept pace. More than 40 per cent of Harlem residents live below the poverty line. The access

Who Smokes Cigarettes? More than 30 per cent of men and more than 25 per cent of women in the United States smoke, and the age group with the highest percentage of smokers is young adults, aged 25 to 44, according to a study reported in December 1989 by the U.S. Centers for Disease Control. In all age groups, people with the least education were more likely to be smokers.

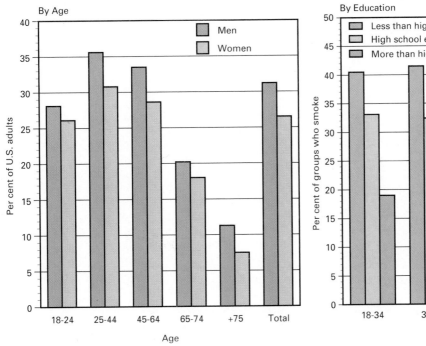

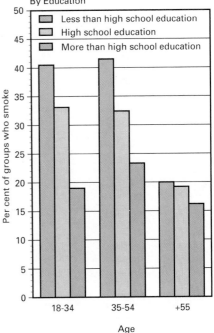

Source: U.S. Centers for Disease Control, 1987 and 1988 data.

Electromagnetic Radiation Dangers: Fact Vs. Fiction

There was a great deal of public concern during 1989 and 1990 about possible health risks—including cancer—from exposure to the electric and magnetic fields associated with power transmission lines and ordinary household appliances. The concern was set off, in part, by a June 1989 report from the U.S. congressional Office of Technology Assessment (OTA) that stated "the evidence now available is too weak to allow firm conclusions" about whether such fields pose a health risk or not. But, the report cautioned, "the emerging evidence no longer allows one to categorically assert that there are no risks."

Electric and magnetic fields exist wherever there is electric power. They surround electric shavers, hair dryers, electric blankets, TV sets—any appliance when it is turned on.

The electromagnetic fields associated with electric power are part of the electromagnetic spectrum, which also includes radio waves, microwaves, infrared light, visible light, ultraviolet rays, X rays, and gamma rays. The only differ-

ence in the various waves is their *frequency*, the rate at which they vibrate, or cycle, per second. Household electric current in the United States and Canada has a very low frequency of only 60 cycles per second. At the other end of the spectrum, gamma rays and X rays are very high frequency forms of electromagnetic radiation. Gamma ray frequencies start at 10^{21} cycles per second (written as a 1 followed by 21 zeros).

High-frequency electromagnetic waves, such as X rays and some ultraviolet rays, can deposit large and potentially damaging amounts of energy into tissues. These waves can break apart the chemical bonds that hold atoms together. If these reactions damage genetic material, they can set off changes that result in the uncontrolled cell growth of cancer. Ultraviolet radiation from the sun, for example, has been linked to skin cancer.

Electromagnetic waves of extremely low frequencies, however, are not energetic enough to break chemical bonds or even heat water in body tissue. In addition, as the OTA report noted, "all cells in the body maintain large electric fields across their outer membranes." Some of these are greater than those generated by appliances. Because of this, most researchers have been skeptical of reports indicating that electromagnetic fields associated with power transmission lines and household appliances could harm

Making and Measuring Electromagnetic Fields

Electricity and magnetism are closely related. Electric current can create a magnetic field, and a magnetic field can be used to create an electric current. The strength of both electric and magnetic fields declines with distance from the source.

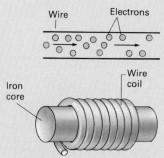

Electromagnets, such as those used in the motors of electric appliances, are made by passing an electric current through a wire wound around an iron core, *above*. The iron core intensifies the magnetic field produced by the electric current. The strength of a magnetic field is commonly measured in units called gauss. The strength of Earth's magnetic field, for example, is somewhat less than 1 gauss, or 1,000 milligauss (mG).

Electric fields produce electric current, the flow of electrons through a wire, *left*. The electric fields we are most familiar with are produced by batteries and power plants. The strength of an electric field is measured in volts per meter (V/M).

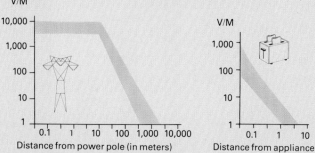

Electric field strengths

Electric fields associated with high-voltage transmission lines, *above left,* are more powerful than electric fields around small appliances, *above right*. The intensity of the electric field can be up to 10,000 V/M 10 meters (30 feet) away from the base of the power pole. The electric field strength next to a small appliance can be up to 1,000 V/M, but it drops off 1 meter (3 feet) away.

health. One of the first studies to make such a finding was reported by researchers in the Soviet Union in 1972. Since then, many more studies have been performed. And the OTA report found that studies done so far have demonstrated that cells can be sensitive to even fairly weak low-frequency fields. But no one knows whether this sensitivity can lead to harm.

A theory of how low-frequency fields might trigger cancer was proposed in the late 1980's by cancer researcher W. Ross Adey of Loma Linda University in California. He suggested that external electromagnetic fields might disrupt the electrical signals at cell membranes, which cells use to communicate with one another. These signals are essential for controlling cell growth.

In April 1990, the results of a laboratory study by researchers at Columbia University and Hunter College, both in New York City, indicated that low-frequency electromagnetic radiation might influence how genes behave in cells. Every cell contains a complete copy of all the body's genetic material. But not all of the genes in any cell are *expressed*, or turned on, at one time. During expression, copies of turned-on genes are made in the cell nucleus and sent out to assemble proteins from material in other parts of the cell. The New York researchers reported that the copying rate for five genes in the cells they studied increased 100 to 400 times when exposed to extremely low-frequency electromagnetic waves.

Nevertheless, the effects of exposure to extremely low-frequency electromagnetic radiation remains a controversial issue. According to most experts, there is still great uncertainty about how much risk extremely low-frequency fields might pose. For most hazards, such as poisonous chemicals, one can safely assume that if a small dose is bad, more is worse.

But there is no clear way to measure or even define doses associated with electromagnetic fields. A dose could be measured in terms of the strength of an electric or a magnetic field. These fields vary according to their source, and they always decline with distance from the source. The dose could also be measured in terms of electromagnetic frequency or the period of exposure. For example, a person is exposed to the powerful magnetic field of a toaster for only a few minutes but can be exposed to that of an electric blanket all night long.

Scientific data do not clearly support one measurement of dose over another as being a reliable indicator of low-frequency electromagnetic risk, the OTA report observed. "The implication of this is that practical regulatory standards which set a simple 'safe' field strength limit cannot be adequately" determined, the OTA said.   [Janet Raloff]

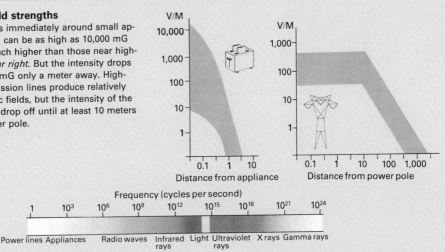

Magnetic field strengths
Magnetic fields immediately around small appliances, *right,* can be as high as 10,000 mG (10 gauss), much higher than those near high-power lines, *far right.* But the intensity drops to less than a mG only a meter away. High-power transmission lines produce relatively weak magnetic fields, but the intensity of the field does not drop off until at least 10 meters from the power pole.

Distance from appliance

Distance from power pole

Frequency (cycles per second)

| 1 | 10^3 | 10^6 | 10^9 | 10^{12} | 10^{15} | 10^{18} | 10^{21} | 10^{24} |

Power lines Appliances   Radio waves   Infrared rays   Light   Ultraviolet rays   X rays   Gamma rays

Electromagnetic spectrum
Electromagnetic fields associated with power lines and appliances are part of the electromagnetic spectrum. So are radio waves, microwaves, visible light, ultraviolet light, X rays, and gamma rays. These are different forms of electromagnetic waves, and they differ only in their *frequency* (number of vibrations, or cycles, of the waves per second). The highest frequency waves are gamma rays, with frequencies above 10^{21} cycles per second (1 with 21 zeros behind it). Waves associated with power lines and appliances have a very low frequency of only 60 cycles per second. The highest frequency waves, including X rays and ultraviolet rays, damage living tissue. But scientists know little about the effects of low-frequency 60-cycle waves on living things.

Source: Data on field strengths from the Department of Engineering and Public Policy, Carnegie Mellon University, Pittsburgh, Pa.

to primary care physicians is nearly 75 per cent lower in Harlem than in the rest of New York City.

Wiping out diseases. Two diseases afflicting millions of people throughout the world can probably be stamped out, according to a report in April 1990 from the International Task Force for Disease Eradication, a worldwide group of scientists. The task force judged that Guinea worm disease, also called *dracunculiasis*, a painful infestation with a parasitic worm that afflicts 10 million people a year, and poliomyelitis, which causes paralysis in about 250,000 people a year, could be eradicated if global leaders made the commitment and provided the necessary resources.

The scientists noted that smallpox has already been successfully eradicated. The last known case of smallpox occurred in 1977.

Eosinophilia-myalgia syndrome. In November 1989, public health officials in New Mexico, Minnesota, Oregon, and New York reported an epidemic of a rare blood disorder called eosinophilia-myalgia syndrome (EMS). The disease is characterized by a marked increase in *eosinophils*, a type of white blood cell, and by severe muscle pain and weakness. Other symptoms include joint pains, shortness of breath, cough, rash, tissue swelling, fever, skin thickening, and hair loss.

Public health officials in New Mexico were the first to investigate EMS after being notified of the illness in three patients who had been taking the dietary supplement L-tryptophan to relieve such disorders as insomnia, depression, and premenstrual syndrome. There is no proof that the supplements provide any health benefit.

The investigation expanded rapidly and soon involved the CDC. By May 1990, more than 1,400 cases of EMS and 21 deaths had been reported in the 50 states, the District of Columbia, and Puerto Rico.

In November 1989, the U.S. Food and Drug Administration (FDA) advised consumers to discontinue use of tablets containing L-tryptophan. The next month, the FDA ordered a nationwide recall of all products in which L-tryptophan was the sole or a major component.

In April 1990, CDC researchers reported evidence linking many U.S. cases of EMS with a single manufacturer of L-tryptophan supplements. They theorized that the tablets may have become contaminated at the manufacturing plant. As of mid-1990, intensive efforts were still underway to pinpoint the specific factor or factors in L-tryptophan products responsible for EMS.

An outbreak of Legionnaires' disease in Bogalusa, La., in the fall of 1989 was traced to a previously unrecognized source of spread for this illness, a bacterial infection that frequently develops into pneumonia.

Legionnaires' disease was first identified in 1976 following an outbreak of severe pneumonia in people who had attended an American Legion convention in Philadelphia. Since then, many outbreaks of the illness have been linked to the presence of the bacterium *Legionella pneumophilia* in the water in large air-conditioning systems.

Between Oct. 10 and Nov. 13, 1989, 33 people in Bogalusa were hospitalized with pneumonia caused by Legionnaires' disease. In January 1990, epidemiologists from the Louisiana Department of Health and Hospitals reported that the outbreak was caused by a supermarket mist machine contaminated with bacteria.

Investigators from the state health department compared 28 victims of Legionnaires' disease with 56 controls—people who did not have the disease. Compared with the controls, the people with Legionnaires' disease were far more likely to have shopped at a certain supermarket in the 10 days before they became ill and to have purchased produce items located close to an ultrasonic mist machine used in the store as a humidifier. The investigators analyzed water from the mist machine and found Legionnaires' disease bacteria.

The outbreak emphasized the importance of following manufacturers' recommendations for maintaining and cleaning ultrasonic mist machines. It also demonstrated the potential for Legionnaires' disease to originate in previously unrecognized sources of infection.   [Richard A. Goodman]

In WORLD BOOK, see PUBLIC HEALTH.

Science Student Awards

Winners in the 49th annual Westinghouse Science Talent Search were announced on March 5, 1990, and winners of the 41st annual International Science and Engineering Fair were named on May 11. Science Service, a nonprofit organization in Washington, D.C., conducts both competitions.

Winners of the 8th annual Duracell NSTA Scholarship Competition, a contest for high school inventors, were announced on March 20, 1990. The National Science Teachers Association (NSTA), an organization of science educators, administers the event.

Other student competitions in 1989 and 1990 included international olympiads in chemistry, mathematics, and physics, all held in July 1989.

Science Talent Search winners. The 40 finalists were chosen from 1,431 seniors from high schools throughout the United States. The top 10 finalists received scholarships totaling $110,000 provided by the Westinghouse Electric Corporation of Pittsburgh, Pa.

First place and a $20,000 scholarship went to 17-year-old Matthew P. Headrick of the University of Chicago Laboratory Schools High School. He isolated for the first time the gene necessary for nitrogen fixation in freshwater blue-green algae. In this process, bacteria and certain types of algae take nitrogen from the air and convert it into a form plants can use.

Second place and a $15,000 scholarship were awarded to David R. Liu, 16, of Poly High School in Riverside, Calif. Liu developed a computer model that simulates how the human nervous system processes visual information.

Third place and a $15,000 scholarship went to 17-year-old David M. Shull of Henry Foss High School in Tacoma, Wash. Shull inserted the genetic material DNA (deoxyribonucleic acid) into white blood cells by using electricity to create temporary openings in the cell membranes.

The winner of fourth place and a $10,000 scholarship was Soojin Ryu, 18, of the Bronx High School of Science in New York City. Ryu studied immune-system molecules called *human leucocyte antigens* (HLA's), which

First-place winner in the 49th annual Westinghouse Science Talent Search in March 1990 was Matthew P. Headrick, center, of the University of Chicago Laboratory Schools High School. Second place went to David R. Liu, right, of Poly High School in Riverside, Calif., and third place was won by David M. Shull, left, of Henry Foss High School in Tacoma, Wash.

Science Student Awards

Continued

Jerry Pratt of Ashland High School in Ashland, Wis., displays the invention that won him first place in the 8th annual Duracell NSTA Scholarship Competition in March 1990. The device, called the "Knock-Out" Keyless Door Lock, can be programmed to open in response to a particular knock.

are found on the surface of white blood cells. She found that there are two types of HLA's that apparently have different functions in activating the body's immune responses.

Fifth place and a $10,000 scholarship went to Joshua B. Fischman, 17, of Montgomery Blair High School in Silver Spring, Md. He won for developing a computer program to investigate mathematical expressions called p-adic continued fractions.

The sixth-place winner, who received a $10,000 scholarship, was Royce Yung-Tze Peng, 17, of Rolling Hills High School in Rolling Hills, Calif. Peng wrote a computer program to explore the mathematical properties of two joined *planar* (flat) surfaces.

Seventh-place winner and a $7,500 scholarship went to Laura A. Ascenzi of the Bronx High School of Science for a sociological survey on values and parent-child relationships.

Eighth place and $7,500 went to Andrew M. Lines, 17, of Yorktown High School in Arlington, Va., who wrote a computer program to map the smallest surface area needed to span a given number of points or lines.

Ninth place and $7,500 went to Mina Kim Yu, 17, of Thomas Jefferson High School for Science and Technology in Alexandria, Va. She determined the molecular structure of complex chemicals using *iodide reagents* (iodine-containing compounds that cause chemical reactions in the presence of certain other chemicals).

Tenth place and $7,500 were awarded to Bianca D. Santomasso, 17, of Stuyvesant High School in New York City, who studied how cancer cells spread from a primary tumor to secondary sites.

Science fair winners. The 41st annual International Science and Engineering Fair took place May 6 to 12 in Tulsa, Okla. The 754 contestants were chosen from finalists at local science fairs in the United States and other countries.

Two students, judged the best of the 754 contestants, won a trip to the Nobel Prize ceremonies in Stockholm, Sweden, in December 1990. The winners were Joshua Fischman, who had won fifth place in the Westinghouse Science Talent Search, and Alexander Jacques

Fleming, 18, of Glynn Academy High School in Brunswick, Ga. In addition, one, two, three, or four First Award winners were selected in each of 13 categories. The 34 First Award winners of $500 each were:

- Behavioral and social sciences. Erik J. Edoff, 15, Athens High School, Troy, Mich; James M. Turner III, 16, Patrick Henry High School, Roanoke, Va.
- Biochemistry. Tessa L. Walters, 16, San Gabriel High School, San Gabriel, Calif.; Tae Hoon Kim, 18, Bullard High School, Fresno, Calif.; Elissa M. Blum, 18, Paul D. Schreiber High School, Port Washington, N.Y.
- Botany. Kelly R. Lindauer, 17, John F. Kennedy High School, Denver; Ching-Ling Teng, 17, Taipei Municipal First Girls' Senior High School, Taiwan; Lori A. Stec, 17, Detroit Country Day School, Birmingham, Mich.
- Chemistry. Matthew Webster, 16, St. Paul's School, London; Wade William Butin, 17, Klein High School, Klein, Tex.
- Computer science. Douglas B. Opfer, 18, Leto Comprehensive High School, Tampa, Fla.
- Earth and space science. Christopher Robinson Mullis, 18, Providence Day School, Charlotte, N.C.; Arturo P. Saavedra-Garcia, 16, Southwestern Educational Society, Mayaguez, Puerto Rico.
- Engineering. Fleming; James C. Ellis, 18, Immaculata High School, Somerville, N.J.; Mark Kevin Woehrer, 18, Bishop Neumann High School, Wahoo, Nebr.; Hugh Greene, Jr., 17, Brewer High School, Somerville, Ala.
- Environmental sciences. Sam Houston, 16, Decatur High School, Decatur, Ala.; Karen Elizabeth Boyle, 17, Braintree High School, Braintree, Mass.; Jay Bhama, 17, Plymouth Salem High School, Canton, Mich.; Keith Curtis, 17, Detroit Country Day School.
- Mathematics. Fischman; Daniel K. Dugger, 17, Nova High School, Davie, Fla.
- Medicine and health. Melissa Kaye Mouldin, 14, Rockledge High School, Rockledge, Fla.; Raymond D. Meng, 18, East Pennsboro Area High School, Enola, Pa.; Tahira Yasmeen Boyd, 18, Kenwood Academy, Chicago.
- Microbiology. Rebecca Penelope Wiggins, 17, Parkway West High

Parrots Make a Comeback in the Arizona Mountains

The thick-billed parrot, *right,* once common in Arizona and New Mexico, is being reintroduced into Arizona's Chiricahua Mountains, *map, below,* by state and federal wildlife officials. The parrots disappeared from the United States in the late 1930's as the result of being hunted and having their forested mountain habitats destroyed by logging activities. The birds survived, however, in the Sierra Madre range of northern Mexico.

Wildlife workers try to restore the wings of a parrot, *below left,* damaged by smugglers attempting to keep the bird from flying away. Thick-billed parrots had been confiscated at the Mexican border from people who were trying to smuggle them into the United States for sale as pets. In 1986, 29 of the confiscated birds were restored to flying condition and released. By 1990, only 10 or 12 of those parrots were still in Arizona; the others had been killed by hawks or had flown back to Mexico. The program is continuing, using parrots raised in captivity and released in mountainous areas, *below right,* where other thick-billed parrots have been sighted.

fools enemies into thinking the snake is lying still when in fact it is slithering away. Speckled snakes, on the other hand, try to "disappear" by becoming motionless and blending with their surroundings. Among Northwest garter snakes, there are individuals with either stripes or speckles and with the tendency to either flee or hide.

Brodie studied 474 baby garter snakes. He classified the skin color and pattern of each snake and then let it "run" on a circular Astroturf race track. He noted such behaviors as how fast each snake moved, how far it slithered before stopping, and whether it displayed any defensive behavior.

Striped garter snakes tended to flee in a fairly straight line and at a constant speed, whereas speckled snakes often stopped suddenly and remained motionless. Thus, it seems that the inheritance of a stripe makes a garter snake prone to fleeing, and inheriting a speckled pattern appears to be linked with a tendency to hide.

Follow that albatross. Biologists in Beauvoir, France, reported in February 1990 just how far the wandering albatross wanders. The scientists used satellites to track six male albatrosses in early 1989. They found that the birds made food-gathering trips of up to 14,500 kilometers (9,000 miles) and lasting as long as 33 days.

The researchers went to Possession Island in the southwestern Indian Ocean, where the birds breed. There, they outfitted the six males with small transmitters. Every two hours, one of two satellites picked up and recorded signals from the transmitters and then transmitted the data to earth. In this way, the scientists were able to plot the birds' movements and to correlate them with wind and weather patterns.

The albatross can fly so far, the researchers said, because it rides the wind. On return trips, when the six birds studied flew into the wind, they zigzagged back and forth, tacking as a sailboat might. The scientists said the albatross can lead this wandering life style only because it lives in a part of the world where frequent storms generate strong, regular winds.

Lost lemur found. The hairy-eared dwarf lemur, an animal that scientists had thought was extinct, still lives in the rain forests of Madagascar. That news was reported in December 1989 by West German zoologist Bernhard Meier, who found several of the tiny primates during a visit to the large island off the east coast of Africa earlier that year.

The hairy-eared dwarf lemur measures just 30 centimeters (12 inches) from its ears to the tip of its tail and weighs less than 85 grams (3 ounces). The species was known to zoologists only through five museum specimens.

A dog accompanying Meier's group found three dwarf lemurs in a burrow, and a guide caught one of them. The scientists measured the animal, took its picture, and then released it.

Desert survival, fish style. When it comes to being a tiny fish in a big desert, genetic diversity increases one's chances for survival, geneticists at Rutgers University in New Brunswick, N.J., reported in September 1989.

The scientists studied the Sonoran top minnow, a small, endangered fish found in springs in the Sonoran Desert of Arizona. They collected 10 female top minnows from each of three natural springs—Monkey Spring, Sharp Spring, and Tule Spring—one month before the females laid their eggs. In the laboratory, after the fish had laid their eggs and the eggs had hatched, the researchers raised the young in tanks. Each tank held the offspring of just one female.

For three months, the researchers kept track of the growth rate and survival of each young fish. They also recorded the number and size of the eggs produced by the female offspring.

Even though conditions in the laboratory's tanks most closely resembled those of Monkey Spring, the offspring of the fish from that spring did less well than the other young fish. The Monkey Spring top minnows survived an average of nine weeks, were smallest, grew the slowest, and produced the fewest number of eggs. The Sharp Spring top minnows grew fastest and largest, lived an average of 10½ weeks, and produced twice as many eggs as the Monkey Spring fish.

Previously, the scientists had found that the Sharp Spring top minnows were also the most genetically diverse. In contrast, they found almost no ge-

Zoology

Continued

netic variation among the Monkey Spring top minnows.

Conservationists hoping to increase the number of top minnows had been raising Monkey Spring fish in hatcheries and setting them free in streams. The conservationists have since switched to raising top minnows with greater genetic diversity from other springs, which should increase the numbers of this species.

Thriving without diversity. Genetic diversity may not be very important for the naked mole rat. In April 1990, zoologist Hudson K. Reeve of Cornell University in Ithaca, N.Y., reported finding very little variation in the genetic makeup of these small hairless mammals. Naked mole rats, which live in large underground colonies in Africa, are the only mammals known to have a social system similar to that of ants, termites, and honey bees, animals that share tasks beneficial to the group as a whole.

Reeve worked with geneticists to make "DNA fingerprints" of 50 naked mole rats from four colonies in Kenya.

DNA fingerprints are patterns based on variations in DNA, or deoxyribonucleic acid, the molecule of which genes are made. Only individuals with exactly the same genes—in the case of human beings, identical twins—have the same DNA fingerprint.

Reeve and his colleagues looked at three segments of DNA from each mole rat. The individuals sampled included 23 adults that had been caught in the field and 27 that were born in the laboratory. All the mole rats had died by the time that Reeve did his study; he conducted his research with tissues that had been saved from the animals.

The patterns produced by the mole rats' DNA were all surprisingly similar. Reeve discovered that even animals from different colonies were closer genetically than human brothers and sisters and almost as similar as identical twins. The scientists theorized that this lack of diversity may be due either to the uniform underground environment in which the mole rats live or to the possibility that they evolved from a recent common ancestor.

A barn owl fitted with special glasses sees objects displaced to the right of their actual location in a test at Stanford University in California. When the bespectacled owls were exposed to lights and sounds in a pitch-dark room, the owls consistently turned their heads to the right of where the light and sounds were coming from. When the glasses were removed, the birds looked directly at the lights, but continued to respond to sounds as if they came from off to the right side. This indicated that vision is a stronger sense than hearing in barn owls.

Zoology
Continued

Friendly vampire bats. Believe it or not, bloodsucking vampire bats do have a nice side. In February 1990, zoologist Gerald Wilkinson of the University of Maryland in College Park reported that these flying mammals, found in Central and South America, share food with fellow bats.

Vampire bats live in hollow trees and other dark places during the day. At night, they suck blood from horses or other large animals. They will starve to death if they miss a meal for more than two consecutive nights.

Wilkinson spent several years observing vampire bats in Costa Rica. On more than 100 occasions, he and his research team saw bats *regurgitating* (spitting up) blood to other bats.

Wilkinson discovered that some female vampire bats organize "buddy" systems, in which females and their relatives tend to roost together. Every night in such a group, bats that have successfully fed share blood with hungry bats.

This system benefits everyone. Each night, about 7 of every 100 bats fail to find food. The gift of blood buys those bats another day of life.

Worrisome declines. Birds are disappearing from North American forests, scientists with the United States Fish and Wildlife Service reported in October 1989. The researchers evaluated 20 years' worth of data and found that birds that breed in U.S. and Canadian forests and migrate to tropical forests for the winter declined in number between 1978 and 1987. The cutting down of forests in both North and Central America is apparently to blame.

Amphibians, too, seem to be in trouble. In September 1989, scientists at the first world congress on herpetology, held in England in September 1989, agreed that they were noticing fewer and fewer amphibians. A number of possible causes were cited, including droughts, acid rain, higher levels of ultraviolet light, and increased competition with human beings. [Elizabeth J. Pennisi and Thomas R. Tobin]

In WORLD BOOK, see ANIMAL; ZOOLOGY.

Science You Can Use

In areas selected for their current interest, *Science Year* presents information that the reader as a consumer can use in understanding everyday technology or in making decisions—from buying products to caring for personal health and well-being.

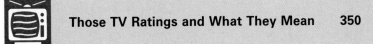
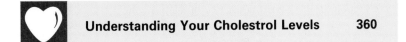

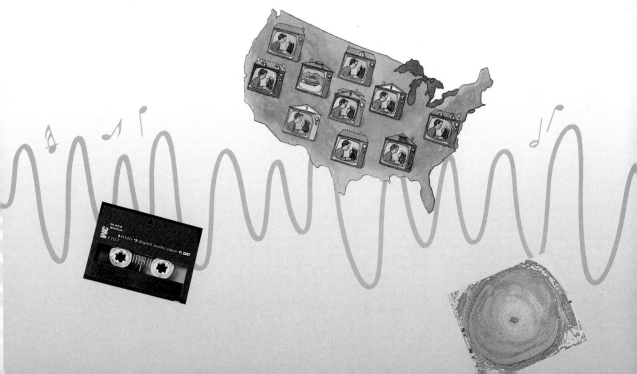

All About DAT

Sound-recording technology for the home entered a new era in June 1990, when *digital audio tape* (DAT) recorders became widely available in the United States. The digital system enables the home recorder for the first time to make a tape copy that is an exact replica, not just an approximation, of the original sounds, on a cassette that is about half the size of a standard audio cassette.

What is digital sound recording and how does the DAT recorder differ from standard tape recorders? Standard tape recorders, also known as *analog recorders*, convert sounds to electrical signals in the form of a wave pattern. Digital recording, however, converts sounds to electrical signals in the form of a numerical code.

Digital sound recording has been used primarily by professional recording studios since the early 1970's. The digital tapes obtained from those recordings were then converted to digital compact discs that could be played on a compact disc (CD) player. The drawback of the CD player, however, is that it can play only prerecorded material; it cannot record. The advantage of the DAT player is that it can both record and play in digital sound.

Analog recording is only a likeness of the original sounds, not an exact copy of those sounds. This is because the wave pattern of the electrical signals cannot be duplicated on the tape exactly. Moreover, because the first analog copy is imperfect, copies made from the copy lose sound quality each

The Difference that DAT Makes
Digital audio recording represents a great advance over traditional analog recording by faithfully duplicating the original sounds. First, sound waves are converted into electrical signals by a microphone.

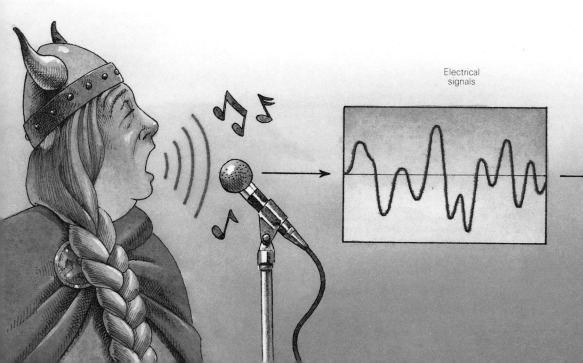

Electrical
signals

time a new copy is made. This is similar to what happens when photocopying a document. The first photocopy is a pretty good likeness of the original. But when a copy is made from the photocopy, it loses visual quality. As additional copies are made from copies, the later generations look very crude indeed.

With digital technology, there is no deterioration in subsequent copies. Each is a perfect replica of the one before it and of the original. This is because digital recording uses a numerical code to represent the original sound as *binary numbers*—a series of 0's and 1's—instead of a wave pattern. These numbers are recorded onto magnetic tape. So each time the tape is copied, only numbers are transferred—not patterns that can become distorted.

In a DAT recorder, the electrical signals that have been converted from sound are sampled at precise intervals of 44,100 times per second. Microprocessors, like those used in computers, assign each sample a 16-digit code of

zeros and ones that corresponds to the *frequency* (pitch) and *amplitude* (loudness) of the sound sample. There are more than sixty-five thousand 16-digit codes to represent all of the sounds in the range of human hearing.

A DAT recording also is free of *tape hiss*, an annoying noise that occurs with analog recordings. In an analog recording, tape hiss is unavoidable because in converting electrical signals to a wave pattern the tape moves over the recording heads, creating a sound with a frequency that can be heard. In recording music with an analog recorder, the voice or music signal usually overpowers the noise of the tape, and so the tape hiss goes unnoticed. But even with the best analog recorders, tape hiss cannot be completely eliminated, and it is usually apparent during relatively quiet moments in a musical passage. A DAT recording, however, has no background noise from the tape, again because the recording is made of numbers, not wave patterns.

The one visible difference in DAT

Then, microprocessors in a digital audio tape recorder sample the signals at precise intervals and assign each sample a 16-digit code of 0's and 1's that corresponds to the pitch and loudness. When the recording is played back, the listener hears sound waves representing the exact original sounds.

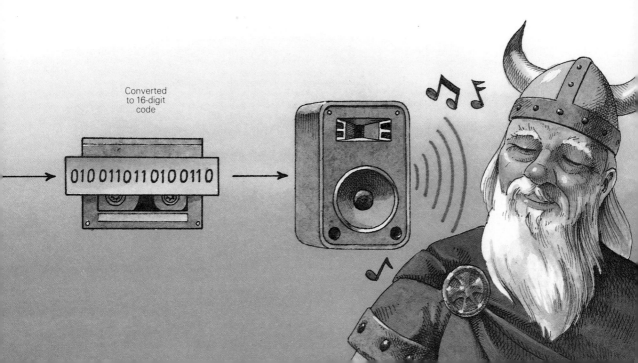

Converted
to 16-digit
code

010 0110 11 0100 110

recording is the tape cassette that is used. It is about half the size of a conventional analog audio cassette and has a hinged lid that makes it resemble a miniaturized videocassette tape. In fact, a DAT recorder operates much like a videocassette recorder (VCR). The DAT recorder's *magnetic recording heads*—the part of the recorder that "writes" the numerical code on the tape—are mounted in a rotating drum. When the DAT cassette is placed inside the recorder, the machine opens the hinged lid of the tape cassette, extracts the tape, and wraps it around the rotating head drum, just as a VCR does with a videocassette.

Also like a VCR, the tape records in one direction only. Standard analog audiotape can be recorded in two directions, which is done by flipping the cassette shell from side A to side B. Nevertheless, a DAT tape offers more recording time on one side than does an analog tape.

This is partly because of the speed at which the recording heads on the drum rotate. As the recording heads rotate, they "write" the numerical code information on the tape in a diagonal track from the bottom to the top of the tape. The track is virtually microscopic—only 0.0136 millimeters (mm) wide. (One millimeter equals 0.04 of an inch.) The tape itself moves at a speed of 8.15 mm per second, and the recording head drum rotates at 2,000 revolutions per minute. This combination yields what is called a *writing speed* of 3.133 meters (123 inches) per second—the rate at which information is laid down on the tape. A DAT recorder's writing speed is 65 times faster than that of analog audio recorders. The combination of fast writing-speed, microscopic track-size, and thin but high-density magnetic tape yields up to 120 minutes of continuous recording time using one side of a cassette. By comparison, the longest analog cassette pro-

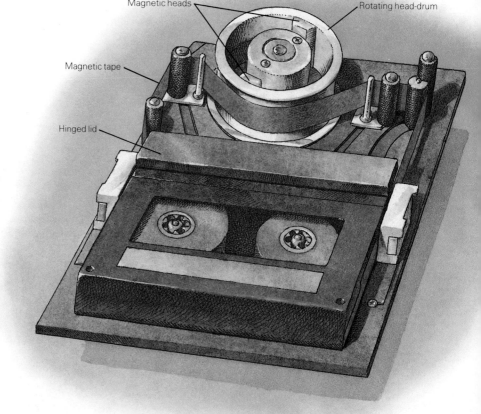

Magnetic heads

Rotating head-drum

Magnetic tape

Hinged lid

The DAT player works like a videocassette recorder. When a DAT cassette is placed inside the player, the machine opens the hinged lid of the cassette, extracts the tape on spools, and runs it against a rotating head-drum with two magnetic heads that alternately scan the tape up and down diagonally. The magnetic heads read the 0's and 1's, which are then reconverted to sound.

A DAT cassette fits easily in the palm of a hand and is smaller than a standard analog cassette but has a recording time of 120 minutes. The cassette records on one side only, so a person wanting to record a symphony or opera can record without interruption for up to two hours.

vides about 120 minutes of recording time using two sides of the cassette. People who don't like to hear their favorite symphonies interrupted when an analog recorder changes sides benefit from a DAT recorder's ability to play and record music for up to two hours on one side only.

This recording time of two hours is available using four of the five recording modes that a DAT player offers. These recording modes yield different levels of sound quality. The fifth mode is for dictation and operates at a slower tape speed, to make about four hours of recording time available.

The high-fidelity capabilities of DAT players have caused concern in the music industry. Recording company executives feared DAT's potential for allowing *illegal pirating*—making duplicate tapes in large numbers to sell at a profit without paying royalties to the record companies or artists involved. They were also concerned that friends would copy one another's tapes, also leading to decreased tape sales. Although home DAT recorders were demonstrated as early as 1986 in Japan, legal wrangling over these concerns postponed the introduction of DAT players in the United States until 1990.

To prevent pirating, electronics manufacturers agreed in 1990 to build into every DAT recorder a Serial Copy Management System (SCMS). The SCMS circuitry prevents a DAT recorder from making a copy of a DAT copy. In other words, a person may make a DAT copy of a digital audio compact disc but cannot make a DAT copy of the first copy.

If a person attempted to copy a DAT copy, the recorder would flash a "copy prohibit" message and fail to operate. The SCMS works by using digital subcodes encoded on virtually all compact discs and prerecorded DAT cassettes.

When a person begins to make a first DAT tape from a compact disc, the SCMS circuit makes note of the disc's subcode and adds a subcode of its own to the tape. This second code identifies the tape as a copy. Should someone attempt to copy the copy, the second code triggers the SCMS circuit and prevents further duplication. If the person wanted another DAT copy of the compact disc, it would be necessary to record the additional copy from the disc once again.

Analog sound sources—such as standard, long-playing records (LP's), conventional audio cassettes, and radio broadcasts—do not have the subcodes found on compact discs. Accordingly, the first DAT recording from these sources is the digital original. Only when a second DAT recorder is used to copy this tape does the DAT recorder imprint a subcode identifying the tape as a copy. So it is possible to make two DAT copies from an analog source before SCMS would prevent further duplication.

This SCMS circuit is considered by many to be an elegant compromise between the concerns of the music industry and technological progress. It lets people make digital copies for personal use. At the same time, it foils the mass-production needs of criminal piracy, thus paving the way for the new era now beginning in digital home recording.   [Stephen A. Booth]

Those TV Ratings and What They Mean

Television ratings have become an important part of American life, even though they do not indicate whether a show is artistically "good" or "bad" or for what age group it might be suitable. Ratings for television estimate only how many people watch a particular program. Nevertheless, these all-important numbers help determine what programs will be aired and when, and how much advertisers will be charged for commercials during a particular TV show.

National TV ratings, which might seem to be shrouded in mystery, are calculated from the actual viewing habits of some 4,000 households selected to represent the entire population of the United States. Information about who in each household watches which channel and when is used to create the ratings.

This might sound simple, but methods of collecting the data are very complex. In June 1990, the TV networks began to question the validity of the statistics. Until then, the sole source

of national TV ratings was Nielsen Media Research of Northbrook, Ill. Now, the networks are planning to conduct their own ratings research. This is but the next chapter in the story of how TV ratings are made.

In the early 1960's, Nielsen emerged as the dominant provider of national TV ratings. At that time, the company asked viewers in specially selected households to keep weekly diaries of programs they watched. This relied, however, on the viewer's memory instead of recording actual viewing.

But in 1987, Nielsen started using interactive People Meters—remote-control devices connected to TV sets. The People Meters do not require people to remember what they watch. Viewers only need to punch in a number on the remote-control device that tells the People Meter who is watching television and what channel they are watching.

Because it would be far too expen-

A family taking part in a Nielsen ratings survey uses a remote control device to trigger a People Meter placed atop their TV set that logs what TV program they're watching.

The creation of TV ratings begins when members of a Nielsen household activate a People Meter to tell which TV shows they are watching. The meter is hooked to the telephone line.

The next day, advertisers and TV executives can learn how many people watched each program.

Each day, a record of what was watched is relayed to Nielsen's computer in Dunedin, Fla., near Tampa, for analysis. The computer produces ratings for each program.

sive to meter all of the nation's 92.1 million TV households, Nielsen tracks the viewing of what it calls a "carefully selected cross-section" of about 4,000 American households to estimate national viewing. The cross-section is determined by geographic region. For example, if 7 per cent of all U.S. households with a television set are located in New York state, then 7 per cent of Nielsen's sample of 4,000 households will be located in New York state.

The numbers collected by Nielsen are reported as a *rating* and a *share* of the TV audience. Both numbers are percentages, but they are percentages based on different measurements. A rating is calculated on the basis of all households with television sets. A share is calculated on the basis of all households with a television set turned on. For example, a 100.0 rating would

mean that all of the 92.1 million households with a TV would have the set turned on and all would be tuned to the same program at the same time. A 100 share would mean all the TV households with a TV turned on were tuned to the same program. But a program with a 100 *share* would have only a 50.0 *rating* if half the country's TV sets were turned off at the time the program was on.

Ratings allow advertisers to compare the performance of shows at different times of the day because the ratings are measured as a percentage of all households with TV's. Shows telecast during the prime-time hours of 8 p.m. to 11 p.m. Eastern Standard Time typically earn the highest ratings on television because more homes have television sets turned on during those hours than at any other time of day.

Shares enable advertisers to compare

351

the performance of one show against others being shown at the same time because shares measure the percentage of people viewing the show in homes with the television turned on at that time. A show might have a low rating because it's on at 3 a.m., but if half the homes using television at that hour are tuned into the show, it would have a 50 share and be considered a success.

Ratings are used as a way to determine the cost of commercial time, and so they have become an important factor in deciding the fate of TV shows. The value of TV commercial time is calculated on the basis of *cost-per-thousand*—that is, the cost to reach viewers in 1,000 households. This means TV networks and TV stations can earn more money by selling commercial time during high-rated shows rather than during low-rated ones.

For example, let's assume that a network sells 30 seconds of commercial time at a $10 cost-per-thousand—about the current rate for prime time—during a show with a 10.0 rat-

ing. A 10.0 rating equals 10 per cent of the 92.1 million TV households in the United States, or 9,210,000 homes (9,210 units of 1,000). At a cost of $10 per thousand homes ($10 × 9,210), the 30-second commercial would be sold for $92,100.

At the same $10 cost-per-thousand, a 30-second commercial during a show with a 1.0 rating would cost only $9,210. A 1.0 rating equals 1 per cent of the nation's 92.1 million households or 921,000 homes (921 units of 1,000). If a show's rating gets too low, of course, the show will be canceled.

Ratings are subject to a margin of error because they are based not on a count of all TV households, but on the sample of 4,000 Nielsen households. According to Nielsen, statistical studies have shown that if, for example, 20 per cent of all U.S. homes were actually watching a program, about a thousand samples of 4,000 households would register ratings between 18.2 per cent and 21.8 per cent. This tells Nielsen that their rating will be plus or minus 1.8 per cent of the actual rating. Advertisers who buy commercial time and TV networks and TV stations that sell the time find this margin of error acceptable.

Because there are 92.1 million American television households and

TV Ratings

Nielsen's TV data are broken down into two categories—ratings and shares. A rating is the per cent of all households with a TV set that watched a particular television program. Ratings are highest during the prime-time evening hours when most people are watching TV.

Here, 9 of 10 homes with TV's are watching the same program. So the program's rating is 90.

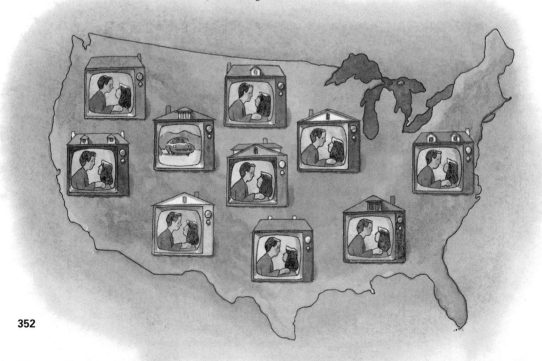

4,000 households are selected, every TV household has a 1 in 23,000 chance of becoming a national "Nielsen family" (92.1 million ÷ 4,000 = 23,025). If a selected family accepts the offer to become a Nielsen family, it agrees to become a part of the sample for two years. After two years, Nielsen selects a new household.

Once a family agrees to take part in the measurement of its viewing habits, Nielsen installs People Meters within the home. Not only does the device indicate family members watching TV, but it also has buttons labeled for visitors. The meter records the time the set is turned on, which channel is being watched (including cable channels), when the channel is changed, and when the set is turned off.

The meter is hooked up to the household's telephone line and is programmed to call Nielsen's operations center in Dunedin, Fla., each night to relay all the data to a central computer. The computer instantly matches the viewer's number with the TV channel or channels that were watched during the day. Processing of data begins at 3 a.m., and national ratings are available that afternoon.

Who will collect future TV ratings and how is far from certain. One next step may be the development of a "passive" People Meter, which would allow Nielsen to measure ratings instantly because the device would instantly relay its data to Nielsen's computer. Many people are alarmed about the project because the passive People Meter would likely include a small camera that scans the room and compares faces it "sees" with images stored in its computer memory.

They believe the passive People Meter would be an invasion of privacy and violate personal freedoms. But advertisers, researchers, and many in the television industry believe a passive People Meter would merely yield the most accurate reflection of who watched what program when. The passive meter would also track whether people were watching the various commercials because it could "see" if people stopped viewing the television during commercials.

Nielsen executives say the passive People Meter is the "logical evolution," because it requires no effort on the part of the viewer.   [Wayne Walley]

TV Shares

A share is the per cent of all households with a TV turned on that watched a particular program. A share takes into account the fact that not all households watch TV at the same time.

Here, only 5 of 10 households have a TV turned on, but all 5 are watching the same program. So the program's share is 100.

New and Better Bikes

Bicycles have changed radically in the past 40 years thanks to the development of new materials for making frames and the application of aerodynamic design. In the 1980's, new materials for making bicycle frames made possible widespread distribution of the *all-terrain* or *mountain bike*. The frame of the mountain bike consists of hollow, large-diameter, thin-walled tubes made of a lightweight aluminum alloy. The result is a bicycle that is light enough for easy handling but rugged enough to cross just about any terrain—from mountain trails to the open road to city streets with potholes and high curbs.

Mountain bikes have become extremely popular in the United States. In fact, half of the 10 million bikes sold in the United States in 1989 were mountain bikes.

As the bicycle industry enters the 1990's, another material—carbon fiber—promises to make popular a bicycle frame that is even lighter and sturdier than the mountain bike. Carbon-fiber frames weigh less than 1.4 kilograms (3 pounds), compared with the 5.4-kilogram (12-pound) weight of mountain bike frames.

The construction of a carbon-fiber frame starts with a synthetic fabric woven from carbon-based strands of yarn. The yarn is similar in appearance to fiberglass strands, but far stronger. The yarn is woven into tough carbon-fiber cloth, which is transformed into a rigid material by saturating it with epoxy. In finished form, it is approximately five times as strong and twice as stiff as the steel alloys used in traditional, 10-speed road bikes.

At first, carbon fiber was used only to replace the metal tubes that made up the bicycle frame. The carbon-fiber tubes were then joined together by metal fasteners. Although the frames were lightweight, they occasionally gave way where two or more tubes were joined.

An important advance, however, came in the late 1980's when California-based Cycle Composites, Inc., originated the Kestrel bicycle frame. It is a one-piece structure with large diameter tubes and a smoothly blended frame. As a result, the hollow frame tubes do not have to be connected to each other by metal fasteners. The only metal components used in this bicycle make up the pedal crank, the gears and chains, and the wheel axles.

Because of their one-piece structure and the incredible strength of carbon fiber, Kestrel frames are far stronger and more durable than bicycle frames made of other materials. The aluminum alloy tubes that make up the frames of mountain bikes, for example, are bonded together with epoxy, and the chromium-steel alloy tubes of road bikes are welded together. Both types of frame have potential weak spots where the tubes are welded or bonded together, unlike the one-piece carbon-fiber frame. And with the virtual absence of metal parts, the carbon-fiber frame is more durable because it cannot rust or corrode.

Carbon fiber is also a good weight-bearing material. The greatest stress points on a bicycle frame are at the steering head, where the frame tubes meet to form the pivot point for the steering, and at the pedal cranks, because these points are where most of the rider's pedaling force is applied. With metal frames, these stress points must be reinforced, adding more weight to the bicycle. But with carbon fiber, the frames can be reinforced by aligning the threads with the direction of stress. The carbon-fiber frame can withstand the great stresses placed on it, without adding any weight to the frame.

Because the new carbon-fiber technology has only recently been introduced to bicycle manufacturing, the price range for a carbon-fiber frame is beyond the $150 to $300 most consumers expect to spend for a new bicycle.

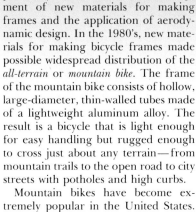

Mountain, or all-terrain, bicycles, with their wide tires and rugged, sturdy frames, have made cycling over rough, hilly terrain a new recreational pursuit.

These bikes range in price from $600 to $1,800, though the price may drop.

Competitive bicycle racers have benefited greatly from the new carbon-fiber materials. Not only is carbon fiber lightweight, making it easier to pedal a bicycle faster, but it also can be used to increase a bicycle's speed by reducing the wheels' *aerodynamic drag*—the force that resists the forward motion of an object through the air and thus slows it down.

The shape of an object moving through the air influences the amount of drag. As air flows around the spokes of a bicycle wheel, the air becomes very turbulent, and this creates a lot of drag. Carbon fiber, however, can be used to make smooth, solid wheels—known as *disk wheels*—without spokes. These wheels have greatly improved the bicycle's aerodynamic efficiency because their smooth shape and lack of spokes greatly minimize turbulence. The international organizations that oversee competitive bicycle racing have long forbidden any addition to a bike that is done solely for the purpose of aerodynamic streamlining. The same governing bodies, however, have ruled that wheels formed entirely of carbon-fiber disks are legal because they also are weight-bearing structures and thus have more than one purpose.

The new materials seem to hold promise for all bicycle riders, whether their interest is racing, fitness, recreation, or just running errands. Bicycles have become increasingly lighter, stronger, more durable, and easier to pedal. And as the bicycle industry enters the 1990's, its products are likely to become even stronger and more streamlined. [Norman S. Mayersohn]

Comparing bicycles made of different materials

	Road bike (chromium-steel alloy frame)	Mountain or all-terrain bike (aluminum alloy frame)	Road or mountain bike (carbon-fiber frame)
Bicycle Type			
Advantages	Lightweight; easy to pedal; fast; aerodynamic styling; can be used for competitive racing.	Lightweight; easy to pedal; rugged, sturdy frame with fat tires can be ridden on mountain terrain or over potholes and high curbs of city streets; straight-across handlebars enable rider to sit up.	Lightest weight available; strongest frame; can be adapted either for competitive racing by using aerodynamic styling and skinny tires or for mountain trail and city street use by using straight-across handlebars and fatter tires.
Disadvantages	Skinny, puncture-prone tires not suited to rough terrain or city streets with potholes and high curbs; dropdown position of handlebars on most models requires an awkward riding crouch.	Fat tires and lack of aerodynamic styling make it unsuitable for competitive road racing; not as fast or as lightweight as road bikes.	Even the least expensive model is extremely expensive.
Price Range	$230 to $10,000	$170 to $3,400	$600 to $12,000

Walking Toward Better Health

Walking is the way most of us get around most of the time. When we walk, we put one foot in front of another, but at least one foot is on the ground at any point during a step. When we run or jog, there is a point during each step when both feet are off the ground. So people think of walking as slow and running as fast. But that is not necessarily the case.

Racewalking is an Olympic event. World-class racewalkers can finish the 50-kilometer walk in under 4 hours—that's much faster than most people can run the distance. An increasing number of people are beginning to think of walking as a way to get the exercise they need to stay healthy. This type of walking is known as *fitness walking*, *exercise walking*, or *pace walking*. It can have the health benefits of running or jogging without putting too much stress on muscles and bones.

Exercise pace walking is not to be confused with racewalking, which involves a complex gait in which the knees are kept straight, the elbows are bent, and the hips swivel constantly. Pace walking is not as fast as racewalking, but it is faster than a casual stroll. A fast pace walker can do a runner's Olympic-length marathon (42.2 kilometers, or 26 miles and 385 yards) in less than five hours. This is a walking pace of 8.8 kilometers (5½ miles) per hour.

In exercise pace walking, you not only walk quickly but also add a strong arm-swing. A comfortable and effective way to do pace walking is to walk fast with a medium-length stride. Keep your back straight, your shoulders dropped and relaxed, your head up, and your feet pointed straight ahead.

Swing your arms and keep your elbows bent. To avoid creating tension in your arms, don't clench your fists. Your arms should be angled slightly across your chest. You should feel a tug at the back of your shoulder at the end of each backswing. On the foreswing, your hand should come up to about midchest level.

With each step, you land on your heel and roll forward along the outside of your foot, pushing off with your toes. Since both feet never leave the ground at the same time, you will sharply diminish the pounding that your feet and joints take when you run or jog and land with all your weight on your forefoot. The objective is to develop a smooth, rhythmic, quick, comfortable stride that will raise your heart rate into the aerobic range.

The healthy aerobic heart rate falls within a range that varies with age. To find out what is appropriate for your age, subtract your age from the number 220. The range, as determined by the American College of Sports Medicine, is from 70 per cent to 85 per cent of the resulting figure. For a 15-year-old person, the heart rate after vigorous, aerobic exercise should range from about 143 to 174 beats per minute. For a 40-year-old, it would range from 126 to 153 beats per minute.

Aerobic exercise is any exercise that uses oxygen from inhaled air as the source of energy for muscle contraction. Aerobic exercise significantly raises the amount of oxygen that your

Walking at a brisk pace strengthens a person's cardiovascular system, burns up calories, creates a feeling of well-being, and helps keep a person of any age fit.

How to Do Exercise Walking

To obtain the greatest health benefits from exercise walking, the exerciser should walk at a brisk pace of about 5.5 kilometers (3 miles) per hour and swing the arms across the chest. Walking must be done on a regular basis for at least 20 minutes three times a week. The brisk pace not only burns calories but also strengthens the cardiovascular system.

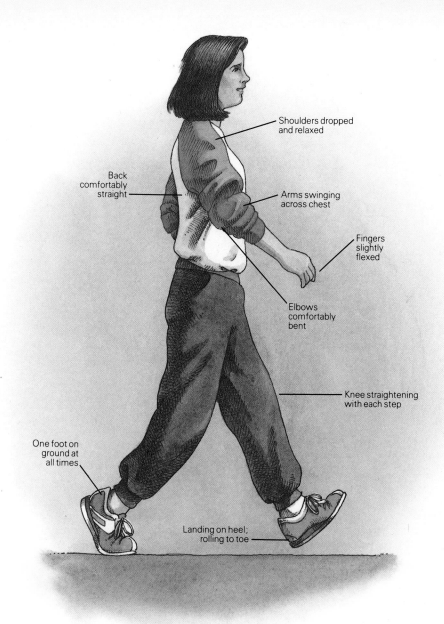

Shoulders dropped and relaxed

Back comfortably straight

Arms swinging across chest

Fingers slightly flexed

Elbows comfortably bent

Knee straightening with each step

One foot on ground at all times

Landing on heel; rolling to toe

Burning Up Calories

In addition to strengthening a person's cardiovascular system, exercise walking burns calories and helps reduce weight. The table below compares the number of calories burned for various walking paces with everyday physical activity and other forms of exercise.

Activity (10 minutes)	Body weight (in pounds)				
	100	125	150	175	200
Walking, 2 miles/hour	23	29	35	40	46
Walking, 4 miles/hour	42	52	62	72	81
Walking upstairs	118	146	175	202	229
Walking downstairs	46	56	67	78	99
Baseball (excluding pitcher)	31	39	47	54	62
Basketball	46	58	70	82	93
Bowling	45	56	67	78	90
Cycling, 13 miles/hour	71	89	107	124	142
Dancing (vigorous)	39	48	57	66	75
Dressing or washing	21	26	32	37	42
Football	55	69	83	96	110
Golfing	26	33	40	48	55
House-painting	23	29	35	40	46
Making beds	25	32	39	46	52
Reading or watching TV	8	10	12	14	16
Running, $5\frac{1}{2}$ miles/hour	73	90	108	125	142
Shoveling snow	53	65	78	89	100
Sleeping	8	10	12	14	16
Standing	10	12	14	16	19
Swimming (crawl)	32	40	48	56	63
Tennis	44	56	67	80	92
Typing (electric)	15	19	23	27	31
Washing windows	29	35	42	48	54
Writing	12	15	18	21	24

NUMBER OF CALORIES BURNED BY PHYSICAL ACTIVITY

Source: K.D. Brownell, University of Pennsylvania.

muscles take out of the bloodstream. It increases your heart rate because your heart must pump faster to supply the needed oxygen.

How do you know when you are exercising aerobically? The simplest way is to count your heartbeats by placing two fingers on your neck just in front of the diagonal bands of muscle that run from under the ears to the collarbones. Halfway down one of those muscle bands you should be able to feel your pulse coming from one of the arteries that supply blood to your neck and head. Count the number of pulses that occur during one minute to find your heart rate. Never feel for your pulse on both sides of your neck at the same time, however, because you could cause yourself to pass out.

Doing aerobic exercises on a regular basis helps train both the heart and the skeletal muscles to function longer and stronger. Aerobic exercise can significantly lower the risk of heart disease, high blood pressure, and certain kinds of diabetes. Under proper supervision, aerobic exercise is also helpful in managing depression, stress, and asthma, especially in children. To gain the health benefits of aerobic exercise, you should work out for about 20 minutes three times a week.

Exercise walking is not only good aerobic exercise; it also produces just enough stress on bones to benefit older women, who are at risk of developing *osteoporosis*, a disease that causes bones to become brittle and so increases the likelihood of fractures. Bone tissue responds to repeated, moderate stress—like that from exercise walking—by increasing bone density, which, in turn, helps strengthen the bones and prevents them from becoming brittle.

Some people use weights while they walk. It is better to wear ringlike weights around the wrist than to carry weights in your hands. Squeezing hand weights can increase both arm tension and blood pressure. Both wrist and ankle weights are safe up to a maximum of 1 kilogram (2.2 pounds). Weights can be worn around the waist if they are positioned over the hips. But pace walking with weights in a backpack is not a good idea, because this can constrict breathing.

To avoid injury and pain while exercise walking, it's important to wear the right shoes. The shoes should fit like a glove, touching your foot in as many places as possible, but without squeezing. A good fit is essential to avoiding blisters and to prevent your foot from sliding around inside the shoe, which can lead to the pain of muscle or joint injury.

The front part of the shoe should be flexible where it bends under the ball of your foot. The heel should be reasonably well cushioned, though you don't need as much cushioning as you do for running. Nevertheless, a good quality running shoe is also ideal for regular exercise walking.

For most people, the hard part of regular exercise is the "regular," not the "exercise." You have to find or make the time to do it. And once you've made the time, you have to stick with it, something that's not always easy to do.

One suggestion for how to become a regular exerciser is to begin gradually. Keep your initial workouts brief and concentrate on doing them regularly. Work up to a routine of walking 20 minutes a day three times a week.

A number of health studies have shown that it is the regularity of the exercise that brings the greatest health benefits. For example, after a seven-year study of 12,138 middle-aged men, doctors at the University of Minnesota in Minneapolis reported in 1987 that those who rarely exercised had a 30 per cent greater chance of dying of coronary artery disease than those who engaged in regular physical activity. The same study found that those who took part in light or moderate physical activity on a regular basis, such as walking, for 30 to 60 minutes a day reduced their risk of dying of coronary artery disease at the same rate as those who took part in more strenuous physical activity.

Such findings should provide motivation for exercising on a regular basis—and motivation is essential. You have to want to exercise because of how it will make you feel about yourself. Most people have that inner motivation. It's just a matter of uncovering it and maintaining it. If you do that, you'll become a regular exercise walker for life.   [Steven Jonas]

Understanding Your Cholesterol Levels

Millions of Americans concerned about the risk of heart disease have been having their blood cholesterol checked, and are talking and worrying about the results. Some can recite their levels of cholesterol and its "good" and "bad" components as easily as their own age. Yet United States government data indicate that 64 million Americans still have cholesterol levels that are dangerously high.

Reducing the amount of cholesterol circulating in the blood can substantially reduce the risk of a heart attack. But it requires knowledge about how people can change their cholesterol levels.

In an unclogged coronary artery, *top right,* there is plenty of room for blood to flow. In an artery clogged with cholesterol-laden deposits of plaque, *bottom right,* the passage is very narrow. It can easily be clogged by a blood clot, and a clogged coronary artery can cause a heart attack.

Cholesterol is a fatlike substance found in all animal cells and thus all foods of animal origin. Cholesterol is essential for life. The human body needs cholesterol to manufacture cell membranes, nerve tissue, hormones, and bile acids used to digest food.

Your body manufactures cholesterol and can make enough to meet these needs—even if your diet contains no cholesterol. About 60 to 70 per cent of the body's cholesterol·is produced in the liver and is carried in the blood to cells throughout the body. The body of a normal adult produces about 1,000 milligrams (mg) of cholesterol each day. This is a very small amount—only about 0.004 ounce. People with certain hereditary disorders produce much more. Many people add to the liver's cholesterol production by consuming large amounts of dietary cholesterol in eggs, butter, and fatty foods. Thus, both heredity and diet can determine a person's blood cholesterol level.

A high level of blood cholesterol has been recognized as one of several controllable risk factors for coronary artery disease (which results from the build-up of fatty deposits in arteries of the heart). Other risk factors include high blood pressure and cigarette smoking.

Coronary artery disease is the underlying cause of most heart attacks, which kill about 550,000 people in the United States each year—more than cancer or any other disease. Most heart attacks occur because deposits of cholesterol and other material build up inside the coronary arteries, much like rust in an old water pipe. Total blockage of the artery cuts off blood flow to the muscular wall of the heart, destroying part of the heart muscle.

Laboratory tests of blood samples are used to determine the build-up of cholesterol in the arteries. A person's blood cholesterol level is expressed in milligrams per deciliter (mg/dl). There are 28,350 milligrams in 1 ounce. A deciliter is one-tenth of a liter—about one-tenth of a quart. The average cholesterol level among Americans—men and women, aged 35 to 57—is 210 mg/dl. So the amount of cholesterol present in the blood is tiny.

Doctors once thought that cholesterol readings in the low 200's were harmless. Most physicians became concerned only if a patient's cholesterol level rose above 250. Then, in November 1986, researchers at Northwestern University in Chicago and the University of Minnesota at Minneapolis, after studying the medical records of 356,222 men aged 35 to 57, found that the risk of a fatal heart attack actually begins to rise steeply at cholesterol levels above 182. Men who have cholesterol readings above 264 have heart attack death rates four times higher than those with cholesterol readings between 167 and 181.

Most physicians now use guidelines established in 1987 by the National Cholesterol Education Program (NCEP), a coalition of government and private groups led by the federal government's National Heart, Lung, and Blood Institute in Bethesda, Md. The NCEP regards blood cholesterol levels under 200 as "desirable." Readings of 200 to 239 are considered "borderline-high," and those of 240 and above are considered "high."

The NCEP recommends that people whose cholesterol levels are between 200 and 239 but who do not have coronary disease or at least two risk factors should go on a low-fat, low-

Researchers have found that not only is total blood cholesterol an important factor in cardiovascular health, but the type of cholesterol also is important. High-density lipoprotein (HDL) helps eliminate excess cholesterol from the body, while low-density lipoprotein (LDL) increases surplus amounts of cholesterol.

Cholesterol Levels and What They Mean

Level of cholesterol	Treatment generally recommended
Desirable level Less than 200 mg/dl.	None. Cholesterol level should be checked every five years.
Borderline high 200-239 mg/dl.	Reduce total fat intake to less than 30 per cent of daily calories and saturated fat intake to10 per cent of calories. Begin aerobic exercise (after checking with your physician).
Borderline high with risk factors 200-239 mg/dl plus two or more risk factors (being male, having high blood pressure, smoking, having diabetes, being severely overweight, having low levels of high density lipoproteins, or having a family history of early coronary heart disease).	Restrict saturated fat to 7 per cent of daily calories. If six months of dieting alone fails to reduce cholesterol levels, combine dieting and treatment with cholesterol-lowering drugs under the supervision of your physician.
High 240 mg/dl or higher.	Same as borderline high with risk factors.

Types of Cholesterol in the Blood

HDL	LDL	Important Ratios
• Often called "good" cholesterol. • Levels of 35 mg/dl are desirable. • Levels may be increased by exercise.	• Often called "bad" cholesterol. • Levels less than 130 mg/dl are desirable. Borderline high-risk levels are 130-159 mg/dl, and high-risk are 160 mg/dl and above. • Levels can be reduced by low-fat diet, but a more stringent diet or medications may be necessary.	• Proportion of HDL may be more important than overall cholesterol. • To find ratio, divide total cholesterol by HDL level. • Example: 180 (total) ÷ 50 (HDL) = 3.6. • Ratios above 4.5 signal heart disease risk.

Source for top chart: Adapted from the National Cholesterol Education Program.
Source for bottom chart: National Cholesterol Education Program and various studies.

cholesterol diet. The risk factors include cigarette smoking, high blood pressure, obesity, diabetes, physical inactivity, and being a male. People with readings of 200 to 239 who do have coronary disease or two risk factors and all people with readings of 240 or above should have an additional test for lipoproteins. Lipoproteins determine what has come to be called "good" or "bad" cholesterol.

Technically, cholesterol is not a fat but a fatlike substance called a *lipid*. Like fats, cholesterol does not mix with water. In order to transport cholesterol in the blood, which is mostly water, the liver wraps cholesterol in packages of protein. The packets—part lipid (cholesterol) and part protein—are called *lipoproteins*.

There are two kinds of lipoproteins, high-density lipoproteins (HDL's) and low-density lipoproteins (LDL's). HDL cholesterol has become known as the "good" form of cholesterol. Like garbage trucks, HDL's scoop up surplus cholesterol from the bloodstream and transport it back to the liver for elimination from the body. Some scientists even believe that HDL's may remove cholesterol from deposits in the coronary arteries. The NCEP says that desirable HDL levels are 35 mg/dl or above.

LDL cholesterol is the "bad" form of cholesterol. LDL's are delivery trucks that transport cholesterol from the liver for deposit in cells. If there is too much LDL in the blood, the excess fatty substance can be deposited on coronary artery walls.

The NCEP says that a "desirable" level of LDL's is less than 130 mg/dl. Borderline high-risk levels are 130 to 159 mg/dl. High risk is 160 mg/dl and above.

The NCEP recommends that people with LDL readings of 130 to 159 who do not have coronary disease or two risk factors should go on a low-fat, low-cholesterol diet. They should be retested annually. People with readings of 130 to 159 who also have coronary disease or who have two risk factors may need a more stringent diet or medications.

A number of studies suggest that the ratio of total cholesterol to HDL may be a more sensitive way of measuring heart attack risk than overall blood cholesterol levels. The ratio is calculated by dividing the total cholesterol level by the HDL level. Thus, a person with a total cholesterol level of 180 and an HDL level of 50 would have a ratio of 3.6. Researchers believe that a ratio above 4.5 signals an elevated risk for a heart attack.

People can lower the ratio by either decreasing their total blood cholesterol level or increasing their HDL level. Studies suggest that every 1-milligram increase in HDL reduces the risk of a heart attack by 6 per cent.

Eliminating fats and high-cholesterol foods from the diet, maintaining normal weight, and exercising can decrease total cholesterol and boost HDL levels. Details of low-fat, low-cholesterol diets can be obtained from local chapters of the American Heart Association or your family physician.

Increasing consumption of certain forms of dietary fiber also can help reduce total blood cholesterol. The kind of fiber found in oat bran, dried beans, and some fruits and vegetables may be especially beneficial.

Generally, a person who begins a low-fat, low-cholesterol diet should see a drop in blood cholesterol levels within two to three weeks. Some people can reduce their cholesterol readings by 30, 40, or 50 points by simply following such a diet, losing weight, and exercising regularly. The average reduction from a low-cholesterol diet is 10 per cent.

Other people, however, still may require cholesterol-lowering drugs, which are available only with a doctor's prescription. Some cholesterol-lowering drugs not only reduce total cholesterol but also have a beneficial effect in reducing LDL cholesterol levels.

While there is a definite link between cholesterol and heart disease, many questions remain. For example, most research on cholesterol and heart disease was done on middle-aged men, so scientists do not know whether women and elderly people also benefit from reducing their cholesterol levels. A great deal more remains to be learned about cholesterol and healthy hearts, but meanwhile, everyone is advised to keep a close watch on his or her own blood cholesterol.   [Michael Woods]

World Book Supplement

Five new or revised articles reprinted from the 1990 edition of *The World Book Encyclopedia.*

Computers come in a wide range of sizes. A *mainframe* computer system may fill a large room, *above.* A *personal computer, left opposite page,* fits on a desk top. The tiniest computers consist of a *microprocessor,* a chip that fits through the eye of a needle, *right opposite page.*

Computer

Computer is a machine that performs calculations and processsses information with astonishing speed and precision. A computer can handle vast amounts of information and solve complicated problems. It can take thousands of individual pieces of data and turn them into more usable information—with blinding speed and almost unfailing accuracy. The most powerful computers can perform billions of calculations per second.

Computers handle many tasks in business, education, manufacturing, transportation, and other fields. They provide scientists and other researchers with a clearer understanding of nature. They give people who work with words an effective way to create documents. They enable designers and artists to see things that have never been seen before. Computers produce new information so quickly and accurately that they are changing people's views of the world. For these and other reasons, the computer is one of the most interesting and important machines ever invented.

The most common type of computer, by far, is the *digital computer. Digital* means *having to do with numbers.* Digital computers perform tasks by changing one set of numbers into another set. All data—numerals, pictures, sounds, symbols, and words—are translated into numbers inside the computer. Everything a digital com-

puter can do is based on its ability to perform simple procedures on numbers—such as adding, subtracting, or comparing two numbers to see which is larger. Digital computers are so widespread that the word *computer* alone almost always refers to a digital computer. The largest digital computers are parts of computer systems that fill a large room. The smallest digital computers—some so tiny they can pass through the eye of a needle—are found inside wrist watches, pocket calculators, and other devices.

All digital computers have two basic parts—a *memory* and a *processor.* The memory receives data and holds them until needed. The memory is made up of a huge collection of switches. The processor changes data into useful information by converting numbers into other numbers. It reads numbers from the memory, performs basic arithmetic calculations such as addition or subtraction, and puts the answer back into the memory. The processor performs this activity over and over until the desired result is achieved. Both the memory and the processor are *electronic*—that is, they work by sending electrical signals through wires.

The smallest digital computers consist only of the memory and the processor. But larger digital computers are part of systems that also contain *input equipment* and *output equipment.* The operator uses an input device, such as a keyboard, to enter instructions and data into the computer. After processing is complete, an output device translates the processed data into a form

The contributors of this article are David Gelernter, Associate Professor of Computer Science at Yale University; and Keith Ferrell, Features Editor for COMPUTE! *Publications.*

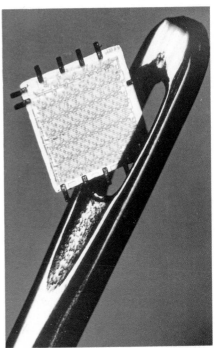

understandable to the user—words or pictures, for example. Typical output devices include printers and visual displays that resemble television screens.

People can think about problems and figure out how to solve them. But computers cannot think. A person must tell the computer in very simple terms exactly what to do with the data it receives. A list of instructions for a computer to follow is called a *program.*

People have used calculating devices since ancient times. The first electronic digital computer, built in 1946, filled a huge room. Since then, rapid improvements in computer technology have led to the development of smaller, more powerful, and less expensive computers.

In addition to digital computers, there are two other general types of computers: *analog computers* and *hybrid computers.* Analog computers work directly with a physical quantity, such as weight or speed, rather than with digits that represent the quantity. Such computers solve problems by measuring a quantity, such as temperature, in terms of another quantity, such as the length of a thin line of liquid in a thermometer. *Hybrid computers* combine the features of analog and digital computers. They have many of the same kinds of parts as an analog computer. But like digital computers, they process data by manipulating numbers. This article focuses on digital computers. For information on analog computers, see **Analog computer.**

The importance of the computer

Computers are tremendously important in a variety of ways. For example, they simplify many difficult or time-consuming tasks to an extraordinary degree. They provide businesses, governments, individuals, and institutions with an efficient way to manage large amounts of information. Computers also help people to understand

things better by allowing them to make models and test theories.

The value of computers lies in their ability to perform certain basic tasks extremely quickly and accurately. These tasks include (1) solving numerical problems, (2) storing and retrieving information, and (3) creating and displaying documents and pictures.

Solving numerical problems. One of the most important and most difficult jobs performed by computers is the solution of complicated problems involving numbers. Computers can solve such problems amazingly quickly. In many cases, the solutions show how certain things work, behave, or happen.

In engineering and the sciences, the knowledge of how something works is often expressed in the form of an *equation.* An equation is a two-part mathematical sentence in which the parts are equal to each other. Engineers and scientists use equations or groups of equations to show how various things relate to one another. They use the solutions to these equations to predict what will happen if certain elements of a situation or an experiment are changed. Engineers and scientists rely on computers to solve the complicated sets of equations that they use to make predictions.

For example, with the help of a computer, an engineer can predict how well an airplane will fly. A large, complex set of equations expresses the relationships between the various parts of an airplane and what happens when the airplane flies. The engineer enters the numbers for the size and weight of a certain airplane's parts. The computer then solves the equations for this particular airplane. Based on the solutions, the engineer can predict how well the plane will fly. The engineer then might decide to change the size or weight of one of the airplane's parts to change the way it flies. Thus,

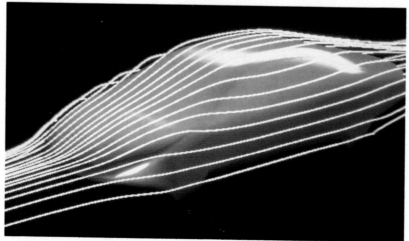

Computers enable engineers to predict how a machine will work. The photo at the left shows a computer image of a car being tested for wind resistance.

© Hank Morgan, Photo Researchers

the computer helps the engineer *simulate* (imitate) various conditions.

Computers help people develop and test scientific *theories*. A theory is a proposed explanation for how or why something happens. Theories, like known relationships, are often expressed as equations. Some equations are so complicated or time-consuming to solve that it would be impossible to develop the theory without the help of computers. Computers are particularly useful in developing and evaluating theories about things that are difficult to observe and measure.

For example, an astronomer can use the problem-solving ability of computers to develop theories about how galaxies are formed. First, the astronomer proposes a set of equations about a group of stars. A computer performs the calculations needed to solve the equations. The astronomer can then use the solutions to predict the shape of the galaxy that the stars should form if the theory is correct. To test the theory, the astronomer can observe a real galaxy to see if it has the predicted shape. If the galaxy's shape agrees with the theory, the astronomer becomes more convinced that the theory is correct. If the galaxy's shape does not agree with the theory, the theory is wrong. The equations must be changed, and new calculations must be performed.

In economics and finance, computers solve equations to make predictions about money. Many of the equations that economists and business people use to make long-range predictions are extremely complicated.

But some of the most widely used of all computer programs rely on fairly simple equations. Such programs help people and businesses figure out their taxes, create budgets, and calculate the value of their investments.

Storing and retrieving information. People use computers to store unbelievably large quantities of information. Information stored in a computer is sometimes called a *database*. Databases can be enormous—for example, a nation's entire census might be contained in a single database. A computer can search a huge database quickly to find a specific piece of information. In addition, the information can be changed easily and quickly—often in less than a second.

The efficiency with which computers store and retrieve information makes them valuable in a wide range of professions. For example, scientists use computers to store and quickly find results of experiments. Libraries use computer catalogs to hold information about their collections. Hospitals use computers to maintain records about their patients. Governments store election returns and census information on computers.

All kinds of businesses rely on computers to store large quantities of information about their employees, customers, and products. Computers also allow markets for stocks, bonds, currency, and other investments to keep track of current prices around the world. Banks maintain many kinds of records on computers, such as account balances and credit card information. Anyone who uses an *automatic teller machine* (ATM) is using a

John O. Hallquist © Discover Publications

A computer simulation can accurately represent an operation, situation, or system. The first three photos above show computer-generated images of a bomb's nose cone striking a steel plate. The fourth photo—which shows an actual nose cone after a test—reveals the great accuracy of the computer simulation.

© Ken Sherman, Bruce Coleman Inc.

Banks rely on computers to execute transactions and to keep track of prices in the markets for stocks, bonds, and currency.

computer terminal. When an identification card and number are entered, the ATM can provide account information, dispense cash, and transfer funds between accounts.

Creating and displaying documents and pictures. Computers can store a huge number of words in a way that makes it easy to manipulate them. For this reason, *word processing* is one of the most important and widespread uses of computers. A *word-processing program* allows people to type words into a computer to write articles, books, letters, reports, and other kinds of documents.

Word-processing programs make it easy for people to change text that has been typed into a computer. For example, they can quickly correct typing or spelling errors. Words, sentences, and entire sections of a document can be added, removed, or rearranged. If a computer is connected to a printer, the document may be printed onto paper at any time. Business people, journalists, lawyers, scientists, secretaries, and students are among those who benefit from word-processing programs.

Computers are also important in the publishing industry. For example, most books, magazines, and newspapers are typeset by computers. In addition, a process known as *desktop publishing* enables people to design and produce newsletters and other documents on personal computers. Documents created in this manner look almost as if they have been professionally typeset.

Computer graphics—the use of computers to make pictures—make up one of the most fascinating and fastest-growing areas of computer use. Computers can produce pictures that look almost like photographs. First, the computer solves equations that predict how an object should look. It then uses these predictions to display a picture on a computer terminal screen or to print a picture on paper.

Computer programs that perform *computer-aided design* (CAD) are important in many fields, particularly engineering and architecture. CAD programs create pictures or diagrams of a new object. They then solve equations to predict how the object will work. Engineers and architects use CAD programs to design airplanes, bridges, buildings, cars, electronic machinery, and many other machines and structures.

Computers also can produce pictures by converting information into pictorial form. The pictures can serve a variety of purposes. For example, computers enable business people, economists, and scientists to plot graphs from lists of numbers. In a technique called *computerized tomography,* or the *CT scan,* a computer uses X-ray data to construct an image of a body part on a screen. Doctors use these images to diagnose diseases and disorders (see **Computerized tomography**). Sophisticated radar systems use computers to produce detailed pictures, often for military use.

Computer graphics also are used to create electronic video games. Terminal monitors or TV screens can display game boards and moving pictures. The player may use a keyboard or some other device, such as a *mouse* or a *joystick,* to play computer games.

Other uses. Many complex machines need frequent adjustments to work efficiently. Small computers can be installed inside these machines and programmed to make these adjustments. In modern automobiles, such *embedded* (enclosed) computers control certain aspects of operation, such as the mixture of fuel and air entering the engine. Today's commercial airliners and military planes carry computers that help control the aircraft. Embedded computers also control the movements of industrial robots and guide modern weapons systems,

© Brownie Harris, The Stock Market

© J. Wilson, Woodfin Camp, Inc.

Computer-aided design programs are important in many fields. An engineer, *top,* uses a light pen to modify the design of an airplane. A fashion designer, *above,* can consider her design in various colors and patterns on a computer screen.

such as missiles and field artillery, to their targets.

Computers can help solve many complicated problems that do not involve numerical equations. Doctors, for example, investigate illnesses, decide on diagnoses, and prescribe treatments. They solve such problems by applying their knowledge and experience, not by solving equations. A branch of computer science called *artificial intelligence* uses programs that help solve problems by applying human knowledge and experience. Artificial intelligence systems called *expert systems* enable computers programmed with vast amounts of data to "think" about numerous possibilities—such as diseases that certain symptoms could indicate—and make a decision or diagnosis.

Computers also can be used to communicate information over long distances. They can send information to each other over telephone lines. As a result, computers keep banks, newspapers, and other institutions supplied with up-to-the-minute information. A *computer network* consists of many computers in separate rooms, buildings, cities, or countries, all connected together. Computer networks allow people to communicate by using *electronic mail*—a document typed into one computer and "delivered" to another. Such documents generally travel in only a few minutes, even if they are being sent over a long distance.

Computers also are used in teaching. Programs that perform *computer-aided instruction* (CAI) are designed to help students at all levels, from elementary school through the university level. The student sits at a computer terminal. The terminal's screen displays a question for the student to answer. If the answer is wrong or incomplete, the computer may ask the student to try again. It then may supply the correct answer and an explanation. CAI also is used in some adult education programs and as part of the employee-training programs of some corporations.

Basic principles of computers

A computer receives individual pieces of data, changes the data into more useful information, and then tells the operator what the information is. For example, a person who wants to find the sum of four numbers enters them into the computer. In only a fraction of a second, signals that represent these numbers are changed

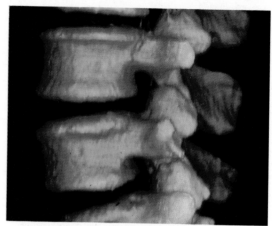

© CNRI/SPL from Photo Researchers

Computers use X-ray data to generate three-dimensional images of body parts such as the human spine, *above.* The images help doctors identify disorders without performing surgery.

into signals that represent the sum. The computer then displays the sum for the user.

How a computer operates. People use input devices to enter data into computers. One of the most common input devices is the *computer terminal,* which looks like a typewriter keyboard combined with a television screen. Data that are typed on the keyboard appear on the screen. At the same time, the data go to the memory. The memory also stores a program—the step-by-step series of instructions for the computer to follow. The processor manipulates the data according to the program.

The processed information is sent to an output device, which presents it to the computer user. In many cases, the computer terminal that served as the input device also acts as the output device, and its screen displays the results. Printers are another important kind of output device. *File storage devices* are used to save information and programs for future use.

All data handled by computers, including words, enter the processor in the form of digits. Computers commonly use the digits of the *binary numeration system* (see **Numeration systems** [The binary system]). Un-

© Brownie Harris, The Stock Market

Computers help meteorologists forecast the weather by solving equations that describe the behavior of the atmosphere.

© James Wilson, Woodfin Camp, Inc.

Computer games entertain children and adults. Many games display detailed moving pictures on monitors or TV screens.

Schools use computers as a teaching aid. An elementary-school teacher and his students work at a computer, *above*.

© Lawrence Migdale, Photo Researchers

like the familiar decimal system, which uses 10 digits, the binary system uses only two digits: 0 and 1. These digits are called *bits*. Different combinations of bits represent letters, symbols, and decimal numerals. Each such combination of bits is called a *byte*. For example, according to one standard code, the binary representation for the letter A is 100 0001, while the binary representation for the letter Z is 101 1010. Each symbol and decimal numeral also is represented by a specific combination of 0's and 1's.

Each of a computer's thousands of tiny electronic circuits operates much like an ordinary light switch. When a circuit is off, it corresponds to the binary digit 0. When a circuit is on, it corresponds to the digit 1. Binary digits, like decimal numbers, can be added, subtracted, multiplied, and divided. Thus, a computer can perform all the basic arithmetic operations.

Computer hardware and software. The physical equipment that makes up a computer system is called *hardware*. Hardware includes input and output devices, file storage devices, the memory, and the processor. The input and output devices and the file storage devices also are known as *peripheral equipment*.

Computer *software* consists of the programs that a computer uses to perform a task. People can either create or purchase software. Computers have vast and varied capabilities because of the many different kinds of available software.

Kinds of computers

Computers vary widely in size, speed, and ability. The size of a computer partly determines the kinds and number of jobs it can do. But even a small computer can perform complicated tasks. For example, a modern desktop computer has more computing power than the huge, room-filling computers of the early 1960's.

The *microprocessor*—an electronic device consisting of thousands of transistors and related circuitry on a sili-con chip—plays an important role in almost all modern computers. A single microprocessor has the computing power of a larger computer but generally costs far less. The small size and relatively low cost of microprocessors have made them valuable as components in computer systems.

Digital computers may be grouped into three categories: (1) embedded computers, (2) personal computers and workstations, and (3) mainframes. The borders between these categories change constantly as smaller, more powerful computers are developed.

Embedded computers control the operation of various types of machinery. Virtually all embedded computers are microprocessors. Such machines as automobiles, digital wrist watches, telephones, and videotape recorders contain embedded computers.

Personal computers and workstations are computers used by one person at a time. Such a computer usually fits on a desk top, and some personal computers can be held on the lap or in the hands. People commonly use personal computers for such activities as word processing, storing and updating information, performing simple calculations, and playing computer games. These computers also are valuable to business people, who use them to manage information about their inventories, customers, and employees.

Personal computers contain one or more microprocessors. By modern standards of computer speed and

Computer terms

Binary code is used by computers to represent information. It consists of the 0's and 1's of the binary numeration system.
Bit, an abbreviation of the term *binary digit,* may be either the digit 0 or 1.
Byte is a group of bits that act as a single unit of information, such as a letter or numeral.
Database is an organized collection of information stored on a magnetic disk or other direct-access storage device.
File storage device is any device used to save information until it is needed again.
Hardware refers to the physical parts of a computer system.
Input is any information that a user enters into a computer.
Mainframe is a large, powerful computer that many people can use at once. It can store large amounts of information.
Memory is the part of a computer that stores information.
Microprocessor is a miniature electronic device consisting of thousands of transistors and related circuitry on a silicon chip. The device is often called a "computer on a chip" because it can hold the processor and some memory.
Modem is a device that allows computer users to communicate with one another over telephone lines.
Network is a system consisting of two or more computers connected by high-speed communication lines.
Operating system is a type of software that controls the operation of a computer system.
Output is any result provided by a computer.
Peripheral equipment consists of input devices, output devices, and file storage devices.
Personal computer is a desktop or handheld computer designed for general-purpose use.
Program is a set of instructions to be carried out by a computer, written in a computer language.
Simulation is the representation or imitation of a situation or system on a computer, usually with a mathematical model. The purpose is to predict and analyze what is likely to occur under various conditions.
Software refers to the programs used by a computer to perform desired tasks.

capacity, personal computers execute programs slowly and have limited memory and file storage capacity.

Workstations are more powerful than personal computers, and better suited to solving difficult engineering, graphics, or scientific problems. Workstations are generally connected to form computer networks. These networks allow operators to exchange information very rapidly. They also enable printers and file storage devices to be shared by many workstations. One important type of computer network, the *local area network* (LAN), connects workstations located within the same building or in neighboring buildings. A *wide area network* (WAN) links workstations over large areas.

Mainframes are fast computers with large memories and file storage systems. These powerful computers solve very complicated problems and manage huge quantities of information. Most mainframes are housed in several large cabinets. Some mainframes do a single job, such as copying and storing the information generated by a laboratory experiment. Others perform many different tasks. *Minicomputers* and *superminis* have many of the capabilities of mainframes, but they are smaller and less expensive.

On a large mainframe, hundreds of people may be *logged on* (running programs) at one time. The use of a single powerful computer by many users at once is called *time-sharing*. The mainframe appears to run many programs at the same time. However, the computer actually switches rapidly from program to program, doing a bit of work on one and then hurrying on to work on another.

The fastest mainframes are called *supercomputers*. Supercomputers solve numerical problems as quickly as possible based on existing technology. They are used to model weather systems, to design cars and aircraft, and in many other ways. But supercomputers are rare, because they are extremely expensive. Individual supercomputer users—mostly scientists and engineers at large scientific installations—sometimes run programs by means of long-distance computer networks.

In recent years, mainframes known as *parallel computers* have provided great increases in speed over other computers. Most computers have a single processor. But a parallel computer has many processors that all operate at once. Each processor can work on a separate piece of a program. As a result, the program can be run much more quickly than on a computer with only one processor. The fastest supercomputers in the world are parallel computers. But parallel computers may even serve as especially fast workstations.

How a computer works

Computers can perform many different activities because they can store huge lists of numbers and do arithmetic very rapidly. All computers work essentially the same way. A computer *encodes* (translates) numbers, words, pictures, sounds, and other forms of data into the 0's and 1's of the binary numeration system. The computer's processor manipulates the binary numbers according to specified instructions. All changes of the data are accomplished by performing arithmetical calculations on these binary numbers. Thus, the binary numbers that represent the data are changed into binary numbers that represent the desired information. The re-

sults are *decoded* (translated back) from binary numbers into decimal numbers, words, pictures, or some other form.

The operation of a computer can be broken down into three steps. They are (1) entering and encoding data and instructions, (2) processing data, and (3) decoding the results and producing output. The storing of information occurs during all three steps of the computing process.

Entering and encoding data and instructions is performed using input equipment. This section explains how the computer encodes data entered through a terminal. It also describes a number of other input devices.

Terminals enable computer users to type *characters* (letters and numerals) directly into the computer. A terminal includes a keyboard unit and a *monitor*. The monitor usually consists of a *cathode-ray tube* (CRT). A CRT is a vacuum tube with a screen like that of a television (see **Vacuum tube**). The CRT display makes it possible for the user to check the data being entered into the computer and to make corrections if necessary.

As each character is typed, the circuitry inside the terminal puts the character's binary code into a temporary storage location called a *buffer*. As soon as a code appears in the buffer, the processor executes an instruction that moves it from the buffer to the computer's memory. The monitor also has a buffer. Whenever the processor sends a code into this buffer, the corresponding character appears on the screen.

Other input devices are also used with monitors. For example, some terminals enable users to communicate with the computer by drawing pictures or diagrams directly on the screen with a light pen. Such units encode drawings directly from the monitor. A device called a *mouse* can be used to give commands to a computer. When this handheld box is moved on a flat surface, it causes a pointer to point at a specific instruction or piece of data displayed on a monitor. Clicking a button on the mouse causes the instruction to be carried out or the data to be moved or changed.

Modems are devices that allow computers to communicate with other computers by using telephone lines. A modem translates sounds into tones that represent binary numbers. It can send the tones over the phone lines to other modems.

Disk drives and tape drives perform many functions in the operation of the computer. One of these functions is providing input in binary form. A disk drive is a machine that, among other things, reads 0's and 1's that are magnetically encoded onto disks. This information then goes to the buffer and the memory. A disk system provides quick and direct access to specific information located anywhere on a disk. Flexible magnetic disks called *floppy disks* or *diskettes* are widely used to provide input to personal computers. *Hard disks* are used with larger computer systems, as well as with some personal computers.

Tape drives and magnetic tapes work in much the same way. However, a tape must be unwound or rewound to the location that contains the desired information. As a result, it takes longer to read information from a tape than from a disk.

Optical scanners also read data and instructions. Some scanners optically sense bar codes and other

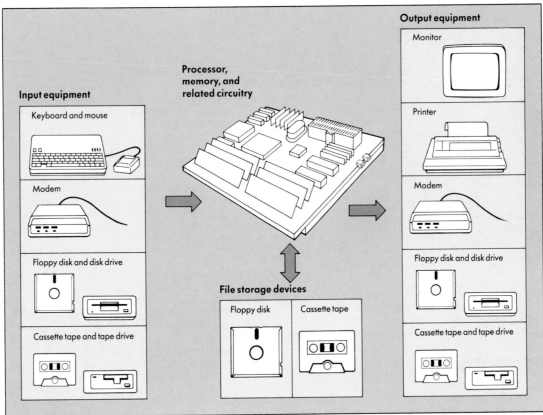

Input equipment

Keyboard and mouse

Modem

Floppy disk and disk drive

Cassette tape and tape drive

Processor, memory, and related circuitry

File storage devices

Floppy disk

Cassette tape

Output equipment

Monitor

Printer

Modem

Floppy disk and disk drive

Cassette tape and tape drive

WORLD BOOK illustration by William Graham

How a computer works

Computer systems come in a wide range of sizes and contain varying types of equipment. Nevertheless, all digital computers work essentially the same way. The diagram above illustrates the flow of information through a personal computer system. A human operator uses *input equipment* to provide data and instructions to the computer. The *processor* then performs calculations on the data, while the *memory* stores information during processing. The results then are sent to the *output equipment,* which presents them to the user. *File storage devices* enable information to be saved for future use.

marks printed on identification and credit cards, grocery items, or documents. They then change these codes into electrical signals. Other scanners read information from *compact discs* or *optical disks.* Such disks contain digitally encoded information that can be read by a laser beam.

Other input devices include a *joystick* for moving figures about on a screen and a *graphic tablet* consisting of a pad and a special pen for producing illustrations. Such devices are used with some personal computers. *Voice activators* enable computers to understand spoken words. Some mainframes obtain input by means of *card readers,* which take information from punched cards. The pattern of punches represents letters, numbers, and other symbols. Card readers once were popular, but today they are used less frequently.

Processing data. The processor, also called the *central processing unit* or *CPU,* is the heart of the computer. It manipulates the binary numbers that represent input according to a program, and converts them into binary numbers that represent the desired result.

Since the development of the *integrated circuit* in the 1960's, the processor in many computers is contained on a single microprocessor—a silicon chip no larger

than a fingernail (see **Integrated circuit**). All of the devices and wires that make up the processor are packed onto the surface of the chip. Silicon is one of a group of materials called *semiconductors* (see **Semiconductor**). The circuitry on the chip contains many tiny devices called *transistors.* A transistor can either stop electric current or allow it to flow (see **Transistor**). The processor of a computer consists of two parts: (1) the *control unit* and (2) the *digital logic unit.*

The control unit directs and coordinates the operations of the entire computer according to instructions stored in the memory. The control unit must select the instructions in proper order because their sequence determines each step in the operations. Each set of instructions is expressed through a binary *operation code* that specifies exactly what must be done to complete a job. The operation code also provides information that tells where data for the processing operation are stored in the memory. The control unit interprets the instructions and relays commands to the logic unit. It also regulates the flow of data between the memory and the logic unit and routes processed information to output or file storage devices.

The digital logic unit, sometimes known as the

Astrid & Hans Frieder Michler/SPL from Photo Researchers

An integrated circuit contains all of the tiny devices that make up the processor on a single, tiny chip. This photo, taken through a microscope, shows a portion of such a chip.

arithmetic/logic unit or *ALU,* manipulates data received from the memory. It carries out all the functions and logic processes required to solve a problem. Computers use logic to perform arithmetical calculations—addition, subtraction, multiplication, and division.

In the digital logic unit, electronic circuits called *registers* temporarily store data from the memory. The data consist of electrical signals that represent binary digits. An electrical signal that has a low voltage level represents 0, and a signal that has a high voltage level represents 1.

To carry out an arithmetical calculation, the electrical signal for each input travels on a wire to another circuit. The answer comes out on a wire from the other end of the circuit. There are a number of basic circuits. Three such circuits are the *AND-gate,* the *OR-gate,* and the *NOT-gate* or *inverter.* The basic circuits are combined in different ways to perform arithmetic and logic operations with electrical signals that represent binary digits. For example, one combination of logic circuits performs addition. Another combination compares two numbers and then acts on the result of the comparison.

After an operation has been completed, the result may be sent to the memory for storage until it is needed for another operation. In many cases, the result is sent to an output device or a file storage device.

Decoding the results and producing output. People use *output equipment* to get information from computers. Output equipment translates the electrical signals that represent binary numbers into a form that the user can understand. Often, it also serves as input equipment. There are many types of output devices, such as terminals, printers, modems, and disk and tape drives.

Terminals, in addition to serving as input equipment, display output on the monitor. As information travels from the processor to the terminal, it moves through the buffer that was used in the input function. On a terminal,

a user can receive data in the form of words, numbers, graphs, or pictures.

Printers produce output on paper. Like terminals, printers have buffers. To print a character, the processor puts the binary code for that character into the printer's buffer. The printer prints the character that corresponds to the code. Some printers operate much like typewriters. Others use heat, special chemicals, lasers, or combinations of these methods to place characters on paper.

Modems, which translate sounds into binary numbers during the input function, can also provide output by translating binary numbers into sounds. As a result, they enable users to receive information from distant computers.

Disk drives and tape drives also serve as both input and output equipment. Magnetic disks and tapes receive output in binary form. The drives interpret binary information from disks and tapes and present it to the user, often on a monitor. Output data presented on disks and tapes can easily be put back in the computer when needed.

Other output devices include *plotters, key punch machines,* and *audio devices.* Plotters use pens to create drawings, diagrams, and graphs on paper or clear plastic. Key punch machines record data by punching holes in cards or paper tape. Audio devices produce spoken words through a type of telephone or loudspeaker. Such devices are becoming increasingly important.

Storing information. Computers can store information in two types of locations during the computing process—the memory and file storage devices. Memory, which is built into the computer, holds instructions and data during processing. File storage devices provide long-term storage of large amounts of information.

Memory, also called the *internal memory* or *main memory,* stores information and programs inside the computer. The memory receives data and instructions from an input device or a file storage device. It also receives information from the processor. The memory stores only the information that is currently needed by the processor. After the processor has finished with it, the information is transferred to file storage devices for permanent storage or sent directly to an output device for immediate use.

The devices and wires that make up the memory can be built from integrated circuits that fit onto one or more chips. The circuits, wires, and transistors form many *memory cells* capable of storing binary digits. These cells are arranged into groups. Each group is assigned an *address*—a number that makes it possible to locate specific pieces of information quickly.

File storage devices, also called *auxiliary storage units,* can store huge amounts of information for long periods of time. Such units are slower than the memory that is built into the computer. But they can hold much more information, and they are less expensive. For this reason, file storage devices are commonly used to store large quantities of data, programs, and processed information.

The most important file storage devices are magnetic disks and magnetic tapes. Disks and tapes are operated by disk drives and tape drives, which also serve as input and output equipment. These units encode data onto the surfaces of disks and tapes by turning the electrical

BASIC language

```
10   SUM = 0
20   READ LENGTH
30   COUNTER = LENGTH
40   READ NEXT
50   SUM = SUM + NEXT
60   IF COUNTER = 1 GOTO 90
70   COUNTER = COUNTER − 1
80   GOTO 40
90   AVG = SUM/LENGTH
100  PRINT AVG
110  DATA 7, 35, 9000, 876, 29, 87, 90, 153
120  END
```

APL language

```
NUMBERS ← (35, 9000, 876, 29, 87, 90, 153)
LENGTH ← 7
SUM ← +/NUMBERS
ANSWER ← SUM ÷ LENGTH
```

Machine language

1. Load the first number on the list into a box called R1.
2. Load the length of the list into a box called R2.
3. If the number in R2 is 1, go to step 7.
4. Add the next number on the list to the number in box R1.
5. Subtract 1 from the number in box R2.
6. Go back to step 3.
7. Divide the number in box R1 by the length of the list.
8. The answer is now in box R1.

Programming languages enable people to write instructions that a computer can translate and execute. The languages allow the programmer to concentrate on the basic ideas of an operation, instead of on the details of what the machine must do. The BASIC and APL programs shown above both contain instructions for finding the average of a list of numbers. The steps in machine language show how a computer interprets and executes this type of program in any language.

signals that represent the 0's and 1's of binary code into magnetism. Every 0 is represented on the disk or tape by a little magnet pointing in a certain direction, and every 1 by a magnet pointing in the opposite direction. To read information from a disk or tape, the drive unit translates the magnetic signals into electrical signals and sends them to the memory. Magnetic disks and tapes are said to contain *random-access memory* (RAM) because the information on them can be searched or replaced with ease.

Some other types of file storage devices contain *read-only memory* (ROM)—information that the computer cannot change. ROM units may consist of a compact disc, a cartridge, or a silicon chip. They are used to store large databases and programs for computer games.

Programming a computer

Programming involves the preparation and writing of detailed instructions for a computer. These instructions tell the computer exactly what data to use and what sequence of operations to perform with the data. Without programs, a computer could not solve problems or deliver any other desired result.

Some people prepare their own computer programs. But in many cases, computer scientists and other computer specialists called *programmers* write instructions for computers. They use *programming languages* that consist of letters, words, and symbols, as well as rules for combining those elements.

A computer cannot work directly with a program written in a programming language. The instructions must be translated into a *machine language* composed of binary digits. These digits represent operation codes, memory addresses, and various symbols, such as plus

and minus signs. Machine language is also known as *low-level language.*

Special programs called *compilers* and *assemblers* translate programming languages into machine language. Another special type of program called an *operating system* contains instructions for the operation of a computer. It controls the input and output devices, and it reads and responds to user commands. It also places programs and data into the memory and makes sure that the processor executes the right programs. Thus, the operating system combines the many separate parts of a computer into a single useful system.

Compilers, assemblers, and operating systems may be viewed as "smart programs" because they enable a computer to understand complicated instructions. The user communicates with the smart program, and the smart program communicates with the computer. A computer combined with a smart program acts like a different, smarter computer. This combination is called a *virtual machine.*

Preparing a program begins with a complete description of the job that the computer is to perform. This job description is obtained from the person for whom the program is being prepared, such as a business manager or an engineer. It explains what input data are needed, what computing must be done, and what the output should be. Computer programmers use the description to prepare diagrams and other pictorial aids that represent the steps needed to complete the task. The programmers may produce a diagram called a *systems flow chart* that shows how all the major parts of the job fit together systematically.

After a computer program is written, it is tested on the computer for mistakes. Computer experts refer to mistakes in programs as "bugs" and the testing of programs as "debugging."

A program generally is entered into a computer in what is known as an *interactive environment*. In such an environment, the programmer enters part of the program on a computer terminal. The computer's operating system responds immediately, telling the programmer how the computer will interpret each instruction. The programmer then can analyze each response. Programs that result from this interaction between the programmer and the computer generally are stored on some type of file storage device until needed.

Using programming languages. Computers appear to work directly with programming languages. But the smart program, not the computer, actually understands these languages. The smart program translates a program into machine language. It then enters the translated version into the computer's memory. The processor reads and executes each translated instruction.

There are many different *high-level* programming languages. Some of them closely resemble the language of mathematics. Others enable programmers to use symbols and various everyday expressions, such as "READ," "PRINT," and "STOP." All high-level languages are designed to let the programmer concentrate on the basic ideas of a task rather than on the details.

The language that a programmer uses depends largely on the job to be done. If a task involves processing business data, the programmer would most likely use COBOL (*CO*mmon *B*usiness *O*riented *L*anguage). However, programming a computer to solve complicated scientific problems might require the use of a mathematically oriented language, such as FORTRAN (*FO*rmula *TRAN*slation).

Some high-level languages can be used for business, technical, or scientific programming. Such languages include APL (*A P*rogramming *L*anguage); C; and LISP (*LIS*t *P*rocessor).

Another commonly used programming language is BASIC (*B*eginner's *A*ll-purpose *S*ymbolic *I*nstruction *C*ode). BASIC is well suited for writing relatively simple programs for personal computers. Many elementary schools and high schools that offer a course in programming teach BASIC because it is easy to learn and to use. Pascal, named for the French mathematician and scientist Blaise Pascal, also is taught in many schools.

Some computer programs may be written in an *assembly language*. This kind of language is harder to use than a high-level language. The programmer must state each instruction very precisely, with much more detail than is needed when using a high-level language.

The computer industry

The manufacture, development, sales, and servicing of computer hardware and software make up one of the largest and most important industries in the world. Governments, institutions, and virtually all industries rely upon computers. By the year 2000, the computer industry is expected to be the second largest industry in the world in terms of annual revenue. Only agriculture will be larger.

The first commercial digital computers were manufactured in the 1950's. Throughout the 1950's, as the importance of computers increased, people's acceptance of them increased as well. More than 10,000 computers were in operation by 1961. Ten years later, the number of computers exceeded 100,000. By 1990, there were about 100 million data-processing computers—that is, computers that require input and output equipment—in operation worldwide.

The United States has the largest computer industry in the world, employing more than 1 million people. It also has more computers than any other country—more than 50 million, or about half the world's computers. Japan ranks second with more than 9 million computers, about 11 per cent of the world total. European countries account for nearly 25 per cent of all computers. The Union of Soviet Socialist Republics (U.S.S.R.) has less

Computer firms manufacture hardware, software, and supplies. In this photo, quality control workers check computers on an assembly line.

than 1 per cent of the world's computers, but is working to develop a computer industry.

The economic growth of the computer industry has matched the increase in the number of computers. The United States produced about $1 billion worth of computers in 1958. Ten years later, the figure had reached $4.8 billion. By 1978, United States manufacturers produced more than $16.6 billion worth of computer equipment each year.

In the late 1970's, the computer industry's rate of growth increased dramatically. Advances in both computer technology and manufacturing technology enabled the United States to sell computers worth more than $30 billion in 1981. By 1990, the U.S. computer industry's annual revenues had topped $100 billion, and they continued to grow.

Manufacturing. From a few dozen companies in the early 1960's, the computer industry has grown to more than 10,000 firms around the world. These companies manufacture computers and such peripheral equipment as modems and printers. They also develop and publish software and provide various computer supplies, such as magnetic disks.

Some companies produce entire computer systems, ranging from personal computers to supercomputers. Many companies manufacture computer components, including processors. Some companies produce input and output equipment, such as terminals and printers. Other important products of the computer industry include equipment that increases a computer's abilities to provide visual and audio output, and the network boards and cables used to create computer networks.

The largest computer manufacturer in the United States—and the world—is International Business Machines Corporation (IBM). By the late 1980's, IBM's annual sales had topped $50 billion. Digital Equipment Corporation (DEC) ranks second in the United States, with more than $9 billion in sales in 1988. Unisys is the third largest U.S. manufacturer, with more than $7 billion in annual sales in the late 1980's. Other leading U.S. computer companies include Apple, Compaq, Cray, Tandy, and Zenith.

The largest computer manufacturer outside the United States is Japan's Fujitsu, followed closely by NEC Corporation, also of Japan. Each company had sales of more than $9 billion in 1988. The leading computer companies in Europe include Groupe Bull of France, Italy's Olivetti, and Siemens AG of West Germany.

Research and development. The constant increase in computer power is a major reason for the computer industry's success. Such increases result from computer science research and development, which take place at businesses and universities throughout the world.

One area of great interest to computer researchers and manufacturers is memory speed and capacity. As software becomes more complex, it requires more computer memory in order to operate properly. At the same time, sophisticated software can manipulate increasingly large amounts of data, which occupy more space in the computer's memory.

The storage of information files is another important area of study. Researchers work to develop increasingly compact ways to store data, such as on magnetic disks, compact discs, or other devices.

Artificial intelligence is an exciting area of software research. Experts in this field design computer systems to perform tasks that appear to require intelligence, such as reasoning and learning. In this manner, artificial intelligence experts hope to increase the ability of computers to respond to problems in a "human" manner. See **Artificial intelligence.**

Sales. Computers are sold in a variety of ways. Large manufacturers of computers have teams of sales professionals. These teams call on corporations and institutions, analyze their needs, and provide the appropriate combination of hardware and software. Another method of computer sales is the *value-added reseller* (VAR). A VAR purchases computer systems and components from a variety of sources. It then sells the finished products to computer users.

Retail outlets play an increasingly important role in the sale of personal computers. Chains of computer stores sell many personal computers. Some general merchandise stores also sell computers.

Service and repair. Because people depend on their computers, it is important to have the machines serviced periodically and repaired promptly when necessary. Many computer manufacturers offer service contracts that provide for regular maintenance and prompt repairs. When a large computer system breaks down, service technicians must visit the computer itself. Some large businesses and institutions have their own computer maintenance staffs.

Many retail outlets that sell personal computers also offer repair service to their customers. These retailers allow their customers to bring computers back to the shop for servicing or repairs.

Careers. There are many career opportunities in the computer industry. Computer engineers are probably the most technically specialized computer experts. Hardware engineers design the circuits that are engraved on chips, and they develop and design the wiring that lets information flow smoothly through the computer. Engi-

© Mark Sherman, Bruce Coleman Inc.

A repair specialist services a personal computer, *above.* Many computer makers and dealers provide repair services.

Computer programmers write instructions for computers to follow. This programmer is entering a program into a computer.

neers also design the technical aspects of memory, file storage, and peripheral equipment.

Computer programmers write the instructions that make computers operate properly. Systems analysts determine the most efficient use of computers for a particular situation. They study entire computer systems—hardware and software—and the purpose a computer is intended to serve.

Software publishers make up another career area. People in this field issue programs, write and edit instruction manuals, and provide technical services for customers.

Many career opportunities in computers exist outside the computer industry itself. For example, data processors enter information into computers. Workers in many industries oversee the computers that control machines.

Some of the industry's most successful individuals are self-taught. But most computer careers call for a college degree. College courses that help prepare students for careers in computers include programming, electrical engineering, systems analysis, and data processing.

The development of the computer

The ideas and inventions of many engineers, mathematicians, and scientists led to the development of the computer. The ancient abacus served as the earliest sort of calculating device. But its use was limited by the need to move each counter individually (see **Abacus**).

Early calculating devices. The first true calculating machines were developed in the 1600's. In 1642, the French mathematician, scientist, and philosopher Blaise

Pascal invented the first automatic calculator. The device performed addition and subtraction by means of a set of wheels linked to each other by gears. The first wheel represented the numbers 1 to 10, the second wheel represented 10's, the third stood for 100's, and so on. When the first wheel was turned 10 notches, a gear moved the second wheel forward a single notch. The other wheels became engaged in a similar manner.

In the early 1670's, the German mathematician Gottfried Wilhelm von Leibniz extended the usefulness of Pascal's calculator. Leibniz's improvements included gear and wheel arrangements that made multiplication and division possible.

Leibniz also sought a counting system that would be easier for a machine to handle than the decimal system. He developed the binary system of mathematics in the late 1600's. Binary mathematics uses only the 0 and the 1, arranging them to represent all numbers.

An important contribution to the development of binary mathematics was made in the mid-1800's by George Boole, an English logician and mathematician. Boole used the binary system to invent a new type of mathematics. *Boolean algebra* and *Boolean logic* perform complex mathematical and logical operations on the symbols 0 and 1. Thus, a mechanical representation of binary mathematics would require the representation of only those two digits. This advance had a major effect on the development of computer logic and computer languages.

Early punched-card computing devices. A French textile weaver named Joseph Marie Jacquard made the next great contribution to the development of the computer. In the weaving process, needles directed thread to produce patterns. In 1801, Jacquard invented the *Jacquard loom,* which used punched cards to automate this process for the first time. The cards had patterns of holes punched in them, and were placed between the rising needles and the thread. The presence or absence of a hole could be compared to the two digits of the binary system. Where there were holes, the needles rose and met the thread. Where there were no holes, the needles were blocked. By changing cards and alternating the patterns of punched holes, it became possible to mechanically create complex woven patterns.

The punched cards of the Jacquard loom inspired the English mathematician Charles Babbage. During the 1830's, Babbage developed the idea of a mechanical computer that he called an *analytical engine.* He worked on the machine for almost 40 years. When performing complex computations or a series of calculations, the analytical engine would store completed sets of punched cards for use in later operations. Babbage's analytical engine contained all of the basic elements of an automatic computer—storage, working memory, a system for moving between the two, and an input device. But the technology of Babbage's time was not advanced enough to provide the precision parts he needed to construct the machine, and he lacked funding for the project. Babbage, like others of his time, also lacked an understanding of the nature and use of electricity.

The first successful computer. In 1888, American inventor and businessman Herman Hollerith devised a punched card system, including the punching equipment, for tabulating the results of the United States cen-

The first analog computer. Vannevar Bush, an American electrical engineer, worked to develop a computer that would help scientists. In 1930, he built a device called a *differential analyzer* to solve differential equations. This machine was the first reliable analog computer. It derived measurements from the movements of its gears and shafts.

The first electronic computers. Some scientists and engineers saw greater computing potential in electronics. The first semielectronic digital computing device was constructed in 1939 by John V. Atanasoff, an American mathematician and physicist. In 1944, Howard Aiken, a Harvard University professor, built another early form of digital computer, which he called the Mark I. The operations of this machine were controlled chiefly by electromechanical *relays* (switching devices).

In 1946, two engineers at the University of Pennsylvania, J. Presper Eckert, Jr., and John William Mauchly, built the first fully electronic digital computer. They called it ENIAC (*E*lectronic *N*umerical *I*ntegrator *A*nd *C*omputer). ENIAC contained about 18,000 vacuum tubes, which replaced the relays that had controlled the operation of Mark I. The machine weighed more than 30 tons (27 metric tons), occupied more than 1,500 square feet (140 square meters) of floor space, and consumed 150 kilowatts of electricity during operation. ENIAC operated about 1,000 times as fast as the Mark I. It could perform about 5,000 additions and 1,000 multiplications per second. ENIAC also could store parts of its programming.

Although ENIAC performed its work rapidly, programming the huge machine took a great deal of time. Eckert and Mauchly next worked on developing a computer that could store even more of its programming. They worked with John von Neumann, a Hungarian-born American mathematician. Von Neumann helped assemble all available knowledge of how the logic of computers should operate. He also helped outline how stored-programming techniques would improve computer performance. In 1951, a computer based on the work of the three men became operational. It was called EDVAC (*E*lectronic *D*iscrete *V*ariable *A*utomatic *C*omputer). EDVAC strongly influenced the design of later computers.

Bureau of the Census

The punched-card tabulating machine invented by Herman Hollerith was the first successful computer. It was used to compute the results of the 1890 United States census, *above*.

sus (see **Census**). Hollerith's machines used electrically charged nails that, when passed through a hole punched in a card, created a circuit. The circuits registered on another part of the machine, where they were read and recorded. Hollerith's machines tabulated the results of the 1890 census, making it the fastest and most economical census to date. In a single day, 56 of these machines could tabulate census information about more than 6 million people.

Hollerith's tabulator enjoyed widespread success. Governments, institutions, and industries found uses for the machine. In 1896, Hollerith founded the Tabulating Machine Company. He continued to improve his machines during the following years. In 1911, he sold his share of the company. Its name was changed to the Computing-Tabulating-Recording Company (C-T-R). In 1924, the name was changed to International Business Machines Corporation (IBM).

UPI/Bettmann Newsphotos

ENIAC, completed in 1946, was the first fully electronic digital computer. The enormous machine was invented by J. Presper Eckert, Jr., *front left,* and John W. Mauchly, *center.*

Also in 1951, Eckert and Mauchly invented a more advanced computer called UNIVAC I (*UNIVersal Automatic Computer*). Within a few years, UNIVAC I became the first commercially available computer. Unlike earlier computers, UNIVAC I handled both numbers and alphabetical characters equally well. It also was the first computer system in which the operations of the input and output equipment were separated from those of the computing unit. UNIVAC I used vacuum tubes to perform arithmetic and memory-switching functions.

The first UNIVAC I was installed at the U.S. Bureau of the Census in June 1951. The following year, another UNIVAC I was used to tabulate the results of the United States presidential election. Based on available data, UNIVAC I accurately predicted the election of President Dwight D. Eisenhower less than 45 minutes after the polls closed.

The miniaturization of computer components. The invention of the transistor in 1947 led to the production of faster and more reliable electronic computers. Transistors control the flow of electric current in electronic equipment. They soon replaced the bulkier, less reliable vacuum tubes. In 1958, Control Data Corporation introduced the first fully transistorized computer, designed by American engineer Seymour Cray. IBM introduced its first transistorized computers in 1959.

Miniaturization continued with the development of the integrated circuit in the early 1960's. An integrated circuit contains thousands of transistors and other tiny parts on a small silicon chip. This device enabled engineers to design both minicomputers and high-speed mainframes with tremendous memory capacities.

Despite the shrinking size of their components, most computers remained relatively large and expensive. But dependence on computers increased dramatically. By the late 1960's, many large businesses relied on computers. Many companies linked their computers together into networks, making it possible for different offices to share information.

During the 1960's, computer technology improved rapidly. Different kinds of circuits were placed on silicon chips. Some of the circuits contained the computer's logic. Other chips held memory. By the early 1970's, the entire workings of a computer could be placed on a handful of chips. As a result, smaller computers became possible. The central chip that controlled the computer became known as a *microprocessor.*

The personal computer. The first personal computer, the Altair, was introduced in 1975. Only electronics hobbyists bought these computers.

In 1977, two American students, Steven P. Jobs and Stephen G. Wozniak, founded the Apple Computer Company and introduced the Apple II personal computer. The Apple II was much less expensive than mainframes. As a result, computers became available to people other than computer specialists and technicians. Personal computers were purchased by small and medium-sized businesses that could not afford mainframes or did not need the immense computing power that mainframes provided. Millions of individuals, families, and schools also bought them.

In 1981, IBM entered the personal computer market with its PC. The machine was even more successful than the Apple II. Apple scored another success in 1984 with the introduction of its Macintosh, a powerful, easy-to-use desktop computer.

As computer power increased, so did computer speed. These increases were accompanied by a steady reduction in both size and cost. Modern personal computers are more powerful than UNIVAC I and can be purchased for less than $1,000.

Computers of the future. Computer researchers continue to seek ways to develop faster and more powerful machines and software. Much software research focuses on the further development of artificial intelligence, which is intended to help computers make decisions rather than simply to manipulate data. One type of artificial intelligence, the expert system, translates patterns of experience into software. An expert system responds to input by asking questions and providing responses. In this manner, it constantly narrows the field of inquiry until a solution is achieved.

Much effort also is being devoted to making computers smaller. In the near future, most experts feel that computers will continue to be built from integrated circuits. But some scientists foresee the production of biological computers, which will be grown rather than manufactured. In addition, some experts believe that computer technology will develop methods of storing data on individual molecules. A molecular storage system could contain all of the knowledge of the human race in a space smaller than a paperback book.

Problems of the computer age

Because computers provide such convenient storage for large amounts of information, less and less information is stored on paper. Much of the convenience of computers stems from their ability to form networks by means of telephone lines. But a computer that makes up part of a network resembles a room with many doors. Intruders who slip through these "doors" are difficult to trace. For this reason, computer designers work to safeguard stored information from unauthorized access, as well as from system breakdown or failure.

Computers and privacy. Many people fear that their right to privacy is threatened by the possible misuse or unauthorized disclosure of information in computer databases. Databases often contain private and personal information, such as medical, banking, or tax records. Other databases pertain to business plans or inventions that a company must conceal from competing companies. Still other databases store top-secret military information or other kinds of data important to a nation's security. Today, laws control the disclosure of data.

Computers and security. Computer operating systems are designed to prevent unauthorized entry into a computer, but computer crimes sometimes occur. Industrial spies and thieves often use telephone lines to gain access to computers. Some of these criminals steal or change the information in a computer database. Others steal money by using the capability of computers to transfer funds electronically from one account to another. Major problems can result if someone obtains illegal access to secret information in government or corporate databases. Sometimes, people within an organization commit computer crimes. Other crimes are committed by outsiders who create chaos by breaking into computer systems.

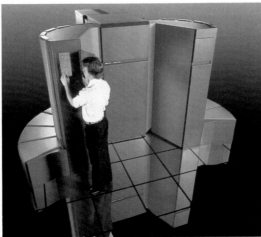

A supercomputer can solve large, complicated numerical problems with amazing speed. The Cray supercomputer shown above generated a detailed image of part of the main engine of a space shuttle, *below.*

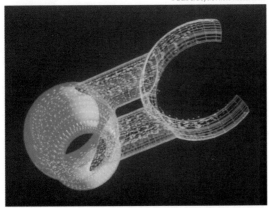

In the late 1980's, computer experts became aware of a dangerous type of program called a *computer virus.* A computer virus is designed to do mischief, sometimes by deleting or changing information and sometimes by simply inserting a message. A virus eventually enters a computer's operating system. It spreads by rapidly making copies of itself, thus "infecting" the other computer systems in a network. This process can quickly overload huge computer networks.

Various methods help safeguard computer systems and databases. Protective measures are built into many computer operating systems to prevent access by invaders. Many computers require a user to enter a secret password. Some systems automatically scramble information so that it can only be decoded by authorized personnel. Careful protection of these passwords and codes helps decrease the likelihood of illegal access.

Other problems. Computers are valuable in many ways. But if a computer breaks or is damaged, the people who rely on it face great difficulties. Until the computer is fixed, these people may be worse off than if they never had a computer at all. For example, informa-

tion may be lost if a computer system suffers damage in a natural disaster, such as a fire or flood. Computer breakdowns and faulty programming in business organizations delay transactions, disrupt work, and create inconveniences for consumers. An undetected computer malfunction at an air traffic control center could cause a collision. A computer failure at a national defense installation could have even more serious consequences.

Computers, together with their programs, are the most complicated machines in history—and, arguably, the most useful. Modern industrial societies depend on computers in the home, school, and workplace. As computers become more powerful and widespread, computer education must continue to increase as well.

David Gelernter and Keith Ferrell

Analog computer is a device that solves problems by measuring a quantity, such as weight, speed, or voltage. Many familiar devices, including speedometers and thermometers, work as analog computers. Analog computers once performed much of the world's calculation. They reached the peak of their popularity in the 1940's. During World War II, they were used to work out the paths of bombs and bullets. The development of *digital computers* since the war has limited the use of analog computers. A digital computer uses numerical digits that represent a quantity, rather than measuring quantities directly. Most computers today are digital.

An analog computer replaces a calculation with a physical system that performs the calculation. For example, the rise and fall of mercury in a thermometer imitates the movement of the temperature. A slide rule is a kind of analog computer that imitates a calculation by representing numbers with lengths. The rule typically consists of three parallel strips, each with a different scale printed on its edges. Moving one strip in relation to another increases or reduces their combined length, making it possible to multiply, divide, and perform more complex operations (see **Slide rule**).

An electronic analog computer represents numbers with electrical quantities, especially voltages. It manipulates voltages much as a slide rule manipulates lengths. In this way, the computer can solve engineering and scientific problems. Electronic analog computers are useful for representing quantities and processes that change continuously. They are also well-suited for building models that *simulate* (duplicate) the behavior of systems. For example, computer *simulations* reproduce the motion of aircraft, spacecraft, and oceangoing ships under various conditions. They are used to test a craft's performance or train its crew.

Certain limitations make it difficult for analog computers to compete with digital computers. Although analog computers can be extremely fast, they are not as accurate as digital computers. This is mainly because analog computers work with varying quantities that cannot be measured precisely. Digital computers count rather than measure, and so their accuracy is limited only by the number of digits they can handle. In addition, digital computers are more versatile than analog computers. Most analog computers are set up to solve only one kind of problem and must be rewired to solve other problems. Devices called *hybrid computers* combine the speed of analog computers and the accuracy of digital computers.   A. K. Dewdney

Computer graphics are images created by a computer. These images include diagrams, cartoon animations, and even highly realistic pictures. The process by which computers draw, color, shade, and manipulate images is also known as computer graphics. Computer graphics enable us to gather, display, and understand information quickly and effectively. Computer graphics can even produce images of objects and processes that we have no other way of seeing, such as the inside of a molecule or the operation of a black hole.

Computer graphics have numerous uses in a wide variety of fields. Businesses follow sales from charts and graphs made by computers. Computer graphics help engineers create and test designs for such products as automobiles and aircraft. Through computer graphics, architects can view building designs drawn in three dimensions from any angle. Scientists use computer graphics to design new drug molecules, track weather systems, and test theories that describe how galaxies develop. Physicians use computer images of the inside of the body to locate tumors and other disorders and plan treatment. Computer graphics are also used in art, in the production of cartoons and special effects in motion pictures, and in video games.

Computer graphics are created on a computer display screen, which resembles a television screen. The screen consists of thousands of tiny dots called *picture elements,* or *pixels.* You can see individual pixels by looking closely at the letters that appear on a computer screen. A computer can turn each pixel on and off like a light bulb to make a pattern. Different combinations of pixels can produce any picture we want.

All computers need a *program* that tells them what to do. A computer graphics program directs the drawing on a computer's screen. The program may generate the image itself or it may copy an image from another source. For example, a program that draws molecules might start by solving equations that describe molecular structure. It can then use the solutions to display the shape of a molecule. But a program that copies a photograph might first convert points on the image into a list of numbers. The numbers can then instruct the computer which pixels to turn on and off.   A. K. Dewdney

See also **Computer** (Uses of the computer).

Thomas J. Watson Research Center

Using complex geometric shapes called *fractals,* a computer graphics program can create forms—like these mountains—that resemble the irregular shapes found in nature.

Creating pictures with computers

These illustrations show how computers enable manufacturers to examine and evaluate designs for products like this automobile without building models. The image takes shape in steps.

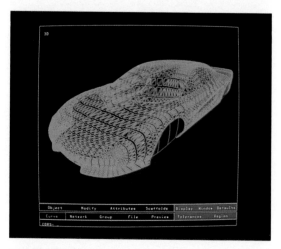

In the first step, the computer "draws" an outline of the automobile with a meshlike pattern of lines.

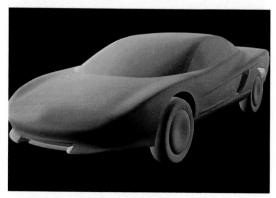

In the second step, the computer fills in the spaces between the lines to show what the automobile's surface looks like.

Evans & Sutherland Computer Corporation

In the third step, the computer adds color, shadows, reflections, and highlights to create a realistic image.

Computerized tomography (CT), *tuh MAHG ruh fee,* is an X-ray system used to produce images of various parts of the body, such as the head, heart, and abdomen. Doctors use CT images to help diagnose and treat diseases. The technique is also called *computed tomography* or *computerized axial tomography (CAT).*

To produce a CT image, the patient lies on a table that passes through a circular scanning machine called a *gantry.* The table is positioned so that the organ to be scanned lies in the center of the gantry. A tube on the gantry beams X rays through the patient's body and into special detectors that analyze the image produced. The gantry rotates around the patient to obtain many images from different angles. A computer then processes the information from the detectors to produce a cross-sectional image on a video screen. By moving the table in the gantry, doctors can obtain many scans of the same organ or even the entire body.

Sometimes an iodine solution, called a *contrast agent,* is injected into the body to make certain organs show up clearly in the CT scan. For scans of the abdomen and pelvis, the patient drinks a barium mixture to outline the inner surfaces of the stomach and bowel.

Doctors use CT scans to diagnose many conditions, such as tumors, infections, blood clots, and broken bones. CT also assists in treating some diseases that might otherwise require surgery. For example, doctors can use a CT scan to guide *catheters* (small tubes) to an abscess in the body and drain pus from the infected area.   P. Andrea Lum

See also **Radiology; X ray.**

Magnetic resonance imaging (MRI) is a technique used in medicine for producing images of tissues inside the body. Physicians use images created by this technique to diagnose certain disorders and injuries.

MRI is an important diagnostic tool because it enables physicians to identify abnormal tissue without opening the body through surgery. MRI does not expose the patient to radiation, unlike tests that use X rays. In addition, MRI lets physicians see through bones and organs. The technique is safe for most people. However, MRI uses a powerful magnet and so cannot be used on people with metal implants, such as pacemakers or artificial joints.

An MRI unit consists mainly of a large cylindrical magnet, devices for transmitting and receiving radio waves, and a computer. During the examination, the patient lies inside the magnet, and a magnetic field is applied to the patient's body. The magnetic field causes nuclei in certain atoms inside the body to line up. Radio waves are then directed at the nuclei. If the frequency of the radio waves equals that of the atom, a *resonance condition* is produced. This condition enables the nuclei to absorb the energy of the radio waves. When the radio-wave stimulation stops, the nuclei return to their original state and emit energy in the form of weak radio signals. The strength and length of these signals—and therefore the kind of image produced—depend on various properties of the tissue. A computer translates the signals into highly detailed cross-sectional images.

An MRI examination is supervised by a *radiologist*—a physician trained in using images for medical diagnosis. The technique is most often used to study the head or

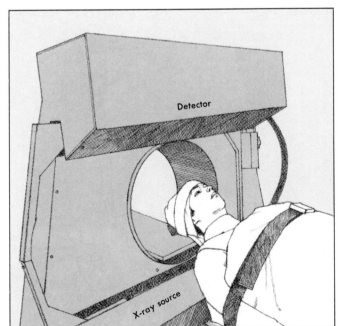
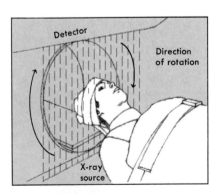
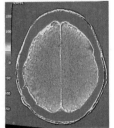

WORLD BOOK diagrams by David Cunningham   © Dan McCoy, Rainbow

A CT scanner is an X-ray machine that makes a cross-sectional view of the brain and other internal organs. It shoots X rays through a patient's body from many angles. An X-ray detector measures the rays that penetrate. A computer reads the data from the detector and then forms an image on a screen. The scanner thus produces a detailed picture of the brain, *right.*

spine. MRI is also used to examine the chest, abdomen, and joints. MRI has a high rate of success in detecting tumors, diseases of the circulatory system, abnormalities present since birth, and some types of injuries.

MRI devices are extremely costly and must be housed in special facilities. As a result, they are found chiefly in large medical centers. In some regions of the United States, a number of small hospitals share a mobile MRI unit.

MRI technology developed from a related technique called *nuclear magnetic resonance spectroscopy* (NMR spectroscopy). Chemists and other scientists use NMR spectroscopy to obtain detailed information about molecular structure.   Glenn S. Forbes

Positron emission tomography (PET), *tuh MAHG ruh fee,* is a technique used to produce images of the chemical activity of the brain and other body tissues. PET enables scientists to observe chemical changes in specific regions of a person's brain while the person performs various tasks, such as listening, thinking, or moving an arm or leg. Scientists use PET to compare the brain processes of healthy people and people with diseases of the brain. Research is being done to see if it is possible to use these comparisons to identify abnormalities that underlie various brain disorders. These disorders include such mental illnesses as bipolar disorder and schizophrenia, as well as such conditions as Alzheimer's disease, cerebral palsy, epilepsy, and stroke. PET also helps doctors diagnose certain other disorders, including heart disease and cancer.

In a PET scan of the brain, the patient's head is positioned inside a ring of cameralike sensors. These sensors can detect *gamma rays* (short-wave electromagnetic radiation) from many angles. A solution containing glucose bound to a harmless amount of a radioactive substance is injected into a vein. This radioactive *labeled glucose* mixes with the glucose in blood and soon enters the brain.

The radioactive substance gives off *positrons,* particles identical to electrons but carrying an opposite electric charge. The positrons collide with electrons present in brain tissue and gamma rays are *emitted* (given off). The sensors record the points where these rays emerge. A computer then assembles these points into a three-dimensional representation of the emitting regions. This representation is displayed on a video screen as cross-sectional "slices" through the brain.

Colors in a PET image show the rate at which specific brain structures consume the glucose. The rate of glucose consumption indicates how active these structures are during a particular task. For example, if the person having the PET scan looks at an object, the brain region that receives and interprets visual signals will appear red on the screen. Red indicates the highest rate of activity. Other colors that appear in PET images include orange—the next highest rate of activity—yellow, green, and blue, the lowest rate.   Michael E. Phelps

Magnetic resonance imaging is used in medicine. The patient is placed inside a machine that has a huge magnet. The magnetic field causes the nuclei of certain atoms inside the body to line up. The machine then sends out a radio signal, which causes the nuclei to change direction. The changes create signals that a computer translates into an image, such as the one of the normal spinal cord, *right.*

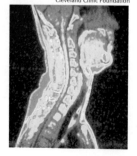

A PET scan produces images of the brain's chemical activity. The patient's head is placed inside a ring of sensors, *above,* which pick up gamma ray signals from the brain. A computer processes these signals to form a cross-sectional color image, *right.* The colors show the rate of activity in specific brain regions. Red indicates a high rate of activity.

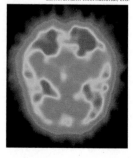

Index

This index covers the contents of the 1991, 1990, and 1989 editions of SCIENCE YEAR, The World Book Science Annual.

Each index entry gives the edition year and the page number or numbers—for example, **91:** 40-41. The number in front of the colon, **91,** indicates the edition year. The remaining numbers indicate the pages on which the desired information may be found—in this example, pages 40 and 41.

All the topics that are indexed are in **boldface** type.

When a topic, such as **CHEMISTRY,** is all capital letters, this means that SCIENCE YEAR has a Science News Update article titled Chemistry. The numbers following the topic indicate where the articles on Chemistry are to be found in the 1991, 1990, and 1989 editions of SCIENCE YEAR:

CHEMISTRY, 91: 258-261, **90:** 239-242, **89:** 239-243

When a topic, such as **Aging,** only begins with a capital letter, this means that there is no SCIENCE YEAR article titled Aging, but information on this topic can be found in the edition and on the pages listed:

Aging, 91: 223-225

When there are many references to a particular topic, they are grouped alphabetically by clue words under the main topic:

CHEMISTRY, 91: 258-261, **90:** 239-242, **89:** 239-243
  Nobel Prizes, **91:** 312, **90:** 291, **89:** 290
  science student awards, **91:** 337

This means that in addition to the general articles about chemistry in the 1991, 1990, and 1989 editions of SCIENCE YEAR, the reader will find references to the Nobel Prize for chemistry in each of the three volumes and a reference to a chemistry award for science students in the 1991 edition.

When an "il." in parentheses follows a page number, the reference is to an illustration only:

Cosmic jets, 91: 73 (il.)

This means that there is an illustration of cosmic jets on page 73 of the 1991 edition.

The various "see" and "see also" cross-references in the index direct the reader to other entries within the index:

Horticulture, see **AGRICULTURE; BOTANY; Plants**

This means that for information on horticulture, look under the boldface index entries **AGRICULTURE, BOTANY,** and **Plants.**

Index

A

Here are your

1991 SCIENCE YEAR
Cross-Reference Tabs

For insertion in your WORLD BOOK

Each year, SCIENCE YEAR, THE WORLD BOOK ANNUAL SCIENCE SUPPLEMENT, adds a valuable dimension to your WORLD BOOK set. The Cross-Reference Tab System is designed especially to help you link SCIENCE YEAR's major articles to the related WORLD BOOK articles that they update.

How to use these Tabs

The top Tab on this page is BALLARD, ROBERT D. There is no such article in WORLD BOOK, so put this Tab in your B volume where it should go alphabetically. (Treat other tabs for which there is no WORLD BOOK article similarly.) Stick the next two Tabs—BEE and BRAN—in the B volume also. Then go on to stick the remaining Tabs in the appropriate WORLD BOOK volumes, and your new SCIENCE YEAR will be linked to your WORLD BOOK set.

Special Report
BALLARD, ROBERT D.
1991 Science Year, p. 112

Special Report
BEE
1991 Science Year, p. 26

Science Year Close-Up
BRAN
1991 Science Year, p. 314

Special Report
COMPUTER
1991 Science Year, p. 68

New World Book Article
COMPUTER
1991 Science Year, p. 364

New World Book Article
COMPUTER GRAPHICS
1991 Science Year, p. 380

New World Book Article
COMPUTERIZED TOMOGRAPHY
1991 Science Year, p. 381

Special Report
CYSTIC FIBROSIS
1991 Science Year, p. 158

Special Report
DEER
1991 Science Year, p. 98

Special Report
EARTHQUAKES
1991 Science Year, p. 10

Special Report
GENETIC ENGINEERING
1991 Science Year, p. 200

Special Report
HUBBLE SPACE TELESCOPE
1991 Science Year, p. 54

New World Book Article
MAGNETIC RESONANCE IMAGING
1991 Science Year, p. 382

Special Report
MICROSCOPE
1991 Science Year, p. 172

Special Report
NEPTUNE
1991 Science Year, p. 142

Special Report
OCEAN (Discoveries)
1991 Science Year, p. 130

Special Report
OCEAN (Ocean pollution)
1991 Science Year, p. 40

Special Report
OXYGEN
1991 Science Year, p. 214

New World Book Article
POSITRON EMISSION TOMOGRAPHY
1991 Science Year, p. 382

Special Report
ZIMBABWE (History)
1991 Science Year, p. 82

D

D-quark, **91**: 326
Dark matter, **90**: 114-127
  Abell 370 and, **89**: 227
  in galaxies, **90**: 226-227
  neutrinos and, **89**: 303
Dart, Raymond A., **90**: 248
Darwin, Charles, **89**: 364-365
DAT, see **Digital audio tape**
Data processing, see **Computers**
Dating methods, **89**: 197-209
  for Milky Way, **89**: 230
  radiometric, **91**: 320
  thermoluminescence, **89**: 215
  see also **Radiocarbon dating**
David, Armand, **91**: 101-102
Death rates, in Harlem, **91**: 331
DEATHS OF SCIENTISTS, **91**: 268-
  269, **90**: 248-249, **89**: 248-249
Debris flow (volcano), **90**: 104, 105
Decaffeination, **90**: 322-324
Deep Rover (submersible), **90**: 33-39
Deep-sea drilling, **90**: 294-296
Deep-sea vents, see **Hydrothermal
  vents**
Deep Tunnel project, **89**: 189
Deer
  excessive breeding, **90**: 316-318
  mating calls, **89**: 318-319
  Père David's, **91**: 99-111
  white-tailed, **89**: 91-103
Defenses, plant, **89**: 119-131
Definition (television), **90**: 200
Deforestation, see **Forest fires; Rain
  forests**
Dehmelt, Hans G., **91**: 312-313
De Hoffmann, Frederic, **91**: 268
Deisenhofer, Johann, **90**: 291
De Mestral, Georges, **91**: 268
DENTISTRY, **91**: 270-271, **90**: 250-
  251, **89**: 250
Deoxyribonucleic acid, see **DNA**
Deprenyl (drug), **91**: 271, 310-311
Depression, **91**: 329-330
Desert, in Biosphere II, **89**: 143, 145,
  148
Desktop publishing, **91**: 266
Deuterium (isotope), **91**: 281, **90**:
  123-124, 305
Devastated zone (volcano), **90**: 101
Devonian Period, **91**: 322
Diaphragm (abdomen), hole in, **91**:
  303
Diastolic pressure, **90**: 328
Dicotyledons (plants), **91**: 209
Diet
  Australopithecus, **91**: 233
  Biosphere II, **89**: 152
  cholesterol level and, **91**: 360-362
  disease and, **91**: 316
  heart disease and, **91**: 301-303, **90**:
    284
  weight and, **89**: 278-279
  see also **Nutrition**
Digestive system
  cystic fibrosis and, **91**: 159-160
  of white-tailed deer, **89**: 96-97
Digital audio tape (DAT), **91**: 278,
  346-349
Digital code
  in cellular phones, **89**: 324

  in fax machines, **90**: 326
Dinosaurs
  artists and, **89**: 60-75
  changing ideas about, **89**: 40-59
  darkness and, **90**: 297-298
  eggs of, **90**: 298, **89**: 297
  new discovery, **91**: 320
Dioxins (chemicals), **90**: 262-265
Disasters, health impact of, **90**: 310
Discovery (space shuttle), **91**: 56, **90**:
  314-315
Discrimination, Genetic, **90**: 171
Disease
  free radicals and, **91**: 224-225
  gene mapping and, **90**: 163-171,
    89: 265
  "magic bullets" against, **90**: 187-
    197
  Pasteur Institute, **89**: 168-181
  see also **Immunology; Medical
    Research; Public health;** and
    specific diseases
Disease-prone personality, **90**: 307-
  308
Disk, of galaxy, **90**: 118, 119
Disk-operating system (DOS), **91**:
  266, **89**: 246-247
Dispersants (chemicals), **91**: 49-51
Disruptive coloration, of insects, **90**:
  80
Diuretics, **89**: 281
DNA (deoxyribonucleic acid)
  AIDS and, **89**: 157
  cystic fibrosis and, **91**: 160, 163-
    171
  discovery of, **90**: 339, 343-347
  fingerprinting, **91**: 343, **89**: 266-267
  gene mapping and, **90**: 162-170,
    89: 265-267
  image of, **91**: 288, **90**: 266
  transfer RNA and, **89**: 265
  see also **Genes; Genetic
    engineering; Genetics**
Dominant genes, **91**: 162
Dopamine (chemical), **91**: 311, **90**:
  288, **89**: 286
Doppler effect
  Doppler radar, **90**: 154
  of galactic arcs, **89**: 225-227
  galaxies, **89**: 207-208, 230-231
  interstellar clouds, **90**: 228
  quasar, **91**: 246
Doppler radar, **90**: 154-157, **89**: 284
Double-hull construction, **91**: 52
Downbursts, **90**: 146-157
Drilling, see **Deep-sea drilling;
  Tunnel construction**
Drones (bee), **91**: 31, 35
Drought
  crop resistance to, **90**: 212
  of 1988, **90**: 128, 133-135, 143, 285-
    286, **89**: 261
Drug abuse
  AIDS, spread of, **90**: 309-310, **89**:
    167
  PCP, **91**: 308-309
  see also **Addiction**
DRUGS, **91**: 271-274, **90**: 251-253, **89**:
  251-253
  computer-designed, **89**: 133-141
  "magic bullets," **90**: 187-197
  plant defenses and, **89**: 120, 130
  see also **Drug abuse;**

  Immunology; and specific
  diseases
Duracell science awards, **91**: 337
Dwarfism, **89**: 218
Dynamic Random Access Memory
  (DRAM), **90**: 242
Dyslexia (disorder), **89**: 287 (il.)

E

Earth Day 1990, **91**: 283
Earth sciences, book on, **91**: 254-255
  see also **Geology;
    Oceanography;
    Paleontology**
Earthquakes, **91**: 11-25
  Armenia, **91**: 272-273
  Los Angeles, **91**: 290, **89**: 271 (il.)
  Macquarie Ridge, **91**: 294
  volcanic activity and, **91**: 317
East Pacific Rise (mountains), **91**: 317
EC-1 (gasoline), **91**: 279-280
Eclipses, **90**: 231, **89**: 234
ECOLOGY, **91**: 274-277, **90**: 254-256,
  380-383, **89**: 253-256
  see also **Ecosystems;
    Environment**
Ecosystems, **90**: 104, 174, **89**: 144
Edgerton, Harold E., **91**: 268
Eggs, **89**: 325-327
Eggs, fossil, **90**: 298, **89**: 55-56, 297-
  298
Egypt, ancient, **89**: 222-223
Einstein, Albert, **89**: 341, 347, 348,
  350
Einstein ring, **90**: 225-227
Electric current, see **Electricity**
Electricity
  electric fields, **91**: 332-333
  solar-powered car, **89**: 258-259
  sources of, **90**: 258-259
Electromagnetic radiation
  dark matter, **90**: 120
  earth's atmosphere and, **91**: 57
  low-frequency, **91**: 332-333
  solar, **90**: 271
  see also **Microwave radiation;
    X rays**
Electromagnetic spectrum, **91**: 57,
  332 (il.), **90**: 119
Electromagnets
  invention of, **89**: 108
  radiation dangers, **91**: 332-333
Electron guns, **90**: 200-202, 205, 208
Electron holes, **90**: 301
Electron microscopes, **91**: 172-174,
  177-179
Electron neutrinos, see **Neutrinos**
Electron-positron accelerators, **90**:
  305-306
Electron spin resonance (ESR), **90**:
  215, **89**: 220-221
ELECTRONICS, **91**: 277-278, **90**: 257-
  258, **89**: 256-258
Electrons
  atomic structure, **91**: 326-328
  microscope and, **91**: 177-181
  oxygen atom, **91**: 218, 222
  superconductivity and, **90**: 301-
    303, **89**: 106-107, 301
  see also **Superconductivity**
Electroporation, **91**: 209

Wilson, Edward, on, **89:** 365-369
see also **DNA; Genetic
engineering; Genetics; Human
genome mapping project**
Genesis (computer), 91: 263, 278 (il.)
Genetic diversity, 91: 342
Genetic engineering
AIDS research, **90:** 196-197, **89:**
159-166
cancer treatment, **90:** 275-276
drug design, **89:** 139
ecology and, **90:** 254-256
foods and, **91:** 200-213
killer bees and, **91:** 38
monoclonal antibody production,
91: 295-296
patents, **89:** 264
plants, **89:** 131
GENETICS, 91: 285-289, **90:** 266-270,
89: 264-269
Watson, James D., and, **90:** 339-
351
see also **Genes**
Genome, 90: 160
see also **DNA; Human genome
mapping project**
GEOLOGY, 91: 290-294, **90:** 270-275,
89: 269-272
books on, **90:** 234
see also **Dating methods;
Earthquakes; Fossils; Volcanoes**
Geosynchronous orbits, 89: 316
Geovision (software), 91: 266
Geysers
ocean, **91:** 130-141
Triton, **91:** 153-154
Gibberellin (hormone), 90: 237
Glaciation
global warming and, **90:** 133
ice ages, **90:** 14, 18-21, 270-274
Global warming, 90: 128-143
clouds and, **91:** 305-308
effects on living things, **90:** 254
hurricanes and, **91:** 304-305
see also **Climate; Greenhouse
effect**
Globular star clusters, 90: 229, **89:**
209, 231-232
Glucose, and brain, 89: 289, 307
Gluon (particle), 91: 328, **90:** 124, **89:**
305
Glyptodon (animal), 90: 15 (il.)
Gneiss (rock), 91: 290
Grand Tour, of Voyager 2, 91: 142-
157
Graphic arts software, 90: 247
Graphical user interfaces (GUI's), 91:
266
Grasshoppers, 89: 129
Gravitational lenses, 91: 247, **90:**
119-120, 225, **89:** 225
Gravitons (particles), 90: 124
Gravity
atmospheres and, **91:** 250-251
black holes, **89:** 346-350
dark matter, **90:** 114-116
plant growth and, **90:** 237
roller coaster and, **90:** 300-301
Great Attractor, 91: 244-246
Great Barrier Reef, 89: 10-23
Great Dark Spot (Neptune), 91: 150
**Great Enclosure (Great Zimbabwe),
91:** 84-89, 95-96

Great Observatories Program, 91: 67
**Great Wall (extragalactic structure),
91:** 244-246
Great Zimbabwe, 91: 82-97
Greece, ancient, 90: 221-222
Green Revolution, 91: 203
Greenhouse effect
drought and, **89:** 212, 261
global warming, **91:** 283, **90:** 130,
135-143
methane and, **90:** 287
ocean temperatures, **90:** 294
ozone hole and, **89:** 89
rain forest destruction and, **90:** 178
Ground water contamination, 91:
228
Grouse (bird), 91: 276-277
Growth hormones
growth hormone releasing factor
(GHRF), **90:** 239-240
somatotropin, in treating livestock,
91: 205, 211, 213
Growth rate (mathematics), 89: 328
Guinea worm disease, 91: 334
Gum disease, 90: 251, **89:** 250
Gun control, 90: 310

H

Habitats
diversity of, **89:** 254
endangered plants, **90:** 236-237
sources and sinks, **90:** 256
Hairy-eared dwarf lemur, 91: 342
Hale telescope, 90: 84, 88-93
Half-life (particle decay), 91: 328, **89:**
200-205
Halley's Comet, 89: 232-233
Halos, extragalactic, 90: 119-123
Handguns, 90: 310
Harbor, of Caesarea, 90: 42-55
Harbor seal, 90: 256
Hard disks, computer, 91: 262
Harlem death rates, 91: 331
Hawking, Stephen W., 89: 341-355
Head winds, 90: 151
Headrick, Matthew P., 91: 335
Heart attacks
aspirin and, **89:** 280, 310-311
cholesterol and, **91:** 360-361, **89:**
291
drugs and, **89:** 251
obesity and, **91:** 301
smoking and, **89:** 277
Heart disease
cholesterol and, **91:** 360-362
cystic fibrosis, **91:** 160-161
diet and, **91:** 301-303, **90:** 284
disease-prone personality and, **90:**
308
free radicals and, **91:** 224-225
lead pollution and, **90:** 265-266
smoking and, **89:** 277
see also **Heart attacks**
Heat, and energy loss, 89: 106
see also **Climate**
Heavy elements, 91: 249, **89:** 226-
227, 230
Heavy water, 91: 281, 326, **90:** 304-
305
Helium, 90: 123, **89:** 208
liquid, **89:** 107, 275, 291

Helper T cells, 90: 196, **89:** 156-157,
167
Hemoglobin, 91: 241, **89:** 237-238
Hemorrhagic strokes, 89: 280
Hepatitis B, 90: 253, **89:** 158-159, 274
Herbicides, 91: 211-212, 230
Heredity, see Genes; Genetics
Herod the Great, 90: 42
Hieroglyphs, 91: 237
Higgs boson, 90: 305
**High blood pressure, see
Hypertension**
High-definition television (HDTV), 91:
278, **90:** 199-200, 208-209
High-density lipoproteins (HDL's), 91:
362
**High-temperature superconductivity,
see Superconductivity**
Hill Ruin (Great Zimbabwe), 91: 84-
95
Hinds (female deer), 91: 103-106
Hipparchus (satellite), 91: 340
Hirschfelder, Joseph O., 91: 268
**HIV, see Human immunodeficiency
virus**
Holocaust survivor studies, 91: 330
Holocene Epoch, 90: 271
Holograms, 90: 209
Homicide, 90: 310, **89:** 311
Hominids, 91: 233
see also **Prehistoric people**
Homo erectus (hominid), 90: 215,
224
Homosexuality, and AIDS, 89: 167
Honey, 91: 31-32
**Honey bees, Africanized, see Killer
bees**
Horizontal faults, 91: 12-13
Hormones
cancer therapy, **89:** 283
human growth, **90:** 239-240
plant, **90:** 235-237, **89:** 237
Horse, native, 90: 15 (il.)
**Horticulture, see Agriculture;
Botany; Plants**
**Hot water vents, see Hydrothermal
vents**
Hubbert, Marion King, 91: 268
Hubble constant, 91: 66
Hubble flow, 91: 244
Hubble Space Telescope, 91: 56-67,
338-339, **90:** 97
Hugo, Hurricane, 91: 304
Human genome mapping project
first linkage map, **89:** 265-267
government involvement, **90:** 267
technology of, **90:** 159-171
Watson, James D., and, **90:** 339-
340, 351
**Human immunodeficiency virus
(HIV), 89:** 156, 273
see also **AIDS**
Human sacrifice, 91: 238 (il.)
Hunting
Père David's deer, **91:** 102
Pleistocene extinctions and, **90:**
21-25
white-tailed deer, **89:** 101-103
Hurricane Hugo, 91: 304
Hybridomas, 91: 295-296, **90:** 190
Hybrids, 91: 202, **90:** 235-237
Hydraulic concrete, 90: 46
Hydrocarbons, 91: 318-319

N

Nakbe (ancient city), **91**: 238
Naloxone (drug), **91**: 300
NASA, see National Aeronautics and Space Administration
National Acid Precipitation Assessment Program, 91: 282-284
National Aeronautics and Space Administration (NASA)
  atmosphere studies, **89**: 80-81, 261
  COBE satellite launch, **91**: 245-246
  deforestation monitoring, **90**: 184
  Io study, **91**: 253
  Space Camp, **91**: 190-196
  Space Telescope, **91**: 56, 61
  supercomputer, **91**: 70
  Voyager 2 probe, **91**: 144-145
National Cholesterol Education Program, 91: 361
National Oceanic and Atmospheric Administration, 91: 304
National Science Foundation (NSF), 90: 178-184
Native Americans, see Indians, American
Natural frequency, in building materials, 91: 19
Natural history, books on, 91: 254-255, **90**: 233-234, **89**: 236
Natural selection, see Evolution
Neanderthals, 91: 237 (il.), **89**: 217
Negative charge, see Electricity
Negative energy, 89: 348
Neptune, 91: 142-157, 338
Nereid (moon), 91: 147
Neural tube defect, 90: 293
Neurons, 91: 309, 310 (il.), 311
NEUROSCIENCE, 91: 308-311, **90**: 288-290, **89**: 286-288
  see also **Brain; Neurons**
Neurotransmitters, 89: 286
Neutrinos
  dark matter, **90**: 125, 127
  mass of, **89**: 303-304
  search for new, **91**: 326-328
  supernova, **89**: 226
Neutron stars, 89: 226, 231
Neutrons, 91: 326
New Madrid earthquake, 91: 13-14
NeXT Computer System, 90: 243
Nicotine, 89: 121, 309
Nielsen Media Research, 91: 350-353
Nightmares, 91: 330
Nimrud (ancient city), 91: 242 (il.)
Nitrogen
  ozone destruction and, **89**: 83
  superconductor coolant, **89**: 107, 275
Nitrogen cycle, 89: 147
Nitrous oxide, 89: 83
No-till farming, 91: 230
NOBEL PRIZES, 91: 312-313, **90**: 291-292, **89**: 290-291
Normal fault (earthquake), 91: 12-13
North American core, 91: 293-294
Novae, see Supernovae
Novgorod (city, U.S.S.R.), 91: 243
Nuclear accidents, 89: 260-261
Nuclear fission, 90: 304
Nuclear fusion

cold, **91**: 325-326, **90**: 239, 258, 304-305
  heavy water, **91**: 281
Nuclear physics, see Physics, Subatomic
Nuclear power
  Argonne National Laboratory, **90**: 358
  experimental reactor, **89**: 260-261
  greenhouse effect and, **90**: 142
  Three Mile Island cleanup, **91**: 279
  see also **Nuclear fusion**
Nuclear waste, 90: 261
Nucleotides (DNA), 90: 162-163, **89**: 265
Nucleus, atomic, 89: 106, 304
NUTRITION, 91: 313-317, **90**: 292-294, **89**: 291-294
  see also **Diet**

O

Oases, Deep-sea, see Hydrothermal vents
Oat bran, 91: 314-315
Obesity, and heart attacks, 91: 301
Observatories, 90: 84-97
  Space Telescope, **91**: 56-67
Occultation, 90: 231
Ocean
  excavation in, **90**: 41-55
  formation of, **91**: 290-293
  Great Barrier Reef, **89**: 12-23
  midwater, **90**: 27-39
  oil spills, **91**: 40-53
  ozone hole and, **91**: 276
  tunneling, **89**: 182-195
  see also **Hydrothermal vents; Oceanography**
OCEANOGRAPHY, 91: 317-319, **90**: 294-296, **89**: 295-297
  Ballard, Robert, and, **91**: 112-129
  Biosphere II, **89**: 145-151
  see also **Ocean**
Ofek (satellite), **91**: 340
Oil, formation of, 91: 318-319
Oil spills, 91: 40-53, **90**: 262
Olestra (fat substitute), 90: 292-293
Oncogene (cancer gene), 91: 313, **89**: 264
Optical digital recording, see CD-ROM; Compact discs
Optical fibers, 91: 184-185, **90**: 39
Optical microscopes, 91: 174-177
Optical processors, 91: 264-265
Optical scanners, 90: 243-244, **89**: 330-333
Optical telescopes, 90: 84-97
  Space Telescope, **91**: 56-67
Orbital speed of stars, 91: 118, **90**: 230
Orbiting Astronomical Observatory, **91**: 56-67
Organization for Tropical Studies (OTS), 90: 173-185
OS/2 (software), 91: 266, **89**: 247
Oscilloscopes, 90: 200-201
Ossuary (mass grave), 89: 219
Osteoporosis, 90: 266
Ovary (plant), 90: 235
Ovens, microwave, 90: 331-333
Owl, 91: 341 (il.)

Oxidation-reduction reaction, 91: 222
Oxides, 91: 216, 222
Oxygen
  aging and disease, **91**: 214-225
  atmospheric, **89**: 147
  deficit of, **90**: 213-214
  ozone, **89**: 82-83
Ozone
  air pollution and, **91**: 79 (il.), 282
  oxygen and, **91**: 217
  plant damage, **89**: 238
Ozone hole
  Arctic, **91**: 284, **90**: 286-287
  causes of, **91**: 217, **89**: 76-89
  ecology and, **91**: 276
  global loss, **89**: 261-262
  Pleistocene extinctions and, **90**: 25
  size of, **91**: 304, **90**: 262, **89**: 261

P

Pace walking, 91: 356-358
Paint, 89: 334-337
PALEONTOLOGY, 91: 320-322, **90**: 297-299, **89**: 297-300
  books on, **91**: 255, **90**: 234, **89**: 236
  see also **Dinosaurs; Fossils**
Paleozoic Era, 89: 199
Palladium (metal), 90: 304-305
Parallel processing (computer), 91: 264, 71
  parallel track program, **91**: 272-273
Paralysis, 91: 299-300
Parapsychology, 89: 309
Parental styles, 91: 330
Parkinson's disease, 91: 310-311, 271, **90**: 288, **89**: 286
Parrot, 91: 341 (il.)
Particle accelerators, 91: 281, 326-327, **89**: 116, 305
  see also **Superconducting Super Collider**
Particle physics, see Physics, Subatomic
Pasteur Institute, 89: 168-181
Patents, on animals, 89: 264
Paul, Wolfgang, 91: 312-313
PCP (drug), 91: 308-309
Pedersen, Charles J., 91: 269
Pegasus booster rocket, 91: 339
Peking man, 90: 215
Pelvis, of Neanderthal, 89: 217
Penicillin, 89: 176
Penrose tiling (crystal pattern), 91: 325
People Meter (television), 91: 350-353
Percentages, 89: 328-329
  television rating, **91**: 351-352
Père David's deer, 91: 99-111
Periodic pattern (crystal structure), 91: 325
Periodontal disease, 90: 251, **89**: 250
Personal computers, see Computers
Personal Information Manager (PIM), 90: 247
Personality, disease-prone, 90: 307-308
Perspiration, cystic fibrosis and, 91: 159-160
Pesticides, 91: 230, **90**: 213, **89**: 213, 263

Contributors

Adelman, George, M.A., M.S.
Editorial Director and Editor,
Encyclopedia of Neuroscience.
[*Neuroscience*]

Amato, Ivan, M.A.
Writer and Editor,
Science News Magazine.
[*Materials Science*]

Andrews, Peter J., M.S.
Free-Lance Writer, Chemist.
[Special Report, *Two Sides of the Oxygen Story; Chemistry*]

Barone, Jeanine, M.S.
Nutritionist/Exercise Physiologist,
American Health Foundation.
[*Nutrition; Nutrition* (Close-Up)]

Booth, Stephen A., B.A.
Electronics and Photography Editor,
Popular Mechanics.
[Science You Can Use: *All About DAT*]

Bower, Bruce, M.A.
Behavioral Sciences Editor,
Science News Magazine.
[*Psychology*]

Boyd, Maria B.
Zoologist and Codirector,
Milu Ecological Research Centre,
Nan Haizi, China.
[Special Report, *Père David's Deer Return to China*]

Brett, Carlton E., Ph.D.
Professor,
Department of Geological Sciences,
University of Rochester.
[*Paleontology*]

Cain, Steve, B.S.
Manager of News and Public Affairs,
Purdue University School of Agriculture.
[*Agriculture; Agriculture* (Close-Up)]

Caulfield, H. J., Ph.D.
Director,
Center for Applied Optics,
University of Alabama in Huntsville.
[*Computer Hardware* (Close-Up)]

Cobun, Peter, B.A.
Associate Editor,
The Huntsville (Ala.) *Times.*
[Special Report,
A Camp for Space Science]

Dewdney, A. K., Ph.D.
Associate Professor,
Department of Computer Science,
University of Western Ontario.
[World Book Supplement:
Computer Graphics]

Fagan, Brian M., Ph.D.
Professor of Anthropology,
University of California, Santa Barbara.
[Special Report,
Mysteries of Great Zimbabwe]

Ferrell, Keith
Features Editor,
Compute! Publications.
[*Computer Hardware;
Computer Software;*
World Book Supplement: *Computer*]

Fisher, Arthur, M.A.
Science and Technology Editor,
Popular Science Magazine.
[Special Report, *The New Microscopes*]

Forbes, Glenn S., M.D.
Associate Professor of Radiology,
Mayo Clinic.
[World Book Supplement: *Magnetic resonance imaging*]

Gelernter, David, Ph.D.
Associate Professor of
Computer Science,
Yale University.
[World Book Supplement: *Computer*]

Goldhaber, Paul, D.D.S.
Professor and Dean,
Harvard School of Dental Medicine.
[*Dentistry*]

Goodman, Richard A., M.D., M.P.H.
Associate Professor,
Department of Community Health,
Emory University School of Medicine.
[*Public Health*]

Hay, William W., Ph.D.
Professor of Geology,
University of Colorado, Boulder.
[*Geology*]

Haymer, David S., Ph.D.
Assistant Professor,
Department of Genetics,
University of Hawaii.
[*Genetics*]

Hellemans, Alexander, B.S.
Managing Editor, Science,
World Book International.
[*Physics, Fluids and Solids*]

Hester, Thomas R., Ph.D.
Professor of Anthropology and
Director,
Texas Archaeological
Research Laboratory,
University of Texas, Austin.
[*Archaeology, New World*]

Howarth, Robert W., Ph.D.
Associate Professor,
Department of Ecology
and Systematics,
Cornell University.
[Special Report,
Oil and Water—A Bad Mix]

Jonas, Steven, M.D., M.P.H.
Professor of Preventive Medicine,
State University of New York.
[Science You Can Use:
Walking Toward Better Health]

Jones, William Goodrich, A.M.L.S.
Acting University Librarian,
University of Illinois at Chicago.
[*Books of Science*]

Katz, Paul, M.D.
Associate Professor and Vice Chairman,
Department of Medicine,
Georgetown University Medical Center.
[*Immunology*]

King, Elliot W., M.A.
Editor,
Optical and Magnetic Report.
[*Electronics*]

King, Lauriston R., Ph.D.
Deputy Director,
Sea Grant Program,
Texas A&M University.
[*Oceanography*]

Lechtenberg, V. L., Ph.D.
Executive Associate Dean of Agriculture,
Purdue University.
[*Agriculture*]

Limburg, Peter R., M.A.
Author and Free-Lance Writer.
[Special Report,
Life at the Deep-Sea "Geysers"]

Lindley, David, Ph.D.
Associate Editor,
Nature Magazine.
[*Anthropology* (Close-Up)]

Lowndes, Jay C., B.S.
President,
Freemen Enterprises.
[*Space Technology*]

Lum, P. Andrea, M.D.
Abdominal Radiologist,
Ottawa Civic Hospital,
Ontario.
[World Book Supplement:
Computerized tomography]

Lunine, Jonathan I., Ph.D.
Associate Professor,
University of Arizona
Lunar Planetary Lab.
[Special Report, *Neptune:
Last Stop on a Grand Tour;
Astronomy, Solar System*]

Maran, Stephen P., Ph.D.
Senior Staff Scientist,
NASA-Goddard Space Flight Center.
[*Astronomy, Extragalactic*]

March, Robert H., Ph.D.
Professor of Physics,
University of Wisconsin.
[*Physics, Subatomic*]

Marino, Roxanne
Research Support Specialist,
Department of Ecology
and Systematics,
Cornell University.
[Special Report,
Oil and Water—A Bad Mix]

Mayersohn, Norman S. B.A.
Contributing Editor,
Popular Mechanics.
[Science You Can Use:
New and Better Bikes]

Merz, Beverly, A.B.
National Editor,
Science and Technology,
American Medical News.
[Special Report,
*Tracking Down a Deadly Gene;
Medical Research; Drugs*
(Close-Up)]

Meyer, B. Robert, M.D.
Chief, Division of Clinical
Pharmacology,
North Shore University Hospital.
[*Drugs*]

Mirsalehi, Mir M., Ph.D.
Assistant Professor,
University of Alabama in Huntsville.
[*Computer Hardware* (Close-Up)]

Moores, Eldridge M., Ph.D.
Professor,
Department of Geology,
University of California, Davis.
[Special Report,
Earth's Deadly Movements]

O'Dell, C. R., Ph.D.
Professor of Space Physics
and Astronomy,
Rice University.
[Special Report,
An Orbiting Eye on the Universe]

Patrusky, Ben, B.E.E.
Free-Lance Science Writer.
[Special Report, *Genetics Heads
for the Supermarket*]

Pennisi, Elizabeth, M.S.
Associate Editor,
The Scientist.
[*Zoology*]

Phelps, Michael E., Ph.D.
Jennifer Jones Simon Professor and
Chief of Nuclear Medicine, University
of California School of Medicine,
Los Angeles.
[World Book Supplement:
Positron emission tomography]

Raloff, Janet, M.S.J.
Environment/Policy Editor,
Science News Magazine.
[*Environment; Public Health*
(Close-Up)]

Roble, Raymond G.
Senior Scientist,
High Altitude Observatory,
National Center for Atmospheric
Research.
[*Meteorology* (Close-Up)]

Salisbury, Frank B., Ph.D.
Professor of Plant Physiology,
Utah State University.
[*Botany*]

Silva, Jessica Ann Morrison, B.S.
Free-Lance Science Writer.
[Special Report,
Invasion of the "Killer" Bees]

Snow, John T., Ph.D.
Professor,
Purdue University.
[*Meteorology*]

Snow, Theodore P., Ph.D.
Professor of Astrophysics,
University of Colorado, Boulder.
[*Astronomy, Galactic*]

Tamarin, Robert H., Ph.D.
Professor of Biology,
Boston University.
[*Ecology*]

Tattersall, Ian, Ph.D.
Curator, Department of Anthropology,
American Museum of Natural History.
[*Anthropology*]

Tobin, Thomas R., Ph.D.
Assistant Professor,
ARL Division of Neurobiology,
University of Arizona.
[*Zoology*]

Visich, Marian, Jr., Ph.D.
Associate Dean of Engineering,
State University of New York.
[*Energy*]

Walley, Wayne, B.A.
Reporter,
Advertising Age.
[Science You Can Use: *Those TV
Ratings and What They Mean*]

Wenke, Robert J., Ph.D.
Associate Professor,
Department of Anthropology,
University of Washington.
[*Archaeology, Old World*]

Woods, Michael, B.S.
Science Editor,
The Blade, Toledo, Ohio.
[Science You Can Use: *Understanding
Your Cholesterol Levels*]

Acknowledgments

The publishers of *Science Year* gratefully acknowledge the courtesy of the following artists, photographers, publishers, institutions, agencies, and corporations for the illustrations in this volume. Credits should read from top to bottom, left to right on their respective pages. All entries marked with an asterisk (*) denote illustrations created exclusively for *Science Year.* All maps, charts, and diagrams were prepared by the *Science Year* staff unless otherwise noted.

Cover NASA

2 Illustration by Robert Bakker; Cystic Fibrosis Foundation; © Paul X. Scott, Sygma; AP/Wide World
3 NASA; © Ken Kerbs; © Chicago Tribune Company, all rights reserved, used with permission; Jet Propulsion Laboratory
4 Runk/Schoenberger from Grant Heilman; © Kathy Dawson; Maja Boyd
5 Computer result prepared by Maria Sundin, Stefan Engstrom, and Bjorn Sundelius, University of Gothenburg, Gothenburg, Sweden, in collaboration with Debra Meloy Elmegreen, Vassar College, and Bruce Elmegreen, IBM Watson Research Center; © Raphael Gaillarde, Gamma/Liaison; Eric and Phyllis Knudsen
8 Richard Hooks*; Robert R. Hessler, Scripps Institution of Oceanography
9 Painting by Ken Marschall from *The Discovery of the Titanic* by Robert Ballard published by Warner/Madison Press Books and protected by the copyright as provided therein; © Flip and Debra Schulke, Black Star
10 © Paul X. Scott, Sygma
13 Oxford Illustrators Limited*; Oxford Illustrators Limited*; U.S. Geological Survey
17 AP/Wide World; Pettersen's Imagecraft*; Pettersen's Imagecraft*
20 Oxford Illustrators Limited*
21 © Susan Lohwasser; © Vitelmo Bertero, Earthquake Engineering Research Center
23 Oxford Illustrators Limited*; © Tom Zimberoff, Gamma/Liaison; © Tom Zimberoff, Gamma/Liaison
24 Oxford Illustrators Limited*
26–27 © Scott Camazine, Photo Researchers
29 U.S. Department of Agriculture; © Scott Camazine, Photo Researchers; Runk/Schoenberger from Grant Heilman
33 U.S. Department of Agriculture
34 © Terry Domico, Earth Images; Grant Heilman
37–38 U.S. Department of Agriculture
41 © Kathy Dawson
43 © Tony Dawson
46–49 Oxford Illustrators Limited*
50 © Kathy Dawson; © Bill Nation, Sygma; © Paul Fusco, Magnum
52 Oxford Illustrators Limited*
53 © Tony Dawson
54–58 NASA
59 Hughes Danbury Optical Systems, Inc.
60 Oxford Illustrators Limited*
63 Oxford Illustrators Limited*; Space Telescope Science Institute; Space Telescope Science Institute
64 National Optical Astronomy Observatory; © Anglo-Australian Telescope Board
65 Art: Oxford Illustrators Limited*—photos: NASA; S.S. Murray, Harvard-Smithsonian Center for Astrophysics; Max Planck Institute
68 NASA
69 Alan Decker, San Diego Supercomputer Center
71 Cray Research, Inc.
72 © Donna J. Cox, National Center for Supercomputing Applications, University of Illinois
74–75 Joshua Barnes
76 Joseph Klemp and Richard Rotunno, National Center for Atmospheric Research/National Science Foundation
77 Reprinted from *Popular Science* with permission © 1990 Times Mirror Magazines, Inc.
78 D. Jackson Coleman and Mark Rondeau, Cornell Theory Center
79 Gregory J. McRae and Armistead G. Russell, Carnegie Mellon University/Pittsburgh Supercomputing Center
80 John Hubbard, Cornell Theory Center
81 Marc A. Berger, Carnegie Mellon University, Michael F. Barnsley, Iterated Systems, Inc., and Mario Perriggua/Pittsburgh Supercomputing Center; Yoichiro Kawachucki

82 Richard Hooks*
85 Joe Rogers*
87 © H. von Meiss, Photo Researchers
88 © Bud Lazarus; © Georg Gerster, Comstock
91 © Tom Nebbia, Aspect Picture Library
92 © Robert Aberman, Werner Forman Archive; © Bruce Norman, Ronald Sheridan Photo Library
93 © Georg Gerster, Comstock
94 © Margie Matter; © Bruce Norman
95 Aspect Picture Library; © Bruce Norman
98 Maja Boyd
101 *Antlers of a Deer*, Handscroll-ink and color on paper by Ch'ien-lung, 1767. Metropolitan Museum of Art, Gift of John C. Gerguson, 1913
102–105 Maja Boyd
106 Joe Rogers*
107–108 Maja Boyd
112 Painting by Ken Marschall from *The Discovery of the Titanic* by Robert Ballard published by Warner/Madison Press Books and protected by the copyright provided therein; Christopher Morrow*
114–117 Christopher Morrow*
118 Steve Boswick*, © National Geographic Society
119 Rod Catanach, Woods Hole Oceanographic Institute
120–121 Christopher Morrow*
122 Painting by Ken Marschall from *The Discovery of the Titanic* by Robert Ballard published by Warner/Madison Press Books and protected by the copyright provided therein; Photographs taken from *The Discovery of the Titanic* by Robert Ballard published by Warner/Madison Press Books and protected by the copyright as provided therein.
123 © Hank Morgan
130 Robert R. Hessler, Scripps Institution of Oceanography
134 Scripps Institution of Oceanography
135 Oxford Illustrators Limited*
138 Woods Hole Oceanographic Institution
139 Woods Hole Oceanographic Institution; Woods Hole Oceanographic Institution; H. W. Jannasch
140 Oxford Illustrators Limited*
142 Francis Reddy
143 Jet Propulsion Laboratory
144 Graham Studios*
145 Jet Propulsion Laboratory; Graham Studios*
146 Jet Propulsion Laboratory; Graham Studios*
147 Jet Propulsion Laboratory
148 Jet Propulsion Laboratory; Graham Studios*
151–157 Jet Propulsion Laboratory
158 Roberta Polfus*
161 Cystic Fibrosis Foundation; Roberta Polfus*
163 Cystic Fibrosis Foundation; Canadian Cystic Fibrosis Foundation
165–171 Roberta Polfus*
172 Oxford Illustrators Limited*
175 © John Reader, SPL from Photo Researchers; © Paul W. Johnson, Biological Photo Service; © M. I. Walker, Photo Researchers; Oxford Illustrators Limited*; Bettmann Archive; Oxford Illustrators Limited*
176 JAK Graphics*; © Leon J. Le Beau, Biological Photo Service
177 NIBSC/SPL from Photo Researchers; CNRI/SPL, from Photo Researchers
178 IBM Research; Oxford Illustrators Limited*; IBM Research
180 Oxford Illustrators Limited*; © M. Isaacson, Cornell University
182 Art: Pettersen's Imagecraft*—photos: © Eric Gravé, Science Source from Photo Researchers; © John Durham, SPL from Photo Researchers; CNRI/SPL from Photo Researchers
183 Art: Pettersen's Imagecraft*—photos: IBM Research; © Gopal Murti, SPL from Photo Researchers; CNRI/SPL from Photo Researchers; IBM Researchers
186 Bob Gathany; © Flip and Debra Schulke, Black Star
187 © Flip and Debra Schulke, Black Star
188 Bob Gathany

World Book Encyclopedia, Inc., provides high-quality educational and reference products for the family and school. They include The World Book Medical Encyclopedia, a 1,040-page fully illustrated family health reference; The World Book of Space Exploration, a two-volume review of the major developments in space since man first walked on the moon; and the Student Information Finder and How to Study Video, a fast-paced video presentation of key study skills with information students need to succeed in school. For further information, write WORLD BOOK ENCYCLOPEDIA, INC., P.O. Box 3073, Evanston, IL 60204-9974.

400